Engels After Marx

Engels After Marx

Edited by

Manfred B. Steger and Terrell Carver

The Pennsylvania State University Press
University Park, Pennsylvania

Library of Congress Cataloging-in-Publication Data

Engels after Marx / edited by Manfred B. Steger and Terrell Carver.

     p.   cm.
    Includes bibliographical references and index.
    ISBN 0-271-01891-7 (cloth : alk. paper).
    ISBN 0-271-01892-5 (pbk. : alk. paper)
    1. Engels, Friedrich, 1820–1895.   I. Steger, Manfred B., 1961–.
    II. Carver, Terrell.
    HX274.7.E53E42   1999
    335.4′092—dc21   99-22631
                                            CIP

It is the policy of The Pennsylvania State University Press to
use acid-free paper for the first printing of all clothbound
books. Publications on uncoated stock satisfy the minimum
requirements of American National Standard for Information
Sciences—Permanence of Paper for Printed Library Materials,
ANSI Z39.48–1992.

For
Henry Tudor
of the
University of Durham

whose untimely death deprived this
volume of an eagerly awaited essay on
Engels's politics, and many other audiences
of his sage and acute contributions to
political theory.

Contents

POLITICS AND SOCIAL SCIENCE

Notes on Contributors

TERRELL CARVER is Professor of Political Theory at the University of Bristol. He has written extensively on Marx and Engels, including *Engels* in the Oxford Past Masters series and Marx for the Cambridge Companions to Philosophy. He is author of *Marx and Engels: The Intellectual Relationship, Friedrich Engels: His Life and Thought,* and a newly published study, *The Postmodern Marx.* He has recently completed new translations in *Marx: Later Political Writings* for the Cambridge Texts in the History of Political Thought, and three of his own books have been translated into Japanese.

JAMES FARR teaches political theory at the University of Minnesota. He is the author of essays on Marx, Dewey, and other figures in the history of political thought, as well as co-editor of *After Marx* and other volumes. His main interests are in the history and philosophy of political inquiry.

MICHAEL FORMAN is Assistant Professor at the University of Washington-Tacoma. He is author of *Nationalism and the International Labor Movement: The Idea of the Nation in Socialist and Anarchist Theory* and of the article "National Minorities and National Self-Determination" in *Global Justice* (spring 1995).

CAROL C. GOULD is Professor of Philosophy at Stevens Institute of Technology and a research associate at the Center for Research in Applied Epistemology in Paris, publishing extensively on issues in feminist, democratic, and socialist theory. She is the author of *Rethinking Democracy* and *Marx's Social Ontology,* and editor of *Beyond Domination: New Perspectives on Women and Philosophy.* Currently she is completing a book, *Hard Questions in Democratic Theory.*

DOUGLAS KELLNER is Professor of Philosophy at the University of Texas at Austin. He is author of *Karl Korsch: Revolutionary Theory; Herbert Marcuse and the Crisis of Marxism; Camera Politica: The Politics and Ideology of Contemporary Hollywood Film* (with Michael Ryan); *Critical Theory, Marxism, and Modernity; Postmodern Theory: Critical Interrogations* (with Steven Best); *Television and the Crisis of Democracy; The Persian Gulf TV War; Media Culture;* and *The Postmodern Turn* (with Steven Best).

PETER T. MANICAS has taught philosophy at Queens College, City University of New York, and more recently in the departments of political science and sociology at the University of Hawai'i at Manoa. His books include *Essentials of Logic, The Death of the State, A History and Philosophy of the Social Sciences,* and *War and Democracy,* along with several edited volumes in logic. He has published articles in the *Journal for the Theory of Social Behavior, History of Political Thought, Philosophy and Phenomenological Research,* and many other journals.

JOSEPH MARGOLIS is Laura H. Carnell Professor of Philosophy at Temple University. He is the author of many books and articles on social philosophy, culture, and science, including *Science Without Unity, Texts Without Referents, The Truth About Relativism,* and *Interpretation Radical but Not Unruly.* Together with Tom Rockmore, he edited *The Heidegger Case.*

SCOTT MEIKLE is Reader in Philosophy at the University of Glasgow. He is the author of *Aristotle's Economic Thought* and is currently preparing a book, *Marx, the Enlightenment, and the Aristotelian Tradition.*

S. H. RIGBY was educated at Sheffield and London Universities and is currently Reader in History at the University of Manchester. He is author of a number of books and articles on Marxism and on social and economic history, including *Marxism and History, Engels and the Formation of Marxism,* and *English Society in the Later Middle Ages.* His main interest is in the relationship between social theory and the writing of history.

TOM ROCKMORE is Professor of Philosophy at Duquesne University and the author of *Heidegger and Philosophy, Before and After Hegel, On Heidegger's Nazism and Philosophy, Irrationalism: Lukács and the Marxist View of Reason,* and *Hegel's Circular Epistemology.* His other books and numerous articles deal with issues in German and French political and social philosophy.

MANFRED B. STEGER is Assistant Professor of Political Science at Illinois State University. He is author of *The Quest for Evolutionary Socialism: Eduard Bernstein and Social Democracy*, editor of *Selected Writings of Eduard Bernstein: 1900–1921*, and has published articles on ethical socialism, German politics, and non-Western political theory. He is currently working on a reader, *Violence and Its Alternatives*, and a book on Mahatma Gandhi's politics of self-control and purification.

PAUL THOMAS is Professor of Political Science at the University of California, Berkeley. His most recent publications are *Alien Politics* and *Culture and the State* (with David Lloyd). He is also co-editor (with Terrell Carver) of *Rational Choice Marxism*. He is currently engaged in a research project on "Scientific Socialism: Career of a Concept."

LAWRENCE WILDE is Reader in Political Theory in the Department of Economics and Politics at Nottingham Trent University. He is author of *Marx and Contradiction*, *Modern European Socialism*, and *Ethical Marxism and Its Radical Critics*, and co-editor (with Mark Cowling) of *Approaches to Marx*.

Acknowledgments

The editors would like to express their appreciation for their publisher's encouragement and support throughout the project. Further acknowledgments, including those to publishers for the use of copyright material, are listed below for each contributor.

Terrell Carver. I am grateful for permission to reproduce material originally published in "'Marx-Engels' or 'Engels v. Marx,'" *MEGA-Studien* 2 (1996): 79–85.

James Farr. For critical commentary or bibliographical assistance, I would like to thank Terrell Carver, Mary Dietz, Jeffrey Isaac, Peter Manicas, and August Nimitz, as well as Barbara Levine and Diane Meierkort of the Center for Dewey Studies at Southern Illinois University.

Douglas Kellner. My chapter draws on research done with Robert Antonio on theories of modernity in classical social theory and is indebted to work done with him over the past decade. Thanks also to Terrell Carver for useful comments and editing.

S. H. Rigby. I am grateful to Terrell Carver for his help in writing this article, even though he can scarcely have agreed with a word of it, and I would particularly like to thank Rosalind Brown-Grant, who suggested a number of improvements to an earlier draft.

Manfred B. Steger. My chapter is reprinted from "Friedrich Engels and the Origins of German Revisionism: Another Look," *Political Studies* 45 (1997): 247–59, by kind permission of the Political Studies Association and Blackwell Publishers.

Note on References

Author-date references refer to lists of references at the end of each
  chapter.
The following abbreviations are used throughout the book:

CW = Karl Marx and Frederick Engels, *Collected Works* (London:
  Lawrence & Wishart, 1975–).
MEW = Karl Marx and Friedrich Engels, *Werke* (Berlin: Dietz Verlag,
  1956–68).
MEGA² = Karl Marx and Friedrich Engels, *Gesamtausgabe* (Berlin: Dietz
  Verlag, 1972–).

A Select Bibliography at the end of the volume covers major works by
  and about Friedrich Engels.

Introduction

Manfred B. Steger and Terrell Carver

The 1989 fall of the Berlin Wall and the collapse of the Soviet Union two years later occurred with little early warning. Before the eyes of an astonished world, the entire edifice of Communist authoritarianism came tumbling down, ushering in a new chapter in modern history. Almost as if to underline the ongoing difficulties of the socialist project, even the much admired "Third Way" of northern European social democracies showed worsening signs of major structural problems. Gradually, social democratic leaders began to abandon their long-standing programmatic commitments to full employment, rising real wages, and large welfare transfers. Caught in the middle of a gigantic, worldwide transition from nationally organized to globally integrated capitalism, both the democratic and authoritarian socialists of the early 1990s found themselves in a seemingly losing battle with the new labor-market internationalism of multinational corporations and the logic of an expanding neoliberalism.

Yet, in the waning years of this century, Francis Fukuyama's triumphant prediction of the impending "end of socialism" has not been fulfilled (Fukuyama 1989). Today, a good number of Eastern European countries are once again led by socialist governments. Most recently, British, French, and Italian voters, too, have expressed their confidence in the political Left, albeit of the rather centrist Tony Blair kind. Turning to the rarefied world of the academy, one finds a strikingly similar picture. In fact, the persistence of strong left voices speaking in distinct political, cultural, and linguistic dialects appears to be even more pronounced in the world of scholars than on the rough turf of "real politics." Indeed, much to the surprise of some academic circles, the momentous changes in Eastern Europe have hardly affected the production of impressive new studies in the history of socialist ideas. If anything, the presumed demise of Marx and Engels's political vision seems to have softened entrenched ideological prejudices, opening the way for a large number of thoughtful reflections on the future of socialism and a reassessment of prominent socialists and their place in modern history (Callinicos 1991; Bronner 1992; Derrida 1994; Roemer 1994; Manuel 1995; Magnus and Cullenberg 1995; Bobbio 1996; Forman 1998).

Placing itself squarely within this "new" tradition of socialist scholarship, the present collection of essays offers a critical reappraisal of Friedrich Engels (1820–95), a pivotal figure of the classical European labor movement. The guiding questions for the book as a whole are: What is the nature of Engels's role as an independent socialist thinker after Marx's death in 1883? What is the theoretical significance and the historical impact of his wide-ranging contributions to philosophy, science, political economy, history, and socialist politics?

Seeking to respond to these questions, *Engels After Marx* deals with Engels "after" Marx in several senses. Chronologically and thematically, the contributors examine main aspects in Engels's thought after the end of his forty-year intellectual relationship with Marx. Politically, the collection attempts to make sense of Engels's work in the aftermath of the 1989–91 revolutions in Eastern Europe. Hermeneutically, the essays search for new readings of Engels's texts; in the spirit of a genuinely "critical" theory, the authors pursue Engels's errors and omissions, uncover his rhetorical maneuvers, and point to insights and conclusions in his thought that appear to have withstood the test of time.

However, before linking this conceptual framework to a detailed overview of the individual contributions to this volume, we must first consider a more fundamental question: Why focus on Engels, as opposed to, say, Marx, Luxemburg, or Lenin? First, there is the compelling reason of topicality. The year 1995 marked the centenary of Engels's death as well as the 150th anniversary of the publication of his classic *Condition of the Working Class in England.* Participants at international conferences held on this occasion in Wuppertal, Engels's birthplace in Germany, in Manchester, where he lived and worked, and at Tokyo Metropolitan University have debated various aspects of his works, as have commemorative essays collected in recent anthologies and special issues of academic journals. Not surprisingly, these renewed considerations of Engels as a thinker and politician have revealed many aspects in his work and influence that still occasion heated discussions (see, for example, Arthur 1996 and Kircz and Loewy 1998).

Second, in spite of the growing body of literature on the subject, Engels is still generally taken for granted and insufficiently scrutinized. The study of his writings often occurs only as a secondary activity, subordinated to or absorbed into the study of the vast body of Marx's own writings. This conveys a rather superficial and sometimes quite distorted portrait of Engels, tending to leave the reader with the impression that Engels's thought may not be a worthy object of study in its own right. As a result, it is still a difficult task to penetrate the popular "Engels myth," which introduces the "General," as he was affectionately called by his party comrades, to new generations of students as the supposedly "lesser half" of Karl Marx—a mere adjunct to a thinker of world-historical importance whom he was fortunate to serve in both intellectual and financial capacities.

As the contributors to this collection point out time and again, nothing could be further from the truth. Although Engels himself at times promoted this subordinate image of merely "playing second fiddle to Marx," one does not have to dig too deep to unearth the impressive intellectual credentials that establish him as an important theorist and politician in his own right. For instance, there can be hardly any doubt that the young Engels of the early 1840s was a more influential and accomplished writer than his famous associate. Impressing on Marx the importance of journalistic clarity while at the same time providing his friend with an outline critique of political economy so evident in the *Economic and Philosophical Manuscripts* of 1844, the 1846 *German Ideology*, and the 1847 *Communist Manifesto*, Engels exerted from the very beginning of their long affiliation a tremendous influence on the direction and quality of their common intellectual and political endeavors. Forced into political exile in England after the unsuccessful 1848 German Revolution, he turned to financially pressing business affairs and soon began to settle into his much overemphasized role as Marx's editor, confidant, and main financial provider. Yet throughout these years, Engels continued to produce such important theoretical works as The *Peasant War in Germany* (1850),

Revolution and Counter-Revolution in Germany (1852), and his famous polemic, *Anti-Dühring* (1878).

From roughly 1859 onward Engels assumed the role of reviewing and popularizing Marx's works, and the two men together worked to gain credence and influence for these ideas through national party organizations, particularly in Germany, and also through the International Working Men's Association, which fostered information exchange and transnational cooperation. It was Engels's specific achievement to present Marx publicly as both scientist and philosopher, and to support this with a biographical narrative linking Marx's intellectual ambitions to socialist politics. Moreover, he not only summarized what he took to be the essence of Marx's work, he also more crucially chose and defined the terms with which most subsequent summarizations of Marx have been constructed.

In setting the scene Engels presented Marx as Germany's premier social scientist precisely because he was expert in French and English political economy, and because his new economics—founded on the "materialist conception of history"—was linked to the nascent proletarian cause in Germany. But it was only after Marx's death in March 1883 that Engels reached the apex of his intellectual career, consciously speaking as the foremost authority on a comprehensive socialist worldview that bore the birthmarks of his own interpretive spin but was mostly ascribed to his dead friend. Already in his eloquent delivery of Marx's funeral address, Engels announced in the name of the late Karl Marx the world-historical importance of a revolutionary proletarian science of truly Darwinian proportions that was based on the centrality of the "dialectic method" (MEW 19:335–37). Eulogizing Marx as a great humanitarian, "beloved, revered, and mourned by millions of revolutionary fellow workers from the mines of Siberia to California," Engels went on to credit his friend with the discovery of a "general law of development of human history" and a "special law of motion" governing capitalist society. Repeated and expanded upon in numerous reviews, prefaces, introductions, and letters related to Marx's work, Engels's somewhat idiosyncratic popularizations set the intellectual framework for the last twelve years of his life. Indeed, his Herculean task of securing worldwide dissemination of a drastically simplified "communist world outlook" bore fruit soon after his death in 1895, when his summarizations surfaced rapidly within the international socialist movement.

On a another theoretical plane, the aging Engels returned to lengthy treatments of philosophy of science in *The Origin of the Family, Private Property, and the State* (1884), *Ludwig Feuerbach and the Outcome of Classical*

German Philosophy (1886) and *Dialectics of Nature* (published posthumously in 1927). Emphasizing the connection between "dialectics" and "material-ism" as fundamental to a "correct" understanding of scientific socialism, Engels cultivated an orthodox interpretation of Marxism that would later find receptive audiences in France and Russia. In addition, much of his intellectual energy was consumed by the onerous task of editing and pub-lishing the remaining volumes of Marx's *Capital*. In many letters to friends and acquaintances, Engels wrote despairingly about the seemingly insur-mountable difficulties of working through Marx's voluminous surviving manuscripts on political economy. The process of molding them into two coherent books took much longer than he expected, and the third vol-ume of *Capital* was not published until 1894. In the end, the completion of this exhausting project turned out to be a rather thankless task, generating more skepticism and hostility than approval from a variety of socialist and nonsocialist critics. In particular, Engels was attacked for not having demonstrated the truth of Marx's claim that the exchange value of commodities on the market was in some sense a representation of socially necessary labor power expended in production throughout the capitalist system.

On the level of practical politics, Engels involved himself in a number of important activities ranging from frequently advising major and minor players in the European labor movement to generating substantial ideas on the founding of the Second International Working Men's Association in 1889. Together with his anointed intellectual "successors" Karl Kautsky and Eduard Bernstein, he also took an active part in the "Marxist" formu-lation of the exemplary and much admired 1891 Erfurt Party Program of German social democracy. He maintained a strong interest in European politics, and he brought his considerable expertise in military affairs to bear on his astute assessment of an increasingly belligerent international environment. Two years before he succumbed to throat cancer in August 1895, Engels returned to continental Europe for a last time. Speaking as the honorary president to the delegates of the Zürich International Labor Congress, he expressed his unwavering optimism about the bright prospects for a socialist future in Europe: "[S]ocialism has now developed into a powerful party before which the whole world of officialdom trem-bles" (Mayer [1934] 1969, 322–23).

After this short excursus into the highlights of Engels's life and work, we must now come back to offering the final justification for this collection's thematic focus—one that is closely related to substantive issues raised in the context of the recent centenary debates. More than most other pivotal

socialist figures, Engels has generated a variety of conflicting interpretations among historians of socialist thought. This can be taken as a clear
indication for both the necessity of further scholarly research on the subject and the existence of important topical issues in Engels's work. Even
more than a century after his ashes were scattered off Eastbourne, his
favorite seaside resort, the nature and extent of his theoretical role following Karl Marx's death has remained a fertile topic among political and
social theorists. In particular, three related themes have formed the core
of contention.

First, did Engels, in his later writings—either mistakenly or intentionally
—embark on a substantial reinterpretation of Marx's work, thereby significantly departing from the latter's intellectual venture? While early
interpretations saw Engels as Marx's "alter ego" (Nikolaievsky and
Maenchen-Helfen [1936] 1976; Mayer [1934] 1969; Stepanova 1958;
Mehring [1936] 1973), the most prominent biographers of the last thirty
years have emphasized significant differences between the two thinkers
(Lichtheim 1961; Tucker 1972; Avineri 1968; Levine 1975; Bender 1975;
Thomas 1976; McLellan 1977; Ball and Farr 1984; Lovell 1984; Carver
1983, 1989). Most recent studies, however, have returned to the guiding
theme of Engels's early biographers, arguing that "dichotomist" accounts
of the last decades seriously downplay Marx and Engels's fundamental
intellectual agreement "on such important matters as humanism, revisionism, determinism, and positivism" (Hunley 1991, 144; Steger 1997;
Rigby 1992; Kellogg 1991; Stanley and Zimmermann 1984; Welty 1983).
While all the intricate aspects of the Marx-Engels intellectual relationship
may never be settled to the full satisfaction of all participating parties, this
question nonetheless continues to hover over much of the current scholarship on Engels.

Second, can Engels's interpretation of dialectical materialism be linked
to the rather simplistic amalgam of positivism and materialist dogmatism
made famous by Lenin and Stalin as "socialist ideology" (Henderson 1976,
734; Jordan 1967, 332–33)? While there may be some support for the claim
that the textual and argumentative bases for Engels's dialectical materialism remain shaky with respect to Marx's work, other plausible arguments
advance the thesis that Marx himself was using similar terminology to
describe his own ideas on this issue (Hunley 1991, 125–26). Even if one
assumes that a canonical Bolshevist understanding of philosophy of science is latent in Engels's views on dialectical materialism, it is only with
Lenin's highly influential 1902 pamphlet *What Is to Be Done?* that one
encounters the explicit formulation of a Soviet-style "scientific ideology."

The best way of addressing this question might be to put renewed research efforts into an investigation of the link between Engels's understanding of philosophy of science and Marx's own writings on the subject.

Third, is there such a thing as an authentic Marxism, traceable in genealogical fashion from contemporary socialists back to Marx and Engels? Does it even make sense to raise this question? As the long history of socialist factionalism and sectarianism shows, questions of Marxist legitimacy and authenticity have been at the root of numerous political and theoretical battles. But aside from the problems regarding what elements should be included in a genuinely Marxist tool kit and who passes the ultimate judgment in what context, the tentative formulation of an even remotely satisfactory answer to this question must employ a strong research focus on Engels after Marx. After all, any useful interpretive insight can only arise from a thorough reading of the later Engels; only then can one ponder if he was a faithful or deceitful messenger of the original doctrine (whatever that might be), and whether he should be regarded as the founding father of Soviet ideology or a Marxist revisionist à la Bernstein. In either case, these and other weighty questions of socialist thought converge in the person of Friedrich Engels. Ignaz Auer, the legendary party secretary of classical German social democracy, accurately captured the central role of Engels only a few days after his death in 1895: "The Old Man is irreplaceable in questions of scriptural interpretation. With all due respect for the younger Church Fathers, the rich experience and authority of Engels is absent. Accordingly, we'll have to do without a 'Source of Truth' for a while, which may turn out to be a quite unpleasant experience" (Steger 1997, 71).

Although a century has passed since then, we have still only begun to explore the richness of Engels's texts. To some extent this is because the methodologies available for doing this have changed over time, particularly with the development of hermeneutics in Continental philosophy and the philosophy of speech acts in the British linguistic tradition. The "linguistic turn" has made the process of interpreting texts in context and texts out of context far more complex and far more exciting than was the case even twenty years ago. Opening the section on philosophy and theory, Terrell Carver situates "the Engels-Marx question" within an interpretive frame to which biography and autobiography are made relevant, but problematic, with respect to Engels. More particularly he considers the complex question of authorial voice in the works Engels wrote jointly with Marx and those he wrote and published under his own name. He finds a number of different "voices" speaking to readers, and discusses Engels's "revoicing" of Marx, culminating in his editorial work on *Capital*, volume 3. Carver argues that this work is a crucial end point in the Engels-Marx question, in that a "reliable" Engels will underwrite traditional Marxism, and an "unreliable" Engels will unravel it.

Engaging with the philosopher Engels, Joseph Margolis argues that there is something philosophically Engelsian that is well worth salvaging today, provided that this reading is conducted in a new way. Margolis is keen to move an evaluation of Engels away from Marxist orthodoxy (whether he was its creator or not), and away from traditional terms of debate, particularly those that pit Engels against Marx, as well as those that try to identify the two. Arguing that Engels's famous letter to Bloch represents a formula of "canny intelligence," Margolis finds an objectivity in Engels that assigns explanatory power in history to "nominal" rather than "real" essences. This locates the materialist theory of history in human praxis, though not in individual wills. Precisely what counts as the "engine" of historical change will vary with the society and indeed with the theorist, who makes a political judgment about what history effectively is. Margolis reckons that in this way Engels avoided the ontological problems associated with traditional materialisms and traditional idealisms, and that this is no mean feat for someone who was self-schooled in philosophy.

Though philosophy of science is itself a recent invention, Peter T. Manicas in his chapter employs it as a framework for investigating the relationship between scientific socialism and dialectical materialism. Putting Marx's reputed philosophy of science to one side, Manicas attributes scientific socialism predominantly to Engels, and explores the similarities and differences between Engels's concept of science and concepts of science developing both earlier and later, particularly positivism in its late-nineteenth- and early- to mid-twentieth-century forms. Engels's engagement with these issues in philosophy of science was conducted largely in terms of an opposition between materialism and idealism, and his "dialectics," according to Manicas, deals with them very inadequately.

Scott Meikle, by contrast, foregrounds the relationship of Engels's philosophizing about science to Marx's work, particularly *Capital*. Arguing that Engels had a taste for speculative metaphysics and was further drawn into a Victorian vogue for science, Meikle suggests that Marx's own conception of science was made unintelligible through Engels's efforts. Marx relied on conceptions of science that antedated both Hegel and Engels and were largely derived from Aristotle. Meikle explores Marx's thought in relation to empiricist concepts of explanation and a supposed opposition between science and ethics, and concludes that an Enlightenment framework, imposed by Engels, has tied Marx paradoxically to the bourgeois concerns and commitments that he was anxious to overthrow.

Moving on to philosophy of history, S. H. Rigby surveys the philosophical underpinnings of Engels's historical materialism, arguing that Engels shifted from an anthropogenetic to a pragmatological outlook in the mid-1840s, and that the pragmatological view was further developed, particularly with regard to gender, after 1883. Rigby rejects the view that Marx's ideas were substantially different from those of Engels, and the view that Engels's late adherence to a nomological conception of history —history as a law-governed natural process—entails a rejection of, or incompatibility with, his previous work. Examining the nomological view of history in two versions—"diluted" and "concentrated"—Rigby concludes that Marxist historiography inevitably lapses into an implicit explanatory pluralism.

Tom Rockmore links Marxism, as largely Engels's construction, with the long tradition of philosophical belief that to know is to know absolutely, or to know the thing-in-itself, which Kant claimed was not possible. While both Engels and Lukács appealed to Hegel's system as one that could indeed generate positive knowledge of the real world and thus solve the problem contra Kant, Rockmore denies that this can be so of Hegel, or of knowledge. Thus Engels set Marxism a problem for itself that it could not resolve, and Lukács, as the superior philosophical mind, was correct to criticize Engels's reading of Kant, yet just as unsuccessful in finding a solution. Rockmore's conclusion is that Marxist philosophy, for all its claims, has been elaborated within a very traditional philosophical form.

Bringing this section to a close, Douglas Kellner takes up the theme of modernity, arguing that Engels preceded Marx in theorizing the distinctive features of the modern world. Besides inspiring Marx's critical theory of modern society and critique of capitalism, Engels is also valuable in the context of social theory as it has developed. Kellner remarks on Engels's skill in structural and dynamic analysis at the level of society, and on his ability to use Hegelian dialectical thought in mapping complexity, relating constituent parts to each other and to the whole social system. This kind of theorizing is also distinctive in its emancipatory vision, embodying hopes for progress, freedom, democracy, and socioeconomic and individual development that are constitutive of modernity itself.

Opening the section on politics and theory, Manfred B. Steger looks again at the relationship between Engels and the revisionists in Germany around the turn of the last century. Steger argues that Engels's political and philosophical ideas of his later years were developed in a party-political context, and that the influence worked both ways: abstract discussions of theory and tactics influenced the balance of power in socialist party politics, and the situation in the socialist party influenced the theoretical positions espoused. At a time when revolution was unlikely, Engels's attempts to reconcile the tactics of parliamentarism with revolutionary optimism actually devalued theory and paved the way for Eduard Bernstein's reformist politics and consequent revisionism. For Engels theoretical questions were never "merely theoretical."

Lawrence Wilde examines Engels's politics in the context of European social democracy as it developed after the 1850s, when Engels attempted to fashion a compromise between revolutionary insurrectionism and electoral reformism, a strategy of "revolutionary electoralism." Wilde argues that there was nothing contradictory in principle with this, but that its application developed tensions within the international socialist movement. Wilde then follows these through—reform versus revolution, the army versus the people, and nationalism versus internationalism—concluding that Engels's attempts to work these tensions out politically were largely ill informed and ill judged.

In a controversial account, Paul Thomas argues ambitiously that Engels's ideas were significantly at variance with Marx's and that this had important political as well as intellectual effects. Characterizing Engels as a *simplificateur*, Thomas sees in his work a scientism that is "radically, and demonstrably, at variance with Marx's approach, method, and even subject matter." In Germany this was developed as a *Weltanschauung* and in Russia as dialectical materialism, effectively marginalizing Marx and his work, as exegetes got to work on the philosophical complexities these two systems inevitably generated. Thomas discerns a link between domination-and-control philosophies of nature and authoritarian political practices, and goes on to contrast Marx's epistemology and politics with Marxism. Paying tribute to the early Engels, Thomas concludes that the later Engels would never be of much interest without Marx, and that the Marx that one finds there is a myth.

Michael Forman reconsiders Engels's record on the "national question" in terms of self-determination and state formation and then on further questions posed by nationalism in socialist politics. While committed to an overall doctrine of international working-class solidarity that transcends national boundaries, Engels's thought and practice derived from two somewhat incompatible sources: a critical theory of capitalism developed together with Marx's, and a radical republicanism that derived from his earliest experiences in politics. On Engels's view a cultural politics of nationality was defensible in socialist terms if it was in the larger interests of the working class, but he also sometimes slipped into a Hegelian view of history as cultural metaphysics. Engels's analysis usefully pointed to the way that capitalism plays on cultural division, dividing the working class and setting it against the democratic and proletarian internationalism that he, and other socialists, espoused.

Unlike Marx, Engels contributed overtly to the theorizing of gender and the movement for women's equality. Carol C. Gould evaluates his classic *Origin of the Family, Private Property, and the State* and the way that it has been treated in the feminist tradition. Feminists have criticized Engels for an overly simple, "materialist" explanation of women's oppression, for the ad hoc and tautological character of some of his argumentation and "evidence," and for his insensitivity to issues of culture and identity, particularly in societies outside the industrialized countries of Europe. The continuing strength of Engels's approach, however, is that it is nonbiologistic and complexly historical, emphasizing economic factors and yet normatively political. Of all Engels's works, this is the one that has generated the most widespread interest in recent years, and Gould shows how he will continue to have a role in feminist thinking.

Closing the volume, James Farr examines the reception of Marxism in the United States, noting that Engels exerted a uniquely powerful influence over the meaning of Marx's words and the Marxist political trajectory. In particular, the American pragmatist philosopher John Dewey, who was critical of capitalism and sympathetic to socialism, rejected Marx and Marxism, but in Farr's view this was a rejection of Engels-as-Marx. Dewey's antipathy was by no means crudely ideological, but because of his unique stature in American intellectual life, his hostility set the tone for many other intellectuals, and this had a distinct political effect. He maintained this position even against attempts by his students, among them Sidney Hook, to make some headway with him in distinguishing Marx's thought from Engels's glosses. Engels's Marxism thus lived on in Dewey's writings as a philosophical system that he characterized as uniformitarian, absolutistic, positivistic, and monistic, but failed to distinguish from Marx's quite contrasting ideas.

In *Engels After Marx* we hope that we have revived Engels "in the round" and that readers will find stimulus in the contrasting views held by contributors, and indeed by the editors. We have made no attempt to bury Engels under fulsome praise or to exhume him for an auto-da-fé. There will be no conclusive account of Engels's work in "Philosophy and Theory" or in "Politics and Social Science." His legacy is controversy, and that is achievement enough.

References

Arthur, Christopher J., ed. 1996. *Engels Today: A Centenary Appreciation.* London: Macmillan.

Avineri, Shlomo. 1968. *The Social and Political Thought of Karl Marx.* Cambridge: Cambridge University Press.

Ball, Terence, and James Farr, eds. 1984. *After Marx.* Cambridge: Cambridge University Press.

Bender, Frederic L., ed. 1975. *The Betrayal of Marx.* New York: Harper & Row.

Bobbio, Norberto. 1996. *Left and Right: The Significance of a Political Distinction.* Chicago: University of Chicago Press.

Bronner, Stephen Eric. 1992. *Moments of Decision: Political History and the Crises of Radicalism.* New York: Routledge.

Callinicos, Alex. 1991. *The Revenge of History: Marxism and the East European Revolutions.* University Park: Pennsylvania State University Press.

Carver, Terrell. 1983. *Marx and Engels: The Intellectual Relationship.* Bloomington: Indiana University Press.

———. 1989. *Friedrich Engels: His Life and Thought.* London: Macmillan.

Derrida, Jacques. 1994. *Specters of Marx.* New York: Routledge.

Forman, Michael. 1998. *Nationalism and the International Labor Movement: The Idea of the Nation in Socialist and Anarchist Theory.* University Park: Pennsylvania State University Press.

Fukuyama, Francis. 1989. The End of History? *National Interest* (summer): 3–18.

Henderson, W. O. 1976. *The Life of Friedrich Engels.* 2 vols. London: Frank Cass.

Hunley, J. D. 1991. *The Life and Thought of Friedrich Engels: A Reinterpretation.* New Haven, Conn.: Yale University Press.

Jordan, Z. A. 1967. *The Evolution of Dialectical Materialism: Philosophical and Sociological Analysis.* New York: St. Martin's.

Kellogg, Paul. 1991. Engels and the Roots of "Revisionism": A Re-evaluation. *Science and Society* 55:158–74.

Kircz, Joost, and Michael Loewy, eds. 1998. Friedrich Engels: A Critical Centenary Appreciation. *Science and Society* 62 (special issue).

Levine, Norman. 1975. *The Tragic Deception: Marx Contra Engels.* Oxford: Clio.

Lichtheim, George. 1961. *Marxism: A Historical and Critical Study.* New York: Praeger.

Lovell, David W. 1984. *From Marx to Lenin.* Cambridge: Cambridge University Press.

Magnus, Bernd, and Stephen Cullenberg, eds. 1995. *Whither Marxism? Global Crisis in International Perspective.* New York: Routledge.

Manuel, Frank E. 1995. *A Requiem for Marx.* Cambridge, Mass.: Harvard University Press.

Mayer, Gustav. [1934] 1969. *Friedrich Engels: A Biography.* New York: Howard Fertig.

McLellan, David. 1977. *Engels.* Hassocks, Sussex: Harvester Press.

Mehring, Franz. [1936] 1973. *Karl Marx: The Story of His Life.* Ann Arbor: University of Michigan Press.

Nikolaievsky, Boris, and Otto Maenchen-Helfen. [1936] 1976. *Karl Marx: Man and Fighter.* Bungay, Suffolk: Penguin.

Rigby, S. H. 1992. *Engels and the Formation of Marxism: History, Dialectics, and Revolution.* Manchester: Manchester University Press.

Roemer, John E. 1994. *A Future for Socialism*. Cambridge, Mass.: Harvard University Press.

Stanley, John L., and Ernest Zimmermann. 1984. On the Alleged Differences Between Marx and Engels. *Political Studies* 32:226–48.

Steger, Manfred B. 1997. *The Quest for Evolutionary Socialism: Eduard Bernstein and Social Democracy*. Cambridge: Cambridge University Press.

Stepanova, Yelena. 1958. *Frederick Engels*. Moscow: Foreign Language Publishing House.

Thomas, Paul. 1976. Marx and Science. *Political Studies* 24:1–23.

Tucker, Robert C. 1972. *Philosophy and Myth in Karl Marx*. 2d ed. Cambridge: Cambridge University Press.

Welty, Gordon. 1983. Marx, Engels, and "Anti-Dühring." *Political Studies* 31:284–94.

Philosophy
and
Theory

1

The Engels-Marx Question: Interpretation, Identity/ies, Partnership, Politics

Terrell Carver

The Engels-Marx question is a question of interpretation. Interpretation is a matter of dialogue—or rather dialogues—between commentator and text, commentator and audience. There is also a dialogue among the texts themselves—as they are deployed by commentators and readers and thus made to speak to each other, as it were. Between Engels and Marx there was also—in their own time—a dialogue in terms of speech and letters. However, it cannot be assumed that the extant texts as we have them (given that some are lost and some deliberately destroyed) are a "window" on just what this dialogue was. Indeed any dialogue has two sides, and each communicating party may not know exactly what is in the mind of the other.

The problem for the commentator is not that Engels and Marx are dead; the problem would simply recur if they were alive and could be interviewed, separately or even together. No one has transparent access to another mind, and there is little assurance, even within ourselves, that what is in anyone's mind is "made up," even as presented in a text, in the way that commentators generally represent an authorial consciousness. When commentators work from evidence of dialogue, as in an exchange of letters, or from an assumption of dialogue, as in a presumed working relationship, then the ambiguities multiply. Nonetheless, the reportage generated by commentators is generally a genre of assertive certainty. It is my aim to deconstruct this familiar kind of discourse, using Engels and Marx as examples of more general problems, as well as focusing on certain well-known "truths" about the two in order to unsettle almost a century and a half of interpretation. Received truth is in need of constant testing, and the effect of this should be invigorating rather than destructive, as John Stuart Mill famously argued (1989, ch. 2). However, readers will have to judge this particular case for themselves.

Questions, Answers, Dialogue

It is not really possible to ask, What kind of relationship was there between Engels and Marx? and to expect a singular answer, applicable in all circumstances. Indeed, to look for that kind of overarching answer, even in terms of a rough characterization, is to stifle the dialogues among commentators and readers that created the question in the first place. Thus an overall characterization of the "Marx-Engels" or "Engels-Marx" relationship as either "agreement" or "dichotomy" is almost always an attempt *to answer in advance* the textual questions that others—whether readers or commentators—might want to pose. I do not think that this is an acceptable scholarly strategy, since it warps or negates the effort of investigation that scholarship entails, and so renders the activity of inquiry uninteresting. It is the language of power, rather than the language of investigation, which admits of different voices, and different answers to different questions.

Presumptions of certainty are not limited to questions about the Engels-Marx relationship. Much the same difficulties have arisen with the familiar periodizations of Marx's (and sometimes Engels's) own works into "early," "middle," and "late," or into "philosophical," "political," and "economic," or into "prescientific" and "scientific" categories. Are the various texts involved to be interpreted in terms of "agreement" or "dichotomy" (famously as a "break" or "rupture")? Did these various Marxes (and sometimes Engelses) agree with each other, or present contradictory views?

Or, leaving psychological questions aside, are the texts to be interpreted as "consistent," or "developmental," or in some cases as "superseded" but in others as "perfected"? Commentators have created just these kinds of dialogues among the texts that Engels and Marx have left us.

Moreover, Engels is almost universally treated as an adjunct to Marx; Engels is brought onto the stage, as it were, when the "story of Marx" requires him, as indeed happens in the autobiographical paragraphs of Marx's 1859 preface to *A Contribution to the Critique of Political Economy*. In that text Marx told his own story as a way of framing the first installment of his critique of political economy. Engels fell in with this device, at least superficially, in his subsequent writing, whether or not under his own name alone. This was almost universally the case after 1848, and certainly later, after Marx's death, when he came to speak for Marx as well as himself. My point here is that commentators are keen to embed their work in what they term "historical context," which in my view is necessarily a rather "biographical" and ultimately "novelistic" construction. Even very short biographies or autobiographies tell a story.

Authors often have a hand in setting things up contextually for commentators; Engels participated in this process by contextualizing himself in relation to Marx, and contextualizing Marx himself in relation to his own (i.e., Marx's) work, to other thinkers, and to world history at large. The relationship between the two is itself almost always termed "Marx-Engels" rather than the reverse, "Engels-Marx," which—given the nature of this volume—is the way round that I have chosen to characterize it.

Authors, Editors, Readers

The notion of authorship—when it is taken to be a single, consistent voice from an individual or individuals—is itself highly problematic, *even if* it is agreed which text is whose. That is, even if all the major texts in the Marx-Engels oeuvre were assigned unambiguously to *either* Engels *or* Marx as separate authorial identities, or even if they were all assigned to *both* Engels *and* Marx as a joint authorial identity, all these interpretive problems would recur, since no one really believes—despite the genre of assertive certainty that prevails among commentators—that either or both writers (however identity is conceived) always said the same thing about the same subjects in the same way absolutely all the time. Indeed, what commentators think the texts are going to say depends to a great extent on the specific questions they, working as commentators, address to the texts when they construct their interpretations. Paradoxically, however, most commentators are hesitant to say to the reader exactly what questions they are putting to a text, preferring instead a "voice from nowhere" telling it "as it really was."

In this chapter I expand on these hermeneutic and deconstructive themes, paying special attention to the way the texts of Engels and Marx become texts-in-politics. I do this by examining Engels and Marx as authorial and "partner" voices constructed through a biographical tradition. As "context" this traditional narrative frames the texts that readers encounter today. Because of the "coincidence," "division-of-labor," and "convergence" theories that contribute to a narrative of "Marx-Engels partnership," it has become unclear in textual terms whether "Marx" in the texts is one person or two, and therefore precisely whose voice—so we imagine—is speaking to us through the texts we read. Moreover, with respect to Engels we also need a concept of "speaking-for," or "revoicing." In aid of this precision I locate five voices in the extant texts:

- separate signed voices
- a joint anonymous voice
- debating voices
- His Master's Voice
- the Voice from the Tomb

I argue that Engels had a hand biographically and editorially in "revoicing" Marx, and that the presumed authority of this process is now being crucially tested in scholarly debates concerning the publication of *Capital*, volume 3, within the Marx-Engels *Gesamtausgabe*, usually known as MEGA^2. Orthodox narratives of partnership rely on an ultimate identity of authorial voice in Marx and Engels, fulfilled in the latter's posthumous role as editor of Marx's masterwork. Those arguing, by contrast, that vocal unison, or at least harmony, between the two *must be established instance by instance*, rather than *presumed in advance*, point to major discrepancies between Marx's manuscripts, which have now been separately published, and Engels's editorial adjustments thereto. Which is the real *Capital*, volume 3? And which is the real author or "final hand," Engels or Marx?

These questions have a crucial bearing on what the text says when commentators read it and report on it to other readers. Does it convey a consistent argument or theory, or do the words on the page portray a debate, contradictions, or uncertainty? "Reading the words on the page," as an activity, gives the reader a role as commentator, constructing meaning as an interpretation unfolds. With a presumption of authorial, or perhaps in this case editorial-authorial, unity and therefore certainty, the reader will encounter logical and synthetic difficulties. Without such a presumption, the reader will have at least two texts to decipher, perhaps an unusual, but not impossible, arrangement. Editors and commentators presently at work on these texts thus have decisions to make about how to introduce it, how to construct an *apparatus criticus,* even how to arrange the title page for the work and what title to give it. While there may be few readers deeply interested in the production of a text of *Capital,* volume 3 (whatever this might eventually turn out to be), I hope that my general approach, working from the supposedly simple author-text-commentator-reader nexus up to the complexities in which scholars engage when working with Marx's drafts and Engels's editorship, can stretch seamlessly and usefully to the benefit of readers who are in this volume encountering Engels after Marx.

Singularity, Plurality, Ambiguity

What happens when two authorial voices join together? Despite the biographical tradition of lifelong "partnership" initiated by Engels, Marx and Engels only produced three major works together. Interestingly all three works were produced in different senses of "together." *The Holy Family* (published in 1845, their first collaboration) has separately signed individual chapters, and is also uniquely by "Engels and Marx," since Engels had an international reputation as a journalist and socialist at the time, whereas Marx had little readership outside the Rhineland and few publications to his name. Engels complained at the time of writing (1844–45) that Marx's contributions had swamped his own, thus suggesting that the "jointness" between the two might not have been equal in the way that joint authorial attribution implies (Carver 1989, 175–80).

After that, the two worked together on *The German Ideology,* which was planned for publication but never completed, as Marx famously relates in his autobiographical remarks of 1859. Apparently Marx and Engels reached self-clarification (N.B.: according to Marx's comments—does "self" here really refer to two people? or to the same clarification? what did Marx understand here by "we"?), and the large "printer's sheets" on which the two had scribbled were abandoned to "the gnawing criticism of the mice," a typically mordant joke from an ironist of considerable savagery and someone who was always in debt and awaiting publishers' advances. There are passages in *The German Ideology* in which I read dialogue and debate (Carver 1988), rather than two writers groping to agree on a "smooth" text (as is generally presumed by editors, except Hiromatsu, in Marx and Engels 1974), and in any case, given Engels's role as Marx's amanuensis (notwithstanding lengthy passages in Marx's hand as well), the manuscript presents irresolvable hermeneutic difficulties. When is Engels speaking for himself? When is Marx speaking through him, or together with him (and vice versa)? When is Marx speaking for himself against Engels (was there ever any vice versa)?

In any case there is now no way to order the various starts, restarts, and rewrites that reside on the surface of the manuscript sheets, which were themselves divided up in various ways (usually into two large columns) and then filled in at different times in what appears to be a set of odd sequences, accompanied by much crossing out. Reproducing the material as it lies on the page is clearly the best editorial strategy, but then that merely reproduces the textual conundrum: what are these people saying? Are they speaking to each other rather than to readers? to readers in agreement with each other? However, of all the various works attributed to Marx (one way or another), it seems fair to say that *The German Ideology* rates high for sheer originality and stimulus, and the raggedness of the text hardly gets in the way. It is very much the origin of what Marx termed "our outlook," and there is considerable textual overlap with the 1859 preface and other works (Carver 1983, ch. 3).

The Communist Manifesto is the joint work with the fewest authorial problems, in that we have two earlier versions by Engels (a Communist "confession of faith" written in a catechetical style, and a draft on the principles of Communism for a party congress) and surviving documentation indicates that Marx worked on a final draft up to (late) submission for publication in very early 1848 (Marx and Engels 1995, 58–69). A textual comparison between Engels's draft "principles" and the final text as published (N.B.: there are still obscurities in dating the earliest versions) suggests where Marx's influence lay, but no one, not least the two themselves in subsequent comments on the document, disputes that both had a hand in the various versions that went into print. Engels did write in 1869 that the work was essentially Marx's, as was his wont when presenting himself as "second fiddle," yet Marx's authorized "voice." Somewhat contrarily I have argued that the historical passages, for instance, have far more to do with Engels's voluminous earlier writings than with Marx's considerably thinner and more theoretical output. It also seems unlikely that the two authors agreed on the final draft while actually working together, Marx being presumed from circumstantial evidence to have worked alone on the text as the "last hand." Nonetheless everything about this work suggests an unambiguously joint effort—though what is lacking are joint signatures. The *Manifesto* appeared anonymously for obvious political reasons—and neither a jointly written manuscript nor the publisher's copy has survived (Carver 1983, ch. 3; see also Cowling 1998).

The real difficulty here is not the joint authorial voice in the *Manifesto*, but the multifarious character of the audience—the document was written to satisfy a committee incorporating known individual views, and to weld together diverse less well known Communists who met only occasionally, and only to advise and educate each other, rather than to embark on any concerted campaigns or covert actions. There may very well be silences in this text—areas too controversial to cover—and ambiguous formulations to please different people differently. This, of course, increases the complexities in terms of the reception of the work by the wider, diverse audience that the authors presumed was their international readership. Interestingly the *Manifesto* itself promises and encourages translations of its own text into other languages. By the late 1860s and early 1870s, in considerably changed political and personal circumstances, both authors were willing to "own" the *Manifesto* and to have it republished with full authorial attribution and an introduction jointly signed "Karl Marx and Friedrich Engels." But by then the two could also frame it as a historical document and plead other preoccupations in order to forestall any suggestion that they should have updated it or written another manifesto instead.

While Marx and Engels were both alive, the primary authorial strategy of each was to sign himself singularly as himself (although Engels had a rather long history of pseudonyms in his pre-Marx days) and to refer respectfully, if slightly distantly, to the other (from the contemporary perspective) as a distinguished author of personal acquaintance. Engels's *Anti-Dühring*, for example, first appeared as his own journalism in 1877–78, and then shortly after reappeared with an introduction in which Marx was quoted and advertised as a mentor and influence. But in the second edition, published in 1885, two years after Marx's death, the partnership motif appears, and the reader encounters the joint "Marx and I" in a shift of narrative subject. Engels also proudly recounted that Marx had contributed a section on "economics" and that he (i.e., Engels) had adjusted *his* text to reflect this joint, if rather retrospective, input. After Marx's death Engels also provided numerous introductions and prefaces to new editions of Marx's works, all in the same vein, and Marx emerged from Engels's narrative as the presumed "senior partner," once Engels had self-identified as his "junior" (Carver 1983, chs. 3–5).

This "Marx" is a voice that Engels used effectively to recount the "materialist interpretation of history" (a phrase Engels introduced in 1859, but one never picked up verbatim by Marx) and to create the "imprimatur" that drives the partnership narrative in its most stringent form, perfect agreement, or its slightly stress stringent versions, eventual convergence in a "deterministic" system or "division of labor" in complementary fields (Carver 1983, intro.). In the 1885 preface to *Anti-Dühring* Engels relates that he read his entire manuscript to Marx, and so he—Engels—feels confident that Marx agreed with what it says. But why was Engels *reading* to Marx? (Marx could read!) And if he was reading aloud, was Marx listening? Curiously Engels does not report Marx speaking for himself about *Anti-Dühring*. Obviously quite a lot would depend, then, on what Marx is supposed to have meant without speaking, so mysteriously this is a case where Engels finds Marx conveniently speechless. Engels's comment that agreement about *Anti-Dühring* was (in the usual translation) "self-understood between us" (Engels 1969, 13; *selbstversteht* is better rendered as "obvious" or "mutual") suggests that in his view the partnership extended to telepathy, at least from Engels to Marx.

Marx did write a (very short) introduction to Engels's *Socialism: Utopian and Scientific*, itself extracted from *Anti-Dühring* and published (in French) in 1880. Marx indeed recommended the pamphlet to readers for its "political" content, interestingly limiting his endorsement to something narrower than Engels ever claimed, and not spelling out exactly what he meant. Even here, however, "voice" is an issue—Marx signed this rather qualified endorsement of Engels's first major work for many years with someone else's name, that of Paul Lafargue, Marx's son-in-law. Engels, so I have argued, was a genius at consciously taking on complexity in some contexts and then unselfconsciously creating ambiguity out of it (Carver 1981, ch. 7).

The notion of Marx's "imprimatur" is a characteristically Engelsian construction. It raises the question whether one person is right to speak for another and, if so, whether the two speak with one voice. Once one of the parties is dead, the issue becomes even more unclear. Engels made Marx live on, not only by giving him a voice of his own, but also by constructing a narrative through which Engels and Marx seemed to speak in unison, suggesting ventriloquism. Summarizing the position, I list once again the "five voices" lurking within the Marx-Engels "partnership" in specific texts, adding a note to each one stating the usual consequences among commentators:

- separate signed voices, as in *The Holy Family*—generally ignored in commentary
- a joint anonymous voice, as in *The Communist Manifesto*—generally attributed to Marx, rather than Engels, by commentators
- debating voices, as in *The German Ideology*—almost universally homogenized as "Marx and Engels" in commentary
- His Master's Voice, as when Engels regurgitates Marx in reviews and articles—Marx's silences about this activity are read by commentators as "consent" ("tacit," rather than "express")
- Voice from the Tomb, or the "resurrected voice," as when Engels makes the authorial Marx speak from beyond the grave—commentators read this in conjunction with the "partnership" narrative, on Engels's own terms

Revoicing the Voice

Much of the Marx that has come down to us derives from commentary on Engels's Marx, a notion that Engels himself encouraged in (not very) private correspondence, suggesting that his own works made easier reading than the highly intellectual and scientific triumphs of the master (Carver 1983, ch. 5). Many millions more read *Socialism: Utopian and Scientific* and (eventually) *Dialectics of Nature* (edited posthumously from Engels's manuscripts) than ever tackled *Capital*, volume 1, or even *Value, Price, and Profit* (written by Marx in English for workers' meetings). But even when commentators are explicating works by Marx, the overwhelming tendency has been to revoice Marx as Engels constructed him. Engels framed Marx in a biographical narrative about Hegel and dialectical philosophy, thus implying that Marx's aim was system building in some comparable manner, and portraying him as a "scientific materialist" to rival Darwin, as Engels said of Marx in his "Graveside Speech" of 1883 (Carver 1983, ch. 4).

It is interesting that the major texts by Marx that are cited in conjunction with Engels's claims are often footnotes and tangential remarks. The 1859 preface, for example, contains a "guiding thread," which Engels revoiced as a lapidary doctrine, beginning with his book review of the same year. Marx himself consigned these few sentences of text to a footnote to

Capital, volume 1, surely not the place for one of the scientific discoveries of the age. Originally it came from a hastily drafted preface and was intended merely to guide the reader; as a footnote to another text it seems exactly that, a footnote, except when taken—for example, by analytical Marxists—as "Marx" *simpliciter.* There may be a highly ironic authorial strategy in Marx that reverses footnotes to text in terms of speaking to the reader, but as a way of reading Marx, in my view, this focus on footnotes and odd sentences tends toward the cabalistic.

References to Hegel are similarly cast by Marx himself in a prefatory and comparative vein, typically in the second preface to *Capital,* volume 1, in which he comments at length on *someone else's* (a Russian reviewer's) comparison of his (Marx's) method to the one employed by "that mighty thinker" (Hegel). There are few references indeed to "dialectic" in Marx, and none to its centrality to explaining anything and everything (Carver 1981, ch. 5). Marx merely comments that he "coquetted" with Hegelian terminology in the opening chapters of *Capital,* volume 1, and makes a limited number of qualified comparisons elsewhere in the text. My point here with respect to commentators is that these remarks and passages are not so much "taken out of context" as *put into a context* supplied by the Engelsian tradition. In the commentators' texts appears another Marx, another voice, revoiced from Engels.

Voices and Lives

Teleology plays a large part in traditional biographical narrations, in that the young Marx and the young Engels seem destined for each other in their early lives, and their first meetings are invested with world-historical significance. Commentators are generally so uninquisitive about the narrative conventions of the genre in which they write, that it is unthinkable to imagine querying the tradition and possibly presenting the tale another way. The "first meeting" invariably sits within an autobiographical and biographical frame that Engels established. In 1895 (some fifty-three years after the event) Engels wrote to Marx's biographer Franz Mehring, saying that the first meeting between the two (in 1842) was "rather cool," an admission that is paradoxically useful in a hagiographical account. Fortunately the story picks up again in late 1844, after Engels and Marx have corresponded, and they not only meet but agree to collaborate—on *The Holy Family.* In that way they are revoiced in a narrative recounting the founding moments of the partnership, a narrative that benefits from the suspense generated by the nearly abortive first encounter. Had they gone their separate ways in 1842, what would have happened? One can hear the biopic voices ringing through the biographies as these originary encounters are revisited, reenacted, and revoiced.

The "perfect-agreement" and "eventual-convergence" theories, on which the "Marx-Engels" school relies, require the unitary voices detailed in the typology above. The other variant in the "partnership" narrative—the "division-of-labor" thesis—requires something different in terms of voicing Marx and Engels. Engels suggested, once Marx was off the set, that scientific and historical questions were largely, though not wholly, assigned to him—after all, Marx had left publications and notebooks on these subjects. In this way, at convenient moments, the voices of the two can be conveniently different, saying compatible things about different subjects, presumably by agreement, and also conveniently the same, overlapping and making use of each other's materials. Obviously this keeps the voices in time and in harmony—where a commentator requires this—and at these moments the commentator, in whose voice the narrative proceeds, rather conveniently disappears.

A common authorial strategy in commentary is to follow the manuals of style that advise crisp declarative sentences and avoidance of the pronoun "I"—perhaps just lapsing into an indeterminate "we," rather inveigling readers into the illusion that they, too, are helping to write the text as well as reading it. Readers do write texts of their own in their minds as they read, on my view, but for them to have to do so hand in hand with commentators seems an unnecessary renunciation of the authorial voice that readers should retain, independent of commentators who wish to create a "partnership" that is rather to the advantage of one over the other. Overinclusive commentators attempt to make readers into their "junior partner" and so subsume their voices into one that is authorial and authoritative. Engels did much the same with Marx. The Engels-Marx or Marx-Engels riddle will not be resolved by investigating and characterizing "the relationship"; rather, the solution to the riddle is in the genre—when Engels characterized the relationship for the world, he cast it in the language of assertive certainty as "Marx and I."

Dead Authors and Living Texts

The *Marx-Engels Gesamtausgabe*, better known as MEGA², is one of the major academic monuments of the mid–twentieth century, or at least it

should have been. Planned in over a hundred double volumes, and bene-
fiting from the seemingly limitless funds and person-hours that only East
Berlin and Moscow could provide, the operation was carried out—from
the 1960s until about 1990—in staggeringly pedantic textological terms.
The remit was to publish everything that survives by Marx and Engels in
the original language, and to catalogue any missing or doubtful items, as
well as to include third-party letters, other items of interest, and a moun-
tain of information about the manuscript production, publication history,
and contemporary reception of every work. Only the purest principles
and procedures were employed to establish the texts, and the *Apparat*
volume accompanying each volume of text gives details of variants, line by
line and word by word. A fundamental tenet of the operation was that
chronology should play a crucial part in ordering the materials presented,
and that copy-texts for each item would be chosen with that in mind. Obviously, for any given work, the earliest manuscript draft does not necessarily
or even usually represent the copy-text to which early drafts can be related
and from which variant copies, authorial notations after publication, and
further editions and translations can be tracked. Sometimes the choice of
copy-text can be a matter of judgment and therefore subject to debate and
dispute, but the sort of arguments involved follow well-established lines,
and the whole exercise often has the marks of necessary but perhaps
rather boring aridity.

Unsurprisingly, however, for a series produced (till 1990) under orthodox Marxist regimes, there was considerable investment in finding Marx
and Engels to be in "ideological" terms what tradition already decreed
them to be, while also maintaining the reputation of the editorial section
as purely "scientific." In editorial terms Marx and Engels are treated in
MEGA[2] as separate individuals producing separate works, but also working
together and collaborating from time to time, just as surviving documentation indicates. *The German Ideology* presents special difficulties, in that an
apparently collaborative work, interpreted as the production of
a single-voiced "smooth text," comes into question once readers are
equipped with a textological apparatus that identifies each individual's
handwriting, and so a variant interpretation becomes possible—some
passages become a debate, in which one author contradicts the other.
Although material from the opening of *The German Ideology* was included
in the MEGA[2] *Probeband* of the early 1970s, the full text has never
appeared, possibly for reasons of this sort, that is, an unwillingness to
probe too deeply into the particulars of the unitary, joint "voice" that is
presumed to be speaking from the authorized version.

At a certain point in the Marx-Engels story, however, all this breaks down. As MEGA² has advanced through the *Nachlaß*, in which "economic works" relating to the published volumes of *Capital* are treated separately (from all other works, from letters, and from notebook materials), the editorial team (reorganized and refunded since 1990) has reached *Capital*, volume 3. This work is problematic in that it was edited by Engels for publication after Marx's death, and it appeared in 1894 as authored by Marx and edited by Engels. But the manuscripts from which Engels worked were written by Marx in 1861–63, before the final manuscript draft of *Capital*, volume 1, was started. Engels's text is known to depart from Marx's manuscripts at numerous points, and a number of commentators have begun to voice disquiet. The manuscripts have themselves been published in MEGA², working chronologically through Marx's materials. Since these manuscripts have become available, it is not too difficult to compare Marx's thoughts with Engels's published version of *Capital*, volume 3, which of course appeared as the third volume of his masterwork, and the last that would appear. The volumes of supplementary materials published later as *Theories of Surplus Value* count as volume 4 of *Capital* only in a supplementary sense, rather than as a continuation of the analytical presentation of the "economic categories." Undertaking this comparison of Engels to Marx, Norman Levine has complained that Engels "Hegelianized" the text at certain points, and Christopher J. Arthur has argued that Engels introduced the concept "simple commodity production" to the detriment of Marx's argument (Levine 1984, ch. 4; Arthur 1996, ch. 8). This type of work has complicated matters for MEGA² considerably.

In MEGA² terms the problem is the copy-text of *Capital*, volume 3. Is it the 1894 text as edited and published, indeed "completed," by Engels, to which Marx's manuscripts of 1861–63 are a precursor in a rough-and-ready sense? Or is the ur-*Capital*, volume 3, really the 1861–63 manuscripts as Marx left them, to which Engels's editorial emendations and additions are exactly that—variants of a text that can be judged independently as "coming from another hand"? Everyone agrees that Engels's voice in *Capital*, volume 3, as published is that of an editor, speaking first to readers through an introduction and then helping readers through a text in which Marx speaks as author. The problem that has arisen is the extent to which Engels's voice is *additionally* so nearly authorial that the published text is not merely a joint production, but actually an act of clairvoyance, in which Engels—as medium—allows Marx to speak through him from beyond the grave.

Extravagant as it sounds, the latter characterization is the one that suits the "true believers" in the orthodox tradition (which encompasses both biographical narrative and doctrinal substance) and is precisely the "fact" they need in order to finish the tale—that of the Marx-Engels "partnership"—most convincingly, in order to safeguard the "ideology" that is "truly Marxist." What could be better proof that two voices spoke as one than universal recognition that one voice in the ultimate instance was as good as the other? The matter is "ultimate" both in terms of *Capital* as a sequential work and in terms of Engels's career—he died in 1895, just after volume 3 was published.

Conversely, those arguing that unity between the two cannot be assumed, but must be established evidentially instance by instance, are in a strong position to unravel the narrative on which so much Marxist orthodoxy depends, by working backward from the differences that textual comparisons between Marx and Engels can plausibly establish. These differences, so the skeptical analysis runs, are so striking—Engels's work so divergent from the tenor of Marx's analysis—that doubt becomes more strongly justified than ever. Blanket presumptions of "partnership" thus become even more damaging to fresh and stimulating readings of Marx, and indeed to new political challenges to capitalism that might be developed outside the "orthodox" framework of assumptions and "laws."

What would satisfy "the orthodox" is an admission from MEGA² that Marx's 1861–63 manuscripts are forerunners of a copy-text, which ought to be *Capital*, volume 3, as published by Engels. This text would therefore be authorially established by Engels, not merely editorially constructed, though quite how clear this elision of distance—between editorship and authorship—would have to be made is not as yet very helpfully addressed by those arguing for the "orthodox" view. Can Engels be viewed as both author and editor without contradiction?

Contrarily, those in MEGA² who see advantages in preserving a clear distinction between editorship and authorship, and hence between Engels and Marx as "voices," where circumstances suggest that this is indeed the case, need do little more than stick with the chronological principle and hold the line, already visible, between the author's hand (in the 1861–63 manuscripts) and the editor's work (in the 1894 edition). This is just as the MEGA² text would helpfully indicate, provided that the 1894 edition is actually produced in line with the series as currently progressing.

It may well be that some readers will do the textual comparison (between the 1861–63 manuscripts and *Capital*, volume 3, as published in 1894) and conclude that Engels did an excellent job rewriting Marx, and that Engels's "economics," whether conceptually "Hegelianized" or not, is an improvement on Marx's manuscript thoughts, which in any case ante-dated the real beginning of the critique of the economic categories in its worked-out form. It could also be that some readers will conclude that Engels meddled unnecessarily and unhelpfully with Marx's thoughts, which even in the 1861–63 manuscripts are really more in line with the sequential thrust of *Capital* than they are with Engels's version of Marx's methodology and consequent emendations to his text (Vollgraf and Jung-nickel 1994, 3–55; Jahn 1996, 117–26). My point is that MEGA², rather than adopt a view that erases, or tends to erase, the different sorts of read-ings that readers might want to construct, should continue to make it easy for readers to choose.

Interestingly, in 1859, when Engels began giving voice to Marx in earnest, he never actually wrote a promised third section of his 1859 book review of Marx's *A Contribution to the Critique of Political Economy*. Having produced a political biography of Marx to put the first installment of his economic critique into context, and having discussed what Engels termed the "historical" and "logical" methods that Marx supposedly employed, Engels never wrote the advertised summary of the critique itself—a digest of Marx's critical re-presentation of the economic categories. After Marx's demise, however, and due to widespread pressure on Engels as literary executor, Engels evidently overcame this reluctance to engage with Marx's multilayered analysis and difficult modes of conceptualization about "eco-nomic" matters. The results can now be evaluated, provided that Engels retains an editorial, rather than authorial, voice and that one person of the pair does not turn into the other. Otherwise we risk a midrash version of *Capital*, volume 3—something that seemingly looks like Marx, seemingly sounds like Marx, seemingly is Marx—but isn't. Or, to put it the other way round, if Engels speaks for Marx at the end (both of *Capital* and of his life), and if we have to work backward through the Marx oeuvre on the assump-tion that Marx was really Engels all along, I think it is going to be hard work making Marx meaningful.

Difference and Dichotomy

The *presumption of difference*, of course, allows agreement to emerge, if it can be found, and there is little political motivation—that I know of—to ob-scure agreement between the two. But where there is a *presumption of agree-ment*, commentators and readers, in my experience, are rarely encouraged to arrive at difference, precisely because so much political energy has gone into promoting the Marx-Engels "partnership" as a unitary voice behind the texts. Maybe I am wrong in the detailed answers I have come up with when acting as commentator and writing about the Engels-Marx relationship, but I am sure that I was right to ask the questions that I have in this chapter and my preceding works. What disturbs me about counterarguments to my views to date is summed up in the following list of *interpretive moves to avoid*. While there is a certain defensive and self-referential quality to the discussion below, I ask readers to bear with this in the interests of larger and more general scholarly issues.

- *Tradition settles the issue.* For example: "Marxists have always known that Marx and Engels were a partnership and spoke with one voice on all important matters." This is supposed to prove that the interpretive principle of agreement between the two is correct. Actually this is simply reading later situations into earlier ones, and indeed it fails to query how and why those who took this view did so, whether they were right at the time, and whether the view is useful now.
- *Difference and diversity = dichotomy.* For example: "Carver looks for differences between Marx and Engels, so he believes that they always differed." This is untrue in terms of the narrow subject matter I have addressed, and indeed it is the principle that has created the supposed school of "dichotomists." Actually, among those who presume that Marx and Engels *may have differed* in various ways at various times, there is little agreement on exactly what these differences are and what their significance is. Curiously, some commentators have criticized the supposed school for failing to form itself properly on the basis of uniform agreement!
- *New ideas are a new orthodoxy.* For example: "The dichotomists are a fashionable orthodoxy." It has been repeatedly claimed that those few writers who have recently challenged the traditional account of the Marx-Engels relationship (which claim of course ignores the long history of challenges, some of which were almost contemporaneous with the original account given by Engels) somehow constitute an orthodoxy, as well as a school. The number of writers complaining of a "new orthodoxy," in my opinion, currently outnumbers those writers who supposedly constitute it.
- *One person's view is allowed to stand for another's.* For example: "Engels characterized his relationship with Marx, and so that characterization is the right one." This simply disregards the fact that another view would

have been possible if Engels had written these characterizations while Marx was alive. I have argued that due attention must be paid to chronology, and to events—such as Marx's death—within that chronology.

- *Dissolution of chronology.* For example: "Any passage from any work of Marx or Engels can be juxtaposed with any other for whatever reason the commentator has in mind." From this perspective Marx and Engels are presumed as authors really to have been philosophers or scientists and are therefore assumed by commentators to be timelessly consistent and unitarily truthful. This obviously violates the first principle of textual interpretation—that texts ought to be considered in some sort of context, preferably a purposive and political one in the case of Engels and Marx, rather than taken as mere words on the printed page.

- *"Inertia selling," or a requirement to dissent.* For example: "Marx must have agreed entirely with Engels because he did not disagree." This treats the textual record as necessarily complete and as a "window" on whatever was in Marx's mind. We all know—really—that this is an unreasonable and implausible assumption. In any case, the textual record is not necessarily complete, and there are reasons for supposing that those who sorted through it physically, including Engels himself, could have been motivated to remove evidence of disagreement for political and personal reasons. I am not saying that they did, but that the *possibility* must be raised and any interpretation suitably qualified.

- *Phrase snatching/word matching.* For example: "Marx mentioned 'Hegel' and 'dialectic' in his writings, so he necessarily agreed with what Engels said about these subjects." Reasonable interpretations must take the argumentative context of works into account and consider more than isolated words and phrases. Otherwise they will generate readings of Marx and Engels that are incredibly impoverished.

- *Only one reading is possible.* For example: "Interpretation is necessarily 'reading material into conformity' with some already given view." I would argue instead for a presumption that there *may be* multiple variants and irresolvable ambiguities in interpretation, rather than of necessity just one view emerging from the commentator. Overwhelmingly the literature of interpretive commentary is written in an authoritative mode of certainty such that commentators seem to feel they cannot admit to doubt or ignorance. Yet the difficulties of contextual reconstruction are such that there is *almost always* variety among readings.

- *Partnership = a single identity.* For example: "Marx and Engels are presumed to be equally good on any given topic." This ignores the educational, experiential, and intellectual evidence that they had different talents, abilities, backgrounds, and opportunities, and so violates what we know of them as characters with highly individualized life histories. They were different people with different ideas and different backgrounds, strong characters who could develop their own views, collaborate and negotiate with one another, tolerate dissimilarity, and generally engage in debate. Presuming that they were merely two sides of one coin or faithful reflections of each other is simply insulting to them as intellects and demeaning to them as people. In my view commentators must take a "life-world" approach and not treat Marx or Engels as a god or "genius" who is "not of this world."

- *Monomania.* For example: "Marx and Engels had only one agenda together, and whatever they said had to fit whatever that agenda was at any particular time." This seems to me a poor way of reading the rich and varied materials that we are left with, and indeed it is precisely in tackling the difficult area of political complexity that the two were so interesting and intelligent. That is probably a good deal of the reason they are still read today.

A Politics of Self and Other

At a deeper level I would argue more positively that Marx and Engels must be treated much as we would treat ourselves as intellects and as persons. That is, we must presume that they had emotions much as we do, and that they had just as little power to see where their lives were going. For instance, they did not know, when they first met, that they were going to meet again, nor when they met again did they know that they would be— *at times*—working together, living in close proximity, in close correspondence, and in a relationship of financial dependency, for many years to come. Engels was quite entitled to write his account of their relationship from his point of view at the time that he did, and we are quite entitled to examine with considerable skepticism the way he memorialized his relationship with Marx.

Skepticism is not the same as blanket rejection or disbelief or "hatred" of Engels, and indeed the same applies to Marx. Rather it is the service that scholars afford the community at large, for surely it is the scholar's job to raise questions—not to foreclose on them or to narrow unduly the answers that may be provided. Scholars should not follow a methodology of assuming what remains to be demonstrated. If they can demonstrate whatever it is to the satisfaction of their readers, then well and good.

The overarching frame of reference in addressing the issues raised by the "Engels-Marx" (or "Marx-Engels") relationship must be one of open-mindedness, willingness to question, and presumption of complexity. Otherwise interpretations of Marx and Engels will continue to have the stultifying quality that Communist orthodoxy and cold-war reaction *together* imposed on this fascinating legacy. This is to say that there must be a fine balance between an enthusiasm that sympathizes and identifies with Marx and Engels and their political world and a skepticism that questions what they said and how they acted. This should not in fact be too difficult, since I suspect it conforms to the way that most of us live out the relationships from which we construct our intellectual and personal lives—with neither blind faith nor blanket disbelief. Rather, we live in a critical and supportive dialogue with others, at least if we are lucky.

In my view, research on Marx and Engels has barely begun, since there is so much more going on in these texts than the "Marxist"/"cold-war" framework allowed. This is not to say that any and all Marxisms were worthless and insupportable—far from it—but that the possibilities are far wider than the traditional frameworks have generally allowed. Many of the intellectual and political issues remain, of course, but the way in which they are approached—as politics moves on—must perforce be different.

References

Arthur, Christopher J., ed. 1996. *Engels Today: A Centenary Appreciation.* London: Macmillan.

Carver, Terrell. 1981. *Engels.* Oxford: Oxford University Press.

———. 1983. *Marx and Engels: The Intellectual Relationship.* Brighton, East Sussex: Harvester/Wheatsheaf.

———. 1988. Communism for Critical Critics: A New Look at *The German Ideology. History of Political Thought* 9:129–36.

———. 1989. *Friedrich Engels: His Life and Thought.* London: Macmillan.

Cowling, Mark, ed. 1998. *The Communist Manifesto: New Interpretations.* Edinburgh: Edinburgh University Press.

Engels, Frederick. 1969. *Anti-Dühring.* London: Lawrence & Wishart.

Jahn, Wolfgang. 1996. Über Sinn und Unsinn eines Textvergleichs zwischen der Engelsschen Ausgabe des dritten Bandes des *Kapital* von 1894 und den Marxschen Urmanuskripten. *MEGA-Studien* 1:117–26.

Levine, Norman. 1984. *Dialogue Within the Dialectic.* London: Allen & Unwin.

Marx, Karl, and Friedrich Engels. 1995. *Das kommunistische Manifest.* Ed. Thomas Kuczynski. Trier: Schriften aus dem Karl Marx Haus.

———. 1974. *Die deutsche Ideologie.* Ed. Wataru Hiromatsu. Tokyo: Kawadeshobo-Shinsha Press.

Mill, John Stuart. 1989. *On Liberty*. Ed. Stefan Collini. Cambridge: Cambridge University Press.
Vollgraf, Carl Erich, and Jürgen Jungnickel. 1994. "Marx in Marx' Worten." *MEGA-Studien* 2:3–55.

2

A Philosophical Compliment
for Friedrich Engels

Joseph Margolis

If, undertaking to throw light on Friedrich Engels's originality, we step back to appreciate Engels's self-effacing comments vis-à-vis Marx's theorizing power, we may well wonder what remains to be salvaged. The answer, if there is a favorable answer, must be that the total eclipse of Marxism—or, better, what Marx and Engels had begun to discern in the movement of human history—cannot be conceded as a mere entailment of the defeat of world Communism or of the various forms of Marxian socialism that are now in deep retreat.

It's hardly likely that Engels can be reclaimed as an unsung genius who modestly suppressed his own originality or merely deformed his best insights to suit Marx's very different energies. But times have changed, and we may linger a little at all those library shelves that were once devoted to the immense promise of Marx and Engels's unique collaboration. The fact remains: now, at the close of the twentieth century, the whole notion of the historical nature of human existence and the historicized structure of our understanding of the events of social history is almost completely marginalized in the Western world—a fortiori, in the world. We have been effectively thrown back to Kantian and pre-Kantian forms of thought. The entire labor of the various forms of nineteenth-century historicism and social constructivism, spanning at least post-Kantian idealism, Marx and Engels's materialist "reversal" of Hegel, the historicizing and dehistoricizing of the Darwinian themes of social evolution, and, more recently, structuralist and existential, poststructuralist and pragmatist, late Frankfurt-Critical and feminist and third-world improvisations have begun to converge unmistakably toward a completely ahistorical reading of the human condition. It's with that impression of the nearly effective eclipse of the main themes of Marx and Engels's collaboration—particularly, of Engels's own conceptual convictions—that I venture to reread a part of Engels's theoretical remains. I am persuaded that, if, in doing so, we are to reclaim any of Engels's contributions, it (or they) should not be too closely linked to the bare essentials of whatever we choose to regard as Marxist orthodoxy. For one thing, there's little point to anything of that sort now, if Marxist orthodoxy is not to be revived—and it cannot be; and, for another, there's no point in diminishing whatever Engels has to say of continuing interest—the same is true of Marx, of course—about the structure of human life, by tagging it as merely Marxist, if the whole of Marxist orthodoxy must be abandoned. (Although, of course, we have precious little at the moment to put in its place.)

Reading Engels

I insist on the caveat because what I wish to take up *is* usually debated in the context of clarifying the conceptual and explanatory relationship, within the terms of Marxist materialism, between so-called economic (or structural) forces and the superstructural aspects of genuine historical events. That way of reading Engels (the entrenchment of orthodoxy) is far from my purpose, but it is essential, for instance, to Louis Althusser's contrived reading of Engels's well-known letter to J. Bloch, dated 21–22 September 1890. Althusser was so exercised by the letter that he analyzed it in an appendix to the essay "Contradiction and Overdetermination," in which he addresses the question of Marx's having "inverted Hegel," a topic already broached in "On the Young Marx." Both papers are included in Althusser's *For Marx*. In fact, that entire text is devoted to advancing Althusser's structuralist—that is, essentialist, dehistoricized, antihumanist

—reading of Marx: in particular, how to characterize dialectical material- ism scientifically; and, above all, how to place Marx correctly in opposing "humanism."

Althusser saw Engels's letter (and more) as threatening, on grounds of orthodoxy, to restore a "humanist" reading of dialectical materialism. He hastened to block off the implicated recovery. I have no wish to pursue Althusser's structuralist fandango or to enter into battles of political or textual factions that no longer have any turf to defend. There is reason to believe Althusser was not adequately informed about Marx's early writings and that, however interesting the structuralist line may be thought to be, Althusser himself distorts much that rightly belongs to Marx—a fortiori, much that belongs to Engels; and *that* does bear instructively on an appre- ciation of Engels's work.

I trust I may take a moment more to say that Michel Foucault, who plainly came under Althusser's influence while a student at the École Normale Supérieure in Paris, borrowed (as Althusser himself observes ([1977b, 257–58]) the signal notion of a *problématique* (central to Althusser's struc- turalism) but also adjusted it to his own radically historicized purpose (opposed to Althusser's). The point is this: in Foucault's late work, barely a few years before his death (in 1984), the quasi-structuralist notion of a "problematic" undergoes an entirely new turn, which in effect aims at recovering (uneasily, it seems) elements of the very same "humanism" (now, de-essentialized) that Foucault himself had dismissed (in his earlier "archaeologies"), without (yet) supporting any inherent ahistoricism of Althusser's sort, or, further afield, of Saussure's or Lévi-Strauss's. Foucault fails in this last effort, but he points to what must be reclaimed; and, of course, he does this without the least intention of restoring Marxism. I think he would have found a companion in Engels's letter to Bloch.

You may glimpse in this the barest clue to the importance of a question otherwise easily submerged in the sheer vastness (what I can only call the "sloggery") of Marxist scholarship deprived of its earlier political vitality. I suggest that what, now, at the end of the twentieth century (and the sec- ond millennium) needs to be recovered in a workmanlike way—separated, wherever necessary, from what must be utterly discarded in Marxism itself, in Althusser's ultrarational mystifications, and in all those eddies of social analysis that are (now) floundering and have never found their way back to the brave new world that was thought to be ours—is this single theme: the historicity of human life and society mapped in moral, political, explanatory, and ontological terms, so as to recover (i) objectivity, (ii) the inseparability of theory and practice, (iii) the robust reality of individual and aggregated human life, (iv) the validity of political norms and aspirations, (v) valid explanations of historical events, (vi) the effectivity of politically active individual selves, and (vii) the compatibility and congruence of all these factors taken together. The ensemble of this entire tally—the gist of Marx and Engels's work (detached from official "Marxism")—may be neatly recovered from this bit of Engels's late correspondence. There's the soft sell. In the Bloch letter, Engels is at great pains to explain, for posterity, Marx's (and of course his own) theory. My sense is that he succeeds handsomely—well enough to worry Althusser.

Althusser and Engels

I do mean to play Althusser off Engels, but not for the sake of some imagined orthodoxy or textual correctness. I doubt Marx can be made entirely consistent. But since textual considerations are essential in rereading Engels, I cannot neglect them altogether. Althusser reads Engels's letter to Bloch as, at once, weakly confirming Marx's deeper understanding and, more strictly, falling back to an untenable position (ultimately Hegelian). The truth is, Althusser has hit on an absolutely unavoidable puzzle in Marx's thought, as well as in any serious subsequent alternative to dialectical-materialist explanations of human history.

Althusser cites some remarks from the afterword Marx wrote for the second edition of *Capital,* to confirm his own (Althusser's) orthodoxy and to suggest the ultimate error of Engels's formulation (Althusser 1977a, 91–94). As it happens, Leszek Kolakowski mentions the same afterword (without reference to Althusser), remarking that Marx "quotes with approval an account of his method given by a Russian reviewer of *Capital* in 1872, who observed that 'Marx treats the social movement as a process of natural history governed by laws independent of human will, consciousness and intentions,' and that in his system each historical period has its own laws, which give way in due course to those of the next" (Kolakowski 1981, 319–20). The curious fact is, one could easily construe the nerve of Althusser's structuralist reading of *Capital* as entirely adumbrated in that Russian's summary: Althusser does not mention the source in citing the passage, but he interprets Marx very, very closely in terms of the same notion (which, perhaps casually, Marx did approve). What is interesting is that Engels's letter to Bloch may be reasonably thought to address the same question *and* to provide an entirely different reading (from Althusser's) of Marx's theme—one that undercuts, *avant la lettre*, the entire structuralist effort to eliminate "the human subject" (that is, essentialized selves possessing fixed natures). But neither Marx's comment nor Engels's letter assumes a fixed human nature: both provide for the recovery of human agents (as indeed Engels's account requires) without restoring *any* version of the essentialism Althusser opposes. Althusser seems to have thought that the only way to eliminate an essentialist humanism was to eliminate the very agency of individual human selves, to treat them as the "effects" or anonymous sites of certain underlying material processes of human history. That much I have already suggested was accepted by (early) Foucault, despite his not subscribing to anything like Althusser's ahistorical essentialism. Foucault simply construes the process of historical "problematics" as historicized, as lacking any essentialized structures at all (unless, perhaps, when believed to be necessary within the captive thought of one "archaeologized" regime or another). This is the meaning of Foucault's notion of the "historical *a priori*," that is, an a priori read as an artifact of history, as a seeming necessity (Foucault 1970, ch. 10). Furthermore, as I say, Foucault fails to bring his own account to bear on the ineliminable problem of responsibility and political commitment until it is too late; in his last years, he makes a belated attempt to undo the mischief of his earlier archaeologies—which, though not structuralist in a strict sense, were still obviously influenced by the seeming need (probably partly under Althusser's influence) to eliminate any admission of robust human agents.

That maneuver, I think, is precisely what Engels defeats in the Bloch letter well before it appears in print. If that's so, Engels may be credited with a telling clarification of a thesis he and Marx very probably shared, that explains not only a central difficulty posed by dialectical materialism but a difficulty that confronts every serious attempt at historical explanation (aspiring to replace Marxism by resolving its puzzles) that admits objective forms of historical causation. In the orthodox quarrel, which Althusser favors, the issue centers on the relationship between (economic) structures and (intellectual or ideological) superstructures. If the issue were thus (orthodoxly) confined, it would soon lose interest for all those aware of the permanent eclipse of Marxist fortunes. But the truth is, the substratum/superstructure question brings together at least three distinct puzzles that Marxism shares with every informed successor theory that claims to be objective: first, the puzzle about what is *essential* and what is *accidental* in human history; second, the puzzle about how to apportion the power of effective *causality* between habituated and transient "ideas" (to speak loosely); and third, the puzzle about how to understand the conceptual and causal relationship between *collective* practices and the effective activity of *individual* selves formed by the constituting elements of such practices and forming them in turn. These are unavoidable questions that cannot be monopolized by the substratum/superstructure idiom—and yet their resolution bears on its prospects as well. In particular, it bears on our reception of Engels's theory.

Engels and Marx

I have no intention of pitting Engels against Marx. But I must report that, in the last analysis, Althusser makes his case along such oppositional lines. That is, *he* pits Engels against Marx. The story is rather complicated but worth telling. Althusser, whose primary concern is to explain the meaning of Marx's "inverting Hegel," cites the well-known passage from the afterword: "With [Hegel, the dialectic] is standing on its head. It must be turned right side up again, if you would discover the rational kernel within the mystical shell" (Althusser 1977a, 89; also Althusser 1977c). The lesson Althusser draws from this, which seems (to me) entirely sensible as well as justified, is summarized thus: "For all its apparent rigor, the fiction of the *'inversion'* is now clearly untenable. We know that *Marx did not retain the terms of the Hegelian model of society and 'invert' them.* He substituted other, only distantly related terms for them. Furthermore, he overhauled the connection which had previously ruled over the terms. For Marx, *both terms* and *relation* changed in nature and sense" (Althusser 1977a, 109). Althusser's point is simply that Hegel's dialectic was not valid in its abstract form— could not be validly applied, without essential alteration, to *any* human space: that would be contrary (Althusser explains) to Marx's strong insistence on treating theory ("speculative philosophy," say) as a form of, as encumbered by, the historical practice of one society or another. At the very least, to say otherwise would violate Marx's claim, in the afterword, that "each historical period has its own laws, which give way in due course to those of the next." Hegel's dialectic cannot, then, be reconciled with this. Fine. But that hardly explains what Marx must or may have meant in treating "the social movement as . . . governed by laws independent of human will, consciousness and intentions" and hardly demonstrates that Engels failed to provide a plausible reading of the thesis he and Marx shared—the very thesis that might be reconciled with all the items of my earlier tally ([i]–[vii]) without producing paradox, without departing from the sense of the central texts, and (especially) without endorsing anything like Althusser's structuralist reading. The matter is important, because, to be candid, it affords the only possible clue by which "Marxism" may be recovered beyond the precincts of official Marxism. It may, in short, actually provide a minimal doctrine on which the most promising non-Marxist accounts of history may yet join hands with the immense labors Marx and Engels shared. That's not the worst of reasons for rereading Engels.

Althusser is precise in stating his assessment of the argument of Engels's letter: it's meant, he says, to be "a *decisive* theoretical document for the refutation of schematism [roughly, idealisms of Hegel's sort: the universal validity of purely abstract forms like the dialectic] and economism [roughly, the dogmatic doctrine that economic determinism is all there is to—all that is needed for—historical explanation, eclipsing determination "in the last instance"]. No doubt this is only a letter, he says. But we should not conceal the fact that [Engels's] argument for this *basis* [the basis regarding determination "in the last instance"] will no longer answer to our crucial needs" (Althusser 1977a, 117). Althusser worries the text with the ardor of a man who realizes that if he does not defeat its claim, his own authority (as the structuralist theorist of French Marxism during the Stalinist era) will not survive close scrutiny. That was orthodoxy's fear, of course—not my concern. The point is, beneath the fear, Althusser dredges up a first-rate conceptual puzzle that, as it happens, Engels helps to resolve in a first-rate way (in effect, against Althusser himself). We are the beneficiaries of that unequal contest; for, as it happens, the formula, "in the last instance," which Marx surely shared with Engels, *demonstrates* that neither Marx nor Engels had any intention of denying the effective agency of individual selves *in* the historical process. That's worth making clear.

The excerpted letter (included in the English-language version of the 1948 two-volume Russian edition of Marx and Engels, *Selected Works*) is quite brief, but the text must be read with care if we are to appreciate Engels's rigor. I shall have to quote from it at length. The following fixes the thesis that offends Althusser:

> [H]istory is made in such a way that the final result always arises from conflicts between many individual wills, of which each again has been made what it is by a host of particular conditions of life. Thus there are innumerable intersecting forces, an infinite series of parallelograms of forces which give rise to one resultant—the

historical event. This may again itself be viewed as the product of a power which works as a whole, *unconsciously* and without volition. For what each individual wills is obstructed by everyone else, and what emerges is something that no one willed. Thus past history proceeds in the manner of a natural process and is essentially subject to the same laws of motion. But from the fact that individual wills . . . do not attain what they want, but are merged into a collective mean, a common resultant, it must not be concluded that their value is equal to zero. On the contrary, each contributes to the resultant and is to this degree involved in it. (Engels 1950a, 444)

The best way to understand this passage, I suggest, is as a materialist gloss on (or as an analogue of) the Hegelian thesis that individual human agents are, in effect, co-opted by the processes of history, do not know in advance what the *historical import* of their particular actions is, and, in that sense, that human history is collective, anonymous, "unconscious." There's nothing here to support the notion that individual human actions are historically irrelevant, causally ineffective, mere epiphenomenal "effects" of "real" historical forces that function "independently" of human "wills." On the contrary, what Engels very neatly supplies is a schema for understanding the meaning of economic determinism and the supposed role of economic forces that are determinative "in the last instance." We may quarrel with Marx's claim here—I shall come back to that—but Engels addresses a deeper matter.

Engels and History

Engels introduces the model of a parallelogram of forces—and so "naturalizes" history and historical explanation. He does not quite say (though it is implicit in what he says) that human nature is, so to speak, "second-natured," formed by the formative enculturing powers of this society or that. Otherwise, it would make nonsense to say—as in Marx's afterword— that "each historical period has its own laws, which give way in due course to those of the next." Althusser bases his own structuralist reading on that very doctrine. (The idea that human nature is "second-natured" has, via Aristotle, made a small recovery in recent analytic philosophy. But one can see how impoverished its use is in the purely abstract epistemological questions usually pursued [for instance, McDowell 1996]. I take this to suggest the importance of recovering a full-blooded sense of the historical dimension of human cognition.)

The naturalism cuts two ways. On the one hand, there are undoubtedly reductive, physicalist tendencies in Engels. On the other, the incompletely analyzed "materialism" signifies that, *since* the "value" (the causal role) of "individual wills" is not "equal to zero," whatever causal power may be assigned to economic structures cannot fail to be assignable as well (in some suitably diminished measure) to individual wills.

There is only one way to understand the argument: *ontologically,* there is, there can be, no difference in the "material" structure of substrate and superstructure; *existentially* or *causally,* whatever is real in either substrate or superstructure is what is historically effective; *formally,* whatever is causally effective in the play of "individual wills" is a proper component *of* the "unconscious" vectorial result of the "parallelogram" of forces (the "economic" substrate) that produce genuine "historical events"; therefore, in *explanatory* terms, what is "essential" answers to what *is* causally effective in actual history, and what is "accidental" is explanatorily negligible in the idiom in which it (merely) answers to the exercise of an "individual will."

There is certainly a tendency in Marxism—in Marx himself, of course—to favor some sort of essentialism; but there is also a countertendency in Marx (the consequence of the "inversion" of Hegel's dialectic) to reject all essentialisms (see Margolis 1992). I think we can safely say that neither Marx nor Engels (nor Althusser) resolves that puzzle satisfactorily, but also that it cannot, in principle, be satisfactorily resolved in essentialist terms. It must be possible, therefore, to construe the essence/accident idiom in Engels's letter to Bloch (and in a good deal of Marx's writings, of course) as committed to "nominal," rather than "real," essences, meaning that whatever is deemed *real* in the way of causal explanation in history need not, for that reason alone (effectively, cannot), be thought to entail any fixed or invariant structures pertinent to historical explanation. The denial of that finding is, I should add, conceptually incompatible with Marxist historicism—or, for that matter, with any historicism not ultimately subsumed as the mere *Erscheinung* of some ultimately ahistorical Reality. The orthodox textualists may dispute the interpretation of Marx and Engels as they wish. But the verdict is incontrovertible, and the passage from Engels is reasonably hospitable to the interpretation I am proposing. (It cannot be defeated on independent grounds—even if Marx and Engels and Althusser conspired to support essentialism. That's what I have in mind in "saving" Marxism from its own orthodoxy.) There is, I may add, a powerful analogue in evolutionary biology (see Mayr 1982). Engels, I should add, was deeply impressed by Darwin's work.

Seen this way, the essence/accident idiom is simply an "enhanced" rhetorical device for identifying what is deemed *objective* in the way of historical explanation. Marxists will have their own convictions, of course. Here we have no need to ensure more than what to count as "objective" in the way of historical explanation. You see, therefore, where Althusser goes astray —reading in the way he does the Russian reviewer's remark cited in Marx's afterword: "Marx treats the social movement as a process of natural history governed by laws *independent* of human will, consciousness and intentions." *If* the process and the laws were *ontologically* independent (rather than merely not cognitively fathomed by individual agents), Marx would have been committed to some ahistorical invariance *and* to the denial of the primacy of praxis. The idea goes completely against the *Theses on Feuerbach:* for instance, the pregnant affirmation (Thesis VI, an affirmation Engels's letter glosses to advantage) that "the human essence is no abstraction inherent in each single individual. In its reality it is the ensemble of the social relations" (Marx 1977, 157).

Thesis VI must be read in the company of Thesis I, which surely gives the (textual) edge to Engels. But, apart from that, Althusser's structuralism would require a form of cognitive privilege, regarding the "independent" laws of history, that would sanction the worst form of closet "idealism" he himself deplores in Hegel (and, by default, in Engels). You begin to see the canny intelligence of Engels's formula: by analogy with the natural sciences, we work first with what (in the current Anglo-American idiom) may be (though usually disparagingly) called the "folk-theoretic" idiom— the idiom of individual beliefs and desires and interests and objectives— and *then,* at some level of deeper analysis, we conjecture (*a*) *what* the underlying causal process of human history is and (*b*) *how* what is discerned at the level of individual agency is conceptually and causally related to the supposed *real* causal process we have uncovered. What I am saying is simply that Engels's interpretation is more than reasonable, both in orthodox terms and in terms of the needs of *any* would-be account of objective history, and that Althusser's account, epistemically unsound and fraught with paradox, goes wildly and irresponsibly astray (never mind orthodoxy, though Althusser fails there as well).

What Engels effectively shows is that, and why, the reality and explanation of human history cannot be ontologically independent of *whatever* (admitting a nominalized reading of the essence/accident idiom suited to would-be historical laws, or, more safely, suited to causation in history) is admitted at the "folk-theoretic" level at which human individuals ("individual wills") address their own (apparent) interests and act on them. The "parallelogram" of forces that is the "resultant" of all our individual wills (hence produced "*unconsciously* and without volition") belongs *at one and the same time* to what is "structural" and what is "superstructural." There can be no ontological difference, unless at the cost of skepticism or cognitive privilege—or, indeed, of a virulent idealism. That's what Althusser misses. In this sense, Engels clearly salvages a crucial theme for all historicisms (Marxist or not) that mean to invoke objective explanation. History is a folk-theoretic undertaking that is not disqualified from admitting that the meaning of history is "objectively" *not* at all what individual "wills" suppose it to be! That's a significant contribution.

Causation and Explanation

For instance, it follows at once that the difference between what is "essential" and what is "accidental" in "structure" and "superstructure" is a matter of what, precisely, contributes, for the most part, to the causal explanation of genuine "historical events." There can be no separate access to genuine events, essence and accident, the causal explanation of historical events, and the division between what is "determinative . . . in the last instance" and what contributes only modestly (but still *does* contribute), piecemeal, blindly, "unconsciously," *to* the parallelogram of forces. The difference between economic structure and intellectual superstructure *cannot be a principled distinction*—not merely because of questions like those Max Weber and Maurice Godelier pose, but also because, as Engels clearly remarks, the proper measure and form of causal effectivity can only be empirically assigned.

The distinction between structure and superstructure is, perhaps, a matter of political "prudence," *not* a principled ontological distinction at all. It's clear that "materialism" in the Marxist sense is inherently "infected"—as it must be if it is to be relevant to human history—with (as we now say) intentional (or significative) structure. The only "world" Marx and Engels admit is a world *already* construed in terms that bear on the work of human praxis. The "world" is the "objectification" of man's historical praxis (Marx 1964). Anything more sanguine would diminish the primacy of praxis—either in the direction of Althusser's structuralism or in the direction of ascribing some form of "scientific realism" to Marx and Engels (see Wood

1984.) Marx and Engels are not realists in the current philosophical sense. But then, there is no satisfactory version of that sort of (analytic) realism that admits the reality of the human world and history; for, of course, the "realism" of the human world *cannot* be independent of human praxis.

Once you grant the point, you see that it is but a step to grasp as well that the formula, "in the last instance," answers very naturally to Engels's explication of Marx's "discovery" of the law of history (in his preface to the third German edition of *The Eighteenth Brumaire*):

> It was precisely Marx who had first discovered the great law of motion of history, the law according to which all historical struggles, whether they proceed in the political, religious, philosophical or in some other ideological domain, are in fact only the more or less clear expression of struggles of social classes, and [he also discovered] that the existence and thereby the collisions, too, between these classes are in turn conditioned by the degree of development of their economic position, by the mode of their production and of their exchange determined by it. This law, which has the same significance for history as the law of the transformation of energy has for natural science—this law gave [Marx] here, too, the key to an understanding of the history of the Second French Republic. (Engels 1950b, 223–24)

The "parallelogram" is clearly implied: which is to say, economic structures are "in the last instance" decisive because, and only because, *for* history to be decisive, the pertinent economic forces must be intellectually or ideologically manifest to a suitable "degree of development" between conflicting classes! There can be no disjunction. The boldest of Marx's conceptions that this formulation catches up is surely that of the 1844 *Economic and Philosophical Manuscripts*, in the section headed "Estranged Labor," in which he affirms:

> The universality of man [as a "species being"] appears in practice precisely in the universality that makes the whole of nature into his inorganic body that is both (i) his immediate means of subsistence and also (ii) the material object and tool of his vital activity. Nature is the inorganic body of a man, that is, in so far as it is not a human body. That man lives from nature means that nature is his body with which he must maintain a constant interchange so as not to die. That man's physical and intellectual life depends on nature merely

means that nature depends on itself, for man is a part of nature. (Marx 1964, 81)

(I may perhaps be permitted to add, without further comment, that this formulation is distinctly superior to Heidegger's treatment of *Vorhandenheit* and *Zuhandenheit*, in *Being and Time*. In fact, it is difficult to imagine that Heidegger's purple account was not directly influenced by Marx's leaner insight. In any case, Althusser's structuralism makes no sense in the light of such considerations, the point of which must surely have been implicit in Engels's mind.)

If, now, you read Engels's letter to Bloch with Marx's theory of the connection between man and nature in mind, you cannot fail to see the rather elegant simplicity and plausibility of Engels's summary formulation. For what Engels maintains (as does Marx, of course) is that effective history is "the production and reproduction of real [human] life" and that, *within* the terms of *that* process, the distinction between economic structures and ideological superstructures is itself an entirely subaltern—I should say a "prudential"—distinction. Anything more extreme would violate two constraints: one regarding what can only be internal to "real [human] life"; the other, what belongs to the deeper symbiosis between man and nature.

It is very much as if Marx and Engels subscribed to a materialist counterpart of Hegel's phenomenology: man is the reflexive and active site of powers that, abstracted by way of "alienation," yield "objective" (even "inanimate") nature and, abstracted by way of self-conscious praxis, yield the distinction between economic structure and ideological superstructure. Whatever "nature" is, "it" is what it is relative to the historical development of human intelligence: there is an indissoluble ontological linkage between "nature" and "[human] life"; the *objective* picture of both is projected from the inherently historicized process of material forces seen from the side of human understanding, *which is itself a part of what is (serially and critically) objectified as nature.*

Let me risk another passage (the opening lines of the excerpt) from Engels's letter:

> According to the materialist conception of history, [Engels affirms,] the *ultimately* determining element in history is the production and reproduction of real life. More than this neither Marx nor I have ever asserted. Hence if somebody twists this into saying that the economic element is the *only* determining one, he transforms

that proposition into a meaningless, abstract, senseless phrase. The economic situation is the basis, but the various elements of the superstructure: political forms of the class struggle and its results, to wit: constitutions established by the victorious class after a successful battle, etc., juridical forms, and then even the reflexes of all these actual struggles in the brains of the participants, political, juristic, philosophical theories, religious views and their further development into systems of dogmas, also exercise their influence upon the course of the historical struggles and in many cases preponderate in determining their *form*. (Engels 1950a, 443)

It seems impossible to read this in any way in which the distinction between the economic and the intellectual can be more than a distinction of convenience (a "prudential" distinction, if one is thinking of informed and effective power) or, ulteriorly, in any way that "reduces" the ideological to the economic or reduces our cognizing and active powers to inanimate "natural" forces. That's why it seems (to me at least) that Althusser's and the "scientific realist's" maneuvers are similarly motivated, though they proceed from altogether opposite poles. Not only that, but what Engels successfully recovers is the inseparability of effective *agency* (in the aggregated life of individual human beings) and the bare *intelligibility* of human history. The scientific realist risks losing his grip on the human world as such; Althusser "merely" risks losing the coherence of that grip.

Engels adds an extremely perceptive remark immediately following the passage I have just cited. He says: "There is an interaction of all these [superstructural] elements in which, amid all the endless hosts of accidents (that is, of things and events, whose inner connection is so remote or so impossible of proof that we can regard it as nonexistent, as negligible) the economic movement finally asserts itself as necessary. Otherwise the application of the theory to any period of history one chose would be easier than the solution of a simple equation of the first degree." He continues, tellingly: "We make our history ourselves, but . . . under very definite assumptions and conditions" (Engels 1950a, 443).

I feel sure the first part of what I've just cited is what encouraged Althusser to construe Engels as having written at cross-purposes (and ultimately to have failed to cleave successfully to Marx's "doctrine"). But there's no evidence of that. Engels clearly means to say what I take to be the essential point of *The Eighteenth Brumaire* and of Engels's preface, which praises Marx's historical acuity regarding the dawning import of large events that cannot be read off the ephemera of individual motivation.

That is surely the same point as the one made in the Bloch letter: "super-structure"—ideological or intellectual or political or literary or similar seeming "accidents" of history—lacks historical meaning *until*, within the terms of *such* "interaction," what we rightly judge to have been historically "necessary" emerges, "asserts" itself.

Materialism and History

What is deemed necessary there *is* the *economic:* it's not that the economic "finally" emerges from the ephemera—a real stream of events that flows independently of the accidents of individual life, or a secret stream that, independently, flows through what, by the distraction of the false cunning of individual understanding, is perceived to be a mere scatter of individual events rather than the fully structured, profoundly interlocking, deeper process that it is. Both of these readings are delusions of the structuralist sort. Engels's point is plainly: "We make our history ourselves."

What this means is that Marx and Engels are Hegelians of a sort; that is, *they* believe that the objective meaning of history belongs to the collective features of a particular ethos. They believe its intelligible pattern cannot be read off the individual acts of particular persons described and explained in the conventional terms favored by those same agents—who do not normally view what they do in terms of a larger history, who directly address matters in whatever idiom (practical, moral, political, religious, ideological, entrepreneurial, or what have you) obtains in their immediate society. It would not be possible for *history* to be explicable in such terms alone; one needs a sense of the underlying engine of the historical process. Marx and Engels thought they perceived the force of history in class conflict. They may have caught a glimpse of the causal process, but history shows they cannot really have been right. Now, at the end of the century, faced with the emergence of an entirely new global economy and a new productive technology, we are obviously not clear about what to count as the engine of history.

Having said that, I hasten to say as well that that's not the important thing about Engels's contribution. If it were, then the collapse of Marxism would have put an end to all that. No, Marxism, we now see, is (and was) a sturdy exemplar of a more general insight that Engels clarifies in his letter. There needn't be any uniquely correct objective history. Perhaps all histories are the artifacts of historical interests, and perhaps historical interests cannot themselves be made entirely "correct" in any sense that departs very far from the reported interests of aggregated agents living in their self-declared societies. If so, then the connection between "accidents" and "essences" is even closer than Engels allows, and entirely opposed to what Althusser maintains (against Engels). Perhaps, then, historical objectivity is itself a critically fashioned artifact projected by certain imaginative members of such societies.

In any case, Engels's insight does not really depend on the validity of Marxism or on there being any uniquely valid alternative doctrine to Marxism. What Marx and Engels confirm is the viability and good sense of a materialist theory of history. By "materialism" is meant, then, a theory that (i) features certain *effective forces* of historical change (ii) that are entrenched in a society's praxis, (iii) *objective* at least to that extent, (iv) subject to critical revision in terms of a measure of predictive and explanatory success (as of the market's behavior and the like), (v) that enable us to make coherent sense of the meaning of some larger changes in our history, in accord with prediction and purposive commitment, and (vi) that draw out what is explanatory and directive in a normative way from imputed processes suitably abstracted (as by a "parallelogram" of forces) from the aggregated individual acts of the members of a particular society.

I cannot see that such a theory of history leaves anything out that must, in principle, be included. It need not insist on historical necessities, as Marx (and Engels) and Hegel often do (in rather different ways). It needn't insist on "world history," if by that is meant (in the Hegelian sense) that one or another society houses a process of objective history that explains and gives significance to some single inclusive history of the entire world. It needn't be committed to any form of teleologism. And it needn't oppose or disjoin the physical and intentional aspects of history or causality (which, of course, Marxism does not). I suggest that this is part of the permanent legacy of Marxism and a sufficient reason for complimenting Engels.

References

Althusser, Louis. 1977a. Contradiction and Overdetermination. In *For Marx*, trans. Ben Brewster, 87–128. London: New Left Books.
———. 1977b. A Letter to the Translator. In *For Marx*, trans. Ben Brewster, 257–58. London: New Left Books.

―――. 1977c. On the Young Marx. In *For Marx*, trans. Ben Brewster, 49–86. London: New Left Books.

Engels, Friedrich. 1950a. Engels's Letter to J. Bloch (21–22 September 1890). In Karl Marx and Friedrich Engels, *Selected Works*, 2:443–44. London: Lawrence & Wishart.

―――. 1950b. Preface to the Third German Edition of Marx's *Eighteenth Brumaire*. In Karl Marx and Friedrich Engels, *Selected Works*, 1:223–24. London: Lawrence & Wishart.

Foucault, Michel. 1970. *The Order of Things*. New York: Vintage.

Kolakowski, Leszek. 1981. *Main Currents of Marxism*. Vol. 1, *The Founders*. Trans. P. S. Falla. Oxford: Oxford University Press.

Margolis, Joseph. 1992. Praxis and Meaning: Marx's Species Being and Aristotle's Political Animal. In *Marx and Aristotle: Nineteenth-Century German Social Theory and Classical Antiquity*, ed. George E. McCarthy, 329–53. Savage, Md.: Rowman & Littlefield.

Marx, Karl. 1964. Economic and Philosophical Manuscripts (First Manuscript). In *Karl Marx: Early Writings*, trans. and ed. Tom Bottomore. New York: McGraw-Hill.

―――. 1977. Theses on Feuerbach. In *Selected Writings*, ed. David McLellan, 156–58. Oxford: Oxford University Press.

Mayr, Ernst. 1982. *The Growth of Biological Thought*. Cambridge, Mass.: Harvard University Press.

McDowell, John. 1996. *Mind and World*. Cambridge, Mass.: Harvard University Press.

Wood, Allen W. 1984. *Karl Marx*. London: Routledge & Kegan Paul.

3

Engels's Philosophy of Science

Peter T. Manicas

Neither Marx nor Engels wrote what we would call a "philosophy of science." If we want to construct one, we must be anachronistic, since "philosophy of science" is a very recent invention. Their situation and, accordingly, their problems are not ours. Still, the effort is required, since their socialism—in explicit contrast to all others—was called by them "scientific." Moreover, for historically pertinent reasons, it is Engels's later writings that contain his efforts at articulating what I am calling his philosophy of science, and, of even greater importance, it was just these efforts that laid the foundation for dialectical materialism, the "official" philosophy of twentieth-century Marxism-Leninism.

It can hardly be doubted that "dialectical materialism" has been one of the most influential general philosophies of the twentieth century. In terms of sheer numbers, no philosophy has ever counted as many adherents. It became, of course, the philosophy of the Soviet Union and was a critical part of the education of all Soviet citizens. After the Second World War, it also became the official philosophy of much of Eastern Europe, and then, as part of Maoist philosophy, was the basis of education in China. The distinction between "metaphysics" and "dialectics," still in common use in the former Soviet Union and in China, appeared first in Engels.

I believe that to make a case that Marx was a "dialectical materialist" as that has come to be understood (Carver 1983), one would have to ignore much of what Marx wrote, and I believe also that the philosophy of science that is constructable from what Marx had to say (Sayer 1979), including what was not intended for publication by him, differs significantly from the one that I construct from Engels's texts. I do not in what follows attempt to make such a case.

The Immediate Background

Marx, of course, was deeply immersed in the fundamental problems of philosophy, but in a well-known text he insisted that the demands of "the critical critics" could be realized only by "the negation of philosophy as philosophy" (Easton and Guddat 1967, 256). By the 1850s, Marx and Engels turned to other matters. It was easy for later thinkers to believe that having "settled accounts" with "the German ideology," Marx and Engels would thereafter do "science." But two problems went unnoticed, problems that by the 1870s had become very clear to Engels.

First, they had not escaped *having* an epistemology and an ontology. Engels, of all people, knew that such an escape was quite impossible. "Natural scientists believe that they free themselves from philosophy by ignoring or abusing it," he wrote. "They cannot, however, make any headway without thought, and for thought they need determinations." Taking these unreflectively from common sense or from the "little bit of philosophy compulsorily listened to at the University," or "from uncritical and unsystematic readings," they are "no less in bondage"; indeed, they are held in bondage to the "worst vulgarized relics of the worst philosophers" (Engels 1972, 209–10). Sadly, as I have tried to show elsewhere (Manicas 1987), this remains true, especially of too much of what is written—and done—by otherwise highly sophisticated social scientists.

Second, a host of pressing questions were generated by the claims, from the *Communist Manifesto* onward, that their socialism was scientific. Unfortunately, the very idea of science was still much contested. Not only could competing conceptions make their own cases, but a "scientific socialism" could be—and is—subject to some profoundly different understandings. Engels tried to meet the challenge and to clarify their position. Whether he did this well or badly is of some importance. "Scientific socialism" owes much to Engels.

Like all of us, Engels was time-bound; but he was neither philosophically unsophisticated nor ignorant either of the science of his day or of the debates about the science of his day. To carry out his project of clarification Engels studied current science. He tells us that he "went through as complete as possible a 'molting' . . . in mathematics and the natural sciences, and spent the best part of eight years on it" (Engels 1935a, 16). The inquiry was hardly without its presuppositions. Engels was clear on this. Having already arrived at "a conception of nature which is dialectical and at the same time materialist," he needed "to convince [himself] in detail . . . that the amid the welter of innumerable changes taking place in nature, the same dialectical laws of motion are in operation as those which in history govern the apparent fortuitousness of events" (Engels 1935a, 16).

The direct motivation for Engels's belated efforts to answer these questions was attacks on Marx and Engels by socialists who were materialists, committed, like Engels, to the idea that "science" was the only way to truth (Carver 1983, ch. 5). Engels's first response was *Herr Eugen Dühring's Revolution in Science* (1877/78), first published in *Vorwärts* and then as a book, generally known as *Anti-Dühring*. Three chapters then became the widely circulated *Socialism: Utopian and Scientific* (1880; English trans., 1892, with a new introduction by Engels). In *Ludwig Feuerbach and the Outcome of Classical Germany Philosophy* (published in 1886 in *Die Neue Zeit* and then as a book in 1888), Engels returned to older issues regarding the relation of their philosophy both to Feuerbachian materialism and to the "old materialism" of Karl Vogt, Jacob Moleschott, and Ludwig Büchner (Gregory 1977). Engels worked on the materials to be found in his *Dialectics of Nature* between 1873 and 1886, but the incomplete text we have was not published until 1927. It is the last of Engels's belated efforts to set out a "dialectical" view of science. But before turning to Engels's responses to the challenges, it will be helpful, perhaps essential, to set out the philosophical context of this response.

What Is Philosophy of Science?

What we think of as "philosophy of science" is a recent invention, dating only from the 1950s. The idea of science, at that time, was quite unproblematic—even if, as I would insist, it should not have been. Assuming then that everyone knew what science was, it was further assumed that philosophy of science could provide a "rational reconstruction," showing in detail both its "logic" and the ground of its claims to truth. It was conceived, accordingly, as a part of analytic epistemology. It could offer a clear account of scientific terms and of theory, of scientific explanation, and of how scientific propositions are warranted. Given such a "rational reconstruction," it could then address unresolved questions, for example, regarding the unity of the sciences or the "reduction" of theory, and it could offer normative advice regarding successful scientific practice. It could show, for example, how cognitive meaning was given to theoretical terms in a scientific vocabulary.

Philosophy of science in the present century, of course, is dominated by writers we think of as "logical empiricist," even though there was room in the argument for differences, regarding, for example, whether the appropriate logic for science aimed at confirmation or falsification, whether "instrumentalist" or "realist" interpretations of theory were preferred (or perhaps, as Ernest Nagel insisted, there was no real difference on this score), and whether and how science could be "unified."

In speaking then of Engels's philosophy of science, we need to notice that, first, there is little in his writings that even looks vaguely like philosophy of science in this sense. As noted (though this cannot be overstated), at the time that he was writing, the idea of science was not settled. "Science" (*epistēmē, scientia, Wissenschaft*) still very much carried its older sense: the use of reason and observation to find knowledge. Moreover, such knowledge could be of God as well as of Man and Nature. As Benton (1979, 108) has said, Engels did reflect on the epistemology and methods of science, but he shared with many of his contemporaries a vocation in offering "a general account of the nature and structure of the world, its interconnections and forms of motion, as well as a conception of the place of the human species in that world—its origins and prospects." There is, thus, no oddity in seeing that much of the argument over the idea of science was between idealists and materialists—what may seem for us, wrongly in my view, very much dated metaphysical concerns.

But we need to notice, second, that logical empiricist philosophers of science have a general metaphysics, or philosophy of nature, even if it was thought otherwise. For example, a presupposition of the analytic-synthetic distinction, as that became received dogma, was that there was no necessity in the world. Engels insisted that this could not be true. Of course, the logical empiricist project began to unwind just as it became a standard subdiscipline of philosophy. Today, at least among philosophers, all of its main propositions have been challenged. Moreover, we are today much less convinced that we even know what science is. Like it or not, we may still be concerned with the questions that concerned Engels. There may be, accordingly, lessons still to be learned.

Three views prevailed in philosophy in the middle of the nineteenth century: idealism, materialism, and positivism. But bad textbooks have contributed to considerable confusion over all three. If we are to locate Engels's philosophy of science properly both in terms of its historical place and with regard to contemporary debate, it will pay us to get as straight as possible on all three (Mandelbaum 1971).

Positivism

Auguste Comte, the philosopher who coined the term "positivism" (and "sociology"), also gave us an adequate characterization of positivism. Its key, if not defining, feature is this: positivism rejects metaphysics, understood as inquiry into existences that go "beyond" experience. For Comte, metaphysics was the near relative of theology in that "the mind supposes, instead of supernatural beings, abstract forces, veritable entities . . . inherent in all beings and capable of producing all phenomena." The positivist, by contrast, has "given over the vain search after Absolute notions, the origin and destination of the universe, and the causes of phenomena" (Lenzer 1975, 72). Comte, influenced by Kant, had no interest in explaining the subjectively phenomenal. Moreover, once Hume's notion of causality became widely taken for granted, positivists, too, could search for causes, except that they would now be construed as "invariant relations." Comte is not rejecting causes as empirically knowable constant conjunctions. He is rejecting the idea of causes as productive powers that have witnessable effects, both with regard to the relation of noumenal "objects" and with regard to nonempirical "forces." I should emphasize that the doctrine just defined might equally be termed "empiricism," owing as much as it does to the British empirical tradition, which takes a decisive turn with Berkeley's critique of matter and includes Kant, who, once awakened from his dogmatic slumber by Hume, sought to find a firm basis for the new science.

There are, of course, enormous differences between philosophies of science rooted in British empiricism and those rooted in Kant, even if by the end of the nineteenth century points of critical potential difference—whether, for example, causality is to be understood as an a priori category of mind or as a psychological propensity—tended to be less important. But regarding the present problem, they are in total agreement. As Lenin (1970, 88) rightly notes, "they both *in principle fence off* the 'appearance' from that which appears, the perception from that which is perceived, the thing-for-us from the 'thing-in-itself.'" Of course, it is true, as Lenin further notes, that "Hume does not want to hear of the 'thing-in-itself,' he regards the very thought of it as 'metaphysics' (as the Humeans and Kantians call it); while Kant grants the existence of the 'thing-in-itself,' but declares it to be 'unknowable,' fundamentally different from the appearance, belong to a fundamentally different realm, the realm of the 'beyond' (*Jenseits*), inaccessible to knowledge but revealed to faith." On the present definition, positivists restrict scientific knowledge to the phenomenal or empirical, and for purposes of science, they put aside metaphysical questions about the "ultimate" character of "the external world."

The Humean critique of causality relates to a second feature of positivism/empiricism. If explanation cannot proceed from principles that go beyond those directly derived from observation, what counts as a scientific explanation? For the positivist, as Comte insisted, "what is now understood when we speak of an explanation of facts is simply the establishment of a connection between single phenomena and some general facts." This, of course, is what we now call "the covering-law model of explanation." Science, accordingly, aims to establish "general laws." Positivists gave this idea a definite and clear sense: "general laws" were "invariable relations of succession and resemblance." While the constraint that such relations be invariable raised enormous problems, it was taken for granted that general laws were empirical: whenever this, then that. The difficulty, recognized, for example by John Stuart Mill, was how to distinguish "empirical laws," understood by him, rightly, to lack any sort of necessity, and "ultimate laws," which give us license to infer from the past to the future. Contemporary empiricist philosophers continue to struggle to understand why only some regularities support counterfactual conditionals, often thought to be the test of a general law.

We might note in passing that late-nineteenth-century positivists, for example, Ernst Mach and Pierre Duhem, held that science does not even try to explain; it only describes. Writing in 1906, Duhem contends, for example, that "to explain . . . is to strip reality of the appearances covering it like a veil, in order to see bare reality itself," but this is metaphysics. For him, "A physical theory is not an explanation. It is a system of mathematical propositions deduced from a small number of mathematical principles, which aim to represent as simply, as completely, and as exactly as possible a set of experimental laws" (Duhem 1954, 7, 19).

Putting aside the enormous sophistication produced by logical empiricist philosophers in this century (drawing on late-nineteenth-century arguments by Mach, Hertz, Poincaré, and others), and putting aside differences between them, we can say with some assurance that mainstream, taken-for-granted logical empiricist philosophy of science is positivist in the sense defined by Comte. Engels's relation to positivism will require discussion.

Materialism

What then of materialism? First, there is the question whether materialism is a metaphysical position. Some have denied this; but these writers have tended to conflate positivism and materialism, despite explicit disavowals of materialism by positivists, beginning with Comte but including Herbert Spencer, Thomas Henry Huxley, Mach, and, in recent philosophy, Rudolf Carnap.

It is true that materialists and positivists agree in holding that theological propositions have no place in science. But they do this for very different reasons: materialists, for ontological (metaphysical) reasons—there are, for them, no nonmaterial beings; positivists, because they reject metaphysics as scientifically irrelevant. Positivists can be agnostics, theists, or atheists; they can be empirical realists or phenomenalists; and they can follow either Hume or Kant with regard to their epistemology. In any case, they need not assume that "reality" is "material," or, better, that the independent existence of "matter" assures the existence of a world independent of "mind." We need a definition that allows for a positivist rejection of metaphysics, but one broad enough to include all sorts of materialists. Mandelbaum writes:

> Taken in its broadest sense, materialism is only committed to holding that the nature of that which is self-existent is material in character, there being no entities which exist independently of matter. Thus, in this sense, we would class as materialist anyone who accepts all of the following propositions: that there is an independently existing world; that human beings, like all other objects, are material entities; that the human mind does not exist as an entity distinct from the human body; and that there is no God (nor any other non-human being) whose mode of existence is not that of material entities. (1971, 22)

In this sense, materialists are all atheists (but may be pantheists or secular humanists), and they are metaphysical realists, however much they may differ regarding questions of how the independently existing world is known and how mind is to be accounted for. Idealists, then, deny a self-existent material reality. Neo-Kantian and Hegelian versions, of course, have been the historically most important versions of idealism.

Feuerbach, Dühring, Büchner, Moleschott, and Vogt rejected idealism for materialism. Mandelbaum says that, strictly speaking, Feuerbach was not a materialist, since, on his reading, Feuerbach rejected metaphysics for "anthropology." Since Feuerbach explicitly rejected idealism and theism, and since both Marx and Engels understood him to be a materialist, we should include him under our broad definition. Feuerbach's views, like John Dewey's and perhaps also Marx's, fit, though not neatly, into the three-part scheme. That is, one might prefer to offer a fourth category, for example, naturalism or humanism. Marx was explicit, of course, in arguing that there was truth in both idealism and materialism, and that his view, naturalism or humanism, was a resolution of supposed differences. I see nothing like this in Engels. A main problem is to see just where Engels departs from these other "materialists." But we need first to see where Engels stands on positivism.

Engels and Positivism

Engels never directly confronted positivism. Although in both the *Feuerbach* and the *Anti-Dühring* Engels ranges widely across pertinent philosophical issues, he never mentions Comte or positivist philosophy. Comte is mentioned twice in the *Dialectics of Nature,* in his outline and then in a fragment on the question of the classification of sciences. Engels notes there that this classification was "copied from Saint Simon" (Engels 1972, 250). Among the natural philosophers, Hermann Helmholtz is treated most prominently (as we shall see), but no mention is made of Kirchoff, Ostwald, or Mach, all of whom promoted positivist versions of science (Passmore 1966). Their main contributions come slightly after Engels had completed his "molting," and this may explain their absence.

Indeed, for Engels, there are but "two great camps": idealists and materialists. "Those who asserted the primacy of spirit to nature and, therefore, in the last instance, assumed world creation in some form . . . comprised the camp of idealism. The others, who regarded nature as primary, belong to the various schools of materialism" (Engels 1935b, 31). For him, "the great basic question of all philosophy, especially of modern philosophy, is that concerning the relation of thinking to being" (30). Engels says that this question has two sides: one is distinctly metaphysical in precisely Comte's sense. It engages in what, for Comte, is a "vain search" for "absolute notions." For example: "Did God create the world or has the world been in existence eternally?" It seems clear enough for Engels that this question was not only intelligible but forced: one had to be either an idealist or an materialist.

Engels's dichotomy was Lenin's point of departure against the Machists, surely the most important of the late-nineteenth-century positivists. In his important (and too little studied) *Materialism and Empirio-Criticism* (published in 1908), Lenin defended Engels's materialism against those "bold warriors who proudly allude to the 'modern theory of knowledge,' 'recent philosophy' (or 'recent positivism'), the 'philosophy of the natural sciences' or even more boldly, 'the philosophy of natural science of the twentieth century'" (Lenin 1970, 7). For Lenin, these views, for all their arrogant claims to have settled matters regarding science, were all idealist. Indeed, they were unsophisticated, even incoherent, idealisms to boot. The ground for Lenin's conclusion, of course, had been given by Engels's "two great camps" dichotomy.

The "other side" to Engels's "great basic question" is this: "What relation do our thoughts about the world surrounding us stand to this world itself? Is our thinking capable of the cognition of the real world" (Engels 1935b, 31). This problem was an old one in philosophy, as in ancient skepticism, but as Engels recognized, it had, by the time that he was writing, definitely taken the form of what Rorty (1979, 139–40) has usefully called "veil of ideas" skepticism: "the problem of getting from inner space to outer space—the 'problem of the external world' which became paradigmatic for modern philosophy."

Idealists have no difficulty with an answer, since, as Engels summarizes things, "what we perceive in the real world is precisely its thought-content —that which makes the world a gradual realization of the absolute idea has existed somewhere from eternity, independent of the world and before the world" (Engels 1935b, 32). Engels here suggests that this answer, at best, is trivial. No one would deny that "thought can know a content which is from the outset a thought-content," but "what is here to be proved is already tacitly contained in the presupposition," a consequence of what Ralph Barton Perry was later to term "the ego-centric predicament" (1955, 129). But having bought into the problem—at least so it seems—he does not here give a materialist answer to the question he has raised.

It is fair to say, I think, that Engels foundered badly on this question. Most of his remarks are fragmentary and unclear at best. In a letter to Conrad Schmidt, written in 1895, he gave what is perhaps the clearest statement of his position:

> The identity and thought and being, to express myself in Hegelian fashion, everywhere coincides with your example of the circle and the polygon . . . the concept of a thing and its reality run side by side like two asymptotes always approaching each other yet never meeting. But although a concept has the essential nature of a concept and cannot therefore *prima facie* directly coincide with reality, from which it must first be abstracted, it is still more than fiction, unless you are going to declare all the results of thought fictions because reality has a long way to go round before it corresponds to them, and then only . . . with asymptotic approximation. (Marx and Engels 1942, 527)

Engels surely assumes reality is whatever it is, quite independent of our cognition of it, and that knowledge must "mirror" it. Moreover, he seems not in the least concerned with developing Marx's powerful suggestions in the *Theses on Feuerbach,* well summarized by Avineri (1975, 68): For Marx, "getting acquainted with reality constitutes shaping and changing it. Epistemology ceases to be a merely reflective theory of cognition, and becomes the vehicle for shaping and molding reality." Engels's concern with Feuerbach, unlike Marx's, is not as much Feuerbachian epistemology as his views of religion and morality. These need not be pursued here.

Engels well recognized, however, that positivist (including Kantian) epistemologies had to be rejected. Thus, he could *not* have said, with some of the positivists, for example, Duhem, that our concepts and ideas are *convenient* fictions, useful in prediction and control, and that is the end of the matter. Nor, in Kantian fashion, could he have said that by virtue of the a priori forms of intuition, empirically real spatiotemporal objects exist *only* in our representations of them.

Engels and the "Agnostics"

Kant's transcendental idealism did undercut skepticism regarding the empirical world; but it did this at a price that Engels could not pay. Kant had affirmed that there are existences that are not empirically real, and that these are causally implicated in our experience, but, as noumenal, they are unknowable things-in-themselves. Indeed, his transcendental skepticism, as Kenneth Westphal (1997, 3) argues, was "an integral part of Kant's aim 'to deny knowledge in order to make room for faith,' where this 'faith' in fact amounts to practical knowledge of the reality of freedom and God."

That Engels had little patience with "agnostics" is clear in the remainder of the argument in the *Feuerbach*. After suggesting that idealists trade fallaciously on the truism that whatever is known is known in terms of concepts and ideas, he considers Hume and Kant as two "who question the possibility of any cognition (or at least an exhaustive cognition) of the world" (Engels 1935b, 32).

Engels seems to hold (with Hegel) that a theory of knowledge must guarantee, at least ideally, an exhaustive cognition of the world, and he seems confident that the (positivist, "agnostic") posture has already been refuted. He asserts first that "what is decisive in the refutation of this view has already been said by Hegel—in so far as this was possible from an idealist standpoint" (Engels 1935b, 32). He does not say what Hegel said to refute this, but a footnote provided by the Soviet editor of the text, L. Rudas, calls our attention to Engels's historical materialism. As opposed to the "the agnostic" view of Kant and Hume, that "it is possible that we can correctly perceive the properties of a thing but are not able to grasp the thing itself by any sense or thought process," Engels argued: "To this Hegel has replied long ago; if you know all the qualities of a thing, you know the thing itself; nothing remains then but the fact that the said thing exists outside of us, and as soon as your senses have taught you this fact, you have grasped the last remnant of this thing, Kant's celebrated unknowable thing-in-itself" (Engels 1935b, 32). This is hardly an adequate summary of Hegel's refutation. It seems to capitulate to the egocentric predicament that whatever is known is experienced, and merely to ignore Kant's main point. On the other hand, if some recent scholarship is correct (Inwood 1987), Hegel's own tendency "is to dismiss Kant's views without explanation" (Sedgwick 1993).

Hegel had undermined Kantian dualism, of course, but at a price. Whether one terms this an "objective idealism" or an idealism in "a thoroughgoingly new sense of the word" need not be here answered (Findlay 1966; Pippen 1989, 1993; Sedgwick, 1993). Similar, but quite impossible to develop here, would be the effort to see precisely what features of Hegel's systematic philosophy Engels appropriated and assumed. We would likely begin with Hegel's analysis of "the Matter of Fact," "The Thing," "Properties," "The Law of Phenomena," and the notion of "A Force and Its Manifestation." All of this, of course, is included—but is also obscured—by saying that Marx and Engels found it necessary to stand Hegel on his head. Indeed, if Engels read Hegel in the way that Westphal reads Hegel, Engels's appropriation was more in the way of a reconceptualization than a turning upside down. Westphal insists, rightly, I think, that Hegel's main objection to Kant was his transcendental skepticism. Hegel offered instead an idealism that was an epistemological realism: "Hegel's brand of idealism is a kind of ontological holism according to which all parts of the world are fundamentally interrelated, where these interrelations are fundamentally conceptual relations. On his view, concepts are, in the first place, structures in the world. Only on this basis do concepts become, in the second place, conceptions in our language and in our heads as well" (Westphal 1989, 142).

Sedgwick (1993) constructs a Hegelian line of argument that could easily have appealed to Engels. She writes:

> A proper appreciation of the role of the "I think" yields the conclusion that we have no cognitive access to an extra-conceptual content. From the fact that we have no access to an extra-conceptual content it follows that we cannot invoke that content as evidence that there are limits to what we can know, or as evidence that what we know is "mere appearance." We have therefore no grounds for restricting the objectivity of our concepts to an objectivity that is merely "for us" and not also attributable to things themselves. Since for Hegel there are no intuitions which are not for us conceptualized intuitions, there can be no appeal outside the determinations of thought to secure the objectivity of the concept. The objectivity of a concept is a function not of its being "anchored" in empirical intuition, but of its relation to other concepts in the system of *a priori* thought-forms. (283)

It is easy to show, I think, that Engels did agree with Hegel that "all parts of the world are fundamentally related." But why hold that the relations are "fundamentally conceptual," still less that they are knowable a priori? On "materialist" grounds, the world was self-subsisting, and the system of "thought-forms" could then be merely a "reflection" of the "dialectically" constituted material reality. I will return to this.

Positivism and Transcendental Realism

Further insight into Engels's "realism" is provided by his second line of argument against the unknowable thing-in-itself. Engels writes:

> The most telling refutation of this as of all other philosophical fancies is practice, experiment and industry. If we are able to prove the correctness of our conception of a natural process by making it ourselves, bringing it into being out of its conditions and using it for our purposes into the bargain, then there is an end of the Kantian incomprehensible "thing-in-itself." The chemical substances produced in the bodies of plants and animals remained such "things-in-themselves" until organic chemistry began to produce them one after another, whereupon the "thing-in-itself" became a thing for us. (Engels 1935b, 33)

Engels insists that, given their "theoretical and practical refutation" by Hegel and then by the achievements of recent science, the efforts of neo-Kantians in Germany and Humeans in England are "scientifically a regression and practically merely a shamefaced way of surreptitiously accepting materialism while denying it before the world" (Engels 1935b, 33).

Engels holds that science has itself established some form of materialism. His appeal to practice in support of this suggests another line of argument. We have empirical knowledge of the properties of the "things" of experience, but we have more than this. As opposed to Kant, we now also have knowledge of what underlies and produces these properties. Science has generated and tested theories about heretofore unwitnessable causal mechanisms. To take Engels's example, in molecular chemistry, given our theory, we are able to identify alizarin, $C_{14}H_6O_2(OH)_2$, the compound that produces a distinctive red color. Knowing exactly what it is gives us the capacity also to produce it synthetically from coal tar.

We can, perhaps, get clearer on this critical issue by considering what had been a problem since Newton, the status of "forces" in nature. Put briefly, because Newton was with those who, "rejecting substantial forms and occult qualities, have endeavored to subject the phenomena of nature to the laws of mathematics," he famously declared *hypothesis non fingo*—after it had been charged that his notion of universal gravitation had reintroduced "occult qualities." In his second letter to Bentley, Newton wrote: "You sometimes speak of Gravity as essential and inherent to matter. Pray do not ascribe this notion to me; for the Cause of Gravity is what I do not pretend to know, and therefore would take more time to consider it" (quoted by Harré [1964, 107]). Looking for the "Cause of Gravity" is precisely what Comte would have called "the vain search" for "absolute notions." While Newton offered a number of highly speculative, though mechanical, accounts of the mechanism of gravitation, he was never satisfied with his efforts. Many writers, including Engels, were led to conclude that even if Newton had allowed for the existence of nonobservables, for example, atoms, he was positivist in disclaiming appeal to unobservable "forces." Indeed, the problem reappears in a number of places in Engels's writings.

Engels argues, rightly, I think, that "the notion of force is derived from the activity of the human organism within its environment." Because our actions can give motions "a predetermined direction and extent," "the idea of *causality* becomes established." He asserts that "the empiricism of observation alone can never adequately prove necessity. *Post hoc* but not *propter hoc*" (Engels 1972, 228). And, "Hume's skepticism was correct in saying that a regular *post hoc* can never establish a *propter hoc*. But the activity of human beings *forms the test* of causality" (230). Although it is hardly clear, Engels would seem to assent to the idea that causes are productive powers in *some* sense (Harré and Madden 1975). But if this is so far innocent, if, "in order to save having to give the real cause of a change brought about by a function of our organism, we substitute a fictitious cause, a so-called force corresponding to the change, then we carry this convenient method over to the external world also, and so invent as many forces as there are diverse phenomena" (Engels 1972, 80). This looks very positivist. Instead of appealing to a force, we should identify the "general laws" governing phenomena: the conditions that are invariantly associated with the outcome. This view, expressed by Comte, had been articulated by Berkeley in his critique of matter. For Berkeley, "the set of rules, of established methods, wherein the Mind we depend on excites in us the idea of Sense, are called the *laws of nature;* and these we learn by experience" (1901, 1:273). In terms reminiscent of Berkeley, Engels writes: "When we know how much mechanical motion a definite quantity of heat motion is converted, we still do not know anything of the nature of heat. . . . To conceive heat as a form of motion is the latest advance of physics, and by so doing the category of force is sublated to it" (Engels 1972, 281). And earlier: "In mechanics, the causes of motion are taken as given and their origin is disregarded, only their effects being taken into account" (Engels 1972, 86). That is, it seems that once one has the "general laws," there is no need to search for metaphysical causes.

But an alternative interpretation is possible. Again, Engels holds that Hegel was on the right track. But instead of pursuing his very fragmentary reference, it will be better to pursue this problem by considering Engels's criticism of Helmholtz: "Saying that a force explains some outcome adds nothing. Indeed, with just as much right as Helmholtz explains physical phenomena from so-called refractive force, electrical force of contact, etc., the mediaeval scholastics explained temperature changes by means of *vis calorifica* and a *vis frigifaciens* and thus saved themselves all further investigation of heat phenomena." Again, it might appear that Engels is taking a rather straightforward positivist line here. But I think that this is not the case. His point, rather, is that inquiry has been prematurely foreclosed. On this view, which surely would be endorsed by Helmholtz, the problem was to identify the causal mechanisms, named by the "force," witnessable or not, that would explain the outcome. On this view, "refractive force" is a promissory note for a mechanism yet to be fully theorized and confirmed. Thus, according to Engels, by acknowledging that forces name "objectified natural laws," "the conditions for which are still rather complicated," Helmholtz should also see that the appeal to forces as explanations is not a vindication of our knowledge, but is a sign of "our lack of knowledge of the nature of the law and its mode of action" (Engels 1972, 82).

Some of these "conditions" may be directly known; others will have to be inferred. Thus "atoms and molecules cannot be observed under a microscope, but only by the process of thought" (Engels 1972, 205). One way to proceed is to hold that the problem of going from what is in experience to what is not in experience is not philosophical but scientific. That is, we reject transcendental skepticism and give scientific reasons for the inference from what is known (in experience) to what is unknown (not in experience but nonetheless knowable). Although the problem needs to be developed in considering Engels's materialism, we can note here that on this view there need be no commitment to an unknowable substratum—matter. For example, the mechanical theory of heat, he says, is "a hypothesis," "inasmuch as no one has up to now seen a molecule, not to mention one in vibration" (Engels 1935b, 76). That "vibrating molecules" were not "seen," however, was not a reason to eliminate them from playing explanatory roles. Indeed, in a fragment in the *Dialectics of Nature*, Engels refers to Newton as an "inductive ass" (Engels 1972, 205). I think that the Soviet editor guesses correctly that this refers to Newton's *hypothesis non fingo*, which Engels likely did see as an unwarranted restriction on scientific explanation. This suggests that Engels gave a positivist reading of Newton from an antipositivist point of view.

On this interpretation, Engels (like Helmholtz) assumes a realism of the sort more recently defended by so-called critical realists (Bhaskar 1978; Harré 1987). While there are points of difference, these writers accept the idea that a valid scientific explanation can appeal to what is, in principle, a nonobservable causal mechanism that *produces* empirical outcomes.

Since the issues continue to haunt philosophy of science (and general epistemology), we might here consider another alternative to the problem of experience and reality, implicitly rejected by Engels and explicitly rejected by Lenin, who assumed that he was elaborating the views of Engels. They are the views of Engels's approximate contemporary Helmholtz.

Engels understood Helmholtz to be a neo-Kantian, and this was correct. But was he, as Lenin argued, inconsistently also a materialist (Lenin 1970, 220)? Because Helmholtz insisted that "our concepts and ideas are effects wrought upon our nervous system and our consciousness by the objects that are perceived and apprehended," Lenin held that he was a materialist. Helmholtz had written: "[T]he word *Ursache* (which I use here precisely and literally) means that *existent something which lies hidden behind the changes we perceive*. It is the hidden but continuously existent basis of phenomena" (1971, 521). The question is: What is the character of this "existent something"? Lenin assumed, presumptuously, that it must be material.

For Helmholtz, there are objects "outside" of us, and perception will be explained physiologically. But, he writes, "none of our sensations give us anything more than signs for external objects . . . and we learn how to interpret these signs only through experience and practice" (1971, 196). Our perceptions are mediated, are but "representations" of the world "out there."

Lenin seems to have supposed that this was a Kantian move, and, depending on how one reads Kant, it might well be. It is clear, in any case, that for Helmholtz there is a structured, independently existing world and that trial-and-error learning gives us knowledge of it. Whether this could be termed Kantian (or neo-Kantian) again depends on how one reads Kant (Westphal 1997; Allison 1989).

But however this may be, why did Lenin reject this approach? What bothered Lenin (Engels is silent on this) was the idea that experience was a "sign" and *not* an "image" or "reflection" of the independently existing external world. Lenin is clear that "if sensations are not images of things, but only signs or symbols which have 'no resemblance' to them, then Helmholtz's initial materialist premise is undermined; the existence of external objects becomes subject to doubt; for signs or symbols may quite possibly indicate imaginary objects, and everybody is familiar with instances of such signs or symbols" (Lenin 1970, 222). Lenin is uncomfortable with Kantian transcendental doubt. The question of what exists independently of us is open. But it is more open than Lenin seems to realize. Lenin seems not to notice that, on the one hand, such doubt surely does make possible a transcendental idealism—Kant's preferred position. As noted, contrary to Lenin, Kant did not withhold causal powers from the thing-in-itself.

But, on the other hand, Helmholtz was adamantly realist. Lenin quotes him: "[T]he realist hypothesis is the simplest we can construct; it has been tested and verified in an extremely broad field of application" (Lenin 1970, 222). This surely sounds much like the Engels approach discussed in the foregoing. It left Lenin unsatisfied. One can only wonder why. Probably what bothered Lenin was that this was a representational theory of perception, according to which it does not follow that, because we see, for example, a red apple, there is a red apple "out there." On the Helmholtzian view, there is an object in real space and time, describable in terms of physics and chemistry, and, as a function of our optical and central nervous system, we see this object *as* a red apple. Unlike Hegel, but like Engels, Lenin was trapped in the mirror metaphor. Like Engels, he wanted a "reflection," a correspondence of concept and reality.

Of course, we can only speculate, finally, regarding why both Engels and Lenin were unimpressed with this sort of transcendental realist answer to the problem they had struggled with. Quite probably, Engels's view that Hegel had already solved the problem was sufficient to prevent him from pursuing this line. But whether Hegel's solution was available to his materialism still needs to be considered.

Against "Old Materialism"

Engels rejected "the shallow and vulgarized form in which the materialism of the eighteenth century continues to exist today [1888] in the minds of naturalists and physicians, the form which was preached in the 'fifties by Büchner, Vogt and Moleschott" (Engels 1935a, 35–36). For reasons having to do with the condition of science itself, this materialism was "predominately mechanical." It mistakenly applied mechanistic standards, still valid in physics, to chemical and biological phenomena.

Engels is not a reductionist in at least one of the obvious senses of that term. He seems to have agreed with Comte that nature is stratified in the sense that higher levels, for example, the organic, depend upon lower levels, for example, the chemical and physical, and that each level exhibits "higher unities." He wrote: "If I term physics the mechanics of molecules, chemistry the physics of atoms, and furthermore biology the chemistry of proteins, I wish thereby to express the passing of each of these sciences into another, hence both the connection, the continuity, and the distinction, the discrete separation between the two" (Engels 1972, 252). One may wish that Engels had said more on this critical issue, but especially on the question of the human sciences, where on occasion, at least, he leaves himself open to a reductionist reading. Most critically, of course, is how Engels would treat consciousness. (I have in mind an argument in Engels 1935b, 59, against the "old materialists.")

Engels identified a second "specific limitation" of older materialism, also the result of the state of natural science in the eighteenth century. This limit was its "inability to comprehend the universe as a process—as matter developing in a historical process" (Engels 1935b, 37). The idea that we think of the universe in terms of process is, of course, critical and requires us to see how Engels's dialectics is his response. But the text raises a prior and important question, relevant to much of the foregoing. It is the idea that matter develops in a historical process. This is at best perplexing, especially if, as is usually the case, matter is conceived as a "substance" capable of carrying properties. I conclude that this was not Engels's conception, but again, he is nowhere clear about what he does mean.

I noted earlier that we can give scientific reasons for the inference from what is known to what is unknown (but knowable) and that, on this view, there need be no commitment to an unknowable substratum—matter. Nowhere, as far as I can tell, does Engels consider Berkeley's critique of matter as *inessential* to science. Moreover, even if science required something external to mind, as Kant had argued, this did not need to be "material substance." It could be a self-subsisting external world. The point may be missed.

One could hold that the atoms of physics are *real bodies* much in the way that Galileo and Locke seem to have understood them. One can hold to this and still repudiate matter as *substance*—as Locke had done. As Engels says: "[M]atter as such is pure creation of thought and an abstraction. We leave out of account the qualitative differences of things in lumping them together as corporeally existing things under the concept matter. Hence matter as such, as distinct from definite existing pieces of matter, is not anything sensuously existing" (Engels 1972, 255).

Of course, all abstractions are creations of thought, but some might not be "pure" creations of thought, in the sense that there is a reality to which they refer. Consider here both the abstraction "canine" and, as in Marx, "abstract homogeneous labor." However, if an abstraction is a "pure creation of thought," then may we not say that there is nothing real to which it refers? That is, while there may well be subatomic particles, atoms and molecules—in addition to the visible things of nature—there is no such thing as homogeneous, undifferentiated matter, a substance or substratum in which properties inhere. Engels would not be bothered by the empiricist critique of matter, since, on this view, he has shifted ground: there can be no question that there are independently existing things that are mind-independent. That philosophers have thought otherwise is evidence of their ingenuity and, perhaps, of the fact that modern epistemology was founded by theologically motivated philosophers. Another way to put this is to say that Engels has no patience with skepticism regarding either empirical or transcendental reality. Materialists affirm an independently existing natural world; accordingly, the real questions about it are now scientific: how do we explain the phenomena of experience?

It is thus that the progress of science proves materialism. It did not prove the existence of matter, but it did establish the truth of the realist hypothesis, which, as Helmholtz had said, "has been tested and verified in an extremely broad field of application."

It is now easy to make sense of the idea of matter developing in a historical process. Some of these existences at least have "histories" in a fairly straightforward sense. The solar system developed from "rotating nebular masses," and organisms evolved from the nonliving. In a sense, then, everything in the universe changes, is in process, and at least with regard to some of these things, we need "history" if we are to understand their origin and perhaps also their nature. As opposed to Dühring, who "reduces motion to mechanical force," *"motion is the mode of existence of matter"* (Engels 1935a, 71). Or as Engels insisted in *Dialectics of Nature:* "Motion, as applied to matter, is change in general" (Engels 1972, 248). On the present reading, this would mean that everything that exists is changing, a key feature of Engels's dialectical view of nature. Indeed, the laws of motion are, for Engels, dialectical laws.

Dialectics

I have avoided engaging what is surely the most distinctive and influential feature of Engels's philosophy of science. The fundamental notions of dialectics as set out by Engels are familiar enough. Indeed, in the hands of his erstwhile epigones, they have been too familiar, reduced to postulates that presumably characterize all of reality and that thus call for an appropriate sort of thinking, one that is not found in the work of bourgeois philosophers and scientists—Hegel excepted.

The subheading in *Dialectics of Nature* to the section entitled "Dialectics" reads: "the general nature of dialectics to be developed as the science of interconnections, in contrast to metaphysics" (Engels 1972, 62). That this is a "science of interconnections" is, I think, most critical, since it strongly suggests that Engels did follow Hegel in holding that "all parts of the world are fundamentally interrelated"—except of course that Engels's holism was materialist. Thus: "The whole of nature accessible to us forms a system, an interconnected totality of bodies, and by bodies we understand here all material existences extending from stars to atoms, indeed right to particles, in so far as one grants the existence of the last named" (70; see also Engels 1935b, 58).

Engels identifies "three great discoveries" that have propelled "by leaps and bounds" a dialectical view of the universe: the discovery of the cell, the transformation of energy, and Darwinian theory (Engels 1935b, 58). He follows Hegel in saying that this understanding is not metaphysics, presumably because dialectics does not investigate "things as given, as fixed and stable," but instead investigates processes. The "laws of dialectics" are "abstracted" from "the history of nature and human society." They are "nothing but the most general laws of these two aspects of development, as well as of thought itself." And indeed they can be reduced to three:

- the law of the transformation of quantity into quality and vice versa;
- the law of the interpenetration of opposites;
- the law of the negation of the negation.

All three were developed by Hegel, but his mistake "lies in the fact that these laws are foisted on nature and history as laws of thought, and not deduced (inferred) from them. . . . If we turn the thing round, then everything becomes simple, and the dialectical laws that look so extremely mysterious in idealist philosophy at once become simple and clear as noonday" (Engels 1972, 62). The famous "placed upon his head" metaphor, articulated in *Feuerbach* (Engels 1935b, 54), becomes here "turn the thing round," which is perhaps preferable. We *infer* the laws from independently existing reality; they are abstractions from it. Of course, "dialectical logic" contrasts with "the old formal logic" in that it denies that cause/effect, negative/positive, chance/necessity, and identity/difference are exclusive polarities. Presumably, dialectical thought enables us to grasp dialectical reality. Indeed, as suggested earlier, we have knowledge to the extent that our thoughts "mirror" this reality. But as opposed to idealism, dialectical thought is not constitutive of reality. What then is the character of a dialectical reality, and how does a dialectical logic help us? There are two critical questions.

The first, of course, is the problem, already discussed, of how ideas are presumed to "mirror" or to be "conscious reflexes" of an independently existing reality. I noted that Engels foundered badly on this problem. Nor, parenthetically, can it be said that Lenin's efforts in *Empirio-Criticism*, following Engels, helped at all. Terrell Carver has raised a second problem. He asks: "If the 'dialectic of concepts' is 'the conscious reflex of the dialectical motion of the real world'—nature and history—where 'these laws assert themselves unconsciously'—how is it that these laws, which could with sufficient sophistication be perceived by men, [could] then be applied 'consciously'?" (Carver 1983, 140). What would be the result? Would the result be, Carver wonders, a reduction in the "'seeming accidents' through which 'external necessity' is asserting itself?" To answer this, we need to raise questions regarding the character of the three laws as universally pertinent. They seem either to do too little or to do too much.

Many pages of *Anti-Dühring* are devoted to illustrating the three laws. One may concede that, for example, one can generate the series of normal fatty acids, each qualitatively different, by "the simple addition of elements" (Engels 1935a, 145). But we can reasonably ask, will this be true of all qualitative change? Surely there are qualitative changes and differences, for example, aging or tensile strength, that involve some other mechanisms?

The point is clearer with regard to the third dialectical law, referred to by Engels as "the kernel" of the dialectical process. Dühring had made a "shrill attack" on Marx. It is well responded to by Engels, who, quoting the famous text from Marx's *Capital*, shows that there are no dialectical miracles in which the contradictions of thesis-antithesis magically bringing forth a synthesis. Instead, Marx proceeded empirically, "on the basis of historical and economic facts." The contradictions in the system of capitalism are concrete and specific. There are structural requirements that, if reproduced, produce consequences inconsistent with continuing system reproduction. This, for capitalism, is the "negation of the negation." But as Stedman Jones (1973, 22) pointed out: "Engels has proved something else, something that he did not intend to prove and something which he does not seem to be aware of having proved: that is, that the

Hegelian dialectic of *Capital* is superfluous, that fundamental dialectical laws . . . are mere redescriptions of processes which have been established by quite different means." The point is easily generalized. The law is a general law that "holds good in the animal and plant kingdoms, in geology, in mathematics, in history and philosophy." Of course, Engels is able to give (as with the first dialectical law) a host of illustrations. But he gives away the problem when he acknowledges that "[i]t is obvious that in describing any evolutionary process as the negation of the negation, I do not say anything concerning the *particular* processes of development" (Engels 1935a, 160). As Engels well recognized, for each of these particular processes of change, there are particular mechanisms. Marx proceeded *empirically;* so does the geologist, biologist, and so on. The problem with the laws of dialectics is not that they are miraculous or mysterious, but that they are very nearly vacuous. In this, they compare neatly with Herbert Spencer's inductively generated supergeneralization, "the law of evolution," to wit: "There is a change from an incoherent homogeneity to a coherent heterogeneity, accompanying the dissipation of motion and the integration of matter" (1976 [1850], 325). One might hold, however, that unlike the Spencerian law, dialectical laws are heuristically valuable, since they guide us in our search for knowledge. This is surely contestable.

First, the appeal to dialectics has, if anything, tended to foreclose inquiry prematurely. That is, just as with the appeal to "force" as explanation, it has been all too easy for inquirers to assume a dialectical process (to which one or more of the laws applies) and then to fail to see that one needs, as Engels acknowledges, to be empirical, to identify the particular mechanisms at work. Calling for "dialectical thinking" is too often an excuse to abandon the analysis, to flee in the face of causal complexity, or sometimes to assume an account in which Humean causes get caught in an unhelpful, potentially infinite regress. Engels was acutely sensitive to this sort of thing, but his own famous "in the last analysis," with regard to historical causation, is a symptom of this unfortunate tendency. One does not need dialectics to affirm that effects can be causes and that, for many processes at least, what causes change is often itself changed. Although Dühring was mistaken about Marx's *Capital,* one may wonder how many of "Marx's faithful followers" have rested content with the assertion that some process is "dialectical." Worse, how many have used the idea like a bludgeon against the unconvinced?

Second, Engels is committed to rejecting the "old method of investigation and thought which Hegel calls 'metaphysical.'" The approach erroneously prefers "to investigate things as given, as fixed and stable" (Engels

1935b, 55). In *Anti-Dühring* he writes: "To the metaphysician, things and their mental images, ideas, are isolated, to be considered one after the other apart from each other, rigid, fixed objects of investigation given once and for all. He thinks in absolutely irreconcilable antithesis. . . . Positive and negative absolutely exclude one another; cause and effect stand in an equally rigid antithesis one to the other" (Engels 1935a, 28). And in *Dialectics of Nature* we read: "The *law of identity* in the old metaphysical sense is the fundamental law of the old outlook: *a = a*. Each thing is equal to itself. Everything was permanent, the solar system, stars, organisms. This law has been refuted by natural science bit by bit. . . . Abstract identity, like all metaphysical categories, suffices for ordinary use, where small dimensions or brief periods of time are in question. . . . For natural science in its comprehensive roles, however, even in a single branch, abstract identity is totally inadequate" (1972, 216).

There are at least three questions. First, are there any "things" that are not impermanent? Second, do "things" lack "identity" because they change? And third, can we dispense with "things" and think only in terms of "processes?"

One can admit that all the "things" in empirical reality are in process, changing and impermanent, but do we want to include here the theoretical "things" of particle physics or of molecular chemistry? And if we do, what sense are to we make of this? Thus, we may admit with Engels that "the plant, the animal, every cell is at every moment of its life identical with itself and yet becoming distinct from itself . . . in short, by a sum of incessant molecular changes which make up life" (Engels 1972, 214). Still, it is the plant or the cell that undergoes change. Indeed, we can explain the change of cell (and of a plant) by seeing that in transaction with other structures, its molecular structure is being altered.

It seems, indeed, that in order to explain change, we need abstract identity. We know, for example, that water can change: it can become salty or evaporate or freeze. It cannot explode. These are "natural necessities," which, although denied by empiricisms, seem ill suited to Engels's dialectical view. Molecular chemistry tells us what water *is*. It is *essentially* H_2O. By virtue of its molecular structure (and the laws of chemistry), it has the causal powers it has. Contrary to the empiricist view, there is necessity in what it can and cannot become. No doubt this idea, clear enough in Marx, is also being promoted by Engels. And of course, water does none of these things of itself and in isolation. To explain what it has done or is likely to do, we need to see exactly how it stands to other "things" with other causal powers. Here Engels might have followed Marx and held that "things" (including systems like capitalism!) have "tendencies" such that how they change and what they change to are a function of what they are—the law of identity in "the old metaphysical sense." But we need also to add here that nothing in this view commits us to the idea that any particular outcome is inevitable. If the water is to become salty, then NaCl must be added to it, and this may or may not happen. If capitalism is be replaced by socialism, then a great many things will need to happen.

This last remark suggests the final problem. Dialectical laws seem to do too much. Here we need to seek the sense of Engels's often repeated claim that nature and history are "governed by inner, hidden laws." For example: "Nothing of all that happens—whether in the unnumerable *apparent* accidents observable upon the surface of things, or in the ultimate results which *confirm the regularity underlying these* accidents—is attained as a consciously desired aim" (Engels 1935b, 58, emphasis added). Granted that "in so far as we ignore man's reactions upon nature"—an assumption made at our peril—natural outcomes are not "consciously desired." But what are we to make of the emphasized phrases here? Despite what appears as accidental, are outcomes necessary? Later, in commenting on history, Engels writes: "Historical events thus *appear* on the whole to be likewise governed by chance. But where *on the surface* accident holds sway, there actually it is always governed by inner, hidden laws and it is only a matter of discovering these laws" (Engels 1935b, 58).

David-Hillel Ruben suggests that the "rational kernel" in Hegel's philosophy that Engels wanted to appropriate was this: "There is no special reason why a materialist outlook should not stress the necessary development, opposition, and change in things—which is what Engels as well as Marx took to be the rational core of the dialectic—without asserting that the finite necessarily changes into the infinite, or subject to object; only the latter of which are genuinely idealistic formulations" (1979, 55). This could well be correct, but much depends upon how necessary development, opposition, and change are to be construed. There are two more or less obvious construals.

First, they may be construed so that there is both necessity and contingency in the world. On this construal, causal powers are natural necessities (Harré and Madden 1975), but since outcomes are always conjunctions of a contingent collocation of causes, they are contingent. They can be explained but are not in principle predictable. The second construal denies this. Presumably, with knowledge of "the hidden, inner laws," explanation and prediction will be symmetrical. Hegel's idealist eschatology is replaced by a materialist eschatology.

The main question can be simply put: Is there for Engels genuine contingency in nature and in history? Many commentators (Bender 1975; Lichtheim 1963; Avineri 1975) have concluded that there is not. As Steven Philion reminds me, Joseph Ferraro (1992) thinks otherwise.

Ferraro argues that a dialectical understanding of necessity allows for chance. What could this mean? Ferraro argues rightly that Engels rejected "determinism" as that is usually understood. On this view, not only is everything caused, but all outcomes are produced by "an irrevocable concatenation of cause and effect, by an unshatterable necessity of such nature indeed that the gaseous sphere, from which the solar system was derived, was already so constituted that these events had to happen thus and not otherwise." Engels argues that that "with this kind of necessity . . . we do not get away from the theological conception of nature." Whether it is the eternal decree of God or Kismet or necessity, for science it is all the same. We cannot trace "the chain of causation," and hence, "necessity remains an empty phrase" (Engels 1972, 219).

This would seem to allow for genuine chance and thus to be decisive in favor of Ferraro's reading—except that Engels has already rejected the "metaphysical" opposition between necessity and chance. As Engels understands this view, what (in positivist terms) is "brought under laws" is thus explained and comes under the heading of necessity. What cannot be so explained is a chance occurrence. For Engels, "[a]nyone can see that this is the same sort of science as that which proclaims natural what it can explain, and ascribes what it cannot explain to supernatural causes; whether I term the cause of the unexplicable chance, or whether I term it God. . . . Both are only equivalents for: I do not know, and therefore do not belong to science" (Engels 1972, 218). Given that Engels acknowledges that we shall not (in his example) be able to account for *all* the properties of a single "pea-pod," it is unclear why he objects to "metaphysical" chance. He seems to think that this trivializes necessity. Thus, "[i]f the fact that a particular pea-pod contains six peas, and not five or seven, is of the same order as the law of motion of the solar system . . . then as a matter of fact chance is not elevated into necessity, but rather necessity degraded into chance" (220). A move hinted at by Ferraro, who sees that Engels frequently notices that laws of nature apply *ceteris paribus*, would allow that the laws of motion, construed as natural necessities, and some fact about a particular pea-pod are *not* "of the same order." For example, while the Galilean law tells us that free-falling bodies near the earth *must* fall sixteen feet in the first second of time, what any particular body will do is not predictable, since there are no bodies in free fall. Engels writes: "*The eternal laws of nature* also become transformed more and more into historical ones. That water is fluid from 0°–100°C. is an eternal law of nature, but for it to be valid, there must be (1) water, (2) the given temperature, (3) normal pressure" (238).

This would seem to be a confusion. The laws of chemistry are not "transformed" into historical laws even if they must be applied concretely and therefore historically. What, in any particular case, H_2O does will be a function of all the other causes operating at that time and place. Moreover, these particular collocations of causes are, as Engels sees, historical. It is just here where we have genuine contingency. On this view, contingency is not to be identified with chance, if that means absolute inexplicability. Everything is caused and, in principle, can be explained, even if, in principle, it cannot be predicted. But it follows also that, for example, evolutionary history could have been different (Gould 1986). Another way to say this is *that while there are laws of nature, there are no historical laws.*

The foregoing, I believe, is perfectly consistent with Darwin, whose "epoch-making work," for Engels, was the fatal blow against "metaphysics." But Engels was not, however, clear on any of the critical issues. And he was not clear, I think, precisely because of his commitment to Hegelian holism (Stedman Jones 1973). In *Dialectics of Nature,* after rejecting determinism and the (metaphysical) opposition between chance and necessity, he writes: "In contrast to both conceptions, Hegel came forward with the hitherto quite unheard-of propositions that the accidental has a cause because it is accidental, and just as much also has no cause because it is accidental; that the accidental is necessary, that necessity determines itself as chance, and on the other hand, this chance is rather absolute necessity" (Engels 1972, 220). Many readers, perhaps content with their capacity "to think dialectically," have concluded that for Engels, "in the last analysis," there is no genuine contingency in nature or in history. It is just this view that ultimately has been the disaster for the "scientific socialisms" that, philosophically, have been dialectical materialisms.

References

Allison, Henry E. 1989. Kant's Refutation of Materialism. *Monist* 72:190–207.
Avineri, Shlomo. 1975. *The Social and Political Thought of Karl Marx.* Cambridge: Cambridge University Press.
Bender, Frederic L. 1975. *The Betrayal of Marx.* New York: Harper & Row.

Benton, Ted. 1979. Natural Science and Cultural Struggle: Engels on Philosophy and the Natural Sciences. In *Issues in Marxist Philosophy*, ed. John Mepham and David-Hillel Ruben, 2:101–42. Brighton, East Sussex: Harvester.

Berkeley, George. 1901. *Works*. 4 vols. Ed. A. C. Frazer. Oxford: Clarendon Press.

Bhaskar, Roy. 1978. *A Realist Theory of Science*. 2d ed. Atlantic Highlands, N.J.: Humanities Press.

Carver, Terrell. 1983. *Marx and Engels: The Intellectual Relationship*. Bloomington: Indiana University Press.

Duhem, Pierre. 1954. *The Aim and Structure of Physical Theory*. Princeton: Princeton University Press.

Easton, Loyd David, and Kurt H. Guddat, eds. 1967. *Writings of the Young Marx on Philosophy and Society*. Garden City, N.Y.: Anchor.

Engels, Frederick. 1935a. *Herr Eugen Dühring's Revolution in Science* [*Anti-Dühring*]. New York: International Publishers.

———. 1935b. *Ludwig Feuerbach and the Outcome of Classical German Philosophy*. New York: International Publishers.

———. 1972. *Dialectics of Nature*. Moscow: Progress Publishers.

Ferraro, Joseph. 1992. *Freedom and Determination in History According to Marx and Engels*. New York: Monthly Review Press.

Findlay, J. N. 1966. *The Philosophy of Hegel*. New York: Collier.

Gould, Stephen Jay. 1986. Evolution and the Triumph of Homology: Or Why History Matters. *American Scientist* 75:50–59.

Gregory, Frederick. 1977. Scientific Versus Dialectical Materialism: A Clash of Ideologies in Nineteenth-Century German Radicalism. *Isis* 68, no. 242:206–23.

Harré, Rom. 1964. *Matter and Method*. London: Macmillan.

———. 1987. *Varieties of Realism*. Oxford: Basil Blackwell.

Harré, Rom, and Edward H. Madden. 1975. *Causal Powers*. Oxford: Basil Blackwell.

Helmholtz, Herman. 1971. *Selected Writings*. Ed. Russell Kahn. Middletown, Conn.: Wesleyan University Press.

Inwood, Michael. 1987. Kant and Hegel on Space and Time. In *Hegel's Critique of Kant*, ed. Stephen Priest, 49–64. Oxford: Oxford University Press.

Lenin, V. I. 1970. *Materialism and Empirio-Criticism: Critical Comments on a Reactionary Philosophy*. Moscow: Progress Publishers.

Lenzer, Gertrude. 1975. *Auguste Comte and Positivism: The Essential Writings*. New York: Harper & Row.

Lichtheim, George. 1963. *Marxism: A Historical and Critical Study*. New York: Praeger.

Mandelbaum, Maurice. 1971. *History, Man, and Reason: A Study in Nineteenth-Century Thought*. Baltimore: Johns Hopkins University Press.

Manicas, Peter T. 1987. *A History and Philosophy of the Social Sciences*. Oxford: Blackwell.

Marx, Karl, and Frederick Engels. 1942. *The Selected Correspondence, 1864–1895*. New York: International Publishers.

Passmore, John. 1966. *A Hundred Years of Philosophy*. Rev. ed. New York: Basic Books.

Perry, Ralph Barton. 1955. *Present Philosophical Tendencies*. New York: George Braziller.

Pippin, Robert B. 1989. *Hegel's Idealism: The Satisfaction of Self-Consciousness*. Cambridge: Cambridge University Press.

————. 1993. Hegel's Original Insight. *International Philosophical Quarterly* 33:285–96.

Rorty, Richard. 1979. *Philosophy and the Mirror of Nature*. Princeton: Princeton University Press.

Ruben, David-Hillel. 1979. Marxism and Dialectics. In *Issues in Marxist Philosophy*, ed. John Mepham and David-Hillel Ruben, 1:37–85. Brighton, East Sussex: Harvester.

Sayer, Derek. 1979. *Marx's Method: Ideology, Science, and Critique in Capital*. Brighton, East Sussex: Harvester.

Sedgwick, Sally. 1993. Pippin on Hegel's Critique of Kant. *International Philosophical Quarterly* 33:273–95.

Spencer, Herbert. 1976 [1850]. *First Principles*. Westport, Conn.: Greenwood Press.

Stedman Jones, Gareth. 1973. Engels and the End of Classical German Philosophy. *New Left Review*, no. 79:17–36.

Westphal, Kenneth R. 1989. *Hegel's Epistemological Realism*. Dordrecht: Kluwer.

————. 1997. Noumenal Causality Reconsidered: Affection, Agency, and Meaning in Kant. *Canadian Journal of Philosophy* 27:209–45.

4

Engels and the Enlightenment Reading of Marx

Scott Meikle

The philosophy on which Marx constructed *Capital* is often referred to in the literature rather peculiarly as his "method." This is done apparently in the belief that Marx was a scientist, of the political economic subspecies, and that his work has to be evaluated in the way that science is supposed to be, and that means methodologically. One would expect, then, that this literature would deal with the topics that belong to the philosophy of science: explanation, observation, hypothesis, causation, necessity, induction, deduction, laws, and so forth. Some things of that kind are sometimes dealt with, such as the nature of laws and tendencies in Marx, and the view that he proceeded by successive approximations. What one mostly finds, however, are discussions of such things as form, totality, internal relations, and dialectics. These discussions look more like metaphysics than the philosophy of science. So why should there be this apparent misnomer of "method"? Is it possible that there might be an equivocation or confusion somewhere along the line over the kind of inquiry Marx is pursuing, over the sense in which it may be said to be scientific, or over the kind of explanation he is looking for?

In trying to prize open this set of problems, one is presented with features of Marx's work that are difficult to account for on the common view of him as being primarily an Enlightenment man of science. That Enlightenment view of Marx was not created single-handedly by Engels, but he had a lot to do with it, and through him it became the backbone of what, through Kautsky and other authors of the Second International and with the addition of further distortions, became the official Marxism of the Soviet authorities. The Western Marxist tradition significantly detaches Marx from the Enlightenment and its preoccupations. The Frankfurt School made this a primary objective, though, as we shall see, even they exaggerated Marx's involvement with Enlightenment conceptions of science, and Lukács, in his later work especially, places Marx in the pre-Enlightenment Aristotelian tradition of philosophical reflection (see Lukács 1980, 10, 29–30). My object here is to consider to what degree, if any, *Capital* embodies Enlightenment conceptions of science, scientific explanation, and social science. I argue that Marx's metaphysics and philosophy of science in *Capital* are not as Newtonian as they are made to appear on the view that the object of *Capital* is to lay out the "laws of motion" of market economy, or as Hegelian as they are made to appear on the view that *Capital* is a particular application of the metaphysics and philosophy of science developed by Engels.

Engels and Marx's *Capital*

It would not have been easy for Engels to have acknowledged the Aristotelian philosophical foundation of Marx's thought, even if he had been aware of it. The very name Aristotle was a *bête noir*, still popularly associated in the progressive mind with everything that the men of the Enlightenment opposed: superstition, authority, dogmatism, and religion. To have saddled Marx with such an association would have been tantamount to announcing his marriage to the Queen of the Night. The question did not arise, however, because Engels, who knew little about philosophy of any kind, was entirely unaware of Marx's philosophical provenance. He went on, in spite of that, to provide Marx with a provenance of his own devising that turned Marx into Sarastro.

Marx and Engels were opposites in many ways, as the work of Carver has shown (Carver 1980, 1983, 1984). Marx himself was academically well trained in the classics and in classical philosophy, and he had learned the habit of approaching the things he read with a spirit of skepticism and detachment. He took great pains to get even small points right, and he was impatient with carelessness and lack of judgment in other authors. Intellectual discipline and a sense of proportion are marked features of the first volume of *Capital*, and Marx shows restraint in the theoretical claims he makes on behalf of the work. It was by far the chief of his works published in his lifetime by himself, and he knew that his future reputation would depend on it. He had planned for this, and he prepared the ground with meticulous foresight, publishing its main ideas in a dry run, *A Contribution to the Critique of Political Economy* (1859), some eight years before *Capital: A Critique of Political Economy* (1867) itself appeared. He was shrewder than most in spotting fads, and there is scant evidence that he took a chance with the future reputation of his book by associating it, or its dry run, with any contemporary vogue that might prove ephemeral. He meant his book to be an enduring one, not a tract for the times. Extravagance of thought, inadequate preparation, intellectual indiscipline, lack of a proper skepticism and sense of proportion, and vulnerability to fads were not parts of Marx's intellectual makeup, and they find no place in *Capital*.

Engels was different in every respect. He was drawn into the late-Victorian vogue for physical science, which also produced the "political arithmetic" of neoclassical economics and the positivist movement in philosophy. It would have been difficult for anyone to stay clear of such a powerful vogue, but Engels was especially vulnerable, lacking the intellectual foundation that might have given him a measure of the independence needed to take a less enthusiastic and more qualified view of it. He pitched into it headlong, and came to believe that he would do Marx a great service if he could tap into this vogue for physical science on his friend's behalf, by showing that Marx's analysis of economics and capitalism was really a particular application of a powerful "scientific" metaphysical theory of everything (see Colletti 1973). It was a naive conception in itself, and the state of Engels's preparation for it meant that its execution by him could only have been naive. The taste he had developed for large-scale speculative metaphysics was not backed by a full study of the subject and its history, and he lacked the sense of proportion to realize that he was aiming, with no chance of success, to put himself in the world league of metaphysicians along with Plato, Aristotle, Aquinas, Spinoza, Leibniz, Hume, Kant, and Hegel. Had Engels left things there and kept Marx out of it, his excursus into metaphysics would have earned a place as a minor work of its time and something of a *folie de grandeur*. Unfortunately he did bring Marx into it, and he went so far as to encourage the view that the major strength of Marx's *Capital* lay in its being a particular application of the general metaphysical theory and philosophy of science devised by himself.

Engels's culpability is great, but it is too easily exaggerated today, and there is a tendency that needs resisting to blame him for anything that might be thought a weakness in Marx's own work. There is a case to be made that Marx himself, in carrying his work forward from the *Economic and Philosophical Manuscripts* of 1844 to *Capital* of 1867, was too influenced by the vogue for science or too overtaken by the mass of material he had assembled, with the effect that what was intended to be a critique of economics (or political economy, if you prefer) came out looking too much like an alternative version of it. This failure suited the inclinations of Marx's early and influential commentators, who were more creatures of the Enlightenment than Marx himself was.

Nonetheless, the effect of Engels's intervention was to make the acceptance of Marx's critique of economics conditional on accepting Engels's own set of claims in metaphysics and the philosophy of science. Those claims were contestable at best, and the consequence was that Marx's *Capital* was made conditional on the acceptance of contestable claims. This is not quite the service that Engels may have imagined he was rendering Marx. Engels may have believed he was gaining a wider appeal for Marx's work on market economy and economics by linking it to his own "scientific" metaphysics, but any success he had in achieving that aim was paid for by mortgaging the reputation of Marx's work in the longer term. What he was certainly successful in achieving was attracting to his own work in metaphysics a wider audience and a more serious attention than it would have earned on its own account, by linking it to the strength of Marx's work *Capital*. It is unrealistic to imagine that this was entirely absent from Engels's mind, or that it was no part of his motivation, in doing what he did. He naturally believed in the truth and importance of his metaphysics and philosophy of science, and though this was folly on his part, it did not in itself have implications for the future reception of Marx's *Capital*. But bolting his metaphysics onto Marx's critique of economics, where it unavoidably assumed priority over Marx's work, since Engels's was the theory of greater generality, was an irresponsible act. It put the future reception of Marx's *Capital* at hazard in a way that Marx himself had not done.

Marx knew the difference between entertaining an idea in a subject you are aware that you have not mastered and asserting its unqualified truth. Engels was not sufficiently aware of that difference. Marx made it his life's work to master economics and to get to the bottom of the nature of market economy, and he spent more than twenty years getting on top of the entire literature with the thoroughness and attention to detail he knew such a task required. Marx was careful not to put at risk the future reception of *Capital*, as a work on economics and market economy, by encumbering it with much opinion about things in fields he had not mastered, opinion that ran a risk of being half-baked. Engels squandered that caution, discrimination, and self-control. Engels believed he could master an entire field, a much bigger and more ancient one than Marx had set out to master and one in which Engels had had no education, with just a few years of selective and unguided reading. Bringing such standards to his own work was his business, but it is sad that he should have imposed them on Marx's *Capital.* In Marx's lifetime, from around 1860, Engels decided to become, as he put it, Marx's "second fiddle." After Marx's death he took steps that, whether by design or oversight, made Marx into Engels's second fiddle. One consequence of this was that reflection on the philosophical foundation of *Capital* was sent off on a false scent. The great influence that Engels's work later came to exercise, under the Second and Third Internationals, had the effect of preempting consideration of the philosophical and scientific character that Marx himself had chosen to impart to his own work. In what follows, that character will be examined, and it will be argued that in *Capital* Marx works to a metaphysics and philosophy of science that antedated Hegel and Engels and that is in its essentials largely independent of Hegelianism and Engels's version of it.

Marx's *Capital* and Metaphysics

Marx's *Capital* shows some features that are odd for scientific work, at least as that is most commonly understood today. The first chapter, entitled "Commodities," is a tortuous and difficult inquiry into the nature of a property: the property of exchange value that things come to have when they are made objects of systematic exchange in markets using money. The problem is to find out the nature of that property, and the order of being to which it belongs. To get to the bottom of it Marx has to consider a series of possibilities. Is it a quantitative property, that is, a property capable of magnitude, and of measurement if there is a measure? Is it a relational property, that is, a property that arises only in a relation, as "being married" is a property that can be had only by someone who is in the relation of "being married to" someone else? Thus "having exchange value" would be a property that is had only by things that enter the exchange relation "x of A = y of B." Or is it a property that things have antecedently to their entering the relation of exchange? If so, is it a property of a natural kind that exists alongside the other natural properties that make an artifact a useful thing, or is it a property of a nonnatural kind, an *übernatürlich* property as Marx calls it, which Moore and Aveling translate as a "nonnatural" property? Is it a property in its own right at all, or is it merely a surface appearance of another property that underlies it as its essence? The entire discussion of the forms of value, from the elementary to the general form, is primarily an attempt to identify the nature of a property, and to arrive at a definition of it.

An inquiry into the nature of a property is a metaphysical inquiry, and the terms in which Marx proceeds make it perfectly plain that his inquiry is of that kind. No argument is needed to show this, because the inquiry is paradigmatically metaphysical, and that will be obvious to anyone who knows anything about the subject of metaphysics in philosophy. Metaphysics traditionally is concerned with things and their attributes and with the categories of the predicates in which they are described, logical categories of substance, quality, quantity, relation, and so forth, and its object is to bring into the open, and to articulate consciously, the logical characteristics of the basic concepts and the conceptual structure we all use as speakers of a natural language in thinking and talking about the world and its furniture, and in pursuing any cognitive enterprise, including science. Marx is employing traditional metaphysics in an attempt to track down the nature of a puzzling property, exchange value. In the vernacular of the modern social sciences the term "metaphysics" still sometimes has empiricist or positivist opprobrium attached to it, so that to describe something as "metaphysical" is to say that it is unscientific and purely verbal. This is simply ignorance about philosophy. The positivists indulged in metaphysics as much as anyone, in spite of their huffing and puffing about "eliminating" it.

But a metaphysical inquiry is not necessarily how one would expect a work of science to begin, and this may be one reason why the metaphysical character of Marx's inquiry into the nature of economic value has often remained unidentified or unacknowledged. Marx's own best-known acknowledgment of its metaphysical character is usually regarded as amounting to nothing more than a wisecrack. He observes that the commodity, "at first sight, a very trivial thing, and easily understood," is in fact "abounding in metaphysical subtleties," and here he is speaking literally as well as ironically (Marx 1908, 41). He is implicitly pointing to the irony in the fact that in order to come to understand something as coarse and brutal as the commodity or exchange value, it is necessary to engage in the most refined and general area of thought. But it is necessary, and that is his literal point, and it is this that gives him the occasion for the crack.

Something should be said, by way of digression from the main argument, about the secondary question of where Marx got this metaphysics. Chris Arthur has suggested that Marx drew on Hegel's *Logic* for his use of the categories of quality, quantity, and relation, and this might be partly right (Arthur 1993, 63–87). Hegel's *Logic* is structured around those categories, certainly, as a glance at the table of contents is enough to show, but Hegel drew them from Aristotle's standard work the *Categories,* in which Aristotle divides predicates into ten categories distinguished by their logical properties: predicates of substance, quality, quantity, relation, place, and so forth. (It is worth noting that G.R.G. Mure, in his *Introduction to Hegel* [1940], usefully begins his book with six chapters on Aristotle.)

It might be that Marx drew in part or in whole, for his handling of the categories, from the same sources Hegel used, the *Metaphysics* and the *Organon*. Marx certainly studied the *Metaphysics* in 1841–42, but both works were pretty standard reading for students on the Continent formed in the Aristotelian philosophical tradition, as both Hegel and Marx were, and Aristotle's works became more influential still following the appearance in 1831 of Immanuel Bekker's magisterial edition of the surviving Aristotelian corpus. Both Hegel and Marx worked within the substance-attribute metaphysics of the Aristotelian tradition throughout their lives, and neither had any truck with Anglo-Scottish antisubstance metaphysics (see Meikle 1991). The influence on Marx of Hegel's *Logic* may best be assessed perhaps if it is considered in the wider context of the relation both of them had to Aristotle and the Aristotelian tradition as the concept matrix within which they both developed.

Marx found Anglophone thought, informed as it generally was by empiricist antisubstance metaphysics, gross and opaque, though it seems that he never explicitly acknowledged that the source of this opacity lay in metaphysics, and it may be that he never realized that this is where it lay. Marx never found time to come to grips with philosophy after his student studies of Aristotle, Spinoza, Hume, and others during his time in Berlin in 1842 (MEGA IV.1, 155–288, and IV.1, Apparat, 733–823), though he expressed an intention to, and his knowledge of the Anglo-Scottish style of philosophy was restricted almost entirely to its economic and political dimensions. His later references to Hume, for example, are always to the economic, social, and historical essays, and never to the more general metaphysical and epistemological work in the *Enquiry* and the *Treatise*. This is one indication among many that Marx's reading of philosophers was strictly governed by his determination, arrived at around the time when he prepared the *Economic and Philosophical Manuscripts* of 1844, to master the whole of economic literature, as the key to market economy.

It is possible that there has been a reluctance to recognize the metaphysical character of Marx's first chapter in *Capital*. The word "metaphysics" and its cognates have acquired derogatory uses in the English language, and they are still sometimes used sarcastically and dismissively, though these days it seems mostly by economists. The practice began in the seventeenth and eighteenth centuries, when "metaphysics" became a term of derision that authors of Protestant and commercial culture applied to the Aristotelian philosophical tradition and to the work of their Catholic and anticommercial intellectual opponents both in continental Europe and in the geographical area that came to be known by the political designation of the "British Isles." Hobbes identified "school metaphysics" as belonging to "Popery" and the "Kingdome of Darknesse," and Hume wrote unpleasantly about it, recommending, perhaps jokingly, that it be thrown into the fire and burned (Hobbes 1991, 461–62; Hume 1894, 165).

This opprobrious sense of the word acquired common currency in Anglophone literature of all kinds. Typically, the historian Edward Gibbon contrasts an argument that is "satisfactory and just" with one that is "metaphysical," and the novelist Wilkie Collins uses "metaphysics" to mean vaporous nonsense deriving from continental Europe (Gibbon 1950, 117, 221n; Collins 1949, 399). In the earlier part of the twentieth century this use of the word was injected with new life by the ultra-Humean logical positivists or logical empiricists, whose program was to "eliminate" what they took to be metaphysics. Joan Robinson, Pareto, Schumpeter, and many others in that period used the word in the positivist opprobrious sense to sneer at Marx's analysis of exchange value (Robinson 1964, 29; Pareto 1971, 177; Schumpeter 1954, 61). In view of this history it seems safe to surmise that Marxian authors of mainstream Anglophone culture, and other Marxians impressed by that culture, may have found difficulty in explicitly acknowledging the metaphysical character of Marx's inquiry, even if they were aware of it. But many, in any case, would not have been aware of it, because metaphysics was not only derided but largely removed from a philosophy curriculum that came to be taken up with an empiricist philosophy in which epistemology was promoted to the leading place in philosophizing about the world and its contents. In Anglophone philosophical culture, metaphysics has been readmitted as a respectable part of the subject only gradually in the last few decades, and a distaste for Aristotelian metaphysics is still characteristic of that culture. Given this unfortunate history, it would be reasonable to expect not only some reluctance to identify the metaphysical character of Marx's inquiry into economic value for what it is, but also some incapacity to do so arising from that history.

Capital and Ethics

If the first chapter of *Capital* is metaphysics, what of the rest of the book? Here we encounter further peculiarities, or, rather, things that from an Enlightenment point of view may appear to be peculiarities. It is obvious what is in the rest of the book. It is taken up with three things: first, an account of the lawlike behavior of a market economy, showing it to work systematically and toward an end, the expansion of economic value or capital accumulation; second, an account of the historical process by which market economy came into existence (in part VIII, "The So-Called Primitive Accumulation"); and a third element that it would be vain to try to locate in any particular place, because it suffuses the whole work, a demonstration that in the "economic process" of market economy human good, when it is not thwarted, is served to too limited an extent, and then only accidentally, because human good is not the end the process aims at.

The first of these elements offers a systematic explanation of an area of lawlike phenomena, and as such it is clearly a piece of science (though it must be treated as a separate question whether it is the same kind of science as political economy). The second element is history. The third is ethics because it concerns ends, and its core is human good. So *Capital* appears to be constructed out of metaphysics, history, ethics, and science of some kind, though which kind remains to be seen. This intellectual construction, with these components and taken as a whole, is not easy to place as science. The claim that Marx's construction is science, and that it proceeds from a scientific methodology, is commonly made nonetheless, though without an explanation of how this can be so when the construction has integral components that are so diverse.

This set of components is apt to seem an odd mixture when looked at from the point of view of prevailing opinion about what science is, which does not harmonize well with a mixture of this kind. The least problematical component is the presence of history in part VIII. This may plausibly be regarded as an addendum to the main construction, and one that does not materially affect the character of the construction itself, other than to draw attention to the fact that the market economy is a recent affair, not a natural condition. What is more difficult to handle is the copresence of science and ethics. In premodern European thought such a copresence was not in principle a problem, but in the thought of modernity it has become a big problem. Science and ethics have grown far apart, or are generally thought to have done so. Science is seen as having to do with observations and their explanation, and ethics with telling you how to live, or with norms, values, and their justification. There are philosophical positions that try to maintain linkages between the two, but the mainstream position is strongly in favor of a separation and a fact-value gap, and theories that link them are generally forced to adopt a defensive stance. In the modern conception of social science, the presence of ethics in a theoretical position is apt to be regarded as gravely weakening any claims to be scientific that may be made on its behalf.

A large segment of that literature on Marx which identifies his work as science avoids the problem of finding a way to reconcile the copresence of science and ethics in *Capital* by implicitly or explicitly denying the presence of ethics and representing the science as more or less Newtonian in character. Typical moves here are to claim that Marx thought ethics to be mere ideology, relying on occasional remarks he makes, such as his sarcastic footnote on Proudhon's "justice éternelle" (Marx 1908, 56). Marx's construction is then represented as a quasi-Newtonian science setting out the "laws of motion" of capitalist society. His theory of history is represented as another set of "laws of motion," of human society in general, and the postmarket, or socialist, society of the future is represented as the end state produced by the operation of those two sets of laws. These moves are unconvincing because it is no part of a Newtonian science to reveal what end a system serves or whether that end is good or bad or worth continuing with or better got rid of. But *Capital* does do those things, and so it is not Newtonian and does contain ethics, just as the *Economic and Philosophical Manuscripts* did.

This social scientific, modernist, or Enlightenment view of Marx generally identifies him as one of the three "classical political economists," along with Smith and Ricardo. The difference between them is seen to lie in the fact that Smith and Ricardo established a scientific road in the analysis of human society, and of capitalist society in particular, on which road they stopped short before reaching the end, while Marx followed it to the end, thereby achieving a fuller scientific theory. This view implicates Marx in the development of the progressive and radical Whig thought that produced economics, the Enlightenment program of constructing a rational order of state administration, and modern social science, the early formation of which is well described in Pocock 1975, ch. xiii. In doing this it also places Marx in an intellectual framework in which ethics and thought about ends are marginalized and from which they are eventually excluded altogether. Smith is prepared to think about ends to some degree. His "hidden hand" defense of markets involves distinguishing between the pursuit of money as an end (M-C-M) and the pursuit of human good as an end (C-M-C), and he concluded that business cannot always be relied on to serve human good and needs public regulation to make sure that it does. But on the whole, a reflective concern with ends is not a strong feature of *The Wealth of Nations,* and the presumption is overwhelmingly in favor of one end, the pursuit of wealth as money. In Ricardo the tendency to relegate ethics to the background is even more strongly marked, and in modern economics this original tendency is fully realized in a strategy of avoiding any discussion at all of the end served by the market system by the device of confining discussion of ends to the preference schedules of individual choosers. Marx's *Capital,* on the other hand, is oriented toward the consideration of ends and human good, not in an incidental way, but in a way that is fundamental to the conception and principal purpose of the book. To have drawn Marx's work into the Enlightenment project in the way that his early and influential interpreters did distorted the nature and purpose of his work by diminishing the role of ethics in it and by misrepresenting the nature of the science involved in it, assimilating it to Newtonian Enlightenment conceptions of science and to the work of Smith and Ricardo.

In spite of the fact that ethics had already begun to take a back seat in Smith and Ricardo, many economists subsequently persisted in efforts to keep economics and ethics connected, and the final separation was eventually reached only in 1932 with the publication of Robbins's *Nature and Significance of Economic Science,* in which all connection is deliberately broken. Economics then moved fully into value-free mode and developed further the earlier attempts made by Jevons and others to present economics as a quantitative science, like physics, supposedly every bit as independent of ethics as physics is (see Mirowski 1989, which gives an excellent account of these physical pretensions). Marx's work, from his first serious encounter with political economy in the *Economic and Philosophical Manuscripts* of 1844, moves in the opposite direction, by establishing at its center a conception of human good based on an account of human nature and of what is needed for creatures with the needs and capacities that humans have to flourish as things of their kind. Marx's thinking about this was developed out of his study of Aristotle's *De anima,* the work in which Aristotle sets out his ideas about human nature, of which Marx produced the first German translation, supplying it with notes and apparently intending it for publication. This aspect of Marx's work came to be suppressed in the official Marxist tradition, and as Norman Geras observes (1983), it was, at the time of his writing, a commonplace progressive and peace-loving opinion that the concept of human nature was inherently reactionary and that Marx's views on it were entirely relativistic and historicist.

It was essential to Marx's project to have a clear conception of human nature drawn up, not in economic terms, but in terms theoretically independent of economics, because only if that were so could it operate as a standard against which one might test how well or badly the market economy and its dedicated science of economics were doing in serving human good. Market economy will always pass this test if economics is allowed to get away with defining human nature and human good in economic and utilitarian terms. In order to make the test a real one, Marx foregrounds a conception of human good that is independent of the accounts of human good that political economists and their associated utilitarian philosophers give, and that is why ethics is central to the very conception Marx had of *Capital* as "a critique of political economy," the subtitle he gave the book. In doing this he is engaged in a study very different in nature and aim from what Smith and Ricardo did and from what economics (or political economy, if you prefer) does, and this ought to make us skeptical of the claims that have frequently been made, by Meek and Dobb, for example, that Marx did the same sort of thing as Smith and Ricardo, only better. Ethics has little or no role in the economic work of Smith and Ricardo. This Enlightenment view of *Capital* has recently been restated in an original way by James Buchan (1997), who argues that Marx got it right about money and its effects on human life ("like a bore at a picnic which interposes itself into every relation between human beings"), but that he did this in the *Economic and Philosophical Manuscripts* and later messed it all up by turning it into economics in *Capital.*

Capital and Science

If ethics has this place in Marx's work, then what sort of science could he have been doing that would allow ethics such a place? To approach this issue it is necessary first to raise two further questions: the nature of explanation in *Capital,* and Marx's relation to the philosophical moves from the seventeenth century on, largely made by the English and Scottish writers anthologized as the "British Moralists," which produced modern social science (Selby-Bigge 1897; Raphael 1969).

There are, broadly speaking, two patterns of explanation: hypothetical and categorical. Hypothetical explanation seeks to explain an area of phenomena without making any claim, or any strong claim, to know much, or anything, about the natures of the entities or agents inhabiting the domain, whose operations might be supposed to give rise to the phenomena. Its aim is, as the saying goes, to "save the phenomena," that is, to bring singular events, or idealized singular events, under laws understood as lawlike statements of constant conjunctions of event types, and if that can be done, it is considered an adequate explanation. It works in this way: Adopt the hypothesis or assumption that x and y, and see how much of the phenomena you can explain on that hypothesis. A hypothesis is a good one if it helps to explain a lot. Categorical explanation, on the other hand, seeks not only to bring the phenomena into some sort of order, but to explain why the phenomena occur as they are observed to do, by showing what it is in the natures of the entities or agents inhabiting the domain in virtue of which they so operate as to produce the phenomena that are observed (see McMullin 1984, which also contains an excellent résumé of contemporary views about explanation and relates those views to the two historical traditions in philosophy, the Aristotelian and the Humean empiricist).

It would seem that categorical explanation, if you can get it, will give a fuller understanding because it will answer more questions and because it will be categorical and not dependent on an assumption or hypothesis, which is by definition not known to be true. But you might not be able to get categorical explanation, and in that case you will have to settle for hypothetical explanation. Whether you like it or not, if it is the best you can get, it is what you must settle for. This situation might not be permanent, of course, because there might be no way of knowing what is possible in the future, and categorical explanation remains a possibility even when it is not presently attainable.

The classical source of philosophy of science embodying categorical explanation is Aristotle's *Posterior Analytics,* the inspiration of generations of European scholars and scientists. The book is in two parts, of which the first, book A, deals with the best way to present and organize the results of research into the facts, so that those discoveries are collected into an intelligible whole in which their interrelations and explanation will be made most apparent. Aristotle's recommendation is that the best form of presentation of a science is a formal axiomatized system, something like the systematization of geometry produced by Euclid a generation or so after Aristotle, which was probably inspired by the *Posterior Analytics,* or in some respects like Maxwell's kinetic theory of gases, in which known gas laws are derived from a small number of postulates and axioms. In book B Aristotle deals with the axioms of a science, and these, he says, must provide definitions of essences or natures.

Marx's research led him to the conclusion that the primary nature operating in market economy is economic value and that everything systematic and lawlike in the phenomena observable in market economy arises from it. Marx's theory of market economy as he presents it in *Capital* is not hypothetical; he does not offer a theory that "saves the phenomena" of market economy based on the granting of a hypothesis. The first chapter of the book is not the presentation of a hypothesis, but an analysis and definition of the nature or essence of the property of economic value, and the rest of the book in part sets out to show that the nomological behavior, or lawlikeness, of market economy and the end it aims at arise from the nature or essence of the property of economic value. Chapter 1 of *Capital* corresponds to book B of the *Posterior Analytics,* and much of the rest corresponds to book A. It would appear on the face of it, then, that *Capital,* with respect to the form of explanation it offers for the phenomena of market economy, answers to the form Aristotle recommends in the *Posterior Analytics* for the presentation of a finished science. This is, of course, too big a thesis to be defended here, but if something has been said to make it seem a thesis worth considering, that will be something.

Marx's "method" in *Capital* is not in the least idiosyncratic really, but this is unlikely to be appreciated if its character and lineage in the philosophy of science remains unidentified and unacknowledged. In the literature on Marx's "method" is abundant indication of a tacit admission that Marx is idiosyncratic, and this is not only a mistake but an unjustifiable concession to empiricist metaphysics and philosophy of science. Marx is very traditional in his philosophy of science, as he is in his metaphysics, and the tradition he works from is that which the early modern theorizers of the market, from Hobbes to the Anglo-Scottish Enlightenment, sought to discredit and replace because it did not serve their turn.

Aristotelian ideas about science are perfectly defensible in modern terms, and Barnes, in his introduction to the Clarendon edition of the *Posterior Analytics,* offers a brief outline of such a defense (see also Brody 1980, ch. 6; McMullin 1984). But those ideas have been the target of an unremitting, often intemperate, and almost always ill-informed campaign in the Anglophone tradition since the seventeenth century. Barnes comments on the fact that there is a need to defend Aristotle from his modern detractors: "Yet I cannot help feeling that there is something vaguely absurd in defending the book at all: it is, on any account, one of the most brilliant, original, and influential works in the history of philosophy. . . . How odd to defend—or to doubt—its accomplishments" (Aristotle 1994, xiv–xv). It is odd, but when it comes to Aristotle and the Aristotelian tradition, Anglophone philosophical culture has been very odd. Indeed, uniquely in European culture, it developed a phobic attitude toward Aristotelianism.

The empiricist philosophical tradition is now deeply rooted in Anglophone philosophical culture, and according to that tradition there are no natures or essences, and all explanation must be hypothetical, since, in the absence of natures, categorical explanation must be impossible. More moderate positions are possible. It might be held that in natural science all our best theories are as a matter of fact hypothetical; that the fate of past convictions of having got to the bottom of things, based on theories that were later superseded, has taught us to be less confident about claims to have reached the real essential nature of things in the natural realm. These moderate positions are compatible with the possibility of categorical explanation, and a formulation of them could embody categorical explanation as an ideal that we might hope to reach, and should in any case strive for. It might perhaps be that the true nature of physical reality might for some reason forever elude our fullest understanding, but we do not know now that it will. The immoderate empiricist position is that we do know that now, but the grounds on which it is supposed that we know it are provided by empiricist metaphysics, not by science.

Even if there were grounds for skepticism about the future of human understanding of the natural realm such as might go some way to justify a belief that only hypothetical explanation will ever be attained in that realm, we should still need to consider it as a quite separate question whether there might be a similar reason for skepticism about explanation and understanding of the human social realm. This does not seem plausible, because the phenomena in this realm are of our own making, as are the natures, mainly institutions and forms of organization of our efforts, that inhabit that realm. (The empiricist skepticism about explanation, and metaphysical commitment to hypothetical explanation, even in relation to physics, have not worn well as physics and chemistry have developed in this century [McMullin 1984].) Vico observed that it is difficult to believe that our own institutions could contain a secret that we were incapable of unraveling, and reflections of this kind might justify confidence that in the social realm categorical explanation should be possible. The inner nature of the natural realm may be unintelligible, if the strong antirealists are right, or intelligible, if the strong realists are right. But even the most open-minded and uncommitted person can surely not believe that the first of these can possibly apply to the social realm. If it is right to identify Marx's conception of science as Aristotelian, and if Marx's theory itself is right, then categorical explanation of the nature of market economy is precisely what Marx achieved.

Marx's *Capital* and Ends

We must ask whether—and if so, how—the science in *Capital* can be co-present with ethics, as we earlier saw them to be, without giving rise to the general problems that might possibly be expected to arise when science and ethics are mixed. This part of the plot has already begun to dilute. Marx shows market economy to be an end-directed and lawlike system, and as he unfolds its lawlike nature, Marx and his readers are constantly and necessarily confronted with the disregard of human good that the pursuit of that end necessarily entails. These laws are shown to work through the agency of people whose wills are constrained by them, so that market economy is necessarily associated with a loss of control over social activities and a closing down of the choice of ends to be pursued. The fact that the system has an end built into it means that, for so long as we live under that system, the list of ends to which our collective efforts can be directed has one overriding entry on it, the expansion of value, or capital accumulation. The end-directed nature of the system itself, and the accompanying loss of control over our own activities, makes it difficult for us to intervene with any serious effect to make the system serve human good better than it does, and these are the deeper reasons for Marx's skepticism about the likelihood that efforts at reforming the system will achieve much. If we have handed control of our own affairs to the laws of the market and its end of profit maximization, then we cannot at the same time have that control in our own hands, nor can we reasonably complain that human good is not being sufficiently served.

The discussion of ends is itself part of the scientific examination of the nature of the system. Reaching an understanding of the nature of the system involves recognizing or discovering that it operates in a lawlike way toward the goal of capital accumulation, and that its being lawlike entails that those living in it will lose control over what they do. Entailment is not the right relation here, because having a lawlike system is not an antecedent condition from which a subsequent loss of control follows as a consequence. A lawlike system is one where control over what we do is passed from our hands into the laws of the system, and such laws can exist at all only because they are controls of our behavior that are alternatives to the controlling power of decision making that we are no longer exercising for ourselves over our own affairs. To regain that control, to recover the capacity to choose ends and the capacity to direct means to the pursuit of the ends we choose, necessarily means dispensing with the lawlike system. It is not possible at the same time both to have a lawlike and end-directed system and to exercise control over ends for ourselves. In the nature of the case, we can have one or the other but not both. They are alternatives between which we must choose. Comparisons of Marx's treatment of the "laws of motion" of market economy with a Newtonian treatment of the "laws of motion" of a physical system can at best deal in superficial resemblances. Marx's ideas of what it is to give a scientific treatment of the capitalist entity are entirely misrepresented if his work is assimilated into the Enlightenment idea of science in that way, and the work of Engels encouraged just such an assimilation.

Scientifically examining the nature of a system of this kind unavoidably involves a discussion of ends because the system itself has been found to be a system with an end built into it. Moreover, one of the results of the scientific examination has been that the end in question is one to which there is an alternative, the direct pursuit of human good rather than its indirect pursuit through exchange value and markets, so that in principle we have a choice between these ends. Doing the science of such an object as market economy therefore involves ethics. This is not to say that the scientific inquirer, as a scientist, sticks to the science of analyzing the object and then in a separate operation evaluates the results of the science ethically and makes recommendations for action. Rather, doing the science itself involves an examination of ends and alternatives because the object of the science, market economy, is of such a kind that doing this is part of what is necessary to achieve the comprehension of that object, and what is required for that examination must be part of the science. The nature of the object itself makes this so, and we cannot regard Marx as doing one sort of thing with his scientist's hat on and another sort of thing with his ethicist's hat on.

The alternative course and its end, the direct pursuit of human good, are presented by Marx both as the way people did things before market economy appeared and as the only future alternative to the market, a course to which people will probably have to decide to revert in order to extricate themselves from the sewer they have got themselves into with market economy, and to which capital accumulation is tending and pointing the way in any case. Marx offers an extended account of "those small and extremely ancient Indian communities, some of which have continued down to this day, [in which] production is independent of that division of labor brought about, in Indian society as a whole, by means of the exchange of commodities," and he describes these as "a specimen of the organisation of the labor of society, in accordance with an approved and authoritative plan" (Marx 1908, 350–52). Postmarket society can only be another specimen of the same general kind, and the socialization of labor under market economy is already, Marx thought, leading in that direction.

Marx's understanding is that market economy is a form taken by human society in the course of its development. It is not possible to discuss the form of something without discussing the thing of which it is the form. A form exists as the form of something; forms do not exist on their own, except in Platonic philosophy. Thus, to inquire into the nature of a form is necessarily to inquire into the nature of the thing whose form it is. Where the thing is such that it changes its form in the course of its existence, then the inquiry into any one of its forms will have to take account of its earlier and later forms and of the principles governing the changes from one to another. So the understanding Marx seeks of the nature of market economy, as a form of human society, must involve an understanding of the forms that precede it and out of which it developed, and an understanding of the tendencies of change that are to be observed in the society that has that form, in order to get a handle on a future form that it might pass into. The conclusion he draws from his considerations under this head is that there are only two ways humans can run their affairs: first, by alienating their own powers of decision and control to markets; and second, by exercising their own powers of control through an "approved and authoritative plan." The discussion of "ways of running their affairs" must involve a discussion of the ends served by running them in one way rather than the other, and that is inescapably ethics.

It is perhaps in order to obscure the presence of ethics here, in the interest of making Marx appear more assimilable to Enlightenment ideas of science, that commentators have often preferred to speak of economic "regulators" rather than ends. Perhaps that is also the reason why, encouraged by Engels's "scientific socialism," commentators have represented planning as a technical procedure rather than a practice based on prudence and ethics. As a strategy for marketing Marx it has not paid dividends. Presenting socialism, in Enlightenment mode, as a more rationally organized economic system than capitalism exposed it to the full force of economic criticism by Mises and Hayek, thus allowing critics to engage Marx on their own terrain. Engels helped to lay Marx open to this, not only in his own work but in the ways in which he chose to present Marx's work; for instance, the subtitle Marx himself gave *Capital*, namely "A Critique of Political Economy," was replaced in the English edition of 1887 by the subtitle "A Critical Analysis of Capitalist Production," which gives the work a rather different complexion. Once embarked on this Enlightenment reading of Marx, it is not easy to resist the logic that led Meek to conclude that "the marginalist trend, then, which began in such bitter opposition to Marxism, has in the end resulted in the production of a congeries of theories, concepts, and techniques which have become an indispensable auxiliary to Marxism—and an auxiliary, moreover, whose importance increases, rather than diminishes, as measures of central control over the economy are widened in scope" (1977, 173). Meek expressed these sentiments little more than a decade before the Soviet Union finally collapsed.

Ethics and economics are competitors over the same ground, as rival sources of reasons for decision making in the public realm. So long as market economy remains, economics will prevail in this contest. Marx was not an economist, or even a political economist, and he was not recommending a new economic order, but rather an end to an order that is in its nature economic. The move to postmarket society, in Marx's view, is not a move to a new "economic" order, as official Marxism generally portrayed it, but a move to an ethical order in which cooperative efforts will be life's prime want, not a struggle to get money from "givers of labor," and distribution will be decided, not by markets, but on ethical criteria: as Marx puts it in the *Critique of the Gotha Programme*, "from each according to his ability, to each according to his needs."

Marx's *Capital* and the Good

It seems, then, that science and ethics are copresent in *Capital*, and that the necessity for this arises from the nature of the object studied. Since the object of study is the way we are at present organizing ourselves and our efforts under market economy, why should it seem odd that ethics and science should be mixed in this way? Even economists used to think, until fairly recently, that there had to be an ethical dimension to their study. The shift in economics away from ethics, though it was finally made only in this century, was a long time in the making, and to see this it is necessary to consider the dispositions on the intellectual map before the arrival of the market economy and modern economics.

European thought about human social affairs, before the emergence of "modernity" in the seventeenth century and for long after in many parts of Europe, was developed around a structure that had been inherited from the ancient world. The key figure was Aristotle, and the structure he bequeathed, though much adapted and extended in subsequent centuries, was preserved in its architecture. The structure was simple and elegant, and it consisted in an arrangement of the arts and sciences in a hierarchical structure according to the seriousness of their ends. Those that were less serious were pursued, not for their own sakes, but for the sake of others that were more serious. Aristotle puts it, in terms of activities that were important in his time, thus: "[A]s bridle-making and the other arts concerned with the equipment of horses fall under the art of riding, and this and every military action under strategy, in the same way other arts fall under yet others—in all of these the ends of the master arts are to be preferred to all the subordinate ends; for it is for the sake of the former that the latter are pursued" (*Nicomachean Ethics* I:1094a10–15). The master art, or rather science (*epistēmē*), is *politikē*, or politics, because its end is the good for man, and so its end includes all the other arts and sciences and their ends, and while they are pursued for the sake of it, it is not pursued for the sake of anything else. In this structure, ethics, or *ethikē*, which deals with individual character and conduct, is subordinate to *politikē* because its end or point is a subordinate part of the end of *politikē*, the good for man.

Aristotle was aware that the activity of pursuing money had a dangerous capacity for introducing confusion into orderly thinking about the conduct of human activities. If the arts and sciences that make up the life of society (or "the polis" as Aristotle puts it) are infiltrated by the pursuit of money, and their ends compromised, confused, or subverted, as they tend to be when they are conducted not only for their own intrinsic ends but also for the sake of another end extrinsic to them, getting money, there can be little hope of their being rationally ordered. The polis itself, Aristotle says, comes into existence for the sake of life, but its continued existence is for the sake of the good life (*Politics* I:1252b30–31, 1280a31–32); it is not merely for defense and exchanging goods, it is also a partnership for living well (*Politics* III:1280b29–35). "Even if people living near each other had laws to prevent them wronging each other in the exchange of products—for instance, if one man were a carpenter, another a farmer, another a shoemaker, and others producers of other goods—and the whole population numbered ten thousand, still, if they associated in nothing more than military alliance and the exchange of goods, this would not be a polis" (*Politics* III:1280b17–23). Commerce, or the pursuit of wealth as money, is not good enough for Aristotle, but worse than that, it undermines what he understands to be the fitting use of human capacities, the good for man, and the point of social and political life (Meikle 1995, 71–76).

Such, more or less, was the understanding of European thinkers on matters of society and commerce until the rise of market economy, when the very confusion, subversion, and disorder in social activity that Aristotle himself had feared, but saw only in embryo, arrived with a vengeance. Until that time, the term "oeconomics" had a very different meaning from the one familiar today. Finley begins his book *The Ancient Economy* with some observations about the *Short Introduction to Moral Philosophy* published in 1742 by Francis Hutcheson, professor of moral philosophy at the University of Glasgow and the teacher of Adam Smith. Book III of this work is entitled "The Principles of Oeconomics and Politics," and it opens with three chapters on marriage and divorce, the duties of parents, children, masters, and servants, but it is otherwise exclusively devoted to politics. It is in book II, entitled "Elements of the Law of Nature," that we find an account of property, succession, contracts, the value of goods and coin, and the laws of war. Finley comments that "these were evidently not part of 'oeconomics.'. . . Hutcheson was neither careless nor perverse: he stood at the end of a tradition stretching back more than 2000 years. . . . The book that became the model for the tradition still represented by Hutcheson was the *Oikonomikos* written by the Athenian Xenophon before the middle of the fourth century BC." This was a work of practical advice to the gentleman landowner about the sound management of an estate, its slaves, household, and land. Finley concludes: "There was no road from the 'oeconomics' of Francis Hutcheson to the *Wealth of Nations* of Adam Smith, published twenty-four years later" (Finley 1973, 17–20). Economics was not a continuation of anything that had existed before.

Before market economy it was possible to think of human affairs only in terms of *politikē* and *ethikē,* and these were the only source of reasons for decision making in the public realm. With the arrival of market economy all this changed, and the intellectual map had to be redrawn. The most important kinds of decisions about human affairs came to be removed from the field of *ethikē* and *politikē* altogether and transferred to the province of the new science of economics. Room had to be made for the new science, and consequently *politikē* shrank, eventually to become "politics" and "political science," subordinate to economics, as we see them today. *Ethikē* developed in two ways, one strand losing all connection with the public realm to become concerned with the purely private and personal, and the other strand retaining its public reference but only by becoming little more than an adjunct of economics itself in the form of utilitarianism. These are the revolutionary conceptual dispositions that contemporary mainstream thought has inherited from the early moderns and the Enlightenment.

Marx's work clearly does not conform to these dispositions. Its lack of conformity is not the result of an idiosyncratic "method" made up by himself or acquired from some quirk of nineteenth-century German philosophy. The big conceptual dispositions he deploys in dealing with political economy and the world of money, and the mixture of components characteristic of *Capital*—ethics, categorical explanation, and metaphysics—were those developed over two thousand years of thought about our relations with each other and with the world around us, before the disruptions that arose with the arrival of market economy. The name for what Marx was doing in *Capital* is *"politikē,"* not "economics" or even "political economy." That part of *Capital* devoted to the analysis of market economy, extensive though it is, is a subordinate part of the whole work. Its aim is to reveal the end aimed at by the lawlike operations of the market system. But this aim is subordinate to a further aim, which is to reveal the limitations of the end aimed at by the capitalist system considered as a means to the end of human good, and to uncover the failure of political economy to distinguish means and ends properly, so as to identify market economy as a means not an end in itself.

It is not really so very surprising that Marx should have operated in this way. In doing so he was viewing market society, not in the new Enlightenment terms it had developed for describing and explaining itself, but in the terms of the earlier philosophical tradition, the application of which yielded such an unclouded, unflattering, and unwelcome view of the new commercial society based on M-C-M. It was not without reason that the early Anglophone moderns vented so much spleen on the Aristotelian tradition and subjected it to a persecution that bears comparison with some twentieth-century instances of that noble art. The thought that developed in the premarket period, mostly within the Aristotelian tradition, did so free of contamination by the commodity and value-production. For most of that period there was no such subject as economics, no such thing as economic policy for men of the state to formulate, and no market economy to generate the need for either (see Finley 1973; Meikle 1995, ch. 8). Marxians have often swallowed more than they should, and certainly more than Marx did, of the philosophical radicalism and destructiveness that was necessary to smooth the path for the economic view of the world from the seventeenth century on.

Marx, in the section of chapter 1 titled "The Fetishism of Commodities and the Secret Thereof," uses the term "fetishism" to refer to the confusion by which useful things, artifacts or natural objects in general, come to be thought of as commodities or utilities, as bearers by nature of exchange value. But our ordinary idea of natural things was not the only fundamental idea that was affected by the arrival of the market. The shunting aside of *ethikē* and *politikē* to make room for economics, and the many other changes that had to be carried through in consequence, were adaptations of thought to the market, too. It would be useful to have a collective name for these adaptations, and since they have a common character, it does not seem unreasonable to extend Marx's own term "fetishism" to cover them all. It could then be said that the thought of the premarket period was unfetishized and that it provides categories or conceptual dispositions for thinking about the world and our place in it that were developed by people free to approach those cognitive tasks without the distorting lens that the people of modernity have to look through. Marx gets the initial critical distance he needs from the fetishized thought of modernity and from the perverse entity of market economy, which begets that fetishism, by bringing to bear on the market economy the conceptual dispositions of the older tradition. The early moderns, especially of the Anglophone world from Hobbes onward, had been energetic in plowing up that tradition to make way for their own dispositions. But this process, begun in the seventeenth century and carried forward in the Enlightenment, had had little serious impact on the Rhineland by Marx's time, and he himself was educated in that tradition at Trier High School and at the universities of Bonn and Berlin.

Conclusions

The overall character and the philosophy of science of Marx's inquiry in *Capital*, as we have seen them to be, if they have holes, have none of a shape

that Engels's metaphysical speculations could fill. His speculations can
be imposed of course, as they were under the Second and Third Internationals, and doing that might have seemed like a good idea at the time.
The tenor of intellectual and political life from the turn of the century to
the Second World War was, on the left of center at least, still Whiggish, pro-
gressivist, and impressed by physical science. But these things change, and
those beliefs and values have gone irrevocably. The Enlightenment seems
to be running to the end of its course, and the balance sheet is beginning
to be drawn up. Marx's work can survive this, but not if it is needlessly
bound hand and foot to the Enlightenment. The Enlightenment was primarily an expression of the beliefs, aspirations, and values of the burghers,
and there was always good reason to be cautious about unqualified judgments identifying Marx as a child of the Enlightenment. Western Marxism
has shown this caution. Attempts to interpret Marx primarily in Hegelian
terms, or Kantian terms, or any terms that tie him straightforwardly to the
concerns and commitments of the Enlightenment, locate him in a *bürger-
lich* frame that, analytically and philosophically, he stood aside from.

References

Aristotle. 1994. *Posterior Analytics*. Trans., with commentary, by J. Barnes. Oxford:
    Clarendon Press.
Arthur, Christopher J. 1993. Hegel's Logic and Marx's Capital. In *Marx's Method in
    Capital*, ed. F. Moseley, 63–87. Atlantic Highlands, N.J.: Humanities Press.
Brody, Baruch. 1980. *Identity and Essence*. Princeton: Princeton University Press.
Buchan, James. 1997. *Frozen Desire: An Inquiry into the Meaning of Money*. London:
    Picador.
Carver, Terrell. 1980. Marx, Engels, and Dialectics. *Political Studies* 28:353–63.
———. 1983. *Marx and Engels: The Intellectual Relationship*. Brighton, East Sussex:
    Harvester/Wheatsheaf.
———. 1984. Marx, Engels, and Scholarship. *Political Studies* 32:249–56.
Colletti, Lucio. 1973. *Marxism and Hegel*. Trans. L. Garner. London: New Left
    Books.
Collins, Wilkie. 1949. *The Moonstone*. Oxford: Oxford University Press.
Finley, M. I. 1973. *The Ancient Economy*. London: Chatto & Windus.
Geras, Norman. 1983. *Marx and Human Nature: Refutation of a Legend*. London:
    Verso.
Gibbon, Edward. 1950. *Autobiography*. Oxford: Oxford University Press.
Hobbes, Thomas. 1991. *Leviathan*. Cambridge: Cambridge University Press.
Hume, David. 1894. *An Enquiry Concerning Human Understanding*. Ed. L. A. Selby-
    Bigge. Oxford: Clarendon Press.

Lukács, Georg. 1980. *Labor*. Trans. David Fernbach. Vol. 3 of *The Ontology of Social Being*. London: Merlin.

Marx, Karl. 1908. *Capital*. Vol. 1. Trans. Samuel Moore and Edward Aveling. London: Sonnenschein.

McMullin, Ernan. 1984. Two Ideals of Explanation in Natural Science. *Midwest Studies in Philosophy* 9:205–20.

Meek, R. L. 1977. *Smith, Marx, and After*. London: Chapman & Hall.

Meikle, Scott. 1991. The Metaphysics of Substance in Marx. In *The Cambridge Companion to Marx*, ed. Terrell Carver, 296–319. Cambridge: Cambridge University Press.

———. 1995. *Aristotle's Economic Thought*. Oxford: Clarendon Press.

Mirowski, Philip. 1989. *More Heat Than Light*. Cambridge: Cambridge University Press.

Mure, G.R.G. 1940. *An Introduction to Hegel*. Oxford: Clarendon Press.

Pareto, Vilfredo. 1971. *Manual of Political Economy*. Trans. Ann Schwier. Ed. Ann Schwier and Alfred N. Page. London: Macmillan.

Pocock, J.G.A. 1975. *The Machiavellian Moment: Florentine Political Thought and the Atlantic Republican Tradition*. Princeton: Princeton University Press.

Raphael, D. D. 1969. *British Moralists: 1650–1800*. 2 vols. Oxford: Clarendon Press.

Robinson, Joan. 1964. *Economic Philosophy*. London: C. A. Watts.

Sayer, Derek. 1983. *Marx's Method: Ideology, Science, and Critique in Capital*. Brighton, East Sussex: Harvester.

Schumpeter, Joseph A. 1954. *History of Economic Analysis*. London: Allen & Unwin.

Selby-Bigge, L. A. 1897. *British Moralists*. Oxford: Clarendon Press.

5

Engels After Marx: History

S. H. Rigby

"You have to do your homework. I've swotted it up. I know all
about his family and that man—oh, who was he, his buddy? Engham?"
"Do you mean Engels perhaps?"
"Yes, that's it. You have to know these things."
—Geoff Loynes, professional Karl Marx look-alike,
to a *Guardian* journalist (*Guardian,* 15 June 1994)

To expound the views of any controversial thinker is, inevitably, to develop
them in some definite direction, and the views of Marx and Engels are certainly no exception to this rule (Jordan 1967, xi). In particular, in explicating Marx's views, his exegetes are prone to modernizing him, periodically
bringing him up to date as an existentialist humanist, a structuralist antihumanist, or whatever, so that, like other intellectual giants from the past,
he seems always to have "anticipated and surpassed the most significant
theoretical trends of recent decades" (Shepherd 1989, 91). The problem
is that, once modernized, Marxism has then to be purified of all those elements the reader has come to find unacceptable: "In all of these operations, there is a need for someone on whom everything which Marxists, at

that particular moment, are asking to get rid of can be dumped. That somebody is Friedrich Engels" (Timpanaro 1975, 73–74). As Woolfson said, Engels has come to function as the ballast for the balloon of Marxism: he is the element that has to be thrown overboard if Marx himself is to float ever higher into the intellectual stratosphere (Woolfson 1982, 1). This self-serving demonization of Engels is most apparent in discussions of Marxist philosophy and politics. Twentieth-century Marxists, who otherwise differ profoundly among themselves, have found some measure of agreement in attacking Engels for supposedly transforming Marx's thought from a critique of political economy based on the concept of revolutionary praxis to a passive materialistic science that was to form the foundation for Soviet dialectical materialism (see Rigby 1992a, 4–7; for a recent example, see Thomas 1991, 36–42).

Yet this tendency to separate Marx's views from those of Engels not only is found in relation to their philosophical outlook but also extends to historical materialism. Thus for Kain, Marx and Engels's most important differences lie in their versions of historical materialism rather than in their interpretations of Hegel's dialectic (Kain 1986, 109). Carver also agrees that as Engels's philosophical outlook diverged from that of Marx after 1859, so too did the content of his historical studies (Carver 1983, 142; 1985, 480). Inevitably, Marx's version of historical materialism is presented not just as different from that of Engels but also as its superior, a viewpoint shared by both Marxists and Marxologists alike. Marx is thus credited with a more sophisticated historical understanding than Engels, being aware of the historically specific nature of social "laws" and rejecting Engels's positivist belief in laws that are universally applicable in all societies and even in both nature and human society (Levine 1984, 172, 210; Avineri 1971, 152; Lichtheim 1971, 250–51; Jacoby 1981, 55; Thomas 1991, 41; see also Farr 1986, 215–20). Typically it is Engels who is criticized for propounding a unilinear social evolutionism, whereas the flexible Marx is said to have been conscious of the multilinear nature of human social development (Shanin 1981, 119; 1983, 21–25; Levine 1975, 172–76; 1984, 121–22, 168; Sawer 1977, 334; Krader 1982, 205; Lekas 1988, 69, 148–49, 166). Thus, while Cohen sees Marx and Engels in agreement in their claims for the social primacy of the productive forces (Cohen 1978, 145), Levine and Colletti argue that Marx himself rejected this position even though Engels had mistakenly adhered to it (Levine 1975, 172–76; Colletti 1972, 65; Avineri 1971, 153–54; Jacoby 1981, 55). Similarly Colletti argues that it was Engels who most frequently wrote in terms of base and superstructure, a metaphor that, with its overtones of economic determinism, rarely occurs in the works of Marx (Colletti 1972, 65).

As a non-Marxist medieval historian, I aim here neither to defend Engels nor to debunk him. Rather, my purpose is to engage with his thought so as to arrive at a workable historical and social theory that will suggest new questions for empirical research and generate hypotheses that can be tested against the historical evidence. Since "the time of mass-based social-ist movements which conceived themselves as specifically Marxist may well be up" (Geras 1990, 32), I work on the premise that, as another medieval-ist said when writing about Marxism, it is Marxism's historical theory that now constitutes "the source of all of its value and its justification" (Leff 1961, 7; Rigby 1992b, 14). Indeed, Marx and Engels's theory has been the inspiration for some of the most original, wide-ranging, and theoretically sophisticated historical writing of the second half of this century (see Rigby 1996 for a survey).

An initial difficulty in considering Engels's historical materialism "after Marx" is distinguishing Engels's views after Marx's death in 1883 from those he had propounded earlier in his life. On the one hand, Engels himself believed that he had remained loyal to the fundamentals of his and Marx's earlier positions, as is shown by the continued publication after 1883 of editions of the *Communist Manifesto* (1848), *The Condition of the Working Class in England* (1845), and *Anti-Dühring* (1878) along with its offshoot, *Socialism: Utopian and Scientific*. The bulk of Engels's *Dialectics of Nature* had also been completed before Marx's death (CW 25:xix). On the other hand, even those who see a clear distinction between the views of Marx and Engels argue that the thought of the two men had been diverg-ing long *before* 1883, perhaps even from as early as the 1840s (Lichtheim 1971, 54; Jacoby 1981, 55; Schmidt 1971, 52; Carver 1984, 261–79; Levine 1984, 21; Fetscher 1971, 162). In neither perspective was 1883 a turning point in Engels's intellectual development.

What were the main claims of the version of historical materialism pro-pounded by Engels in the years after 1883, and how can we assess them? Fleischer has usefully distinguished three overarching conceptions of his-tory present within the works of Marx and Engels. The first is the *anthropo-genetic* approach, in which history is seen as having a universal meaning as a teleological process in which humanity eventually overcomes its alien-ation and realizes its true nature. The second is the *pragmatological* out-look, in which "history is regarded as the outcome, more blind than the result of any tendency to a specific goal, of the actions of individuals and groups impelled by their needs in the situations in which they find them-selves" (Fleischer 1973, xlii). The third is the *nomological* outlook, in which "history is regarded as a natural process taking place in accordance with definite laws" (12–13). Here I examine the major historical assumptions underlying each of these outlooks and ask to what extent they are mutually compatible. In particular, did Engels's adherence to a positivist "nomological" perspective in his later works mean that his views had come to differ from those of Marx and that he had forgotten his and Marx's intellectual achievement of the mid-1840s?

The Anthropogenetic Outlook

The anthropogenetic outlook is most evident in the works of the youthful, Hegelian-inspired Engels, where he optimistically argued that the total atomization of society brought about by capitalism was "the last necessary step towards the free and spontaneous association of men" and that the rule of money in society was "an inevitable stage which has to be passed through if man is to return to himself, as he is now on the verge of doing" (CW 2:476). A similar vision of man overcoming his alienation and returning to his true self informs Marx's early writings up to and including his "1844 Manuscripts" (Fleischer 1973, 15; Mewes 1992, 31–32). It has been claimed that, in his later works, Engels abandoned this humanist vision and replaced it with a conception of the Communist future as one enormous factory where the productive forces are liberated rather than human alienation transcended (Levine 1975, chs. 4, 11, 13; Fetscher 1971, 165; Colletti 1973, 178; Easton 1983, 39). In fact, Engels's youthful humanist ideals continued to motivate even the most "scientific" of his later writings (Hunley 1991, 114–17). Thus he praised Hegel for realizing that history was not simply "a wild whirl of senseless deeds" but was "the process of evolution of humanity itself." History was the evolution of man from an animal state toward the freedom and the "really human morality" of a classless society, where he would no longer be the slave of his own social and ideological creations and his true potential would be realized by the "completely free development of his physical and mental faculties" (Engels 1976, 29, 31, 119, 144, 350, 352–53, 361–62; 1968a, 171–75).

The Pragmatological Outlook: Definition and Defense

Yet, while never abandoning the humanist ideals implicit in the anthropogenetic conception of history, Marx and Engels, as early as *The Holy Family*

(1844) and *The German Ideology* (1845–46), arrived at a very different account of historical causation. In these works, Engels offered a critique of his own earlier outlook, rejecting his previous view that had seen history in terms of the teleological unfolding of a series of Hegelian principles (compare CW 3:475–76 with CW 4:614–15). Instead, he adopted the pragmatological outlook in which, as Engels put it in *The Holy Family*, "[h]istory does nothing, it 'possesses no immense wealth,' it 'wages no battles.' It is man, real, living man who does all that, who possesses and fights; 'history' is not, as it were, a person apart using man as a means to achieve its own aims; history is nothing but the activity of man pursuing his aims" (CW 4:93; see also CW 38:12). Similarly, in *Ludwig Feuerbach and the Outcome of Classical German Philosophy* (1888), Engels argued that "[m]en make their own history, whatever its outcome may be, in that each person follows his own consciously desired end and it is precisely the resultant of these many wills in operation and of their manifold effects upon the outer world that constitutes history" (Marx and Engels 1949, 354). It is this admirable view of historical causation that seems to be recommended to us by Elster under the title of "methodological individualism," although, since Elster himself recognizes that "many properties of individuals, such as 'powerful,' are inherently relational so that an accurate description of one individual may involve reference to others," "individualism" may be a misleading label for it (Elster 1985, 5–6, 18; see Warren 1995; Kirkpatrick 1995). In this perspective, Marx and Engels present historical circumstances and social structure in "structurationist" terms (Giddens 1984) as both the condition *and* the outcome of human agency. As Marx wrote in *The Eighteenth Brumaire*, a work that Engels, in his preface to the 1885 edition, praised as a classic application of the theoretical claims of historical materialist method, "men make their own history but . . . they do not make it under circumstances chosen by themselves, but under circumstances . . . transmitted from the past" (Marx and Engels 1962). Indeed Elster speculates that the development of this outlook may have owed a particular debt to Engels, who had "a more sober attitude to history than did Marx" (Elster 1985, 109–10; see also Anderson 1979, 23; Collins 1994, 56–62).

From the mid-1840s to 1883, in *The Condition of the Working Class, The German Ideology, The Poverty of Philosophy* (1847), the *Communist Manifesto*, the 1859 preface, *Capital* (1867), and *Anti-Dühring* (1878), Marx and Engels offered a more precise account of the social "circumstances" within which "men made their own history." In particular, they presented the social structure as a specific hierarchy of forces, a hierarchy often expressed by Marxists by means of the two-storey metaphor of "economic base" and "political and ideological superstructure," a metaphor that would seem to imply that society's mode of production, a combination of its productive forces and relations of production, has a causal primacy (Mishra 1979–80; Lovell 1980, 28).

Yet, in practice, despite the implications of the metaphor of base and superstructure, Marx and Engels's programmatic statements of social theory tended to put forward a *three*-storey model of society. Here a certain level of development of society's productive forces (human labor power, particular raw materials, forms of energy, tools, technology, and scientific knowledge, along with some specific technical division of labor between the producers) forms the basis for a corresponding form of the relations of production, that is, the property relations that determine how individuals obtain access to the productive forces and to the necessities of life that such forces produce (Marx 1971, 20–21; Cohen 1978, ch. 6; Shaw 1978, ch. 2; McMurtry 1978, 71; Van Parijs 1993, 9; Graham 1992, 42–49; Loone 1992, 163). Just as specific relations of production are "appropriate to a given stage in the development of their material productive forces," so, in turn, the relations of production constitute the "foundation on which arises a legal and a political superstructure and to which correspond definite forms of social consciousness" (Marx 1971, 21; 1974, 88). However, the tensions within this structure mean that social change is inevitable. First, change is generated by the conflict between society's developing productive forces and its relatively less dynamic relations of production, which eventually means that from being "forms of development of the productive forces," social relations "turn into their fetters" (Marx 1971, 20–21). Second, change also arises from the social struggles that are inevitably produced by society's class relations (CW 6:482–85; for multiple quotations in support of all of these points, see Rigby 1987, chs 3, 9). Marx and Engels thus offered a "functional explanation" of society's relations of production in terms of their benefits for the development of its productive forces and of the social superstructure in helping to stabilize and perpetuate class relations (Cohen 1980; Carling 1991, ch. 1; Donham 1990, 71–76), while also emphasizing one dysfunctional element inherent in the social system.

Engels remained loyal to this outlook in his writings after 1883, repeating his earlier claims in works such as his preface to the 1885 edition of Marx's *Eighteenth Brumaire, Ludwig Feuerbach,* and his introduction to the English edition of *Socialism: Utopian and Scientific* (1892). Thus in 1885 he argued that all political and ideological struggles in history were "only the more or less clear expression of struggles of social classes" and that, in turn, the existence of specific classes was "conditioned by the degree of development of production and exchange" (Marx and Engels 1962, 246; see Marx and Engels 1949, 153). Similarly in 1892 he defined historical materialism as that "view of the course of history which seeks the ultimate cause and the great moving power of all important historic events in the economic development of society, in the changes in the modes of production and exchange, and in the consequent division of society into distinct classes, and in the struggles of these classes against one another" (Engels 1978, 17). Once more, it is difficult, given the views expressed in *The German Ideology* and the 1859 preface, to see why "historical materialism" should be seen as a theory invented by Engels and attributed to Marx (Carver 1985, 480).

However, in the years after 1883, Engels did not simply expound historical materialism in abstract terms, he also applied it, in detail, in his study of the transition from primitive communism to class society in *The Origin of the Family, Private Property, and the State* (1884). Here Engels explained the end of the relations of production of primitive communism in terms of the "the growth of the productivity of labour" within society, which created a growing social division of labor. As social productivity grew, new social relations emerged, relations involving classes, private property, and exploitation, as "herds and flocks were converted from the common property of the tribe or gens into the property of the individual heads of households" and the land that had belonged to the tribe passed into outright individual ownership (Engels 1968a, 6, 158–66).

It was the appearance of class society that, for Engels, then provided the social basis for the development of the state. The state was "the product of society at a certain stage of development" and, in particular, of the fact that it had been "split into irreconcilable antagonisms which it was powerless to dispel." Yet, although it was the function of the state to alleviate this social conflict, this did not mean that the state was socially neutral. On the contrary, the state was, in general, "the state of the most powerful, economically dominant class which, through the medium of the state, becomes also the politically dominant class." However, here, as in *The German Ideology* and his account of the Revolution of 1848 in Germany, Engels recognized that the social determination of the political superstructure did not mean that the state was necessarily always an "instrument" in the hands of the ruling class. Rather, in certain periods, such as that of absolutism, where the warring classes were in balance and so canceled out each other's power, the state could acquire an unusual degree of independence from the economically dominant class (Engels 1968a, 6, 166, 168; CW 5:90, 195,

200; Engels 1969, 21–22, 33). Indeed, in his 1892 introduction to *Socialism: Utopian and Scientific,* Engels argued that "[i]t seems a law of historical development that the bourgeoisie can in no European country get hold of political power—at least for any length of time—in the same exclusive way in which the feudal aristocracy kept hold of it during the middle ages" (Engels 1978, 27–28).

The Origin of the Family had less to say on ideology, but the views on the social determination of consciousness that Marx and Engels had developed in the 1840s were applied in the detailed account of the transition from feudalism to capitalism that Engels provided in the 1892 introduction. Here, Engels argued, as he had in *The Peasant War in Germany* (Engels 1977, 42), that since Catholicism "surrounded feudal institutions with the halo of divine consecration," every struggle of the rising bourgeoisie against feudalism "had to take on a religious disguise," as in Calvinism, a creed "fit for the boldest of the bourgeoisie of his time." Yet Engels rejected any simple one-to-one formula to explain why particular classes favored specific ideologies. On the contrary, the whole point of his 1892 introduction was to explain in historically specific terms why the French bourgeoisie had embraced materialism as a doctrine of social critique, while the English bourgeoisie clung to a conservative religious piety. He emphasized too the elastic nature of particular bodies of thought, which allowed them to be twisted to different purposes, as when Christianity was used by the propertied to "keep down" the lower orders while also offering a rhetoric of the "poor as the elect" and of class antagonism, which provided the potential for resistance against those seeking to foist religion upon the workers. Nevertheless, while offering a nuanced analysis of the social origin of particular forms of social consciousness, Engels rebuffed any suggestion of their autonomous social power: since juridical, philosophical, and religious ideas were the "offshoots" of society's dominant economic relations, it followed that such ideas could not, "in the long run, withstand the effects of a complete change in these relations" (Engels 1978, 18–32).

It was this hierarchical account of the forces at work in society that Engels was obliged to defend in a fascinating series of letters in the 1890s, where he argued that conceiving of society in terms of "base and superstructure" did not mean that either he or Marx was committed to a form of crude economic determinism. A century after their composition, these texts retain an enduring appeal for those Marxists keen to reject the familiar charge of economic reductionism (Hilton 1990, 178; Thompson 1978, 262; Delany 1990, 43). How did Engels characterize historical materialism in these letters? First, like Marx before him (Marx and Engels 1975, 291–94), Engels rejected the charge that Marxism provided a Hegelian philosophy of history, a lever for constructing history according to some predetermined pattern. Rather, it was "a guide to study," one that put "an end to philosophy in the realm of history" and "required that all history must be studied afresh" (390–91, 393–94, 443). This denial is in one sense welcome but, in another, is also obligatory. After all, no one is ever likely to admit that his thought is dependent upon an a priori framework that does not respect the historical evidence (see Neale 1985, xiii). Even Hegel, who for Engels was the archexponent of such a philosophy of history, had himself rejected such philosophically based historical schemata to which the empirical evidence had to be adjusted (Hegel 1956, 8–9).

Second, in defending historical materialism against its critics, Engels denied that he and Marx had seen history in monocausal or economic reductionist terms. He argued that it was "fatuous" for the critics of Marxism to claim that because he and Marx had denied "an independent historical development to the various ideological spheres which play a part in history, [they] also deny them any effect upon history." To claim that the economic factor was the "only determining one" was to transform the materialist conception of history into a "meaningless, abstract, absurd phrase." Those who alleged that historical materialism denied the active historical role of the political and ideological superstructure were thus "tilting at windmills" (Marx and Engels 1975, 394, 399–401, 435). As examples of the active historical role and "relative independence" of the superstructure, Engels cited the example of the state, which is not just the product of specific economic and social conditions but in turn "reacts ... upon the conditions and course of production" (398–99). "It could scarcely be maintained without pedantry" that of all the many states of northern Germany, Brandenburg became the principal power only "because of economic necessity and not also because of other factors (above all, its entanglement with Poland and hence international political relations)." Nor was it possible "without making oneself ridiculous, to explain in terms of economics the existence of every small state in Germany, past and present," or to prove that the differences between the legal liberty of testators in France and England were "due to economic causes alone." Yet such "accidental factors" could "exert a very considerable effect on the economic sphere" (395–96, 400). Similarly, in the realm of thought, economic factors did not create ideas directly but rather determined "the way in which the body of thought found in existence is altered and developed." The economy's influence thus "operates within the terms laid down by the particular sphere itself" so that in the sphere of philosophy it is "political, legal and moral reflexes which exert the greatest direct influence" (401).

Engels thus characterized the relationship between base and superstructure as one of dialectical interaction (Rader 1979, 3), so that even where some social element is seen as brought into existence by economic forces, it can, in turn, "react on the environment and even on the causes that have given rise to it." It was "metaphysical" and abstract to "see only cause here and effect there" rather than to see the historical process as an "interaction" of elements (Marx and Engels 1975, 395, 399, 401, 435, 442). Political struggles, the state, law, and ideologies all "exercise their influence upon the course of historical development and in many cases determine their *form* in particular." Historical events are thus the product of "innumerable intersecting forces, an infinite series of parallelograms of forces" (394–95, original emphasis). This recognition of the active role of the superstructure was certainly no late revision of Marxism or a concession by Engels to his critics. On the contrary, as early as *The German Ideology*, the first codification of historical materialism, Marx and Engels had referred to the "reciprocal action" of the productive forces, social relations, the state and ideology (CW 5:53).

Finally, however, in order to avoid the bathetic (although highly persuasive) conclusion that "a number of factors have to be taken into account" in historical explanation, Engels did not simply argue that the historical process involved an interaction of multiple forces. Rather, as in *The German Ideology*, he presented the relationship of base and superstructure as "the interaction of two *unequal* forces" (emphasis added). In the interaction of base and superstructure, it is the former that is "by far the strongest, the most primary and most decisive" element, the one that enjoys an "ultimate supremacy" and that "ultimately always asserts itself"—after all, if this were not the case, the economy could hardly be referred to as the "base" in the first place. Thus, however much the state strives for its independence from society, "on the whole, the economic movement prevails." It is not that the base is active and the superstructure is passive, however much Marx and Engels's use of the metaphor of the superstructure "reflecting" the base might have suggested that this was the case (CW 5:36; Marx and Engels 1975, 400; Dobb 1951, 4; John 1953, 4). Rather, the base is the "prime agent," while the superstructure is "secondary" (Marx and Engels 1975, 393–96, 399, 401–2, 441–42; see also Engels 1968a, 6).

Although Engels rejected economic reductionist interpretations of historical materialism, he did concede that he and Marx were, in a sense, partly to blame for them, since in their theoretical assaults upon their idealist opponents they had tended to overstress one side of the interaction of base and superstructure, that is, the economic derivation of "political, judicial and other ideological notions" (Marx and Engels 1975, 433–35). After all, in *Ludwig Feuerbach,* Engels himself had referred to the modern state as "on the whole *only* a reflex, in concentrated form, of the economic needs of the class controlling production" and had claimed that this was even truer in previous economic epochs (Marx and Engels 1949, 358; emphasis added), while in an 1890 letter to Schmidt he saw historians as being able to "deduce" society's political and ideological superstructures from its economic base (Marx and Engels 1975, 393; see also Marx and Engels 1949, 150). Similarly, in *Anti-Dühring,* Engels had claimed that "[f]orce plays *no part*" in the transition from ancient communal property to private property, this transition being "a result of economic causes," and that the "entire process" of the transition to capitalism could be "explained by purely economic causes, without the necessity even in a single instance, to resort to robbery, force, the state, or political interference of any kind" (Engels 1976, 206–8; see, by contrast, 207, 364; Engels 1977, 145–46, 172).

However, Engels argued that, despite the polemical exaggeration of some of his and Marx's programmatic statements, "when it came to applying the theory in practice, it was a different matter and there no error was permissible" (Marx and Engels 1975, 396, 401–2, 433–35, 443). Certainly, for all his criticism of Dühring's stress on the role of political force in history in *Anti-Dühring,* Engels's own historical analysis in *The Origin of the Family* sometimes has a rather similar emphasis. Here, while Engels accounted for the emergence of the Athenian state in terms of economic development and the rise of private property, "without the interference of violence, external or internal," his explanation of the rise of the state among the Germans stressed the importance of warfare, which, with its military commanders and retinues, formed the basis for the development of the state and of classes. Whereas in Athens the state sprang "directly and mainly out of the class antagonism" that had developed within Athenian society; among the Germans "the state sprang up as a direct result of the conquest of large foreign territories" (Engels 1968a, 106–7, 118, 142, 160–61, 166; see Sahlins 1983, chs. 1–3). The problem, then, was not that Engels was unaware of the causal role of the so-called superstructure in history. Rather, it was how this awareness was to be reconciled with his claims for the primacy of the economic base (discussed below).

Never willing to ascribe to Marx a view with which they themselves disagree, a number of Marxists reject the claim that the social primacy of the productive forces was the "real meaning" of Marx's own writings on social

theory, even when it is conceded that Engels himself did adopt this outlook. Instead, they prefer to see Marx as emphasizing the social primacy of
class and of class struggle or at least of the "contradictory unity" of "forces
and relations of production" (Mishra 1979–80, 156; Rosenberg 1981,
11–13; Levine 1987; Mooers 1991, 17–19; Colletti 1972, 65; Ferraro 1992,
ch. 8; Lukács 1972, 136–39). It is certainly true that many of Marx's *specific*
historical analyses and even, at times, his general historical formulations
tend to emphasize the control that society's relations of production exercise over the development of its productive forces and to focus on class
struggle rather than on the growth of the productivity of labor (Rigby
1987, ch. 8; Miller 1991, 102–3; Lekas 1988, 1–3, 105, 138, 153, 199–200;
Katz 1989, 3–4, 173; Wood 1995, ch. 4). Furthermore, it is this interpretation of Marx that has been particularly fertile for Marxist historians (see,
for instance, Brenner 1976). Nevertheless, Marx himself did explicitly
identify Engels's views on "the connection between the productive forces
and social relations" with his own (CW 40:186) and clearly stated that class
struggles, political conflicts, battles of ideas were merely "subsidiary forms"
of the contradiction between society's productive forces and its social relations: "[A]ll collisions in history have their origin in the contraction
between the productive forces and the form of intercourse" (CW 5:74,
81–82). Indeed, in 1852, Marx specifically denied any credit for discovering the importance of class or class struggle in human history and claimed
simply to have discovered that "the existence of classes is merely linked to
particular historical phases in the development of production" (Marx and
Engels 1975, 64), although, in fact, this discovery was in fact a commonplace of eighteenth-century political economists such as Robertson, Smith,
and Millar (Meek 1976, 2, 126, 161–74, 219; Rigby 1987, ch. 5).

Similarly, many Marxists have abandoned the metaphor of base and
superstructure as too economically reductionist in its overtones, and, predictably, it is Engels who has to take the blame for its worst excesses (Colletti 1972, 65; Sayer 1987, 148; Lekas 1988, 229; Wood 1995, 49). Yet the
metaphor of base and superstructure was central to Marx's 1859 preface
(Marx and Engels 1971, 20–21; see also CW 5:53, 55, 89, 329, 335–36, 373;
Marx, 1974, 489), the "clearest and most convincing statement" Marx ever
made about his social theory" (Jackson 1994, 84) and the text to which
he referred the reader of *Capital*, volume 1, as a reliable source of his views
for the "materialist basis" of his method (Marx 1976, 100; see also 175–76).
By definition, no metaphor can ever capture *all* aspects of the reality it is
supposed to illuminate. Nevertheless, even if the metaphor of base and
superstructure is rejected or the notion of the base "determining" the

superstructure is repudiated or watered down, it is the hierarchy of social forces, the "causal asymmetry," this metaphor was supposed to encapsulate that, for better or worse, "gives Marxism its distinctiveness as a theory of the social world and of history" (Lovell 1980, 28; Wright, Levine, and Sober 1992, 59, 133; Graham 1992, 42–44; Cutler et al. 1977, ch. 8; Thompson 1978, 84; Hobsbawm 1973, 278–80).

The Pragmatological Outlook Developed: Gender

If Engels's post-1883 claims about the determination of society's relations of production by its level of development of the productive forces, and of the political and ideological superstructure by its economic base, were familiar from his and Marx's earlier writings, then where *The Origin of the Family* was far more original was in its extension of historical materialism to the analysis of gender relations. Indeed, Engels's work is usually seen as "the definitive Marxist pronouncement on the family and therefore on the so-called woman question" (Vogel 1983, 75). In *The Origin of the Family*, Engels defined historical materialism, as he had in *Anti-Dühring*, as the view that "the determining factor in history is, in the last resort, the production and reproduction of immediate life." However, he now added, this production and reproduction of life actually had a "twofold character. On the one hand the production of the means of subsistence, of food, clothing and shelter and the tools requisite therefore; on the other, the production of human beings themselves, the propagation of the species. The social institutions under which men of a definite historical epoch and of a definite country are conditioned by both kinds of production: by the stage of development of labour, on the one hand, and of the family, on the other" (Engels 1968a, 6).

The most enduring aspect of Engels's work is his emphasis on the *sociological* origins of women's social inequality and on its historically specific nature and meaning (Sayers 1987, 57–58; Collins 1994, 78), even if, in practice, his own analysis was not always free of an implicit "biologism" (Carver 1985, 1994). For Engels, the social superiority that men enjoy over women under patriarchy is not an eternal, *biological* phenomenon but is rather the product of a certain stage of economic development. He argued that each stage of human social evolution was accompanied by a characteristic form of family life: group marriage corresponded to "savagery"; the pairing family to "barbarism"; monogamy to "civilization." Women were by no means the slaves of men in the earliest stages of social evolution. On the contrary, the matrilineal kinship systems and their "supremacy" within the household meant that women were socially esteemed and even "predominant" in primitive times (Engels 1968a, 23–29, 37–42, 49, 53, 74–75, 84, 158, 161–64). Only with the development of new forms of wealth under barbarism, with the growth of agriculture and pastoralism, did men begin to take control of family property and to desire to favor their own children through inheritance, resulting in the "world-historic defeat of the female sex" and their reduction to "mere instrument[s] for breeding children" (53–58, 157–59). Once established, the patriarchal monogamous family had persisted up to the modern day. Patriarchy thus originated as a product of change in society's relations of production and its productive forces and, in particular, from the growth of productive capacity, which had eventually led to the emergence of private property and of class society (62, 65, 68, 74–75). Finally, Engels believed that under capitalism, where the bulk of the population had been stripped of any private property, the material basis of patriarchy was being eroded so that, with the exception of the bourgeoisie, to whom private property rights were crucial, patriarchy was becoming an anachronistic, ideological hangover from the past (65, 70–72). Just as capitalism supposedly produced its own gravediggers in the form of the proletariat, so Engels saw capitalism itself as undermining patriarchy and preparing the way for the sexual equality of the communism of the future.

In presenting the ultimately determining factor in human history as having a "twofold character," the production of the means of subsistence and the production of human beings themselves, Engels has often been seen as a "dualist" who presents production and reproduction, the economy and the family, as "two distinct and co-ordinate aspects of production," each of which has an "equal analytic weight," a dualism that is then equated with that between the realms of class and gender (Hartmann 1981, 17; McDonough and Harrison 1978, 28; Vogel 1983, 31–32, 90). Yet such an equation would be unwise. Although women's role in reproduction is vital for an understanding of their social position, patriarchal relations are by no means confined to the sphere of reproduction and the family but rather permeate all aspects of society, including that of production (Hartmann 1981, 141–45). Furthermore, even if we recast Engels's analysis so that his dualism of production and reproduction is replaced with a broader dualism of class and gender, it would still be misleading to portray Engels as a strict dualist who gave class and patriarchy an equal weight in his analysis. On the contrary, in *The Origin of the Family*, as in *The German*

Ideology, Engels argued that as the productive forces of primitive society had developed and private property emerged, so social structures "based on ties of sex," where the family and kinship functioned as relations of production, had given way to forms of social relations where "the family system [was] entirely dominated by the property system" (Engels 1968a, 6; CW 5:43). It was the growth of the productive forces and the emergence of new forms of property that were the primary dynamic forces in Engels's historical analysis and that were the basis for specific forms of family and gender relations.

Inevitably, a century after it first appeared, Engels's account is open to a number of fundamental empirical criticisms (Coontz and Henderson 1986a, 26, 32; 1986b, 108–9; Saliou 1986, 170; Bloch 1983, 66, 75–77; Godelier 1977, 103; de Beauvoir 1974, 86; Gimenez 1987, 40). Here, however, it is more important to note two broader problems of Engels's analysis. The first is that in associating patriarchy with private property and the monogamous family, Engels tended to present patriarchy as an enduring and uniform social arrangement, even though he recognized that some societies, such as ancient Greece, were more patriarchal than others, such as ancient Rome (Engels 1968a, 68). Yet "patriarchy" as a concept exists at the same level of abstraction as "class society." However, while we have a classification of the specific forms taken by class relations, such as slavery, serfdom, wage labor, and so forth, we have no equivalent typology of the forms taken by patriarchy. It is not just that Engels omitted to produce such a classification. Rather, it is that his association of patriarchy with the transhistorical category of private property positively prevented him from doing so.

Second, as a result of his association of patriarchy with the possession and transmission of "private property," Engels was unable to offer any analysis of how patriarchy is articulated with the property relations or relations of production of specific modes of production (Vogel 1983, 87–88). For instance, under capitalism, even if we confine our analysis to the realm of economics, patriarchy must be examined in terms not only of the transmission of private property but also of the sexual division of labor within paid work, of the role of women as a reserve army of labor, of women's domestic labor in reproducing the commodity of labor power that forms the basis of capitalism, and of the concept of the family wage. Such an analysis would show how patriarchy is structured into capitalism, rather than merely portray it as an ideological hangover from the past (Hearn 1991, 239). However, the fact that patriarchy and class relations may interact and become interdependent does *not* mean that gender relations are therefore socially "subordinate" in the sense that they can be reduced to or explained by their functionality for society's relations of production (Barrett 1984, 132–33).

The Nomological Outlook: The "Diluted" Version

Having considered Engels's shift from an anthropogenetic to a pragmatological outlook in the mid-1840s and his application and development of the pragmatological outlook after 1883, we need finally to consider the third of the historical approaches identified by Fleischer in the works of Marx and Engels, that is, the nomological perspective in which history is "regarded as a natural process taking place in accordance with definite laws." Fleischer claimed that the anthropogenetic, the pragmatological, and the nomological outlooks are, despite their differences of emphasis, by no means mutually exclusive and, indeed, that they "are legitimate only to the extent that they complement each other" (1973, 13). Yet, as Adamson points out (1985, 19–23), there is no inherent reason why this should be the case. Certainly, in presenting history as a law-bound process and in claiming that "the same dialectical laws apply in the development of nature, history and thought" (Engels 1976, 12, 179; 1964, 69, 228), Engels is often seen as having lapsed into a positivist and reductionist materialism that denies the specificity of human history. After all, when an apple falls from a tree or a planet orbits the Sun, it is not "in pursuit of its own aims," as Marx and Engels claimed for human historical agency in their pragmatological outlook. Rather, it is obeying a law that is external to it and over which it has no control. Engels's positivism would thus seem to have led him to overlook the essential differences between the natural and the social sciences (Lukács 1971, 3, 24; Levine 1984; Rubel 1977, 47–48; Sartre 1976, 27–34; Schmidt 1971, ch. 1; Fetscher 1971, 162–79).

In fact, while claiming that the same dialectical laws applied in natural and human history, Engels himself also emphasized that history was *not* literally a "natural process" and that there was, in fact, an "unbridgeable gulf" between human society and the rest of nature (Engels 1976, 34; 1968a, 34–35). He thus rejected reductionist materialism and instead adopted an "emergent evolutionist" position in which he invoked Hegel's holism (Hegel 1987, 183) to argue that an organism or complex system could *not* simply be reduced to its component parts. He explicitly attacked eighteenth-century materialism for presenting man as simply a machine ruled by mechanical laws and for ignoring the fact that although such laws existed in organic nature, "they are pushed into the background by other higher laws." He went out of his way to distinguish humanity from the rest of organic nature by its self-consciousness and its ability to plan and produce, not just to collect (Engels 1964, 22–23, 34–35, 172–86, 217, 228, 234–35, 240, 252, 253, 313; 1976, 29, 144). As he argued in *Ludwig Feuerbach,* whereas in nature "there are only blind unconscious agencies acting upon one another," human history is distinguished by the fact that "the actors are all endowed with consciousness, as men acting with deliberation or passion, working towards different goals" (Marx and Engels 1949, 350–54). Engels thus explicitly rejected the claim that the laws of animal species could easily be transferred to human societies (Marx and Engels 1975, 283–85), even though Marx himself had previously claimed that Darwin's theory of the survival of the fittest "provides a basis in natural science for the historical class struggle" (CW 41:232, 246–47). Far from being a reductionist guilty of simplistically equating human society with the natural world, Engels himself repeatedly condemned capitalism for reducing humanity to an animal-like state in which it was subject to economic laws that asserted themselves over the producers with a seeming "natural necessity" rather than the producers controlling the economy through conscious human control (Engels 1976, 350, 352–53, 361–62; 1968a, 171–73; Marx and Engels 1975, 356). In this perspective, it is capitalism that is reductionist, not Engels's analysis of it.

Engels did, however, see human history as *analogous* to natural processes in two ways. First, although history is the product of conscious agents, their conflicting intentions produce unintended consequences, so that the path taken by historical development is not the consciously desired goal of any subjective agent (Marx and Engels 1949, 353–54). This was a point Engels had made about the law of competition under capitalism as early as his *Outlines of a Critique of Political Economy* of 1843 (CW 3:433–34). Second, although human history seems on the surface to be governed by accident, it is really governed by "inner general laws" (Marx and Engels 1949, 354–55). The key issue then is what Engels meant by these "underlying laws" of history, the real "driving forces" that "lie behind" the conscious motives of men who act in history (149–50, 354–55; Engels 1976, 32–33). In *Ludwig Feuerbach,* Engels specifies their nature in more detail. First, there is the class struggle, a historical force that determines men's motives even when they themselves are unaware of it. Such class conflict is not just the motor of history in modern society but also in precapitalist societies, as in the Roman republic, whose political struggles were, in the last resort, about the issue of landed property (Marx and Engels 1949, 356–57, 359). Indeed, although Marx is sometimes given credit for emphasizing class struggle while Engels is said to have emphasized the productive forces (Jacoby 1981, 55), Engels here gave a far greater emphasis to class struggle than had Marx's 1859 preface, a text written with a wary eye on the Prussian censor (Prinz 1969).

As an instance of class relations and class struggle as driving forces of history, Engels referred to modern history, where "the will of the state is, on the whole, determined by the changing needs of this or that class" (Marx and Engels 1949, 357–58), a claim that, as we have seen, Engels had already applied to precapitalist society in his *Origin of the Family*. Similarly, class relations formed the basis for specific forms of social consciousness, such as philosophy and religion. For instance, the opposition of the bourgeoisie to medieval feudalism took the "theological form" of religious heresy, which adapted the inherited theology of Christianity to the interests of specific social classes (359–63).

In turn, if class and class struggle formed the basis for the state and ideology, Engels's second general "law" of history was that specific class relations were grounded in the needs of particular levels of development of the productive forces, as when feudal social relations became a fetter on the further development of the productive forces, which therefore rebelled against the feudal order: "[T]he result is known, the feudal fetters were smashed, gradually in England, at one blow in France" (Marx and Engels 1949, 357). In other words, the so-called underlying laws or forces of historical development turn out to be, in many of Engels's formulations, simply the constraints on human agency set out in the three-tier model of society familiar from *The German Ideology* and the 1859 preface (CW 5:53–54, 74, 82; Marx 1971, 20). Here, at least, there is no necessary incompatibility between the nomological and the pragmatological outlooks. It is true that Marx himself rarely referred to his claims for the primacy of the productive forces in society or for the historical importance of class struggle as "laws" of history, but nevertheless, these claims seem to have been somewhat more than mere "principles" of historical "interpretation" (Farr 1986, 219–20). Rather, these were causal relations at work in social and historical reality, whether or not some historical interpreter was aware of them.

The Nomological Outlook: The "Concentrated" Version

However, as both Marx and Engels themselves warned, there is a danger that, in any analysis, the laws abstracted from the real world come to be "set over against it as something independent of it, as laws coming from the outside to which the world has to conform" (Engels 1976, 48; see also Marx 1974, 196–97). The result is that these laws—as embodied in the economy, history or the dialectic—are then presented as if they were "a person apart using man to achieve [their] own aims," precisely the conception of history Marx and Engels had criticized in *The Holy Family* and *The German Ideology* (CW 4:93; CW 5:50). An instance of such reification of the economy in Engels's later work seems to be provided by his analysis of changes in the rate of profit, where he argued that the laws of commodity production asserted themselves "without the producers and against the producers, as the natural laws of their form of production working blindly." Here, while each individual capitalist races after the biggest rate of profit, the real "goal" of this race is, ironically, the equalization of the rate of profit. Yet in adopting this logic, Engels transformed the unintended consequences of human action (the equalization of the rate of profit) into a teleological purpose or goal that determined prior human action. When challenged by Sombart in 1895 to explain how consequences that had yet to come into existence could determine prior actions, Engels could only lamely reply that more research was necessary (Marx and Engels 1975, 455). In this instance, the laws of commodity production seem to require the world to conform to them, using individuals as their agents in order to realize their aims.

Perhaps the classic instance of Engels's reification of history into a subject with needs of its own came in his letter to Borgius of 1894. Here he argued that although it was pure chance that any particular individual, such as Napoleon, played a specific historical role, nevertheless, "if one eliminates him there is a demand for a substitute and this substitute will be found, good or bad, but in the long run he will be found." If a Napoleon had been lacking, "another would have filled [his] place, a claim apparently proved by the tautological argument that "a man was always found as soon as he became necessary" (Marx and Engels 1975, 442). As with Hegel's claim that each new philosophy "must have appeared of necessity at the time of its appearance" (Hegel 1988, 93), it is difficult to see how Engels's claim could ever be tested (Hook 1945, ch. 5). Engels seems here to conceive of human agency in Hegelian terms of the "cunning of Reason," which governs the process of history in order to fulfill its own "needs" (Hegel 1956, 9–10, 21, 32–33).

Finally, in his later writings, Engels sometimes lapsed into presenting human history as the expression of the underlying laws of the dialectic, which drive history forward through the existence of contradiction and the unfolding of the negation of the negation, exactly the kind of "Hegelian trash" that he and Marx had rightly criticized in the 1840s (CW 5:247, 305; CW 6:162–63; CW 38:97). The classic instance is Engels's defense in *Anti-Dühring* of Marx's description of the rise of capitalism as the dialectical "negation" of the individual private property of the peasant and the artisan and his claim that capitalism would inevitably beget its own negation, the "negation of the negation," through which private property would be replaced by common possession of the land and means of production (Marx 1976, 874, 929). For Engels, Marx had shown the emergence of socialism to be a process that "must occur in the future ... in accordance with a definite dialectical law" (Engels, 1976, 170–71).

That Marx was capable of conceiving of his own outlook in similar terms is suggested by his postface to the second edition of *Capital*, volume 1, where he approvingly cited a Russian reviewer of the book who had claimed that "Marx treats the social movement as a process of natural history governed by laws not only independent of human will, consciousness and intelligence, but rather, on the contrary, determining that will, consciousness and intelligence." Marx thus showed "the necessity of the present order of things, and the necessity of another order into which the first must inevitably pass over, and it is a matter of indifference whether men believe or do not believe it, whether they are conscious of it or not." To these words, Marx simply added the comment: "[W]hat else is he depicting but the dialectical method?" (Marx 1976, 101–2). For Marx, the dialectical "method" was useful precisely because it was grounded in a particular *ontology,* one that "includes in its positive understanding of what exists a simultaneous recognition of its negation, its inevitable destruction" (103).

It was this Hegelian description of society as "in a fluid state, in motion," and of capitalist society as "full of contradictions" (Marx 1976, 103) that allowed Marx himself to predict that capitalism would, "with the inexorability of a natural process," lead to socialism: the "negation of the negation" (929–30). Here, a Hegelian emphasis on the inevitability of change (Wilde 1989, 93–99) was fused with a positivist evolutionism in order to provide *Capital* with the kind of dialectical happy ending that Shanin rightly criticizes in Engels's *Origin of the Family* (Shanin 1983, 22). Marx's dialectical language had a rhetorical function, for, by invoking the negation of the negation and by showing that the first negation had already occurred, he was able to give a greater credence to the second negation, which was to come (although in the advanced capitalist countries this inexorable process, "palpably evident" in 1867 [Marx, 1976, 91], has yet to occur). Even if we saw Marx's invocation of the negation of the negation and his account of the rise and fall of the capitalist mode of production in terms of the classic Hegelian dialectic of initial unity, separation, and higher unity (928–30) as a mere "coquetting" with Hegelian modes of expression (103), we would still need to ask what impression this rhetoric was supposed to convey. Here Marx invoked the unfolding of the Hegelian dialectic and the inexorability of natural processes in order to predict a future in which the fall of the bourgeoisie and the victory of the proletariat were both "equally inevitable" (930).

The dialectic thus provided Marx and Engels not just with a methodology but also with a set of definite ontological assumptions in both the natural and the human sciences (Wood 1981, 27, 98, 142, 159, 208–18; Edgley 1983, 293). This ontology involved an emphasis on the inevitability of evolution and change (Marx 1976, 101–3, 494), the passing over of quantitative differences "by a dialectical inversion into qualitative distinctions" (423, 443, 448; CW 42:385), the dialectical interpenetration of opposites (CW 41:551, 553; CW 42:138; Marx, 1976, 198–99, 209, 217), and the dialectical unfolding of contradictions (Marx 1976, 103, 198, 217, 235–36, 268, 531, 798–99). Levine argues that, for Marx, Hegel's dialectic was an explanation of structure, whereas, for Engels, it was an explanation of process (Levine 1984, 168). In fact, for Hegel, Marx, and Engels, structure and process formed a unity, since process and movement are themselves generated by inherent structural contradictions. As Marx put it, "[T]he development of the contradictions of a given historical form of production is the only way in which it can be dissolved and then reconstructed on a new basis" (Marx 1976, 619).

Thus Marx and Engels's nomological outlook actually existed in two rather different versions. In its "diluted" version, the "underlying laws" of history that it identified simply turned out to be, in practice, the constraints on human agency set out in the three-tier model of social structure (productive forces, relations of production, political and ideological superstructure) familiar from *The German Ideology* and Marx's 1859 preface (CW 5:53–54, 74, 82; Marx 1971, 20–22). Here, unlike the natural sciences, explanation and prediction do not exist in a symmetrical relationship in the sense that to explain an event is to bring it under some predictive covering law. In history, explanation and interpretation are only possible *after the event*. As Engels said, in the social sciences, unlike in the study of organic nature, "the repetition of conditions is the exception and not the rule, once we pass beyond the primitive state of man," and even where repetitions do occur, "they never arise under exactly the same circumstances." As a result, the "inner connections of the social and political forms" of any particular epoch come to be known, as a rule, "only when these forms have already half outlived themselves and are nearing their decline (Engels 1976, 111–12). As Engels put it in his introduction to the 1895 edition of Marx's *Class Struggles in France*, "[A] clear survey of the economic history of a given period can never be obtained contemporaneously, but only subsequently, after a collecting and sifting of the material has taken place" (Marx and Engels 1962, 119; see also Marx 1976, 168). In this diluted version, the nomological outlook remains an interpretive historical sociology that can only be wise after the event.

By contrast, in its more "concentrated" version, the nomological outlook goes beyond an emphasis on the circumstances that constrain human agency. Instead, it comes to see historical laws as somehow set apart from the concrete individuals that are their agents, as the real movers of historical change. A knowledge of such laws then provides the basis from which to make predictions about the "inexorable" and "inevitable" future course of events. At times, Marx and Engels lapsed into the latter position while never explicitly abandoning their loyalty to the pragmatological outlook they had developed in *The Holy Family* and *The German Ideology*. Of course, Marx and Engels had believed in the inevitability of proletarian revolution in the 1840s (CW 6:42, 496), but then their optimistic predictions had been justified in terms of the realization of the class interests of the proletariat rather than buttressed with appeals to the negation of the negation or the inexorability of natural laws.

The Nomological Outlook: Universal Laws of History and Multilinear Historical Development

For many of Engels's critics, the main problem with nomological historical theory is not that he spoke of historical laws per se. After all, Marx himself referred to the exchange of products in terms of the socially necessary labor time they embodied as a law of capitalism that asserted itself "as a regulative law of nature." "In the same way," said Marx, with a reference to Engels's 1843 *Outlines of a Critique of Political Economy*, "the law of gravity asserts itself when a person's house collapses on top of him" (Marx 1976, 168). What Engels's critics object to is rather that he saw such laws as universally applicable, unlike Marx, who realized that those historical "laws" that do exist are specific to particular modes of production in their workings (Levine 1984, 172, 210; Avineri 1971, 152; Lichtheim 1971, 250–51;

Jacoby 1981, 55; see Marx 1976, 101; 1974, 85–87; CW 42:136). As usual, the reality is rather more complicated than "sophisticated Marx: good; simplistic Engels: bad." After all, Engels was well aware of Marx's comments on the historically specific nature of economic laws and himself warned that "the so-called 'economic laws' are not eternal laws of nature but historical laws that appear and disappear" (CW 42:136; see also Engels 1976, 187, 192–94). It is true that in his "Speech at the Graveside of Karl Marx" (Marx and Engels 1949, 153) and his preface to the 1885 edition of Marx's *Eighteenth Brumaire* (Marx and Engels 1962, 246), Engels *did* refer to Marx's discovery of "*the* great law of motion of history" and "*the* law of historical development," implying, as he said explicitly in *Anti-Dühring*, that there are a "few quite general laws which hold good . . . in all cases" (Engels 1976, 187). However, the universal laws of history that Engels referred to here were simply the familiar claims of the 1859 preface, that is, that given levels of economic development "form the foundation upon which the state institutions, the legal conceptions, the ideas on art, and even on religion, of the people concerned have been evolved" (Marx and Engels 1949, 353) and that the existence of particular classes is "conditioned" by the degree of development of society's forms of production and exchange (Marx and Engels 1962, 246). There is no reason to see Engels here as distorting Marx's own views. After all, Marx himself had gone out of his way in *Capital* to defend his claims for the social primacy of the mode of production of material life and of material interests as being as applicable to precapitalist societies as they were to the modern world (Marx 1976, 175–76; 1974, 489), and he referred his readers to his 1859 preface, where he had claimed that "*no* social order is ever destroyed before all the productive forces for which it is sufficient have been developed" (Marx 1971, 21, emphasis added). Similarly, in *The German Ideology*, Marx had said that "the *whole* development of history" constituted a "*coherent* series of forms of intercourse" in which "*all* collisions" had their origin in the contradiction between the productive forces and society's "forms of intercourse" (CW 5:64, 82, emphases added). Like Engels, who, in his "Speech at the Graveside," referred to both "*the* law of development of human history" *and* the "*special* law of motion" governing the capitalist mode of production (i.e., of surplus value) (Marx and Engels 1949, 353), Marx seems to have believed in the existence both of universal regularities of human history *and* of historically specific laws of society.

An issue closely related to the existence of universal historical laws is the question whether Marx and Engels were aware of the multilinear nature of human social development or whether they conceived of it in unilinear terms. As usual, it is Engels to whom the less attractive position is ascribed, whereas Marx is given credit for appreciating the variety of historical paths taken by particular societies (Levine 1984, 121–22; Sawer 1977, 334; Krader 1982, 205). Shanin, for instance, claims that while Marx became increasingly aware of the plural paths of human history, Engels, by the time of *The Origin of the Family*, had abandoned the concept of a unique Asiatic path of development, which he and Marx had adopted in the 1850s and to which Engels had remained loyal as late as 1878 (Shanin 1981, 119; 1983, 21–25; see CW 39:326–28, 332–34, 339–41, 346–48; Marx 1973, 301–7; Engels 1976, 189, 206, 225, 230–32).

In fact, far from abandoning his views on Oriental despotism after the publication of *Anti-Dühring* in 1878, Engels reissued this work in 1885 and 1894 and even, in 1887–88, planned to publish its chapters on "the role of force in history," which contained most of the work's material on the Orient, as a separate pamphlet (Engels 1968b, 11–12). It was also, of course, Engels who edited *Capital*, volume 3, for publication (1894), a work that included Marx's analysis of tax-rent in the Asiatic mode of production (Marx 1981, 927). If, like Shanin, we see the Asiatic mode as an example of multilinear historical development (though Lubasz argues that, for Marx, it was actually a variant form of the initial social stage of primitive communal property), then Engels employed this concept from 1853 until the end of his life (Shanin 1983, 5; Lubasz 1984).

Nor is it true to say that *The Origin of the Family* offers a unilinear view of world history. On the contrary, Engels explicitly stated here that it was a lack of space that prevented him from discussing Oriental history, and even within his account of Western history he acknowledged the variety of forms of communal property that preceded class society, and offered three alternative routes by which the Greeks, Romans, and Germans arrived at a form of state organization (Engels 1968a, 98, 165–66; 1976, 224). While Engels certainly believed that all of humanity had experienced a state of "savagery" (characterized by hunting and gathering, the use of stone and wooden tools, etc.), he argued that with the advent of "barbarism" (where animals were domesticated and agriculture was introduced), the populations of the Old and the New World each "went on its own special way." Indeed, in the New World, the lower stage of barbarism "was nowhere outgrown until the European Conquest" (Engels 1968a, 25–27). Engels, in his writings on Russia, was similarly aware of the multiple paths of historical development in suggesting that, unlike the West, Russia would not have to go through a long period of capitalist development before it could reach socialism, provided a proletarian revolution was to occur first in the West. Here the Russian peasant commune could "serve as starting point for a communist development," so that Russia could "pass directly to the higher form of communist common ownership" without the need for a stage of capitalism (Marx and Engels 1949, 46–47, 54–56; 1970, 56).

Conclusion: Historical Materialism Assessed

Rather than pit Marx against Engels, I have tried to show here that the diverse historical views expressed by each of the two friends can usually be found somewhere in the works of the other and that, as a result, their historical outlooks shared common strengths and weaknesses. The central problem with Engels's historical thought was not, therefore, that his views diverged from those of Marx. How then can historical materialism be assessed? Marx and Engels's social theory has been criticized in a number of ways.

First, even Marxists have often found it difficult to accept Marx's claims for the social primacy of the productive forces and have tended to adopt an alternative account of historical materialism, one that emphasizes the social primacy of the relations of production and the centrality of class struggle in history. Second, Marx and Engels's claims for the determination of society's political and ideological superstructure by its economic base encounter difficulties in that, as they themselves realized, base and superstructure "interpenetrate" in the sense that so-called superstructural elements of law, politics, and ideology actually enter into the base as its constitutive components: one cannot say that x determines y if y is actually a part of x in the first place (Acton 1962, 164–68, 177, 258; Plamenatz 1984, 283–89, 345; Lukes 1983; Wokler 1983, 229–37; Engels 1977, 39, 146; 1968a, 145; for this view as the strongest reading of historical materialism rather than a criticism of it, see Rader 1979, chs. 1–2, and Sayer 1987, 145; see, however, Rigby 1990, 828–29). In this perspective, "the economy" does not actually exist in any autonomous form, separate from politics and ideology, but is simply an intellectual abstraction. To abstract a concept from reality and then to invert reality and claim that this abstraction is actually the "basis" of it would seem to be a classic instance of the methodology that Marx and Engels themselves rightly condemned as "idealist" (Marx and Engels 1975, 434; CW 5:128–34, 159–60, 269–75, 282, 287). Thus, what presents itself as the most materialist analysis of society turns into its opposite and becomes, with a true dialectical irony, a form of pure idealism (Rigby 1992a, 174–75). Finally, there is the problem that the main claims of historical materialism involve a reliance on functional explanation, a form of explanation that many commentators see as, in general, illegitimate in the social sciences (Tännsjö 1990; for references, see Rigby 1987, ch. 6; 1992a, 182–84).

Let us assume that all of these problems could be overcome. First, let us accept that Marx and Engels's claims for the primacy of the productive forces *could* convincingly be defended or made compatible with Marxist analysis that stresses the historical importance of class and class struggle (Cohen 1988, chs 1, 6, 7; Callinicos 1987, 91–95; Mayer 1994, 55). Second, let us agree that Marxism can successfully address the problem of the interpenetration of "economic" base and political and ideological superstructure by reformulating itself into a claim for the primacy of some broadly defined relations of production, including their legal, political, and ideological components, rather than for the primacy of a narrowly defined "economic" base (Godelier 1978, 1988; Wood 1995, ch. 1). Third, let us assume that Marxism could be supplied with the kind of feedback mechanism that makes functional explanation legitimate in the social sciences (Cohen 1978, 152; Torrance 1985, 388–89; Bertram 1990; Van Parijs 1982; Carling 1991, chs. 1–3). The point here is that even if we generously agreed that the problems of the primacy of the productive forces, of interpenetration, and of functional explanation can be overcome, the hierarchy of social forces characteristic of Marx and Engels's historical thought would still face criticism on philosophical grounds that were first formulated even before historical materialism had ever been devised, that is, from the account of causation and explanation offered in John Stuart Mill's *System of Logic* (1843) (Mill 1970, 214–17; Hospers 1973, 292–96; Ryan 1974, 74–79; Skorupski 1989, 175–77; Ryan 1987, 41–50; Hart and Honoré 1985, 15–22).

As we have seen, in its claims about historical causation and social structure, historical materialism is committed to the legitimacy of the belief that, as Norman Geras puts it, "one thing might just be more important than others" (Geras 1990, 9–11). It was exactly this belief in hierarchies of causes that Mill took as his target in his *System of Logic*. Here he argued that any particular event was the sum total of all the antecedents, negative and positive, that had brought it about, and that it was wrong to hierarchize them, giving a primacy to one antecedent as the real "cause" while relegating all of the others to the position of mere "conditions." Causes exist objectively in the real world and are knowable by us, but which cause we see as primary is a result of our own subjective perception and purposes, a view that has since been supported by thinkers as diverse as Hook, Ryle, Gardiner, Dray, Hart and Honoré, Putnam, and Garfinkel (Hook 1945, 71–74; Ryle 1963, 50, 88–89, 113–14; Gardiner 1961, 10–11, 99–112; Dray 1957, 98–101; Hart and Honoré 1985, 35–37; Putnam 1979, 41–44; 1983, 211–15; Garfinkel 1981, 3–5, 21–34, 138–45, 156–74; see also Cutler et al. 1977, 227–38, 315–16).

Why did Mill adopt this position? When we look at specific explanations, in science, history, and everyday life, we often find that some particular factor is picked out as the key cause of an event or trend because it seems to be the "differentiating factor" in any particular situation (Gorovitz 1965, 701–2). We ask, "Why did the bottle break?" and answer, "Because the stone hit it." Here the stone hitting the bottle is the differentiating factor, the new element, that takes pride of place in our explanation. But what we see as the differentiating factor, naturally, will depend upon what we differentiate that situation from, something which, in turn, will tend to depend upon the subjective *purposes* of our analysis (Mill 1970, 214–16). As Ryle put it, we could equally say that "the bottle broke when the stone hit it because it was brittle," foregrounding the bottle's brittleness rather than the stone as the key cause of its breaking (Ryle 1963, 50, 98–99, 113–14).

Similarly, to turn to a historical example, many historians would argue that the English peasantry managed to end villeinage and win its freedom in the later Middle Ages primarily because the Black Death (1348–49) and later outbreaks of plague had reduced England's population by 50 percent or more, thus giving the peasants a strong bargaining position and allowing them to demand concessions from their lords (see Rigby 1995a, 80–87). It is this new factor of population decline that "differentiates" the situation from that previous and so is seen as the key factor that explains the end of serfdom. Yet, in other cases, a similar decline in population led not to peasant freedom but rather to an intensification of serfdom (Klima 1979). It would seem then that the key issue, the "differentiating factor" at work, was the strength of the peasant community and its ability (or lack of it) to organize to take advantage of the new demographic conditions. Class struggle, not population decline, then comes to have an explanatory primacy because it is the success or failure of the peasantry's resistance to their lords that is the differentiating factor in determining whether demographic decline leads to the end of serfdom or its intensification (Brenner 1976, 1982).

Mill would argue that such debates about historical primacy are futile and irresolvable. What they show is that it is only when we take a mass of conditions as given, as, in Mill's terms, "understood without being expressed" (Mill 1970, 215; Runciman 1983, 193), that we can identify some other factor as having an explanatory primacy. If we take it as given that the bottle is brittle, we can explain its breaking in terms of the stone; if we take it as given that the bottle was hit by a stone, we can explain its breaking in terms of its brittleness. Similarly, if we take it as given that the peasant community in England was relatively strong, we can explain peasant freedom as the consequence of a 50 percent population decline after 1348; if we take it as a given that population declined, we can explain the achievement of peasant freedom in terms of the strength of the peasant community. In reality, of course, the end of serfdom in England was caused both by population decline *and* the strength of the peasantry (not to mention numerous other factors): in historical explanation, as with broken bottles, a number of factors do indeed have to be taken into account. In other words, even if we take from Marxism an emphasis on the "causal pervasiveness" of class, this does not mean that class therefore has to be assigned a causal primacy (Wright, Levine, and Sober 1992, 174). Gratefully accepting from Marxist historiography an indispensable piece of the historical jigsaw does not mean that we have to judge that piece as primary: one piece of the jigsaw is not "more indispensable" than another (Rigby 1995b).

However, let us for a moment imagine that we *could* agree that it was class struggle, not population decline, which was the "key variable" (Brenner 1976, 39–40) in explaining why the English peasantry won its freedom in the later Middle Ages. Immediately, any particular outcome of class struggle would cease to be an explanation and would itself become an *explanandum*. The strength of the English peasantry would then need accounting for in terms of a multiplicity of other factors, including settlement patterns, field systems and modes of agriculture, population density, the role of the state, and so forth (Brenner 1976, 53–56, 61–72; 1982, 50–60, 67, 74–75, 79–85). In other words, in historical explanation we are faced with an infinite regression of multiple factors in which it is arbitrary to pick out any one factor as historically "predominant" or as "the ultimate cause" of the course of history (Engels 1968a, 5–6; 1978, 17; Marx and Engels 1975, 394–95, 401–2, 441–43; Hook 1945, 71–74). This pluralism does not simply threaten to overwhelm Marxist historiography that stresses the primacy of class relations and class struggle (McLennan 1989, 70–77). Rather, since Marx and Engels realized that the pace and form of development of the productive forces themselves required a historically specific explanation in terms of a variety of other factors (see, for instance, CW 5:32, 34, 40,

50–53, 70–75, 83, 303–4, 329, 518; Marx, 1976, 617), such pluralism is also implicit in attempts to explain social change in terms of the growth of the productive forces. While retaining a loyalty to the primacy of this or that social factor in its explicit theory, Marxist historiography inevitably lapses, in its practice, into an implicit explanatory pluralism.

It is this pluralism that explains why Marxism is so easily assimilable into mainstream historiography: it is easily assimilated because—in practice—it is not that different in the first place, a point that is intended as praise of Marxist historiography, not as criticism. We thus tend to arrive at accounts of social structure and of historical change similar to those offered by Weberian-influenced sociologists (Parkin 1979; Mann 1986; Gellner 1988; Runciman 1989), which reject any attempt to specify in advance a necessary primacy of particular forms of social power. If the choice facing us is either Marx or Weber (Callinicos 1995, 110), then many of us would choose Weber—or rather would integrate Marx and Engels's insights into a Weberian framework.

Marx and Engels left us a mass of writings that were written over a long period of time, in different forms and genres, responding to a variety of circumstances, and with a number of different purposes. By selective quotation, one can easily show that Marx and Engels disagreed fundamentally on most issues. In fact, it is pointless to counterpose Marx against Engels when the individual works of each man were so internally contradictory: "[T]he two men agreed even in their inconsistencies" (Gouldner 1980, 274–75; Lekas 1988, 165, 234; Hunley 1991, 144). It is futile to denigrate Engels as a means of avoiding the problems posed by Marx's own works. We have been taught to read for the "best Marx" (Johnson 1982); we must now learn not to read for the "worst Engels."

References

Acton, H. B. 1962. *The Illusion of the Epoch.* London: Cohen & West.

Adamson, W. L. 1985. *Marxism and the Disillusionment of Marxism.* Berkeley and Los Angeles: University of California Press.

Anderson, Perry. 1979. *Lineages of the Absolutist State.* London: Verso.

Avineri, Shlomo. 1971. *The Social and Political Thought of Karl Marx.* Cambridge: Cambridge University Press.

———, ed. 1977. *Varieties of Marxism.* The Hague: Martinus Nijhoff.

Ball, Terence, and James Farr, eds. 1984. *After Marx.* Cambridge: Cambridge University Press.

Barrett, Michele. 1984. *Women's Oppression Today: The Marxist Feminist Encounter.* London: Verso.

Bentley, Michael, ed. 1997. *Companion to Historiography.* London: Routledge.

Bertram, Christopher. 1990. International Competition in Historical Materialism. *New Left Review* 183:116–28.

Blackburn, Robin, ed. 1973. *Ideology in Social Science.* London: Fontana.

Bloch, Maurice. 1983. *Marxism and Anthropology.* Oxford: Oxford University Press.

Brenner, Robert. 1976. Agrarian Class Structure and Economic Development in Preindustrial Europe. *Past and Present* 70:30–74.

———. 1982. The Agrarian Roots of European Capitalism. *Past and Present* 97:16–113.

Callinicos, Alex. 1995. *Theories and Narratives: Reflections on the Philosophy of History.* Cambridge: Polity.

Carling, A. H. 1991. *Social Division.* London: Verso.

Carver, Terrell. 1983. *Marx and Engels: The Intellectual Relationship.* Brighton, East Sussex: Harvester/Wheatsheaf.

———. 1984. Marxism as Method. In Ball and Farr 1984, 261–79.

———. 1985. Engels's Feminism. *History of Political Thought* 6:479–89.

———, ed. 1991. *The Cambridge Companion to Marx.* Cambridge: Cambridge University Press.

———. 1994. Theorizing Men in Engels' *The Origin of the Family. masculinities* 2:67–77.

Carver, Terrell, and Paul Thomas, eds. 1995. *Rational Choice Marxism.* Basingstoke, Hampshire: Macmillan.

Cohen, G. A. 1978. *Karl Marx's Theory of History: A Defence.* Oxford: Oxford University Press.

———. 1980. Functional Explanation: A Reply to Elster. *Political Studies* 28:129–35.

Colletti, Lucio. 1972. *From Rousseau to Lenin.* London: New Left Books.

———. 1973. *Marxism and Hegel.* London: New Left Books.

Collins, Randall. 1994. *Four Sociological Traditions.* New York: Oxford University Press.

Coontz, Stephanie, and Peta Henderson. 1986a. Introduction to Coontz and Henderson 1986c, 1–42.

———. 1986b. Property Forms, Political Power, and Female Labour in the Origins of Class and State Societies. In Coontz and Henderson 1986c, 108–55.

———, eds. 1986c. *Women's Work, Men's Property: The Origins of Gender and Class.* London: Verso.

Cutler, Antony, Barry Hindess, Paul Hirst, and Athar Hussain. 1977. *Marx's Capital and Capitalism Today.* London: Routledge & Kegan Paul.

de Beauvoir, Simone. 1974. *The Second Sex.* Harmondsworth, Middlesex: Penguin.

Delany, Sheila. 1990. *Medieval Literary Politics.* Manchester: Manchester University Press.

Dobb, Maurice. 1951. Historical Materialism and the Role of the Economic Factor. *History* 36:1–11.

Donham, D. L. 1990. *History, Power, Ideology: Central Issues in Marxism and Anthropology.* Cambridge: Cambridge University Press.

Dray, William H. 1957. *Laws and Explanation in History.* Oxford: Oxford University Press.

Easton, S. M. 1983. *Humanist Marxism and Wittgensteinian Social Philosophy.* Manchester: Manchester University Press.

Edgley, Roy. 1983. Philosophy. In McLellan 1983, 239–302.

Elster, Jon. 1985. *Making Sense of Marx.* Cambridge: Cambridge University Press.

Engels, Frederick. 1964. *Dialectics of Nature.* Moscow: Progress Publishers.

———. 1968a. *The Origin of the Family, Private Property, and the State.* Moscow: Progress Publishers.

———. 1968b. *The Role of Force in History.* London: Lawrence & Wishart.

———. 1969. *Germany: Revolution and Counter-Revolution.* London: Lawrence & Wishart.

———. 1976. *Anti-Dühring.* Peking: Foreign Languages Press.

———. 1977. *The Peasant War in Germany.* Moscow: Progress Publishers.

———. 1978. *Socialism: Utopian and Scientific.* Moscow: Progress Publishers.

Farr, James. 1986. Marx's Laws. *Political Studies* 34:202–22.

Ferraro, Joseph. 1992. *Freedom and Determination in History according to Marx and Engels.* New York: Monthly Review Press.

Fetscher, Iring. 1971. *Marx and Marxism.* New York: Herder & Herder.

Fleischer, Helmut. 1973. *Marxism and History.* London: Harper & Row.

Gardiner, Patrick. 1961. *The Nature of Historical Explanation.* Oxford: Oxford University Press.

Garfinkel, Alan. 1981. *Forms of Explanation: Rethinking the Questions in Social Theory.* New Haven, Conn.: Yale University Press.

Gellner, Ernest. 1988. *Plough, Sword, and Book: The Structure of Human History.* London: Paladin.

Geras, Norman. 1990. Seven Types of Obloquy: Travesties of Marxism. In Miliband, Pantich, and Saville 1990, 1–34.

Giddens, Anthony. 1984. *The Constitution of Society: Outline of the Theory of Structuration.* Cambridge: Polity.

Gimenez, Marthe. 1987. Marxist and Non-Marxist Elements in Engels' Views on the Oppression of Women. In Sayers, Evans, and Redclift 1987, 37–56.

Godelier, Maurice. 1977. *Perspectives in Marxist Anthropology.* Cambridge: Cambridge University Press.

———. 1978. Infrastructures, Society, and History. *New Left Review* 112:84–96.

———. 1988. *The Mental and the Material: Thought Economy and Society.* London: Verso.

Gorovitz, Samuel. 1965. Causal Judgements and Causal Explanations. *Journal of Philosophy* 62:695–711.

Gouldner, Alvin W. 1980. *The Two Marxisms: Contradictions and Anomalies in the Development of Theory.* London: Macmillan.

Graham, Keith. 1992. *Karl Marx: Our Contemporary.* Hemel Hempstead, Hertfordshire: Harvester/Wheatsheaf.

Hart, H.L.A., and Tony Honoré. 1985. *Causation in the Law.* Oxford: Oxford University Press.

Hartmann, Heidi. 1981. The Unhappy Marriage of Marxism and Feminism: Towards a More Progressive Union. In Sargent 1981, 1–41.

Hearn, Jeff. 1991. Gender: Biology, Nature, and Capitalism. In Carver 1991, 222–45.

Hegel, G.W.F. 1956. *The Philosophy of History.* New York: Dover.

————. 1987. *Hegel's Logic.* Oxford: Clarendon Press.

————. 1988. *Introduction to the Lectures on the History of Philosophy.* Oxford: Clarendon press.

Hilton, R. H. 1990. Unjust Taxation and Popular Resistance. *New Left Review* 180:177–84.

Hirschkop, Ken, and David Shepherd, eds. 1989. *Bakhtin and Cultural Theory.* Manchester: Manchester University Press.

Hobsbawm, Eric J. 1973. Karl Marx's Contribution to Historiography. In Blackburn 1973, 265–83.

————, ed. 1982. *The History of Marxism.* Vol. 1, *Marxism in Marx's Day.* Brighton, East Sussex: Harvester.

Hook, Sidney. 1945. *The Hero in History: A Study in Limitation and Possibility.* London: Secker & Warburg.

Hospers, John. 1973. *An Introduction to Philosophical Analysis.* London: Routledge & Kegan Paul.

Hunley, J. D. 1991. *The Life and Thought of Friedrich Engels: A Reinterpretation.* New Haven, Conn.: Yale University Press.

Jackson, Leonard. 1994. *The Dematerialisation of Karl Marx: Literature and Marxist Theory.* London: Longman.

Jacoby, Russell. 1981. *Dialectic of Defeat: Contours of Western Marxism.* Cambridge: Cambridge University Press.

John, Eric. 1953. Some Questions on the Materialist Interpretation of History. *History* 38:1–10.

Johnson, Richard. 1982. Reading for the Best Marx: History and Historical Abstraction. In Johnson and McLennan 1982, 153–201.

Johnson, Richard, and Gregor McLennan, eds. 1982. *Making Histories: Studies in History Writing and Politics.* London: Hutchison.

Jordan, Z. A. 1967. *The Evolution of Dialectical Materialism: Philosophical and Sociological Analysis.* London: Macmillan.

Kain, P. J. 1986. Marx's Method, Epistemology, and Humanism. *Sovietica* 48.

Katz, C. J. 1989. *From Feudalism to Capitalism.* Westport, Conn.: Greenwood Press.

Kirkpatrick, Graham. 1995. Philosophical Foundations of Analytical Marxism. In Carver and Thomas 1995, 258–74.

Klima, Arnošt. 1979. Agrarian Class Structure and Economic Development in Preindustrial Bohemia. *Past and Present* 85:49–67.

Krader, L. 1982. Theory of Evolution, Revolution, and the State: The Vital Relation of Marx to His Contemporaries Darwin, Carlyle, Morgan, Maine, and Kovalevsky. In Hobsbawm 1982, 192–226.

Kuhn, Annette, and AnnMarie Wolpe, eds. 1978. *Feminism and Materialism.* London: Routledge & Kegan Paul.

Leff, Gordon. 1961. *The Tyranny of Concepts.* London: Merlin.

Lekas, Padelis. 1988. *Marx on Classical Antiquity: Problems of Historical Methodology.* Brighton, East Sussex: Wheatsheaf.

Levidow, Les, and Bob Young, eds. 1981. *Science, Technology and the Labour Process.* Vol. 1. London: CSE Books.

Levine, Norman. 1975. *The Tragic Deception: Marx Contra Engels.* Santa Barbara, Calif.: Clio.

———. 1984. *Dialogue Within the Dialectic.* London: Allen & Unwin.

———. 1987. The German Historical School of Law and the Origin of Historical Materialism. *Journal of the History of Ideas* 48:431–51.

Lichtheim, George. 1971. *Marxism: An Historical and Critical Study.* London: Routledge & Kegan Paul.

Loone, Eero. 1992. *Soviet Marxism and the Analytical Philosophy of History.* London: Verso.

Lovell, Terry. 1980. *Pictures of Reality: Aesthetics, Politics, Pleasure.* London: British Film Institute.

Lubasz, Heinz. 1984. Marx's Concept of the Asiatic Mode of Production. *Economy and Society* 13:456–83.

Lukács, Georg. 1971. *History and Class Consciousness.* London: Merlin.

———. 1972. *Political Writings, 1919–29.* London: New Left Books.

Lukes, Steven. 1983. Can the Base Be Distinguished from the Superstructure? In Miller and Siedentop 1983, 103–9.

Machonachie, Moira. 1987. Engels, Sexual Division, and the Family. In Sayers, Evans, and Redclift 1987, 98–112.

Mann, Michael. 1986. *The Sources of Social Power.* Vol. 1, *A History of Power from the Beginning to A.D. 1760.* Cambridge: Cambridge University Press.

Marx, Karl. 1971. *A Contribution to the Critique of Political Economy.* London: Lawrence & Wishart.

———. 1973. *Surveys from Exile.* Harmondsworth, Middlesex: Penguin.

———. 1974. *Grundrisse.* Harmondsworth, Middlesex: Penguin.

———. 1976. *Capital.* Vol. 1. Harmondsworth, Middlesex: Penguin.

———. 1981. *Capital.* Vol. 3. Harmondsworth, Middlesex: Penguin.

Marx, Karl, and Frederick Engels. 1949. *Selected Works.* Vol. 2. Moscow: Foreign Languages Publishing House.

———. 1962. *Selected Works.* Vol. 1. Moscow: Foreign Languages Publishing House.

———. 1970. *The Communist Manifesto.* Harmondsworth, Middlesex: Penguin.

———. 1975. *Selected Correspondence.* Moscow: Progress Publishers.

Mayer, Tom. 1994. *Analytical Marxism.* Thousand Oaks, Calif.: Sage.

McCarthy, George E., ed. 1992. *Marx and Aristotle: Nineteenth-Century German Social Theory and Classical Antiquity.* Savage, Md.: Rowman & Littlefield.

McDonough, Roisin, and Rachel Harrison. 1978. Patriarchy and Relations of Production. In Kuhn and Wolpe 1978, 11–41.

McLellan, David, ed. 1983. *Marx: The First Hundred Years.* London: Fontana.

McLennan, Gregor. 1989. *Marxism, Pluralism, and Beyond.* Cambridge: Polity.

McMurtry, John. 1978. *The Structure of Marx's World View.* Princeton: Princeton University Press.

Meek, Ronald L. 1976. *Social Science and the Ignoble Savage.* Cambridge: Cambridge University Press.

Mewes, Horst. 1992. Karl Marx and the Influence of Greek Antiquity on Eighteenth-Century German Thought. In McCarthy 1992, 19–36.

Miliband, Ralph, Leo Pantich, and John Saville, eds. 1990. *The Socialist Register.* London: Merlin.

Mill, John Stuart. 1970. *A System of Logic.* London: Longman.

Miller, David, and Larry Siedentop, eds. 1983. *The Nature of Political Theory.* Oxford: Oxford University Press.

Miller, R. W. 1991. Social and Political Theory: Class, State, and Revolution. In Carver 1991, 55–105.

Mishra, Ramesh. 1979–80. Technology and Social Structure in Marx's Theory: An Exploratory Analysis. *Science and Society* 43:132–57.

Mooers, Colin. 1991. *The Making of Bourgeois Europe.* London: Verso.

Neale, R. S. 1985. *Writing Marxist History: British Society, Economy, and Culture Since 1700.* Oxford: Blackwell.

Parkin, Frank. 1979. *Marxism and Class Theory: A Bourgeois Critique.* London: Tavistock.

Plamenatz, John P. 1984. *Man and Society.* Vol. 2. London: Longman.

Prinz, A. M. 1969. Background and Ulterior Motive in Marx's Preface of 1859. *Journal of the History of Ideas* 30:437–50.

Putnam, Hilary. 1979. *Meaning and the Moral Sciences.* London: Routledge & Kegan Paul.

———. 1983. *Philosophical Papers.* Vol. 3, Reason, Truth, and History. Cambridge: Cambridge University Press.

Rader, Melvin. 1979. *Marx's Interpretation of History.* New York: Oxford University Press.

Rigby, S. H. 1987. *Marxism and History: A Critical Introduction.* Manchester: Manchester University Press.

———. 1990. Making History. *History of European Ideas* 12:827–31.

———. 1992a. *Engels and the Formation of Marxism: History, Dialectics, and Revolution.* Manchester: Manchester University Press.

———. 1992b. Marxism and the Middle Ages. In Ryan et al. 1992, 14–18.

———. 1995a. *English Society in the Later Middle Ages: Class, Status, and Gender.* Basingstoke, Hampshire: Macmillan.

———. 1995b. Historical Causation: Is One Thing More Important Than Another? *History* 80:227–42.

———. 1997. Marxist Historiography. In Bentley 1997, 889–928.

Rosenberg, Nathan. 1981. Marx as a Student of Technology. In Levidow and Young 1981, 8–31.

Rubel, Maximilien. 1977. Friedrich Engels—Marxism's Founding Father: Nine Premises to a Theme. In Avineri 1977, 43–52.

Runciman, W. G. 1983. *A Treatise on Social Theory.* Vol. 1. Cambridge: Cambridge University Press.

———. 1989. *A Treatise on Social Theory.* Vol. 2. Cambridge: Cambridge University Press.

Ryan, Alan. 1974. *J. S. Mill.* London: Routledge & Kegan Paul.

———. 1987. *The Philosophy of John Stuart Mill.* London: Macmillan.

Ryan, Alan, et al. 1992. *After the End of History.* London: Collins & Brown.

Ryle, Gilbert. 1963. *The Concept of Mind.* London: Peregrine.

Sahlins, Marshall. 1983. *Stone Age Economics.* Cambridge: Cambridge University Press.

Saliou, Monique. 1986. The Process of Women's Subordination in Primitive and Archaic Greece. In Coontz and Henderson 1986c, 169–206.

Sargent, Lydia, ed. 1981. *Women and Revolution: A Discussion of the Unhappy Marriage of Marxism and Feminism*. London: Pluto.

Sartre, Jean-Paul. 1976. *Critique of Dialectical Reason*. London: New Left Books.

Sawer, Marian. 1977. The Concept of the Asiatic Mode of Production and Contemporary Marxism. In Avineri 1977, 333–71.

Sayer, Derek. 1987. *The Violence of Abstraction: The Analytical Foundations of Historical Materialism*. Oxford: Blackwell.

Sayers, Janet. 1987. For Engels: Psychoanalytic Perspectives. In Sayers, Evans, and Redcliff 1987, 57–80.

Sayers, Janet, Mary Evans, and Nanneke Redclift, eds. 1987. *Engels Revisited: New Feminist Essays*. London: Tavistock.

Schmidt, Alfred. 1971. *The Concept of Nature in Marx*. London: New Left Books.

Shanin, Teodor. 1981. Marx and the Peasant Community. *History Workshop* 12:108–28.

———, ed. 1983. *Late Marx and the Russian Road: Marx and the "Peripheries of Capitalism."* London: Routledge & Kegan Paul.

Shaw, W. H. 1978. *Marx's Theory of History*. London: Hutchison.

Shepherd, David. 1989. Bakhtin and the Reader. In Hirschkop and Shepherd 1989, 91–108.

Skorupski, John. 1989. *John Stuart Mill*. London: Routledge.

Tännsjö, Torbjörn. 1990. Methodological Individualism. *Inquiry* 33:69–80.

Thomas, Paul. 1991. Critical Reception: Marx Then and Now. In Carver 1991, 23–54.

Thompson, E. P. 1978. *The Poverty of Theory*. London: Merlin.

Timpanaro, Sebastiano. 1975. *On Materialism*. London: New Left Books.

Torrance, John. 1985. Reproduction and Development: A Case for a Darwinian Mechanism in Marx's Theory of History. *Political Studies* 33:382–98.

Van Parijs, Philippe. 1982. Functionalist Marxism Rehabilitated. *Theory and Society* 11:497–511.

———. 1993. *Marxism Recycled*. Cambridge: Cambridge University Press.

Vogel, Lise. 1983. *Marxism and the Oppression of Women*. London: Pluto.

Warren, M. E. 1995. Marx and Methodological Individualism. In Carver and Thomas 1995, 231–57.

Wilde, Lawrence. 1989. *Marx and Contradiction*. Aldershot: Avebury.

Wokler, Robert. 1983. Rousseau and Marx. In Miller and Siedentop 1983, 219–46.

Wood, A. W. 1981. *Karl Marx*. London: Routledge & Kegan Paul.

Wood, E. M. 1995. *Democracy Against Capitalism: Renewing Historical Materialism*. Cambridge: Cambridge University Press.

Woolfson, Charles. 1982. *The Labour Theory of Culture: A Re-examination of Engels' Theory of Human Origins*. London: Routledge & Kegan Paul.

Wright, Erik Olin, Andrew Levine, and Elliott Sober. 1992. *Reconstructing Marxism*. London: Verso.

6

Engels, Lukács, and Kant's Thing-in-Itself

Tom Rockmore

Within Marxism, Engels was widely considered to be a philosopher. In *Ludwig Feuerbach and the Outcome of Classical German Philosophy,* he offered a controversial reading of Kant's concept of the thing-in-itself. This reading was criticized by Lukács in the central essay of *History and Class Consciousness.* He later retracted most of the criticism, notably in *The Young Hegel.*

The aim of this chapter is to consider the importance of Kant's doctrine of the thing-in-itself, Engels's reading of it, and Lukács's criticism of that reading for Marxism. I argue that Kant raises a problem that Marxism must solve in order to succeed according to its own standards. I further argue that Engels significantly misunderstood Kant, but that his misunderstanding has parallels in later naturalized forms of epistemology that address philosophical issues requiring epistemic justification through causal analysis. In this respect, I also maintain that Lukács was initially correct to criticize Engels, even if he was unaware of the issues raised by naturalism, but later in error in retracting his criticism. I finally argue that the work of Engels, hence Marxism, which is based on Engels, fails to resolve Kant's unresolved problem of knowledge of the thing-in-itself, hence fails when judged by its own standards.

Engels as Philosopher

Marxism is often considered to concern philosophy, economics, and politics. This chapter is limited to Marxist philosophy, with special attention to Friedrich Engels. Marxist philosophy originates in the writings of Engels, the first Marxist. Some Marxists draw their insights more from Marx than from Engels and other Marxists, and even from the wider philosophical tradition. Lukács, for instance, is heavily dependent on Hegel and, to a lesser extent, Fichte (see Rockmore 1992a, 1992b). Yet Lukács is an exception. For Marxist philosophy is built mainly on the subsequent development of Engels's insights.

In Marxist circles, Engels was routinely seen as a philosopher, whereas Marx was seen as a political economist or critic, as nearly anything but a philosopher (see Kolakowski 1978, a distinct exception; see also Henry 1978). The philosophical attention to Engels up until the time of the tardy publication of Marx's early, more philosophical writings is explicable by the lack of access to the texts. It is explicable after that time by the need, strongly felt within "official" Marxism, to defend the received Marxist view of Marx. For instance, Althusser's famous theoretical antihumanism (e.g., Althusser 1970), which appeared long after the publication of Marx's early writings, which it attempts to "explain away" in order to defend orthodox Marxism, has little directly to do with Marx, but a great deal to do with the Marxist view of Marx, as based on Engels's writings.

Before the recent political rejection of Marxism in practice occurred, it was standard procedure to look to Engels on questions of philosophical substance. This tendency was due to several distinct factors. One factor, already mentioned, was certainly the fact that many of Marx's earlier, more philosophical texts remained unpublished until relatively recently, when the view of the intellectual division of labor between the founders of Marxism had already been fixed in stone.

A second factor was the well-established tendency to regard Marx and Engels as coequal founders of a new worldview. Thus, through the editorial device of inserting a hyphen between the two names, Marx and Engels, friends and colleagues in life, are forever linked in death in various editions of their writings as the nonexistent but widely celebrated bicephalic entity

Marx-Engels. This practice simply ignores the relevant fact that, although some texts were composed together, most were not. The widespread but unfortunate practice of considering both Marx and Engels as a single entity leads to considerable distortion of their ideas. Marx and Engels, who held very similar, even identical, political views, held demonstrably different, in fact very dissimilar, philosophical views.

A third factor concerned the pronounced stylistic differences between Marx's and Engels's texts. The simple but often simplistic way in which Engels presented frequently complex philosophical issues meant that his writings quickly assumed authoritative stature. Marx is the deeper, more original mind, but his writing is usually difficult and almost never felicitous.

Marx, who was trained as a philosopher, quickly abandoned the academy and the philosophical discipline. Engels, who never entered the academy, studied in the local gymnasium and later attended Schelling's classes at Berlin University as a nonmatriculated student. Engels criticized Schelling in several articles. But on the whole, since he was not a trained philosopher, but rather a philosophical autodidact, his knowledge of and sensitivity to philosophical argument remained primitive at best, certainly primitive in comparison to Marx's philosophical acumen.

The fourth factor followed from Engels's many declarations, in which he often appeared to cast himself in the role of the philosopher while attributing a different role to Marx. One example concerns his account of his own contribution. Engels was personally modest about his own intellectual accomplishment. He accurately stated that Marx, whom he eulogized as "the greatest living thinker," did what he (i.e., Engels) could not have done, and that he had done only what Marx could have done without him (see Friedrich Engels, "Speech at the Graveside of Karl Marx," in Tucker 1978, 681): "Lately, repeated reference has been made to my share in this theory [i.e., Marxism], and so I can hardly avoid saying a few words hereto settle this particular point. I cannot deny that both before and during the forty years' collaboration with Marx I had a certain independent share in laying the foundations, and more particularly in elaborating the theory. But the greater part of its leading basic principles, particularly in the realm of economics and history, and, above all, its final, clear formulation, belong to Marx" (Engels 1941, 42–43n). David McLellan, a qualified observer, believes this claim is too modest (1977, 97). This suggests that Engels's contribution is greater than he suggests, perhaps equal or even superior to Marx's. That would be a false inference, for Engels's statement accurately describes his contribution to his intellectual partnership with Marx. But in another sense his statement is highly misleading. For it suggests, in a way that has unfortunately been decisive within Marxism, that it is Engels who was the philosopher, since Marx was either an economist or a historian, or both.

For these and other reasons, Engels has long enjoyed exceptional status as a preeminent student of classical German philosophy within Marxist circles, but the attention accorded to Engels as a philosopher is out of proportion to his philosophical accomplishment for two reasons. First, his philosophical accomplishment is at best surprisingly modest on any account. Claims that it is more than that are typically unjustified. Second, Marx's own contribution is certainly greater than is usually realized. Since its recent political discreditation, Marxism has fallen into disrepute. There is now little attention to Marxist philosophy and scarcely more to Marx. Yet if Marx were to be omitted from the philosophical discussion, something important would disappear (see Rockmore 1991). There is reason, then, to defend Marx after Marxism, although there is less reason, certainly less reason for philosophical purposes, to defend Engels.

On Engels's Philosophical Writings

Engels wrote a series of works that fall under the heading of philosophy. In *The Dialectics of Nature*, which remained unfinished at his death, he follows Hegel in reinterpreting nature from a dialectical angle of vision foreign to Marx. Lukács criticized Engels's extension of dialectic to nature (see Lukács 1971; for a discussion of Marx's views of nature, see Schmidt 1971). Engels's view represents the basis of what later became known as dialectical materialism, or Diamat. This term, which was apparently coined by Plekhanov in 1891, after Marx's death in 1883, never occurs in Marx's writings. In *Anti-Dühring*, a highly polemical work, Engels presented what Plekhanov—who had taught Lenin philosophy, and who conflated Marx and Engels in typical Marxist fashion—regarded as the philosophical views of Marx and Engels "in their *final* shape" (Plekhanov 1970, 23).

Engels's best-known, most influential exposition of Marxist philosophy is *Ludwig Feuerbach and the Outcome of Classical German Philosophy*. In the short foreword, Engels points to the famous preface to *A Contribution to the Critique of Political Economy*, where "Marx relates how the two of us ... set about working out in common 'the opposition of our view'—the materialist conception of history which was worked out especially by Marx—'to the ideological view of German philosophy, in fact to settle accounts with our previous philosophical conscience" (Engels 1941, 7).

This short work, scarcely longer than a brochure, is important as a canonical source of Marxist philosophy and deserves our close attention. The Marxian conception of ideology suggests an opposition between knowledge, or science, and false opinion, or what Lukács later called false consciousness. Engels here analyzes a perceived opposition between Marxist science and classical German, or what Marxists call bourgeois, philosophy. According to Engels, Marxism is science, more precisely the science of dialectical materialism.

The intrinsic opposition between idealism as mere ideology and materialism as science is further heightened if we note that the term *Ausgang* in the title of the work, here translated as "outcome," in fact means "exit" or "way out" in ordinary German. This term suggests that, if not Feuerbach, at least Marxism takes the discussion beyond classical German philosophy, hence beyond Hegel and beyond philosophy. Engels reports that his purpose in this book is to prove "a short, connected account of our relation to the Hegelian philosophy, of our point of departure as well as of our separation from it" (Engels 1941, 7–8).

Engels's Conception of Classical German Philosophy

Engels's presentation of the new Marxist worldview in his study of Feuerbach is schematic at best. The book is divided into four chapters, the first concerning the historical transition "from Hegel to Feuerbach," followed by accounts of the opposition of "idealism and materialism," and "Feuerbach's philosophy of religion and ethics," and ending in an exposition of "dialectical materialism."

Feuerbach assumes a key role in Engels's discussion as a transitional figure who began a basic change in perspective, an instance of what Kuhn later called a paradigm change. Engels believes that this change occurs in the progression from idealism, which reaches a peak in Hegel's thought, to materialism, whose high point lies in the new angle of vision represented by Marx and himself. The claim that philosophy finds its fulfillment in an extraphilosophic form of science is a further development of the traditional philosophical insistence that philosophy is science. Engels maintains that the new worldview is not philosophy, but that it extends the philosophical tradition on the scientific plane.

The Young Hegelians famously thought that Hegel had brought philosophy to a high point and to a close. Engels shared the Young Hegelian view that it was no longer possible to pursue the road taken by philosophy, which leads up to the Hegelian system. Like the other Young Hegelians, Engels believed that philosophy ended in Hegel's thought. He maintained that when Hegel for the first time grasped the entire progressive development leading up to the present moment, he consciously ended the philosophical quest, understood as absolute truth reached by a single individual. He further maintained that Hegel had shown us the way out of "the labyrinth of 'systems' to real, positive knowledge of the world" (Engels 1941, 15).

Engels's view of Hegel is based on his twofold conviction that philosophical problems can be solved or resolved, and that the relation of thought and being is the watershed problem of all philosophy. For Engels, idealism and materialism are true contraries that divide the philosophical universe between them. "The great basic question of all philosophy, especially of modern philosophy, is that concerning the relation of thought and being" (Engels 1941, 20).

The claim that all forms of thought are either idealism or materialism obviously depends on the definition of these two basic philosophical approaches and on the viability of the distinction between them. Engels understands idealism simplistically as the doctrine that thought is prior to being. This claim is simplistic, since the doctrine as Engels understands it has never been held by any idealist, including Berkeley. Engels proposes two definitions of "materialism" in his book: the view that nature is the sole reality (1941, 17) and the view that it is necessary to sacrifice every idealist fancy that cannot be brought into accord with the facts (43).

Engels stresses the importance of the distinction between ideology and science for knowledge of society. We need, he maintains, to replace the cult of the abstract man with the science of real men and women and their historical development (1941, 41). Just as, with respect to nature, natural science has taken the place of the philosophy of nature, so too, with respect to the social world, a science of society should substitute for philosophy (47). Philosophy is merely a form of ideology occupied with thought as composed of independent entities that develop according to immanent laws (56). It follows that philosophy, which has no redeeming virtues, is unable to come to grips with its own problems, which, however, are real.

Engels on Kant's Conception of the Thing-in-Itself

Despite his rudimentary grasp of fundamental philosophical principles, Engels never hesitates to criticize such philosophical giants as Hegel, a frequent object of attack, or Kant. In part, his view that Marxism constitutes the way out as well as the solution to the problems of classical German philosophy follows from his reading of Kant's thing-in-itself.

It might seem that this technical issue is beyond the scope of Engels's discussion. In fact, it is central to that discussion. Engels argues in effect, as Lukács will later argue, that the problem of knowledge consists in knowledge of society, that classical German philosophy is unable to solve this problem, and that it is solved by Marxism. The problem is that of the essence of capitalist society, depicted as a thing-in-itself, which classical German philosophy can think but cannot know. The uncognizable thing-in-itself represents the insurpassable limit of classical German philosophy, which is surpassed in Marxism, which, for the first time, achieves knowledge of modern society, which it knows as it is, not merely as it appears, namely as a thing-in-itself. If this is true, then Engels must show that, unlike Kant, for whom the thing-in-itself is uncognizable, he, on behalf of Marxism, knows the thing-in-itself, or the essence of modern society.

The only passage where Engels directly considers the thing-in-itself in his study of Ludwig Feuerbach, to the best of my knowledge the only such passage in his writings, occurs in the context of his effort to distinguish between idealism and materialism, in a remark on cognition, which needs to be cited at length:

> [T]here is another set of philosophers—those who question the possibility of any cognition (or at least an exhaustive cognition) of the world. To them, among the moderns, belong Hume and Kant, and they have played a very important role in philosophical development. What is decisive in the refutation of this view has already been said by Hegel—in so far as this is possible from an idealist standpoint. The materialistic additions made by Feuerbach are more ingenious than profound. The most telling refutation of this as of all other philosophical fancies is practice, *viz.*, experiment and industry. If we are able to prove the correctness of our conception of a natural process by making it ourselves, bringing it into being out of its conditions and using it for our own purposes into the bargain, then there is an end of the Kantian incomprehensible "thing-in-itself." The chemical substances produced in the bodies of plants and animals remained just such "things-in-themselves" until organic chemistry began to produce them one after another, whereupon the "thing-in-itself" became a thing for us, as, for instance, alizarin, the coloring matter of the madder, which we no

longer trouble to grow in the madder roots in the field, but produce much more cheaply and simply from coal tar. For three hundred years the Copernican solar system was a hypothesis with a
hundred, a thousand or ten thousand chances to one in its favor,
but still always a hypothesis. But when Leverrier, by means of the
data provided by this system, not only deduced the necessity of the
existence of an unknown planet, but also calculated the position in
the heavens which this planet must occupy, and when Galle really
found this planet, the Copernican system was proved. (Engels 1941,
22–23)

Kant's Thing-in-Itself

In order to discuss Engels's and other Marxist readings of the thing-in-
itself, something must be said about this concept in Kant's theory. This
concept, which is important in Kant's view of knowledge, has attracted
much scholarly attention in a special discussion, which surpasses the limits
of the present paper (see, for example, Prauss 1974). The few words I can
say about it here are intended merely to indicate in minimal fashion some
main aspects of the thing-in-itself within the theory.

For present purposes, suffice it to say that Kant's critical philosophy
depends on a basic distinction between phenomena, or what appears in
experience, and noumena, or the objects of thought that do not and cannot appear. Phenomena, whose appearance constitutes experience and
knowledge, are understood as representing, or standing in for, an independent reality.

In an important letter from the critical period, when he was preparing
the *Critique of Pure Reason,* Kant tells us that he is concerned with the following question: "What is the ground of the relation of that in us which we
call 'representation' [*Vorstellung*] to the object?" (letter to Marcus Herz, 21
February 1772, in Kant 1967, 71).

Kant, who presupposes the concept of the thing-in-itself throughout his
theory of knowledge, refers to it in many passages in the *Critique of Pure
Reason.* In the critical philosophy, this concept functions within a causal
theory of knowledge, in which the independent real world is thought of
as affecting the subject. The subject is both passive with respect to independent reality, which affects it and is the source of the content of experience and knowledge, and active with respect to that content, which it

transforms, or works up, as the objects of experience and knowledge. The thing-in-itself is the independent object, considered as the object of thought, but not of experience.

The main idea can be summarized as the claim, appropriately stated in causal language, since the relation of appearance to object is a causal relation, that the independent object can without contradiction be thought of as the cause and that the appearance can without contradiction be thought of as the effect. In an important passage on the idea of appearance, Kant writes: "If ... appearances are not taken for more than they actually are; if they are viewed not as things in themselves, but merely as representations, connected according to empirical laws, they must themselves have grounds which are not appearances. The effects of such an intelligible cause appear, and accordingly can be determined through other appearances, but its causality is not so determined" (Kant 1961, 466–67 [B 565]). In another passage, he stresses the uncognizable nature of the thing-in-itself in writing that "[t]he thing in itself is indeed given, but we can have no insight into its nature" (514 [B 642]).

Engels's Reading of the Thing-in-Itself

The passage on the thing-in-itself cited above from Engels's study of Feuerbach is a veritable microcosm of the difficulties of the Marxist approach to philosophy. We can easily see the fragile nature of Engels's grasp of the theory he criticizes, which in turn undermines the criticism he proposes, through examining the passage.

The passage occurs in the context of his account of the relation of thought and being, in which Hegel is taken as the illustration of the idealist claim that thought is prior to being. Engels is concerned here with cognition of the real world, cognition that he understands as "a correct reflection of reality" (1941, 21). If this is the normative view of knowledge, then "to know" means "to provide a correct reflection"—one is tempted to say a mirror image—of an independent object. Hegel's view is rejected by Engels on the grounds that he is unable to show that the "identity of thought and being" is in fact demonstrated "by mankind immediately translating his philosophy from theory into practice and transforming the whole world according to Hegelian principles" (22).

Engels's grasp of Hegel is shaky at best. Since Hegel does not make anything like the claim attributed to him, Engels's criticism appears wide of the mark. In the cited passage, Hegel is listed as an authority figure who correctly rejects skepticism about the possibility of any cognition as well as of "an exhaustive cognition." It is correct to regard him as a deep critic of Kantian epistemology. Yet if, as in Engels, "cognition" means "knowledge of an independent real," then Hegel cannot be adduced in support of the position.

Kant invokes his famous Copernican turn, since it is not otherwise possible to justify the claim to know objects given in experience. Following Kant on this point, Hegel's central epistemological insight, described, for example, in the introduction to the *Phenomenology of Spirit*, is that we do not and cannot know objects independent of us. There is an obviously empiricist dimension in German idealism. Kant's critical philosophy combines transcendental idealism and empirical realism. Yet no idealist accepts Engels's view that knowledge requires the correct reflection of an independent reality. For if it were really independent of us, it could not be known, since it would lack an epistemological link to the subject.

Engels's comment that in making something ourselves we put an end to Kant's incomprehensible thing-in-itself indicates that he has not comprehended this important concept. There is a difference between what is comprehensible and what is cognizable. The thing-in-itself is not incomprehensible, although it is by definition outside experience, hence uncognizable. Certainly, as Engels suggests, many things once thought to be uncognizable have later been understood by modern science. Yet this is not and cannot be the case for the thing-in-itself. This concept designates the way something is, independent of the subject, something that, if knowledge necessarily begins with experience, cannot therefore be known.

Lukács on the Thing-in-Itself

Engels's reading of the thing-in-itself, crude by any standard, was criticized by Georg Lukács—a highly significant figure within Western Marxism—in an important passage in *History and Class Consciousness* (1971, 131–33). Marxists, who routinely criticize philosophy, rarely possess a deep knowledge of the philosophical tradition. In this respect, Lukács is an exception. He is arguably the outstanding Marxist philosopher.

Lukács's criticism of Engels's reading of the thing-in-itself is important for two reasons: because he puts it into the context of his own reading of classical German philosophy, and because he wants to free Marxism from its primitive approach to philosophical questions. Like Marx, but unlike Engels, Lukács was a trained philosopher. Lukács needed to confront Engels's discussion of the thing-in-itself, since he himself offered a very different, vastly more sophisticated interpretation of this concept.

In the central essay of his book, Lukács considers the thing-in-itself as an unsolved problem running through classical German philosophy, a problem that is resolved by Marx (see Rockmore 1986; 1992b, 79–152). In Lukács's sophisticated interpretation of Kant, the thing-in-itself has two distinct functions as an epistemological limit and as an ontological source of content. With respect to Kant, he writes: "[W]e see, on the one hand, that the two quite distinct delimiting functions of the thing-in-itself (viz. the impossibility of apprehending the whole with the aid of the conceptual framework of the rational partial systems and the irrationality of the contents of the individual concepts) are but two sides of the one problem" (Lukács 1971, 116).

Since he was deeply knowledgeable about German philosophy, which he interpreted in very different fashion, Lukács could not simply accept Engels's simplistic reading of this concept. In his criticism of Engels, Lukács cites part of the passage cited above, before noting a series of confusions. These include Engels's mistaken claim that the thing-in-itself could be a barrier to the expansion of knowledge, an idea rejected by Kant, and the mistaken view that science and industry constitute practice as understood in philosophy. According to Lukács, science consists in pure contemplation, whereas modern industrial society functions according to natural laws deriving from the private ownership of the means of production.

In the context of the Marxist debate, Lukács's criticism of Engels was obviously important. In correctly treating the texts as more important than claims about them, Lukács left political orthodoxy behind as he moved in the direction of orthodox philosophy. Unfortunately, as early as the next year he felt compelled to renounce this book and to align himself with Marxist orthodoxy. It is regrettable that in his later, Stalinist phase, he felt compelled to retract his earlier criticism (Lukács 1975). In this respect, as in others, he never again reached the level of his early thought.

Lukács and Engels on Science

From Lukács's critique of Engels's criticism of the thing-in-itself emerge two issues regarding their respective grasps of Kant and science from a

Marxist perspective. Engels's reading of the thing-in-itself rests on an opposition between philosophy, which sets up a barrier to knowledge, and science, which knows no barriers and which resolves problems that were often thought to be unsolvable. Lukács correctly responds that knowledge, which, for Kant, can be expanded limitlessly, is limited to the phenomenal world. It is, then, a crude mistake to maintain that we do in fact, or in principle ever could, overcome this distinction through modern science.

Engels's criticism is based on his view of modern science. His remark about the Copernican system betrays an antiphilosophical faith in a particular conception of science as the main, even as the only, source of knowledge. This faith, which can be described as positivism or scientism, is widespread in modern times, and never more so than at present. According to Comte, the founder of modern positivism, metaphysics, which replaced theology, will itself be replaced by science. "Scientism" can be described as the conviction that "science, and only science, describes the world as it is in itself, independent of perspective," in a way that "leaves no room for an independent philosophical enterprise" (Putnam 1992, x). Like the positivists, Engels obviously believes that the questions of science are definitively resolved, since scientific theories, such as the Copernican system, are proven. If this is true, then science can substitute for, and resolve the questions of, philosophy.

Lukács's criticism of Engels is as interesting for what he does not say as for what he does say. What Lukács does not do is to criticize either Engels's view of science or his view of knowledge. He counters Engels, who seems to accord a privileged epistemological status to science, in noting that it does not help us to grasp what philosophers understand as praxis, hence what Marx presumably has in mind. Certainly, there is no passage where Marx even remotely suggests that natural science is what we mean by human praxis. If this is true, then practical questions, or questions of human practice, cannot be resolved through modern science at all.

Engels's view of science as demonstrably true is not widely shared. The results of science are neither analytically true nor self-evident nor intuitively obvious. Science, which is based on experiment and observation, is widely regarded as intrinsically fallible, hence always open to possible refutation (see, for example, Popper 1968). It is true that alizarin can be produced from coal tar. It is not true that the Copernican hypothesis has been proved, although it has indeed proved useful in interpreting data.

In suggesting that science yields anything like a correct reflection of independent reality, Engels departs from Kant, for whom only appearances could be known. Even though he held that knowledge is capable of limitless expansion, Kant denied that we can know things-in-themselves. In that sense, he is a skeptic. Neither Engels nor Lukács, both of whom take a Marxist line, are skeptical at all.

In pointing to the limits of science, Lukács implicitly criticizes Engels's positivist identification of science with knowledge. Yet he does not object to the idea that knowledge is itself limitless. Although Engels and Lukács are critical of classical German philosophy, in this respect both follow the mainline philosophical view, already stated by Descartes at the dawn of modern philosophy. In following the correct method, there is in principle no limit to what can be known with certainty, since "there can be nothing so remote that we cannot reach it, nor so recondite that we cannot discover it" (Descartes 1970, 92).

Lukács and Engels on the Thing-in-Itself

Lukács and Engels, who disagree about science, agree on the relation of philosophy and science concerning the thing-in-itself. Marxism is a dualistic theory, presupposing a relation between appearance and reality. In Kant's critical theory, appearance represents an uncognizable reality. In Marxism, on the contrary, appearance represents no more than a false or merely ideological appearance, provided in bourgeois views of bourgeois society, whose veil of illusion is pierced in Marxist science. Marxism claims to go beyond mere appearance to know the thing-in-itself, not as it merely appears but as it is. As Marxists, Lukács and Engels maintain that only Marxism, or Marxist science, grasps the essence of advanced industrial society, since only Marxism knows the thing-in-itself; only Marxism knows social reality.

Engels and Lukács, who agree that only Marxism knows the thing-in-itself, understand such knowledge in remarkably different ways. Marxism is widely understood as a theory of praxis, or human practice. The difference concerns how human praxis—which, according to Marxism, is the concealed essence of capitalist society, the thing-in-itself uncognizable through capitalist methods—can be known.

Engels's superficial view of knowledge is arguably inconsistent with Marxism. If the thing-in-itself can merely be known through science, then three consequences follow. First, ordinary science—or, as he also says, experiment and industry—is sufficient to know the way the world is. Second, there is no difference between ordinary science and Marxism with respect to the thing-in-itself; both enlighten us by cognizing that which is ordinarily uncognizable through other means. Third, there is no need for Marxism, or the special Marxist science, to grasp the essence of capitalist society.

Lukács clearly saw that in exempting science from the illusions of bourgeois ideology, Engels overlooked its social character, in virtue of which, from the Marxist perspective, it, like all other capitalist forms of cognition, is subject to ideological distortion. That is the point of his remark about Engels's view of science as able to cognize the philosophically uncognizable thing-in-itself:

> He [i.e., the scientist] strives as far as possible to reduce the material substratum of his observation to the purely rational "product," to the "intelligible matter" of mathematics. And when Engels speaks, in the context of industry, of the "product" which is made to serve "our purposes," he seems to have forgotten for a moment the fundamental structure of capitalist society which he himself had once formulated so supremely well in his brilliant early essay. There he pointed out that capitalist society is based on "a natural law that is founded on the unconsciousness of those involved in it." (Lukács 1971, 132–33)

Like Engels, Lukács thought that Marxism showed the way to knowledge of the thing-in-itself. Unlike Engels, Lukács understood that it was not enough to appeal to science. To understand the nature of capitalism, it was further necessary to appeal to Marxism, or Marxist science. Ideology is not merely false; it is also an indication of the truth. Marxism, for Lukács, by knowing the thing-in-itself, which represents the uncognizable essence of capitalist society, resolves the ideological problem that reaches its high point in classical German philosophy. This essence, which cannot be known through bourgeois philosophy, is knowable and known through Marxism. In referring to Marx's theory of commodity analysis as resolving the problem of how to portray capitalist society while laying bare its fundamental nature, he in effect claims that Marx points the way to knowledge of the thing-in-itself: "It is no accident that Marx should have begun with an analysis of commodities when, in the two great works of his mature period, he set out to portray capitalist society in its totality and to lay bare its fundamental nature. For at this stage in the history of mankind there is no problem that does not ultimately lead back to that question and there is no solution that could not be found in the solution to the riddle of ommodity-*structure*" (Lukács 1971, 83).

Marxism and the Thing-in-Itself

The thing-in-itself is a central concept in Kant's critical philosophy. Marxism lays claim to, but fails to demonstrate knowledge of, the thing-in-itself, which Kant regarded as uncognizable. Marxism must claim to know the thing-in-itself. For it claims to surpass classical German philosophy in knowing the social context, which is otherwise inscrutable.

The weakness of Engels's treatment of the thing-in-itself is rooted in the nature of Marxism as a political and a philosophical theory. As a political theory, it focuses on the effort to assume political power. As a philosophical theory, it presents a philosophical analysis, which can and must be judged by standard intellectual criteria, without special pleading. Philosophy has long been concerned with theory of knowledge. At least since Plato, it has been widely believed that to know is to know absolutely, in a way beyond skepticism of any kind.

Modern philosophy mainly offers variations on the theme of a representational, causal approach to epistemology. In simplest terms, Marxism offers a further variation on the same theme with the same intent, that is, unlimited knowledge of the object, understood in this case as modern society. Naturalists tend to think that everything is composed of natural entities and that the acceptable methods of justification are commensurable in some sense with the causal approach of modern science. Naturalists tend to conflate justification with causality.

Engels is close to naturalism. Like naturalists, he mistakenly thinks that through science we can have knowledge of the way the world is. Lukács, who is incomparably better trained in philosophy, merely substitutes a revised form of Marxism, understood as an alternative, not to philosophy, but to Marxism understood as the science that philosophy has long sought to become, with the result that he makes an identical claim.

If this is true, then Marxism's error does not lie in the concern to know the nature of modern society, but rather in the surprising continuity between traditional philosophical and Marxist claims to know. Epistemologically speaking, Marxism proposes a social theory of social knowledge, that is, an approach to knowledge of society grounded in the idea that the real human subject is a social being. If all sciences are finally human sciences, then knowledge of society is limited by the social nature of the human subject.

Engels, who claims that Hegel has shown us the way out of systems to positive knowledge of the real world, was followed on this point by Lukács. Lukács's famous breakthrough to Marxism is largely based on his breakthrough to a reading of Hegel from the Marxist perspective. Yet neither Engels nor Lukács, who appreciated the importance of Hegel for Marxism, appreciated Hegel's essential cognitive insight. This insight can be stated in the form of a familiar slogan, which is not the same as a full discussion: all claims for knowledge are claims made within, hence limited by, the historical moment.

If we know only from the perspective of our time and place, then claims to know the thing-in-itself understood as the essence of society are always historically limited. Marxism cannot claim to go beyond appearance to the social essence, which can only be known as it appears in a given historical moment. Engels may not have been wrong in concluding that much philosophy is wrongheaded, no better than ideology. But he was wrong to maintain that Marxism could surpass mere appearance to grasp reality. Engels, who correctly saw that Marxism needed to come to grips with the thing-in-itself, was incorrect in thinking that Marxism could provide absolute knowledge of society as it is. For we cannot have absolute knowledge, even absolute social knowledge, but only knowledge of how the cognitive object, for instance society, appears at a particular historical moment.

References

Althusser, Louis. 1970. *For Marx*. Trans. Ben Brewster. New York: Vintage.

Descartes, Ren . 1970. *Discourse on Method*. In *The Philosophical Works of Descartes*, vol. 1, trans. Elizabeth S. Haldane and G.R.T. Ross. New York: Cambridge University Press.

Engels, Friedrich. 1941. *Ludwig Feuerbach and the Outcome of Classical German Philosophy*. Ed. C. P. Dutt. New York: International Publishers.

Henry, Michel. 1978. *Marx: A Philosophy of Human Reality*. Trans. Kathleen McLaughlin. Bloomington: Indiana University Press.

Kant, Immanuel. 1961. *Critique of Pure Reason*. Trans. Norman Kemp Smith. London: Macmillan; New York: St. Martin's.

———. 1967. *Philosophical Correspondence: 1759–99*. Ed. and trans. Arnulf Zweig. Chicago: University of Chicago Press.

Kolakowski, Leszek. 1978. *Main Currents of Marxism*. 3 vols. Trans. P S. Falla. Oxford: Clarendon Press.

Lukács, Georg. 1971. *History and Class Consciousness*. Trans. Rodney Livingstone. Cambridge, Mass.: MIT Press.

———. 1975. *The Young Hegel: Studies in the Relations Between Dialectics and Economics*. Trans. Rodney Livingstone. Cambridge, Mass.: MIT Press.

McLellan, David. 1977. *Friedrich Engels*. New York: Penguin.

Plekhanov, George V. 1970. *Fundamental Problems of Marxism*. New York: International Publishers.

Popper, Karl. 1968. *Conjectures and Refutations: The Growth of Scientific Knowledge*. New York: Harper & Row.

Prauss, Gerold. 1974. *Kant und das Problem der Dinge an sich*. Bonn: Bouvier.

Putnam, Hilary. 1992. *Renewing Philosophy*. Cambridge, Mass.: Harvard University Press.

Rockmore, Tom. 1986. *Hegel's Circular Epistemology*. Bloomington: Indiana University Press.

———. 1991. Marx and Perestroika. *Philosophy and Social Criticism* 16:193–206.

———. 1992a. Fichte, Lask, and Lukács's Hegelian Marxism. *Journal of the History of Philosophy* 30:77–96.

———. 1992b. *Irrationalism: Lukács and the Marxist View of Reason*. Philadelphia: Temple University Press.

Schmidt, Alfred. 1971. *The Concept of Nature in Marx*. London: New Left Books.

Tucker, Robert C., ed. 1978. *The Marx-Engels Reader*. New York: W. W. Norton.

7

Engels, Modernity, and Classical Social Theory

Douglas Kellner

Friedrich Engels and Karl Marx were among the first to develop systematic perspectives on modern societies and to produce a critical discourse on modernity, thus inaugurating the problematic of modern social theory. In most of the narratives of classical social theory, Marx alone is usually cited as one of the major founders of the problematic, while Engels is neglected. It is Marx who is usually credited as one of the first to develop a theory of modernity and a critical social theory linking the rise of modern societies with the emergence of capitalism. Yet Engels preceded Marx in focusing attention on the differences between modern and premodern society, and then on the constitutive role of capitalism in producing a new modern world. As I show in this chapter, from the late 1830s into the 1840s, Engels played a leading role in theorizing the distinctive features of the modern world, and he inspired Marx to see the importance of capitalism in constructing a distinctively new modern society. Consequently, I argue that Engels preceded Marx in his analysis of the historical originality and novelty of modern societies and their rupture from traditional societies.

Study of the work of the early Engels and the beginning of his collaboration with Marx thus provides fresh perspectives on their relationship and
the role of Engels in creating their shared theoretical and political positions. The analysis here also suggests that the critical theory of modern
societies and political economy of capitalism remains a major contribution
of Marx and Engels to contemporary thought.

Many interpretations of the relationships between Marx and Engels
stress the differences between them, by emphasizing the scientistic writings of the later Engels, which are contrasted with the more philosophical
works of Marx. But both Marx and Engels were engaged in theorizing
modernity and shared important perspectives on the modern world,
despite some later differences of emphasis in theory and method. It is one
of the merits of Gouldner (1980, 250 ff.) to stress the importance of Engels
in developing the Marxian theory and to defend Engels against attacks that
he was but a crude simplifier of Marx's ideas. Mazlish (1989) also appre-
ciates the importance of the contribution of Engels, while Lichtheim
(1961), Levine (1975, 1984), and many others sharply distinguish between
Marx and Engels, attacking Engels as a vulgar debaser of Marx's ideas.
Although important epistemological differences between their views
would eventually emerge, it is a mistake to downplay the important initial
contribution of Engels and his significance in shaping Marx's vision of
modernity (for discussions of Engels' life and times, see Marcus 1974;
Carver 1989; Hunley 1991; Rigby 1992).

Engels and the Search for the Modern

Engels's father had factories in Barmen and Bremen in Germany, and
Manchester in England, and his son Friedrich was thus able to experience
the modern world in the beginnings of industrialization in Germany.
Some of Engels's initial publications concern the new industrial society
emerging in Germany and what he saw as modern forms of industry, urban-
ization, architecture, culture, and thought. In the series "Letters from
Wuppertal," published in a German newspaper in 1839, Engels describes
the novel industrial conditions in the Wuppertal valley, opening with a
description of the pollution of the Wupper River, caused by dyes from "the
numerous dye-works using Turkey red" (CW 2:7). Engels was nineteen
when he published these revealing analyses of the novel conditions of the
emerging modern industrial society. Self-taught and a voracious reader

with evident literary ambitions, Engels spent much of the time during his apprenticeship in Bremen and later during his military service in Berlin engaged in study and writing. Many of his early writings are collected in CW 2, and I draw upon these texts in this study.

Engels then describes the town of Elberfeld and contrasts it with its neighboring town, his own native Barmen. He lauds the "large, massive houses tastefully built in modern style" that "take the place of those mediocre Elberfeld buildings, which are neither old-fashioned nor modern." The new stone houses appearing everywhere, the broad avenues, the green bleaching-yards, gardens, and the Lower Barmen church were, Engels thought, "very well constructed in the noblest Byzantine style." He concludes that "there is far more variety here than in Elberfeld, for the monotony is broken by a fresh bleaching-yard here, a house in the modern style there, a stretch of the river or a row of gardens lining the street. All this leaves one in doubt whether to regard Barmen as a town or a mere conglomeration of all kinds of buildings; it is, indeed, just a combination of many small districts held together by the bond of municipal institutions" (CW 2:8).

Engels thus characterizes the new modern world in terms of new modern architecture, new industry, and new towns, bustling with variety and diversity. He also describes inebriation in the alehouses, with drunken individuals pouring out of them at closing time and sleeping in the gutter. He blames this situation on factory work and describes the lot of the new industrial working class as a miserable one: "Work in low rooms where people breathe in more coal fumes and dust than oxygen—and in the majority of cases beginning already at the age of six—is bound to deprive them of all strength and joy in life. The weavers, who have individual looms in their homes, sit bent over them from morning till night, and desiccate their spinal marrow in front of a hot stove. Those who do not fall prey to mysticism are ruined by drunkenness" (CW 2:9). Likewise, the "local-born leather workers are ruined physically and mentally after three years of work": "three out of five die of consumption." In sum, "terrible poverty prevails among the lower classes, particularly the factory workers in Wuppertal; syphilis and lung diseases are so widespread as to be barely credible; in Elberfeld alone, out of 2,500 children of school age 1,200 are deprived of education and grow up in the factories—merely so that the manufacturer need not pay the adults, whose place they take, twice the wage he pays a child" (CW 2:10).

Thus, as early as 1839, Engels deplores the horrific working and living conditions of the working class and depicts them as a reprehensible effect of modern industrial development. In the latter part of his "Letters," and in many other newspaper articles written over the next few years, Engels describes in great detail "modern" literature, culture, and thought of the present, equating "modern" cultural tendencies with Enlightenment criticism and the contemporary literature of the "Young Germany" movement, which he champions against reactionary pietistic thought and backward German literature. In his voluminous early newspaper articles and sketches he reveals himself to be, like Marx, a great partisan of modernity, an avatar of modern ideas, as well as a sharp critic of the impact of modern conditions on the working class (see Engels's further works in CW 2).

Engels was sent to England in 1842 to learn the business of industrial production in his father's factory in Manchester, the industrial heart of the most advanced capitalist society of the day. While experiencing first-hand the new mode of industrial production and way of life that accompanied it, young Engels assiduously studied German, French, and English socialism, as well as British political economy. In an article titled "Progress of Social Reform on the Continent," Engels describes the new communist ideas as "not the consequence of the particular position of the English, or any other nation, but ... a necessary conclusion, which cannot be avoided to be drawn from the premises given in the general facts of modern civilisation" (CW 3:392).

Indeed, it is generally accepted that Engels preceded Marx in converting to communism, in that Moses Hess converted Engels in 1842, at a time when Marx was still formally a radical democrat, who acknowledged that he was not thoroughly familiar with the communist ideas (see Riazanov 1973, 43; Carver 1989, 95). Engels, by contrast, began to write newspaper and journal articles promoting communist ideas in early 1843 (see CW 3:379–443; CW 4:212–65), as well as attending meetings and making speeches.

For Engels, it was British political economy that described the workings of the new capitalist economy and provided its ideological legitimation. In the autumn of 1843, Engels accordingly began writing an article on the new modern economic theory and sent it to Marx and Ruge for publication in their forthcoming *Deutsch-französische Jahrbücher*. The yearbook was intended to collect studies by the top German and French radical theorists to help produce a new tendency that would further progressive social change. The first—and only—issue contained an article by "Friedrich Engels in Manchester" titled "Outlines of a Critique of Political Economy."

Engels dissected the forms of private property, competition, trade, and crisis in the newly emerging modern industrial society. His study is fragmentary and highly moralistic, though it contains some good insights into the modern capitalist economy and discloses his early commitments to radical social critique and transformation. He opens by relating the genesis of political economy to the rise of trade and industry, and presents it as a legitimation of the new capitalist social relations, anticipating the Marxist critique of ideology: "[P]olitical economy came into being as a natural result of the expansion of trade, and with its appearance, elementary, unscientific huckstering was replaced by a developed system of licensed fraud, an entire science of enrichment" (CW 3:418).

Engels develops his "outline" as an ideal-type comparison between the mercantile system and "modern economics" (CW 3:420). The new system assumes "the *validity of private property*" (419) and develops into a system of trade (422). Competition is the economists' "principal category—his most beloved daughter, whom he ceaselessly caresses" (431). But competition leads to the monopoly of property and produces an inherently unstable economic system full of conflicts and crises. As noted, Engels's critique of the new modern market economy is highly moralistic. Malthus's theory of population is "the crudest, most barbarous theory that ever existed, a system of despair which struck down all those beautiful phrases about philanthropy and world citizenship. The premises begot and reared the factory system and modern slavery, which yields nothing in inhumanity and cruelty to ancient slavery" (CW 3:420). Trade is "legalised fraud" (422), and to those apologists of the system who argue for its civilizing virtues, Engels contemptuously replies:

> You have destroyed the small monopolies so that the one great basic monopoly, property, may function the more freely and unrestrictedly. You have civilised the ends of the earth to win new terrain for the deployment of your vile avarice. You have brought about the fraternisation of the peoples—but the fraternity is the fraternity of thieves. You have reduced the number of wars—to earn all the bigger profits in peace, to intensify to the utmost the enmity between individuals, the ignominious war of competition! When have you done anything out of pure humanity, from consciousness of the futility of the opposition between the general and the individual interest? When have you been moral without being interested, without harbouring at the back of your mind immoral, egoistical motives? (CW 3:423)

As a Left-Hegelian, Engels is concerned to delineate the series of contradictions between competition and monopoly, supply and demand, wealth and poverty, and the general and particular interest that will eventually lead the system to crisis: "The economist comes along with his lovely theory of demand and supply, proves to you that 'one can never produce too much,' and practice replies with trade crises, which reappear as regularly as the comets, and of which we have now on the average one every five to seven years. For the last eighty years these trade crises have arrived just as regularly as the great plagues did in the past—and they have brought in their train more misery and more immorality than the latter" (CW 3:433). Yet although Engels sees the emerging industrial society as inherently unstable and crisis-prone, he does not grasp any mechanism or tendencies that will lead to a progressive social transformation; he merely cautions as follows:

> But as long as you continue to produce in the present unconscious, thoughtless manner, at the mercy of chance—for just so long trade crises will remain; and each successive crisis is bound to become more universal and therefore worse than the preceding one; is bound to impoverish a larger body of small capitalists, and to augment in increasing proportion the numbers of the class who live by labour alone, thus considerably enlarging the mass of labour to be employed (the major problem of our economists) and finally causing a social revolution such as has never been dreamt of in the philosophy of the economists. (CW 3:434)

During 1843, Engels also composed a review of Thomas Carlyle's *Past and Present*, which, like Engels's work of the period, develops a contrast between modern and premodern society. The review shows Engels at work in researching the contemporary factory system and exploring the development of industrial society. Studies of England—"The Eighteenth Century" and "The English Constitution"—disclose that Engels was also inquiring into the structure and conditions of the modern economy and state, as they emerged in England (CW 3:444–514). In addition to studying industrial production and the political constitution of modern society, Engels explored the new working class life in England, compiling materials for a book that he published in 1845, *The Condition of the Working Class in England*. In this groundbreaking study Engels argues that the history of the proletariat was bound up with the invention of the steam engine and "machinery for working cotton" in the second half of the seventeenth century (CW 4:307). These instruments gave rise to the industrial revolution, which produced new instruments of labor, new industries, a new social structure, and new living and working conditions.

David Riazanov claims that "[t]he term 'Industrial Revolution' belongs to Engels" (1973, 14). But Dirk J. Struik, in notes on the republication of Riazanov's classic study of Marx and Engels, argues: "The term 'Industrial Revolution' was used in France at least as early as the 1820s, in analogy to what was known as 'The Revolution,' the one of 1789. Friedrich Engels, using the term in 1844 and 1845, may well have met it in the French literature and have used it for the first time in the German language. Strangely enough, the term has not been noticed in English before 1884, when the economist Arnold Toynbee used it. Toynbee knew Marx's *Capital*, which uses the term in German" (1973, 223).

Engels claims that "[t]he industrial revolution is of the same importance for England as the political revolution for France, and the philosophical revolution for Germany; and the difference between England in 1760 and in 1844 is at least as great as that between France under the *ancien régime* and during the revolution of July [1830]. But the mightiest result of this industrial transformation is the English proletariat" (CW 4:320). Engels's account begins with a sketch of the living conditions of weavers in preindustrial England, thus setting up a model for distinguishing between premodern and modern societies in the mode adopted by later classical social theory. He describes the "passably comfortable existence" of weavers who worked in their homes, owned their means of production, and had a stable family structure and "leisure for healthful work in garden or field," as well as sports and recreations (CW 4:308f.). Yet Engels does not idealize the previous conditions of the English workers, calling attention to their lack of education, political awareness, intellectual life, and the possibility of a better life. Standard criticism of the text claims that Engels "painted a one-sided picture of the conditions of the English working classes at the time, over-emphasizing the well-being of the workers before industrialization and the subsequent impact of the machine upon them" (Hunley 1991, 16). But the following passage and my discussion raise questions concerning the extent to which Engels did romanticize previous conditions, and I suggest rather that he used the sort of dialectical model of the gains and losses from the industrial revolution that he and Marx were to develop in *The Communist Manifesto* and their other writings. Engels says that previously the workers

> were comfortable in their silent vegetation, but for the industrial revolution they would never have emerged from this existence, which cosily romantic as it was, was nevertheless not worthy of human beings. In truth, they were not human beings; they were

merely toiling machines in the service of the few aristocrats who had guided history down to that time. The industrial revolution has simply carried this out to its logical end by making the workers machines pure and simple, taking from them the last trace of independent activity, and so forcing them to think and demand a position worthy of men. As in France politics, so in England manufacture and the movement of civil society in general drew into the whirl of history the last classes which had remained sunk in apathetic indifference to the universal interests of mankind. (CW 4:309)

Note that Engels adopts the same attitude toward the industrial revolution that he and Marx were later to espouse toward the rise of capitalism and the bourgeoisie in *The Communist Manifesto* and their writings on imperialism. The industrial revolution destroyed the "romantic" conditions of traditional society and violently forced the proletariat into the conditions of modern industrial society. By bringing them into "the whirl of history," the industrial revolution brought them the possibility of achieving human emancipation, of developing their human potentials and faculties to the fullest. This dialectical vision that affirmed both destructive effects and emancipatory possibilities would characterize the work of Marx and Engels throughout their careers.

Engels's humanism is also striking, and indeed a sharp focus of both the early Marx and Engels is their critique of capitalist modernity for what it did to human beings, for its demoralizing, dehumanizing, and oppressive aspects. The first result of the industrial revolution was thus a class structure, divided into the bourgeoisie and proletariat. Engels writes:

> It has already been suggested that manufacture centralises property in the hands of the few. It requires large capital with which to erect the colossal establishments that ruin the petty trading bourgeoisie and with which to press into its service the forces of Nature, so driving the hand-labour of the independent workman out of the market. The division of labor, the application of water and especially steam, and the application of machinery, are the three great levers with which manufacture, since the middle of the last century, has been busy putting the world out of joint. (CW 4:325)

The expression "out of joint" articulates the rupture produced by modern conditions, and Engels also emphasizes the impact of technology, science, and industry on the production of modern societies. Throughout his early writings, Engels presents highly favorable pictures of the progressive effects of science and industry (see, for example, Engels in CW 3:427–28, 440, 478). He provides an account of how the spinning jenny created a new division of labor and new factories for the spinning of cotton, flax, wool, and silk. Invention of the steam engine produced new sources of power and the beginning of a manufacture and factory system. The factory system mechanized agriculture and made possible new large-scale farming, which displaced small farmers, who were forced to seek their livelihood in the newly emergent factory towns.

Throughout the book, Engels describes the novel forms of manufacture, the innovative division of labor, and the new social differentiation produced by the industrial revolution and capitalism. The production of raw materials and of fuel for manufacture produced new mining industries and generated coal mining and iron smelting. The iron industry created new forms of construction, like bridges, and new products, like nails and screws. New industries, like ocean trade, boomed and new forms of transportation and communication emerged, such as roads, bridges, canals, and railroads. But Engels's focus is on the towns, which were a distinctive feature of the new industrial revolution, and the new social structure appearing in the urban centers.

After briefly describing London and other "great towns," Engels zeros in on his own Manchester, the second largest city in England and the capital of the industrial world. (For an excellent study of the city of Manchester and Engels's book on it, see Marcus 1974.) Engels maps out the structure of the city, the class division that cleaves it, and the deplorable working and living conditions of the working classes. For Engels, class division and conflict constitute "the completest expression of the battle of all against all which rules in modern bourgeois society." This battle is fought not only between the different classes, but "also between the individual members of these classes. Each is in the way of the other, and each seeks to crowd out all who are in his way, and to put himself in their place" (CW 4:375). In a later passage, Engels describes the class war typical of modern societies, thus delineating the new forms of division and conflict:

> In this country, social war is under full headway, every one stands for himself, and fights for himself against all comers, and whether or not he shall injure all the others who are his declared foes, depends upon a cynical calculation as to what is most advantageous for himself. It no longer occurs to any one to come to a peaceful understanding with his fellow-man; all differences are settled by

threats, violence, or in a law-court. In short, every one sees in his neighbor an enemy to be got out of the way, or, at best, a tool to be used for his own advantage.... The enemies are dividing gradually into two great camps—the bourgeoisie on one hand, the workers on the other. (CW 4:427; note the anticipation of the class analysis of *The Communist Manifesto* in this passage)

Yet Engels describes the associations that the working class strives to put in the place of competition and is optimistic concerning the revolutionary potential of the proletariat. Throughout the book he describes the cycles of capitalist crisis, which he believes make the collapse of the system inevitable. Anticipating the classical Marxian vision of revolution, Engels claims that if the present trends continue,

commercial crises would continue, and grow more violent, more terrible, with the extension of industry and the multiplication of the proletariat. The proletariat would increase in geometrical proportion, in consequence of the progressive ruin of the lower middle-class and the giant strides with which capital is concentrating itself in the hands of the few; and the proletariat would soon embrace the whole nation, with the exception of a few millionaires. But in this development there comes a stage at which the proletariat perceives how easily the existing power may be overthrown, and then follows a revolution. (CW 4:580)

Marx and Engels, at approximately the same time, arrived at the conclusion that the proletariat was the revolutionary class, but at this time Marx had a much more extravagant, Hegelian concept of the proletariat as revolutionary subject than Engels's more modest sociological and political concept (compare Marx CW 3:175ff. with Engels's *Condition of the Working Class*). Engels is completely confident that a "revolution will follow with which none hitherto known can be compared.... These are all inferences which may be drawn with the greatest certainty.... The revolution must come; it is already too late to bring about a peaceful solution" (CW 4:581). Later, Engels would chide this excessive optimism, but in fact a similar vision of the certainty of the coming revolution would permeate Marx and Engels's works.

Engels thus emerges as one of the first social theorists to attempt to grasp the structure of modern societies, to delineate their fundamental conflicts, and to predict their eventual demise. One is struck by the confidence with which he attempts to delineate the entire situation of the working class in England, attempting to map out comprehensively its working and living conditions, and to lay bare the class structure of modern societies. Moreover, Engels's analysis is a dynamic one, showing the classes in conflict, struggling for control of society. Marcus (1974, 177ff.) claims that in Engels's study of the English working class, one sees a particularly modern mode of thought emerge: the ability of thought to grasp the essential features of a phenomenon, and to distinguish between appearance and reality in producing a comprehensive and systematic analysis of the contemporary social structure.

As Marcus points out (1974, 192), Engels also provides the first full-scale attempt at representing the "culture of poverty." In order to grasp the macrostructure of the new industrial cities, Engels maps out the various connections between neighborhoods, describing and mapping the structure of the city in what can be seen as the first work of urban sociology. Penetrating the heart of darkness of modern industrial society, Engels plunges into the labyrinth of squalid working and living conditions, attempting to make order out of chaos. Using his eyes, nose, ears, and feet, he attempts to map and comprehend the horrific situation of the working class in England, which he takes, as did Marx later in *Capital*, as the model of the modern industrial societies of the future. In mapping this immense complexity, Engels makes use of Hegelian dialectical thought, relating the parts to each other and to the whole social system. For Engels, dialectics is making connections, and he confidently maps out the essential structures of the emerging industrial society. His thought is thoroughly systematic, conceptualizing the parts in terms of the whole and showing how the parts are components of a new modern industrial society.

Yet Engels also maintains a critical posture, describing the horrendous living and working conditions of the proletariat in astonishing detail. His critique is generally moralistic and lacks the concepts of alienation and human nature with which Marx carries out his analysis of labor in the *Economic and Philosophical Manuscripts* of 1844 (see Marx in CW 4). Engels condemns the greed and callousness of the bourgeoisie, recounting in one telling vignette how he described the wretched lot of the workers to a bourgeois associate, who nodded and then said: "And yet there is money to be made. Good day, sir" (CW 4:563). Typically, Engels sees retribution coming in the future revolution, an event to which he and Marx dedicated their lives.

Marx, Engels, and Modernity

Although thinkers like Machiavelli, Vico, Montesquieu, Rousseau, Con-
dorcet, Adam Smith, Comte, Saint-Simon, and Hegel all distinguished
between modern and premodern times, it was Karl Marx and his collaborator Friedrich Engels who produced the first systematic social theory of
modernity, thus initiating the mode of thought associated with classical
social theory. Although previous theorists developed distinctions between
modern and ancient societies, sketched historical stages that described
the transition to a new modern society, and delineated some of its key
distinguishing features, it was Marx and Engels who provided the first rig-
orous and comprehensive historical analysis of the rupture that produced
modernity, and the first systematic analysis of the distinctive structures,
processes, conflicts, and potentials for progressive transformation of modern societies. Combining detailed historical and empirical analysis of capitalist social formations, systematic theoretical conceptualization, radical
social critique, and a call for fundamental social transformation, Marx and
Engels formulated with particular analytical rigor and historical grounding the new forms of social differentiation, conflict, and fragmentation, as
well as the modes of social cooperation and association produced by social
modernity.

Moreover, it was Marx and Engels who initiated a distinctive emancipatory tradition in social theory that critically addressed the structures of
modern society from a standpoint of its higher historical possibilities and
developmental tendencies. In the Marxian vision, the destructive and
oppressive features of modernity would be overcome in a superior stage of
societal development that would fully realize the potentials of modernity.
Thus, whereas Enlightenment thinkers and positivist-technocratic social
theorists like Comte and Saint-Simon embraced modernity and postulated
a utopian future ruled by a technocratic elite who would solve all social
problems and promote social progress, the Marxian theory addressed the
forms of societal crisis and oppression that modernity produced, but saw
the solution to its problems, and its potential for more progressive societal
development, to be immanent features of modern societies rather than
simply normative ideals to be imposed from without.

In the Marxian theory, the motor of modernity was the capitalist mode
of production, with economic development shaping the forms of social,
political, and cultural life, and consequently generating a new modern
social formation. For classical Marxism, the capitalist mode of production
thus produced an entirely new modern world that decisively broke with

the feudal world. For Marxian theory, the concept of modernity is thus constituted by the theory of capitalism as the fate of the new modern world, as the motor and demiurge of modernity.

In this study, I have shown that Engels preceded Marx in developing an ideal-type analysis of the distinction between modern and premodern society, in sketching the outlines of a critique of political economy, and in developing a critique of capitalist society with the intention of overthrowing it for a socialist society. In their collaborative texts of the 1840s, Marx and Engels worked together on this project. When Marx was expelled from Paris in 1845 for publishing in a radical émigré newspaper, he moved to Brussels, where he began his collaboration with Engels. Together they traveled to England to observe the new factories and industrial living and working conditions. Upon their return, they began developing their sketch of the genesis of the modern world and their historical-materialist perspectives in *The German Ideology* (CW 5), written in 1845–46 but never published in their lifetime. The text is important, for it articulates some of their first formulations of the differentiated structure of modern societies, as well as theorizing the new modes of association and cooperation. Marx and Engels also published a joint attack, *The Holy Family* (1845, CW 4), on Bruno Bauer and their former Young Hegelian associates, whom they now considered pseudoradical and idealist. Marx published, in addition, an attack on the economics of Proudhon in *The Poverty of Philosophy* (1846, CW 6:105ff.), declaring the French writer to be trapped in the idealist verbiage of Hegel, thus mystifying the concrete economic phenomena that Marx and Engels were attempting to analyze.

Marx and Engels's vision of history from this period was presented in *The Communist Manifesto,* which sketches in dramatic narrative form their view of the origins and trajectory of modernity (CW 6:477ff.). It appeared in early 1848, anticipating the sequence of revolutions that broke out throughout Europe shortly after its publication. In it Marx and Engels sketch out a contrast between precapitalist societies and the new modern society, where "[a]ll that is solid melts into air, all that is holy is profaned, and man is at last compelled to face with sober senses his real conditions of life, and his relations with his kind" (CW 6:487).

The standard English translations (other than Carver's 1996 version) obscure the important point, implicit in the German, that all previous classes and social groups (*Stände*), as well as "all that is solid," dissolve (*Alles Ständische und Stehende verdampft*). The point is especially important because it distinguishes Marx and Engels's analysis from Hegel's. Hegel believed that the *Stände* would play an important part in integrating individuals into modern society, but Marx and Engels argue that these institutions are disintegrating. Hegel thus ultimately developed a political theory that would unify modern and premodern institutions and conceptions, while Marx and Engels developed a concept of a thoroughly modern society. The passage thus points to the dissolution of the old hierarchical order of society and of previous classes, leaving workers facing the bourgeoisie without intervening classes (Carver's translation reads "Everything fixed and feudal goes up in smoke"—Marx and Engels 1996, 4). The first section of *The Communist Manifesto* is entitled "Bourgeois and Proletarians," and one of the first important points is that during the present era class antagonisms have been simplified, so "society as a whole is more and more splitting up into two great hostile camps, into two great classes directly facing each other: bourgeois and proletariat" (CW 6:485). This two-class vision derived from Engels's *Condition of the Working Class in England* (CW 4), and it would periodically appear in key junctures in their thought, though in some texts they would use a more differentiated class analysis. Indeed, much of the vision of *The Communist Manifesto* was delineated in Engels's early writings, although Marx is usually given credit for drafting its especially expressive prose and dramatic historical narrative (see Berman [1982], who interprets the "Manifesto" as a founding document of social modernity and an example of modernist writing; Carver [1983] argues that much of the historical writing is more like Engels's earlier works than Marx's).

When solid ties of dependence melt in the air, individuals become free to compete with each other and engage in exchange. This produces a wholly disharmonious and conflicted social order, precisely as Engels sketched out in his early writings. Indeed, modern capitalist societies for Engels and Marx were torn by inequalities, class conflicts, and crisis tendencies, which produced an inherently unstable modern social order riven with conflict and subject to crisis and overthrow. Following the hopes of the Enlightenment for a higher stage of civilization, Marx and Engels held that class conflicts between the ruling bourgeois class and the oppressed proletariat would be resolved through victories of the working class, which would create an egalitarian, just, and democratic social order, realizing the ideals of the Enlightenment, the French Revolution, and the emergent socialist traditions and driving modernity to a higher stage of civilization. Marxism thus very much shared the optimistic Enlightenment belief that modern society was on a trajectory of historical progress and that humanity was bound to overcome its limitations and solve its problems en route to a higher stage of human history.

By addressing capitalism in its most advanced setting, British society, Marx and Engels were ideally situated to describe the inner dynamics of the new modern order and to be prescient about changes that came later in other nations. They experienced firsthand the second industrial revolution (with its mechanization, big industry, intensified incorporation of science and technology into the labor process, intensified imperialist competition, and modern state)—a revolution that began in England and quickly spread to the Continent and the "new world" of the Americas. Marx and Engels also experienced the rise of the working-class movement, which increasingly called for sweeping political and egalitarian social reconstruction, and themselves became leaders of the movement.

Marxian theory thus bears distinctly modern hopes for progress, freedom, democracy, and socioeconomic and individual development. To some extent, both the strengths and limitations of classical Marxism are connected with its extremely ambitious hopes concerning the progressive features of the era, which Marx and Engels believed would terminate in creation of a democratic and socialist society that would realize the promises of modernity. The Marxian analysis of the contrast between pre-capitalist and capitalist societies provides the basis of Engels and Marx's concept of modernity, and they present the transition from capitalism to socialism as a process that would fully develop the potential of modernity and produce a higher stage of civilization. The enduring contributions of the Marxian theory are its mode of historical and social analysis, which provides the model for classical social theory, and its insights into the structures, conflicts, and potentials of modern societies.

Of course, it was in their mature writings that Marx and Engels developed their most articulated perspectives on modern society. Between them would emerge important differences regarding their respective uses of the Hegelian dialectical method and the methods of modern science, and their epistemological and methodological differences have been explored in the literature and are the topic of several other chapters in this volume. But this study of the early Engels and the beginning of his collaboration with Marx reveals that Engels should receive more credit for being one of the founders of classical social theory and contributing decisively to the development of the Marxian vision.

References

Berman, Marshall. 1982. *All That Is Solid Melts into Air: The Experience of Modernity.* London: Verso.

Carver, Terrell. 1983. *Marx and Engels: The Intellectual Relationship.* Bloomington: Indiana University Press.

———. 1989. *Friedrich Engels: His Life and Thought.* New York: St. Martin's.

Gouldner, Alvin W. 1980. *The Two Marxisms: Contradictions and Anomalies in the Development of Theory.* New York: Seabury.

Hunley, J. D. 1991. *The Life and Thought of Friedrich Engels: A Reinterpretation.* New Haven, Conn.: Yale University Press.

Levine, Norman. 1975. *The Tragic Deception: Marx Contra Engels.* Oxford: Clio.

———. 1984. *Dialogue Within the Dialectic.* London: Allen & Unwin.

Lichtheim, George. 1961. *Marxism: A Historical and Critical Study.* New York: Praeger.

Marcus, Steven. 1974. *Engels, Manchester, and the Working Class.* New York: Vintage.

Marx, Karl, and Friedrich Engels. 1996. *Later Political Writings.* Ed. and trans. Terrell Carver. Cambridge: Cambridge University Press.

Mazlish, Bruce. 1989. *A New Science: The Breakdown of Connections and the Birth of Sociology.* New York: Oxford University Press.

Riazanov, D. B. 1973. *Karl Marx and Friedrich Engels.* New York: Monthly Review Press.

Rigby, S. H. 1992. *Engels and the Formation of Marxism: History, Dialectics, and Revolution.* Manchester: Manchester University Press.

Politics
and
Social Science

8

Friedrich Engels and the Origins of German Revisionism: Another Look

Manfred B. Steger

Was Friedrich Engels the first Marxist "revisionist"? As is well known, there has been the long-standing charge that Marx's collaborator was, in fact, responsible for "vulgar Marxism"—a "crude" form of positivism and materialist dogmatism that culminated in "Soviet Stalinism" (Levine 1975, 228; Jordan 1967, 332–33). Curiously enough, however, one also encounters the opposite reading, which portrays the aging Engels as moderating his theoretical outlook on the role of force, the value of parliamentary elections, and historical materialism. Indeed, this issue seems to have taken center stage in the last decade of Engels scholarship. While some historians of the German labor movement vehemently reject the notion that, in his last years, Engels substantially altered his views on these matters (Tudor and Tudor 1988, 32–37; Gilcher-Holtey 1986, 126; Gustafsson 1972, 76–79), others suggest a definitive link between the "new" evolutionism of his later writings and the piecemeal reformism of his famous protégé, the "archrevisionist" Eduard Bernstein (Gneuss 1962, 35; Elliott 1967, 71–88; Colletti 1972, 45–108; Heimann 1977, 6; Lehnert 1977, 169–70; Meyer 1977, 101–10; Kolakowski 1978, 109; Stammer 1989, 134–40; Rogers 1992, 58).

Despite their intellectual disagreements, exponents of both sides frequently share a serious interpretive deficiency: the failure to connect their reading of crucial texts to a thorough analysis of their specific political contexts (see, for example, Kolakowski 1978, 98–114; Colletti 1972, 45–108). Without serious consideration of this weighty contextual dimension, however, the quarrel over Engels's alleged revisionism assumes a rather abstract character. As I argue in this chapter, Engels's new position on party tactics and historical materialism cannot be presented as a mere development of "ideas" on a purely theoretical plane. In order to address the full dimension of Engels's possible implication in Bernstein's "evolutionary socialism" (Steger 1997), the critical analysis of Engels's later work must be substantiated by a discussion of its historical setting.

Therefore, the present chapter situates Engels's crucial 1890s letters on historical materialism and his 1895 introduction to Marx's *Class Struggles in France* within the dramatically changed political situation in fin-de-siècle Germany, ultimately explaining his new position as a purely tactical, and at the same time deeply ambiguous, response to concrete challenges at the party level. New political imperatives arising from the regained "legal" status of the German Social Democratic Party (SPD), the intellectual provocations posed by young socialist radicals, and the transformation of social democracy into a mass movement competing for electoral success pushed Engels into endorsing short-term tactics of accommodation while at the same time seeking to maintain his overly optimistic assessment of the potential for a revolutionary seizure of power.

As a result, Marxist theory—though never free of contradictory tendencies (Gouldner 1980)—accumulated even more internal tensions and inadequacies. Forced to respond to a sociopolitical setting that defied revolutionary expectations, Engels attempted to wed gradualist tactics with revolutionary objectives. Consequently he not only lost any meaningful analytical distinction between "evolution" and "revolution," but also compromised Marxism's most ambitious claim: the purported unity of theory and practice. Ultimately, Engels's position contributed to the further decline of the status of "theory" in the SPD and strengthened the role of the instrumentalist party tacticians—the so-called *Praktiker* (pragmatists). Ever further removed from political reality, socialist theory increasingly became a convenient "grab bag" for both orthodox Marxists and the *Praktiker,* who had no difficulty legitimizing their conflicting interpretations.

In fact, in the name of "tactical considerations," theory could be ignored altogether.

Hence Engels's later writings provide a link to Marxist revisionism to the extent that they inspired Bernstein (1993, 28) to draw the full consequences of his mentor's expressed intentions to engage in a "further development and elaboration of Marxist doctrine." However, unlike his master, Bernstein was keenly aware that a fatal crisis of capitalism was not on the horizon and thus took it upon himself to synchronize Engels's revised tactics with his own revisionist model. In the end it was Bernstein, not Engels, who acted on the crucial Marxist imperative for "unity of theory and reality, of formulation and action" (Bernstein in Tudor and Tudor 1988, 324). Realizing that much of what Marx and Engels had to say about socioeconomic development no longer matched a "realistic" assessment of modern capitalism, Bernstein chose to endorse reformist practice and revise Marxist theory—the least damaging alternative available to remedy the "striking divergence between reality and the presuppositions of our theory" (326).

Dawn of a New Era

"February 20, 1890, marks the beginning of the German revolution," an enthusiastic Engels wrote to Laura Marx-Lafargue six days after the SPD's breathtaking electoral triumph (MEW 37:359). Polling almost 1.5 million votes out of close to 10 million, German social democracy had successfully made the transition from a small movement garnering only 314,000 votes two years before Marx's death to a well-organized mass party—the second strongest in the *Reich*. The same year also saw the dismissal of Imperial Chancellor Otto von Bismarck and the lapse of his repressive "Anti-Socialist Laws," which had crippled the German labor movement for twelve years. Gone were the old days of conservative stability under the stalwart triumvirate of Emperor Wilhelm I, Field Marshal von Moltke, and Chancellor Bismarck.

Kaiser Wilhelm II and his new chancellor, Caprivi, eagerly embarked on a "New Course" vis-à-vis the "workers' question," and their calculated moderation was echoed by labor leaders, who refused to jeopardize the expected "legalization" of the SPD in the autumn of 1890. The new era cried out for a fundamental reevaluation of party tactics built on the old political realities of oppression, marginalization, rigid opposition, and underground resistance. True, the long years of illegality had not only strengthened the party's resiliency but had also contributed to the swift dissemination of Marxist ideas. After all, Marxist doctrine would never have planted its roots so firmly into the German labor movement had not actual sociopolitical conditions in the 1880s corresponded to its revolutionary message of an all-out class war. But a window of opportunity— social truce—had at last opened up for German social democracy, and nobody knew that better than Friedrich Engels.

With the prospect of legalization and relatively open electoral campaigns, Georg von Vollmar, Eduard David, and other leaders of the SPD's moderate wing resurrected the old reformist model of social transformation based on the principles of limited interaction with bourgeois parties on particular issues (Gilcher-Holtey 1986, 54–57). While both Engels and August Bebel, his trusted friend and SPD party leader, successfully resisted calls for an absolute "reformism," both men agreed on a temporary strategy of endorsing "gradualism." In their opinion, the rapid growth of the labor movement could only be maintained under conditions of legality and without launching nasty provocations against the kaiser's government. Nothing would be more devastating for German social democracy than a new round of oppressive measures before the labor movement was strong enough to muster a decisive revolutionary response. Reacting to the kaiser's new politics as a mere "tactician" and without even entertaining profound theoretical concerns, Engels repeatedly warned party radicals against premature forms of direct action. For example, pointing to the volatile political climate in Germany, he counseled against SPD-led demonstrations in celebration of "Labor Day." In addition, in a letter to Adolph Sorge, he dismissed calls for a general strike on that day as "horrendous stupidity" (MEW 37:395). Throughout the 1890s, Engels upheld, "for the time being," "peacefulness, legality, and restraint" (MEW 37:366, 381).

In a steady flow of communication with the SPD leadership during his exile in London, Engels argued that socialist success in the "New Era" depended on both clever tactics and a "clear Marxist direction." He thus urged his German comrades to draft a new party program that would replace the old eclectic platform of the 1875 Gotha Compromise. In Engels's opinion, the Gotha Program was fraught with "theoretical inconsistencies" and the "pernicious state socialist terminology" of the legendary Ferdinand Lassalle, the late labor leader and former ideological rival of Karl Marx (for the most detailed account of the events surrounding the drafting of the 1891 Erfurt Program, see Gilcher-Holtey 1986, 60–100). Though the new 1891 Erfurt Program, designed by Engels's main pupils,

Bernstein and Kautsky, did not include his urgent demands for the "creation of a German democratic republic," he nonetheless expressed great satisfaction with the final draft. Once again bowing to political imperatives, Engels accepted Bebel's explanation that such radical stipulations had to be dropped for the sake of maintaining the party's legal status. In the end, fears of government reprisals had outweighed theoretical "correctness."

In fact, what bothered Engels much more than Bebel's extreme tactical caution was the sudden rise of a vociferous radical faction in the SPD known as the Youngsters. These self-proclaimed "revolutionary Marxists," who had begun to exercise considerable influence over a number of socialist newspapers, fiercely attacked the party leadership's gradualist tactics. Attracting scores of young intellectuals to their cause, they accused Bebel and Liebknecht of abandoning revolutionary Marxist principles in favor of a "despicable petty-bourgeois opportunism" (Pierson 1993, 19–33). In this regard, the Youngsters faction resembled the British Social Democratic Federation (SDF), led by Henry M. Hyndman and Ernest Belfort Bax— two self-styled "Marxists" whose rather simplistic reading of *The Communist Manifesto,* combined with their incessant calls for radical measures, had long irked the founders of "scientific socialism." In the past, Hyndman and Bax had found themselves embroiled in a series of nasty clashes with the "General," as Engels was called by his German comrades. As a result, Engels openly warned his London associates against supporting Hyndman's narrowly conceived "vulgar Marxism," which, in his judgment, sought to "transform our theory into the rigid dogma of a purist sect" (MEW 39:245, 308). Seconded by his fellow-in-exile, Eduard Bernstein, Engels was forced to wage an exhausting war of words against the SDF's revolutionary propaganda.

Thus, when Bebel and Liebknecht asked the General for some "authoritative scripture" directed against the Youngsters' left-wing attacks, he hardly hesitated to employ his well-oiled arsenal of anti-SDF invectives in order to teach these "arrogant students, blown-up literati, and other young, degraded upstarts" a lesson in "appropriate political tactics" (MEW 22:66–70, 84; 37:450–51). Scornfully dismissing their radical line as "frantically distorting Marxism," the co-author of *The Communist Manifesto* cheerfully applauded the party for eventually expelling these "rabble-rousing" Youngsters leaders. Just to stay balanced, however, Engels made sure to turn his fury against the *Praktiker* faction as well, calling them "petty bourgeois socialists" who were soon destined to "bite the dust" (MEW 38:448).

There can be no doubt that young Eduard Bernstein was deeply influenced by his mentor's apparent turn toward political pragmatism. It appeared to him as though the fundamentally changed political situation had convinced Engels *in principle* of the general value of parliamentary elections and the "peaceful" transformation of capitalist society. Bernstein seemed to assume that his mentor was moving closer to the kind of Fabian evolutionism that he himself had gradually come to espouse (Steger 1992, 647–63). After all, had not the General, in an interview with the prominent French newspaper *Le Figaro,* redefined his understanding of "revolution" by insisting that the "so-called socialist society" was not a fixed concept, but a constantly changing and evolving social phenomenon, making "us [socialists] all evolutionists" (MEW 22:542)? Didn't he declare it "suicidal" to talk about a revolutionary seizure of power at a time when objective historical developments clearly favored the parliamentarian road, probably putting "social democracy into power as early as 1898" (MEW 22:243, 10)? Finally, didn't he seek to temper the revolutionary fervor of the French Labor Party by warning its leader, Paul Lafargue, against "moving too close to the antiquated principles of Blanquism" (MEW 39:89)?

For a variety of reasons, however, Bernstein naively disregarded the remaining revolutionary core underlying his mentor's mantle of tactical moderation. As Henry Tudor has pointed out (in Tudor and Tudor 1988, 35), the main reason for Bernstein's bad judgment was his fundamentally different conception of the relationship between means and ends. For Engels, whose confidence in revolutionary change remained unshaken, switching political tactics was but a sober act of calculation designed to find the most appropriate and successful mode of action for the SPD. There were no ethical principles involved in calculating the revolutionary advent of proletarian rule along "strict mathematical laws" (MEW 22:250; 38:189). Had Bernstein listened less selectively, he would have easily detected his mentor's purely instrumental attitude: "Setting the moral question aside, as a revolutionary I welcome any means—both the most violent one and the seemingly most restrained—that will lead to the end.... In my opinion, you [Gerson Trier] are mistaken to turn a purely tactical question into one involving principles" (MEW 37:327).

"Honest Ede" Bernstein, on the other hand, deeply abhorring violence as a means of social change in complex, modern societies, sought to escape the amoral, instrumental means-ends calculations of the political realist. Sympathetic to Kant's ideal of the "moral politician," he refused to separate means and ends for purely tactical advantage: "Democracy is both means and end. It is a weapon in the struggle for socialism, and it is the form in which socialism will be realized" (Bernstein 1993, 142). His high moral standards of toleration, cooperation, and the dignity of human life ultimately transcended narrow class interests, constituting a conviction his more sober mentor would have found deeply troubling had he lived through the 1898–1903 "Revisionist Controversy" of German social democracy.

Seen from Engels's perspective, a temporary, purely tactical support of the "parliamentary road" and "legality" was entirely reconcilable with the overall Marxist blueprint of "objective developments" propelling capitalist society toward the great revolutionary abyss. What Engels neglected, however, was the damaging effect of such an instrumental gradualism on the entire body of Marxist theory. After all, Marxism demanded to be judged, not as a traditional science, but as a committed unity of theory and practice, always dependent upon the concreteness of historical events. True, certain elements in the Youngsters' faction could easily be chided for subscribing to a "subjectivist," and even "anarchist," position. Yet the majority of the young intellectuals who had joined the party in the turbulent 1880s embraced revolutionary Marxist theory both as a schematic rationale and as a guide to action. Their radical fervor was deeply anchored in those memorable lines of *The Communist Manifesto* that had so confidently predicted the deepening of economic and political crises, the polarization of society, and the violent seizure of power by the proletariat. For a good many of these "Young Turks," Engels's attack against the Youngsters, coupled with his instrumental defense of reformist tactics, seemed to run counter to the very backbone of Marxist theory—the Marxist materialist conception of history. Indeed, wasn't its central tenet, the growing antagonism between the forces and relations of production, and the subsequent disjuncture between the economic base and political-ideological superstructure, that which made revolution inevitable?

Here was the Youngsters' real challenge to Engels: if theory depended on practice and vice versa, didn't his sudden endorsement of legality and electoral concerns ultimately *have to* translate into a "revision" of theory as well? In fact, their challenge was even more serious in that it did not commence from an abstract critique of theoretical inconsistencies, but was deeply rooted in the immediate political context of German social democracy. Confused about the exact role of economic and political factors in the historical development of capitalism, young party members like Conrad Schmidt, Joseph Bloch, and Franz Mehring wrote to Engels, asking him to elaborate in greater detail on the nature of cause-and-effect relationships between base and superstructure.

Given the existing political pressures from both ideological ends of social democracy, the General's response was predictably ambiguous. One thing was for sure: his new pronouncements differed to some extent from Marx's famous exposition of historical materialism offered in his 1859 preface to *A Contribution to the Critique of Political Economy*. This is not to say that Marx's preface represents the be-all and end-all of historical materialism; surely, a more "idealist" recognition of the active role of superstructural factors can be found in Marx and Engels's works as early as *The German Ideology*. But we must remember that the latter study was not published until much later, and most Marxist socialists identified historical materialism with the very succinct and compact passages of Marx's preface (Bottomore 1983, 206).

Letters on Historical Materialism

From the very outset, Engels's letters indicated that the Youngsters' "rigid" applications of the 1848 *Communist Manifesto* to the historical context of the 1890s were rooted in an overly simplistic understanding of Marx's method. He forcefully reminded his young correspondents that "the whole Marxist conception is not a doctrine, but a method. There are no instant dogmas, only points of reference for further investigation and the method for this investigation" (MEW 37:447; 39:428). But Engels also implicitly acknowledged that those "vulgar" interpretations of historical materialism offered by the Youngsters exposed the existing unstable compromise in Marxist theory between the alleged primacy of causal determination and the role of human volition. Here Engels encountered the following pivotal problem: if the ultimate causes of historical events were to be found neither in ideology (Hegel) nor in the undialectical "old materialism" of Büchner and Dühring, how then was it possible to conceptualize primary sociohistorical structures in terms of which humans have motives and act?

Responding to this challenge in "dialectical" fashion, Engels, in his famous 1886 study of Ludwig Feuerbach, had argued that it was impossible to explain what happened in history by appealing exclusively to the personal motives of individuals: "The many individual wills active in history produce, for the most part, results other than those intended.... Their motives in relation to the total result are therefore only of secondary significance" (Engels 1935, 62). While this explanation successfully set limits to sheer voluntarism and the idealist credo of an "autonomous human consciousness," the exact relationship between ultimate causation operating at the economic base and human will remained unresolved. In his 1890s letters on historical materialism, however, Engels sought to address the "vulgar materialism" of his young critics more directly by moving toward a more "interdependent" model of historical materialism. Enhancing the causal significance of the ideological superstructure, he clearly weakened the economic determinism of Marx's 1859 preface.

To the surprise of his correspondents, Engels acknowledged the presence of "substantial holes" in their "old" conception of history: "[W]e [Marx and Engels] have neglected the formal side in favor of the content: the mode in which mental representations arise" (MEW 39:96). In Engels's letter to Bloch (MEW 37:463), Marx's method suddenly emerged as an extremely complicated model for explaining social change: "According to the materialist conception of history, the production and reproduction of real life are the determining factors only in the last instance.... If somebody twists it into meaning that the economic factor is the only determining factor, then the previous sentence is turned into a meaningless, abstract, and absurd phrase."

Engels probably wouldn't have accepted the charge that he was "revising" historical materialism; in his mind, he was simply defining his and Marx's earlier views with more clarity and greater precision (MEW 37:463). Indeed, he reasserted the pioneering Marxist notion of "ultimate" economic necessity, arguing that human history proceeded in the fashion of natural evolution and its "laws of motion": "[I]ndividual wills tend to conflict with each other, and the result is something that wasn't willed by anybody" (MEW 37:464).

Yet his stronger emphasis on the "interdependence" of base and superstructure gave religious, juridical, and philosophical elements far greater significance than Marx had given to them in his 1859 preface (MEW 39:206). Rather than clarify the role of consciousness in relation to economic factors, Engels's "qualified" historical materialism remained deeply ambiguous, open to a number of different, and even contradictory, interpretations. For example, once Engels allowed that the economic base could be substantially impacted by "relatively autonomous political factors" (MEW 37:490), it took Bernstein only a small change in emphasis to derive his full-blown revisionist proposition: "[I]t is neither possible nor necessary to give socialism a purely materialist basis" (1993, 200).

In other words, Bernstein readmitted political and ideological forces *alongside* purely economic factors, thereby turning Engels's determining "last instance" into the causal pluralism of parallel acting forces, all capable of causing significant and lasting social change. Such "revised" models of historical materialism struggled to retain the explanatory and predictive value of Marx's original emphasis on economic determination: "An economic conception of history need not mean that only economic forces, only economic motives, are recognized. It need only mean that economics constitute the ever-recurring decisive form, the pivot on which the great movements in history turn" (Bernstein 1993, 22). Refusing to drop economics as the *primum agens* of history, and at the same time eager to emphasize the role of ideas, Bernstein's version of historical materialism lost its coherence in a vast number of complex, interacting influences: "Whoever employs the materialist conception of history nowadays is duty bound to use it in its most developed and not in its original form. This means that, in addition to the development and the influence of the forces of production, he is duty bound to take full account of the legal and moral concepts, the historical and religious traditions of every epoch, geographical and other natural influences, which include the nature of man himself and his intellectual dispositions" (16). Indeed, once the methodological basis for the prediction of distinct stages in social development was weakened, socialism reverted from a "science" back to an uncertain ethical enterprise of "Kantian hope." Hence Engels's emphasis on the "relative independence" of ideological factors was not only the point of departure for Bernstein's revisionism, but it also created an opening for "neo-Kantian" socialists like Max Adler, Kurt Eisner, and Karl Vorländer, who sought philosophically to justify their political reformism by wedding Marx's economic analysis with the conceptual framework of Critical Idealism (Keck 1977, 105–19; Van der Linden 1988).

Gareth Stedman Jones (1973, 35) echoes the common assessment of Engels's letters when he notes that "[t]he absence, on the theoretical plane, of any mechanism to connect the determination of the last instance by the economy and the relative autonomy of the superstructure, was reproduced on the political plane in an inability to produce a systematic theory of revolutionary politics." In fact, however, it was the other way around: concrete challenges on the political plane exposed and exacerbated theoretical inconsistencies. This problem—the widening gap between the SPD's practices/tactics as a direct response to political reality and Marxist theory—was enhanced with every month that passed without a proletarian seizure of power. Yet as late as 1895, an optimistic Engels was still preaching his "new tactics" of gradualism as a temporary measure preceding the revolution.

Engels's "Political Testament"

Before moving on to an interpretation of Engels's 1895 introduction to Marx's *Class Struggles in France*—an essay often referred to as Engels's "political testament" (since he died later in 1895)—it is necessary to turn briefly to the ongoing controversy over the "correct" version of the text in question (Steinberg 1971, 115–26; Kellogg 1991, 158–74; Hunley 1991, 96–112; Rogers 1992, 55–58). When Engels finished the draft of his introduction in early 1895, the German Reichstag representatives were hotly debating the so-called *Umsturzvorlage* (revolution bill), a legal blueprint designed once again to curtail the political activities of the labor movement.

Moreover, political events once again dictated theoretical considerations. In order to placate the worried party executive committee, Engels reluctantly agreed to the deletion of certain passages that Conservatives might pick out as "evidence" for the "subversive" plans of social democracy. Before Engels was able to publish his piece, Liebknecht, the editor in chief of the prestigious party organ *Vorwärts*, managed to get hold of the edited copy. Failing to ask Engels's permission, Liebknecht proceeded to revise the essay as he saw fit. The General was furious: "To my great astonishment I saw in *Vorwärts* today an extract from my 'Introduction,' printed and trimmed without my prior authorization in such a fashion that I appear as a peaceful worshipper of legality *under any circumstances*" (MEW 39:452). Insisting that he was advocating such tactics "only for *today's Germany* and even there still *with considerable reservations*," Engels immediately demanded that the edited manuscript he had authorized himself be published in Karl Kautsky's *Neue Zeit* (MEW 39:458). Kautsky obliged, and Engels approved of this version in two separate letters to Bernstein and Richard Fischer (Steinberg 1967, 177, 182–85; Rogers 1992, 56–57).

In 1925, David Riazanov, a Russian scholar and director of the Moscow Marx-Engels Archives, published the deletions made to satisfy the party executive committee, falsely implying that these had occurred against Engels's will. As Kendall Rogers noted, Riazanov's work facilitated the common misunderstanding that Engels's protests against Liebknecht's excerpts in *Vorwärts* were directed instead against the *Neue Zeit* version of the introduction (Rogers 1992, 56). Unfortunately, the lingering confusion over these events makes a number of recent publications on Engels's alleged revisionism close to irrelevant. (Regrettably Paul Kellogg's [1991] "Engels and the Roots of 'Revisionism': A Re-evaluation" is such an example. While Kellogg is correct to claim that the entire text of the introduction was not published until 1930, he fails to make the crucial distinction between the authorized, edited "Kautsky Version" and the unauthorized, edited "Liebknecht Version.") While it is true that even Engels's edited but authorized "Kautsky Version" of his introduction suffered somewhat from the desire of his Berlin comrades not to say anything that might be used as a means to assist in passing the Revolution Bill, the text retained its radical theoretical framework despite its clear endorsement of short-term gradualist tactics. After all, Engels agreed to these changes, thus assuming responsibility for the entire content of the essay. Let us now examine the text itself.

From the outset, Engels reiterated that the revolutionary model developed in *The Communist Manifesto* turned out to be an illusion: "History proved us [Marx and Engels] ... wrong. It showed that the degree of economic development on the Continent was by far not ripe enough to do away with the capitalist mode of production" (MEW 22:513, 515). Here Engels opened himself up to Bernstein's later critique (1993, 8) that he was indulging in a "utopian way of thinking in socialist theory." After all, if Marx and Engels were wrong in 1848, couldn't Engels be wrong again about a pending revolutionary confrontation with the kaiser's regime in 1895?

In line with the overall tenor of the opening paragraphs of his introduction, Engels kept emphasizing that the leaders of a future proletarian "social revolution" could no longer expect to find guidance in the historical precedents of 1789, 1830, and 1848, when "small conscious minorities" led the "dull masses" in "old-style rebellions" characterized by strategies of "street-fighting and barricades" (MEW 22:519, 523). An astute military historian, Engels realized that modern armies were far better trained and equipped to deal with such insurrections than their predecessors fifty years ago; in this regard, the 1871 Paris Commune had taught the proletariat a painful but valuable lesson. The point was to remind overly radical elements within German social democracy to resist the temptation to face the kaiser's armed forces on their own terms. In a nutshell, the labor movement's "old tactics" of confrontation were urgently "in need of revision" (MEW 22:523).

Drawing an analogy to Christianity's slow but successful penetration of the Roman Empire, Engels counseled his comrades to persevere and fight a protracted "war of position," for the main task of the party was to secure the explosive growth of the labor movement. Given Engels's assumption that the historical momentum was on the side of the working class, their ultimate revolutionary goal was actually far easier to achieve under conditions of legality: "The irony of world history turns everything upside down. We, the 'revolutionaries' and 'insurrectionists' prosper far better under legal conditions than under those of illegality and revolution. The parties of the 'order,' as they call themselves, are perishing under the very legal conditions created by themselves ... while we [social democrats], under this legality, develop strong muscles and rosy cheeks and look like life eternal" (MEW 22:525).

Engels recognized the value of universal suffrage as "our best propaganda," a political instrument that "scares off enemies and boosts our morale," in addition to serving as "a perfect gauge that regularly informs us of our growing strength" (MEW 22:519). Elections were nothing but a tool that helped his party identify the crucial historical juncture (which he thought would occur around 1900) at which the majority of the Prussian soldiers would vote socialist, and thus, at the moment of confrontation, would be unlikely to follow the kaiser's orders to shoot their own comrades. Despite his calls for moderation, Engels left no doubt that he expected a revolutionary situation in Germany (MEW 22:524–25). He explicitly stated that the "discipline" and "astonishing growth" of the labor movement would eventually leave the German government no choice but to rescind this "fatal legality." By that time, he hoped, social democracy would be strong enough to win the decisive battle for state power.

Hence, even the revised "Kautsky Version" of his introduction leaves little doubt that Engels intended his new tactic of legality and gradualism as nothing more than a temporary measure: the most appropriate strategy that would buy the SPD time to survive the inevitable confrontation with the kaiser's authoritarian regime. Only the misplaced fervor of short-sighted socialist insurrectionists or a possible European war of "gigantic proportions" could, in Engels's opinion, result in a temporary setback (MEW 22:252–60). Yet ultimately the proletariat would prevail.

On his overall strategy, however, Engels found himself somewhat at odds with important party leaders. Bebel, for example, expected the working class to take power after a general economic breakdown (Steinberg 1976, 71–72; Walther 1981, 135–39), while Liebknecht considered the goal of the SPD's "new tactics" to be the assumption of an absolute majority in parliament and the subsequent *hineinwachsen* (growing into) of the current society into socialism. Conversely, Engels explicitly excluded the possibility that "the socialist party would first gain the majority [in parliament] and then seize power" (MEW 22:280). While the General and the SPD reformists agreed on revised party *tactics*, each clearly subscribed to different conceptual models of what a "socialist transformation of society" in the German context really meant. Still, the new political situation explained why Engels, who had formulated "the classical Marxist definition of 'opportunism' and mercilessly exposed every kind of opportunism in the international labor movement," was prepared to give the SPD "enormous latitude in this regard—as long as it contributed to its smooth growth" (Steinberg 1971, 126).

Conclusions

Continuing to argue for a "temporary" tactics of gradualism, Engels thought he could afford to let his underlying revolutionary theory remain basically unaffected by such instrumental changes. Bernstein, who lived much longer and came to a more realistic evaluation of capitalist development, was the first leading Marxist theorist to anticipate the pernicious long-term ramifications of maintaining the glaring gap between revolutionary theory and reformist practice: the increasing incoherence of Marxist theory, ultimately signifying different things to different people. Hoping to stem this devaluation of socialist theory in an increasingly bureaucratized SPD, Bernstein decided to bring theory once again into accordance with political reality, thus supplying a sophisticated theoretical justification for a liberal, reformist socialism. As Peter Gay (1979, 110) put it so aptly, "[I]f there had been no Bernstein, it would have been necessary to invent him," for the objective political and economic developments in Germany defied Engels's revolutionary expectations.

Hence it is a mistake to approach the matter of Engels's alleged revisionism as a merely "theoretical" question. As I have argued in this essay, the entire gestalt of this discussion needs to be recast by seriously reconsidering the historical and political framework of Engels's later writings. Indeed the conventional focus on abstract textual interpretations should be complemented by an illumination of the political factors that had such an effect on Engels's Marxism and its theoretical premises.

References

Bernstein, Eduard. 1993. *The Preconditions of Socialism*. Ed. Henry Tudor. Cambridge: Cambridge University Press.

———. 1996. *Selected Writings of Eduard Bernstein, 1900–1921*. Ed. Manfred B. Steger. Atlantic Highlands, N.J.: Humanities Press.

Bottomore, Tom, ed. 1983. *A Dictionary of Marxist Thought.* Cambridge, Mass.: Harvard University Press.

Colletti, Lucio. 1972. Bernstein and the Marxism of the Second International. In *From Rousseau to Lenin.* New York: Monthly Review Press.

Elliott, C. F. 1967. Quis Custodiat Sacra? Problems of Marxist Revisionism. *Journal of the History of Ideas* 28:71–88.

Engels, Friedrich. 1935. *Ludwig Feuerbach and the Outcome of Classical German Philosophy.* New York: International Publishers.

Gay, Peter. 1979. *The Dilemma of Democratic Socialism: Eduard Bernstein's Challenge to Marx.* New York: Octagon Books.

Gilcher-Holtey, Ingrid. 1986. *Das Mandat des Intellektuellen: Karl Kautsky und die Sozialdemokratie.* Berlin: Siedler.

Gneuss, Christian. 1962. The Precursor: Eduard Bernstein. In *Revisionism: Essays on the History of Marxist Ideas,* ed. Leopold Labedz. New York: Praeger.

Gouldner, Alvin W. 1980. *The Two Marxisms: Contradictions and Anomalies in the Development of Theory.* New York: Seabury.

Gustafsson, Bo. 1972. *Marxismus und Revisionismus.* Frankfurt: Europäische Verlagsanstalt.

Heimann, Horst. 1977. Die Aktualität Eduard Bernsteins. In *Texte zum Revisionismus.* Bonn: Verlag Neue Gesellschaft.

Hunley, J. D. 1991. *The Life and Thought of Friedrich Engels: A Reinterpretation.* New Haven, Conn.: Yale University Press.

Jordan, Z. A. 1967. *The Evolution of Dialectical Materialism: A Philosophical and Sociological Analysis.* New York: St. Martin's.

Keck, Thomas. 1977. The Marburg School and Ethical Socialism: Another Look. *Social Science Journal* 14:105–19.

Kellogg, Paul. 1991. Engels and the Roots of "Revisionism": A Re-evaluation. *Science and Society* 55:158–74.

Kolakowski, Leszek. 1978. *Main Currents of Marxism.* Vol. 2, *The Golden Age.* New York: Oxford University Press.

Lehnert, Detlef. 1977. *Reform und Revolution in den Strategiediskussionen der klassischen Sozialdemokratie.* Bonn: Verlag Neue Gesellschaft.

Levine, Norman. 1975. *The Tragic Deception: Marx Contra Engels.* Oxford: Clio.

Meyer, Thomas. 1977. *Bernsteins konstruktiver Sozialismus.* Berlin: Dietz.

Pierson, Stanley. 1993. *Marxist Intellectuals and the Working-Class Mentality in Germany, 1887–1912.* Cambridge, Mass.: Harvard University Press.

Rogers, H. K. 1992. *Before the Revisionist Controversy: Kautsky, Bernstein, and the Meaning of Marxism, 1895–1898.* New York: Garland.

Stammer, Gerhard. 1989. *Die Kunst des Unmöglichen oder die Politik der Befreiung: Über Eduard Bernsteins halbherzigen Versuch, Marx mit Kant zu korrigieren.* Frankfurt: Materialis.

Stedman Jones, Gareth. 1973. Engels and the End of Classical German Philosophy. *New Left Review,* no. 79, 17–36.

Steger, Manfred B. 1992. Historical Materialism and Ethics: Eduard Bernstein's Revisionist Perspective. *History of European Ideas* 14:647–63.

———. 1997. *The Quest for Evolutionary Socialism: Eduard Bernstein and Social Democracy.* Cambridge: Cambridge University Press.

Steinberg, H. J. 1967. Revolution und Legalität: Ein unveröffentlichter Brief Engels' an Richard Fischer. *International Review of Social History* 12:177–85.

———. 1971. Friedrich Engels' revolutionäre Strategie nach dem Fall des Sozialistengesetzes. In *Friedrich Engels, 1820–1970*, ed. H. Pelger, 115–26. Hannover: Verlag für Literatur und Zeitgeschehen.

———. 1976. *Sozialismus und deutsche Sozialdemokratie.* 4th ed. Berlin: Dietz.

Tudor, Henry, and J. M. Tudor, eds. 1988. *Marxism and Social Democracy: The Revisionist Debate, 1896–1898.* Cambridge: Cambridge University Press.

Van der Linden, Harry. 1988. *Kantian Ethics and Socialism.* Indianapolis, Ind.: Hackett.

Walther, Rudolf. 1981. "... aber nach der Sündflut kommen wir und nur wir": Zusammenbruchstheorie. In *Marxismus und politisches Defizit in der SPD, 1890–1914.* Frankfurt: Ullstein.

9

Engels and the Contradictions of Revolutionary Strategy

Lawrence Wilde

Scholarly work on Engels in recent years has concentrated on his contribution to the theory of Marxism, presenting a convincing case that what was to become Marxist orthodoxy on the questions of dialectics and materialism differed significantly from Marx's own philosophical outlook (Carver 1989, 1983; Levine 1984, 1975). To complete the picture of the role played by Engels in the invention of Marxism (Rubel 1977, 45–46), we need to examine his attempts to fashion a distinctive Marxist politics in the years following Marx's death. Engels was a consistent advocate of class struggle and social revolution, but in his final years he concluded that insurrectionary tactics had become outdated and suicidal due to the increased coercive power of the modern state. He endeavored to find a *via media* between revolutionary insurrectionism and eternal reformism, which amounted to a strategy of "revolutionary electoralism." Although he was sufficiently astute to recognize that applying this strategy involved a number of contradictions, his attempts to resolve them were often ill considered and delusory.

Engels and European Social Democracy

Before exploring the ways in which Engels confronted the contradictions
of revolutionary electoralism, it is important to recognize his significance
in the emergence of European social democracy. His authority was un-
disputed among Marx's followers, and he maintained a steady stream of
correspondence with leading figures, such as Bebel, Kautsky, Sorge, Bernstein, and Wilhelm Liebknecht in Germany; Paul and Laura Lafargue in
France; Labriola and Turati in Italy; Adler in Austria; and Zasulich, Daniel-
son, and Plekhanov in Russia. Well over a thousand letters sent by him in
the years following Marx's death have survived.

But it was his short book *Socialism: Utopian and Scientific* that set down
the "historical materialist" framework for the political programs adopted
by the social democratic parties that grew in strength across the continent
of Europe in the 1880s and 1890s. Although it appeared first in French in
1880 and then in German in 1882, its influence widened with the publication of a revised German edition in 1891 and the English edition in 1892,
and it played an important role in the adoption of a Marxist program by
the SPD (German Social Democratic Party) at Erfurt in 1891 (Steenson
1981, 192–95). The book had a strong evolutionary flavor, reflecting his
enthusiasm for Darwin. In the revised edition he forecast the gradual
weakening of capitalist power by the formation of oligopolies and the necessary increase in state intervention in the economy. Although this was an
accurate picture of capitalist development, the prediction that no nation
would put up with the barefaced exploitation of huge trusts was wildly
optimistic. Nevertheless, the general interpretation suggested a natural
evolution toward socialist forms crowned at the decisive moment when
"the proletariat seizes the public power, and by means of this transforms
the socialized means of production, slipping from the hands of the bourgeoisie, into public property" (CW 24:325).

Engels did not specify *how* the proletariat was to seize the public power,
and this was to become the central issue in the strategic debate. Kautsky,
who was close to Engels and shared his Darwinian outlook, published a
popular outline of the socialist project, *The Class Struggle*, in 1892, and
in it he argued that it was by no means necessary that a social revolution
"be accompanied with violence and bloodshed" (Kautsky 1971, 90–91). By
this time Engels had decided that the insurrectionism that had been a feature of nineteenth-century revolutions in Europe was no longer a viable
option. In a letter to Paul Lafargue in November 1892 Engels admitted

that he had no answer to the problem of finding revolutionary tactics appropriate to contemporary conditions: "The era of barricades and street fighting has gone for good; *if the military fight,* resistance becomes madness. Hence the necessity to find new revolutionary tactics. I have pondered over this for some time and am not yet settled in my mind" (MEW 38:505). When Engels attempted to clarify the problem in his 1895 introduction to Marx's *Class Struggles in France* (CW 27:506–24), it resulted in a famous controversy. Since this throws light on a range of problems concerned with political strategy, it is worth recounting the main details of the furor.

Extracts edited by Wilhelm Liebknecht and published in *Vorwärts* gave the somewhat misleading impression that Engels had totally renounced the idea of violent revolution and instead endorsed a purely gradualist strategy. In fact, although Engels was an enthusiastic supporter of the politics of the ballot box, he stipulated that socialists must be prepared to use violence if the authorities flouted their own constitution and used coercion against them. In letters to Karl Kautsky and Paul Lafargue, Engels complained of the "nice trick" that had been played on him by Liebknecht to enlist his support for those who favored "peace at any price and . . . opposition to force and violence," and insisted that his approval of electoral tactics applied only to Germany and not necessarily to other countries (MEW 39:452, 458). Even the fuller version that appeared in Kautsky's *Die Neue Zeit* omitted the passage in which Engels argued that street fighting might still be necessary at a crucial moment in a revolutionary situation (CW 27:519). A further four references to the possibility of armed struggle were censored, including mention of the "decisive day" when power would be seized (CW 27:522).

What the episode reveals is the tension involved in promoting the goal of social revolution when the organizational means for achieving it had become dependent on remaining "acceptable" to the state. When the introduction was considered by the SPD executive, four members (Bebel, Fischer, Auer, and Singer) thought it too revolutionary. Not only did Engels insist that revolutionary violence might have a part to play if the state resorted to force, but he reminded readers that all modern states, "without exception," rested on the "right to revolution" (CW 27:521). The SPD leaders were less interested in the rights or wrongs of the argument than the effect of its publication. The 1878 Anti-Socialist Law (*Sozialistengesetz*) had made life desperately difficult for socialist activists until its repeal in October 1890 (Lidtke 1966), and the leaders were naturally sensitive to the possibility that it would be reimposed. The hostility of the state was amply demonstrated in November 1895, when the Prussian authorities dissolved the organizations of the six Berlin districts on the basis of a law dating back to 1850 (Steenson 1981, 114). The restoration of legal status saw an immense leap forward in the strength of the SPD, in terms of membership, electoral support, and a wide range of organizational resources. Under these circumstances, why should the party take the risk of openly discussing the option of revolutionary violence?

When the Anti-Socialist Law was in operation, Engels had expressly rejected the demand of the authorities that German social democracy should cease to be revolutionary, arguing that if it did so, it would uphold the existing political order "for all eternity" (CW 26:308–9). He was clearly worried that a formal renunciation would encourage the development of a form of socialism that would compromise with capitalism. His response to the central committee in 1895, communicated in a letter to Richard Fischer, was that he could not "suffer the thought" that the party would pledge itself to legality in all circumstances, thereby relinquishing the right to "render armed resistance to lawlessness" (MEW 39:424). According to Engels it was always likely that the state would resort to repression, and in these circumstances socialists should make it clear that they would resist. He had made this point in an article in the Italian journal *Critica Sociale* in February 1892, stating that "the odds are ten to one that our rulers ... will use violence against us, and this would shift us from the terrain of majority to the terrain of revolution" (CW 27:271). However, from the point of view of those charged with managing the day-to-day affairs of a mass party, it seemed advisable to suppress all discussion of the possibility of violence. Engels thought that if the party was less than open about the possibility of revolution, it would slide into a position of "peace at any cost." He was anxious to maintain his unflagging commitment to social revolution by whatever means necessary, while favoring political work that clearly favored victory through peaceful means.

There is nothing contradictory in principle about the position outlined by Engels in 1895. Political democracy was to be the means to achieve power, and that power would be defended by revolutionary violence in the event of a preemptive strike by the state or a counterrevolutionary movement by forces representing the old ruling classes. The contradictions occurred when it came to applying the general principle, and Engels saw these tensions at work as he surveyed the growing strength of European social democratic parties and the early years of the Second International. Let us move on to his attempts to resolve these contradictions.

First Contradiction: Reform Versus Revolution

Why should the pursuit of constitutional politics be considered contradictory to the goal of social revolution? Rosa Luxemburg argued in the preface to her pamphlet *Social Reform or Revolution* (1899), "[F]or Social Democracy there exists an indissoluble tie between social reforms and revolution" (Luxemburg 1971, 52). She chose the title precisely in order to refute Bernstein's "revisionist" view that the means and ends *were* contradictory and that the party should abandon its commitment to revolution, a campaign he started immediately after the death of Engels. But revisionism was not simply a set of ideas set down by Bernstein. It was an outlook that reflected the daily life of the movement, including the trades unions, since progress was measured by the movement's ability to improve the lives of the German working class. It was not until after 1905 that the SPD developed a significant bureaucracy of its own (Tegel 1987, 20–24), but already it was clear that a movement building its strength through constitutional means was going to develop a respect for those means and a strong intuition for prudent self-protection (Michels 1959, 367–76).

Engels was well aware that there was a tendency to pursue reforms for the benefit of the working class while losing sight of the necessity of taking social control of the means of production. His letters are scattered with warnings against the "opportunists," "philistines," or the "petty bourgeois element" (CW 47:169, 258, 268, 290, 296, 300). In a preface to *The Housing Question* he outlined the danger of the "petty bourgeois" tendency that had crept into parts of the SPD during the period of the Anti-Socialist Law: "[W]hile the fundamental views of modern socialism and the demand for the transformation of all the means of production into social property are recognized as justified, their accomplishment is declared possible only in the distant, and for all practical purposes, unforeseeable future. Thus, for the present one has to rely on mere social patchwork, and sympathy can be shown, according to circumstances, even with the most reactionary efforts for what is known as the 'uplifting of the laboring class'" (CW 26:427–28). When the law was repealed in 1890 Engels detected a growth of "opportunism" in the social democratic press. He complained of this in 1891 in his comments on the draft program of the SPD, and felt impelled to remind them that although there might well be a peaceful development to socialism in republics like France and the United States, and even in Britain, where the monarchy was "on its last legs," in Germany the socialists would have to smash the fetters of the "semi-absolutist" political order (CW 27:226).

Engels opposed reformist socialism elsewhere in Europe, both in his advice to socialists in the various countries and in his comments on the development of the Second International. He attacked the "Possibilists" in France, and Hyndman's Social Democratic Federation in Britain (CW 27:61; MEW 37:231–32). Not only were these tendencies offering unwelcome rivalry to more militant socialists in their own countries, but in the International they wielded considerable influence when their votes were combined with moderate trade unionists. Engels also opposed the British Fabian Society, denouncing the fixation of its leaders with "money, intrigues, careerism" (MEW 38:446–48; cf. 39:53). Everywhere these tendencies were popular Engels supported the groups who were determined to act independently and explicitly for the victory of socialism against the bourgeois enemy (Steenson 1991, ch. 1). For Engels, socialist politics was always a politics of class struggle.

Engels knew that it was no easy task to maintain revolutionary conviction while pursuing reformist politics, but his reactions to the problem were reckless and exaggerated. He produced three main arguments: first, he held that as a last resort the unity of the party could be sacrificed by a split between Left and Right; second, he invoked the uncompromising socialist instincts of the politically conscious working class as a check on errant leaders; third, he held out the promise that electoralism would deliver power in the near future. He first mentioned the possibility of a formal split in a letter to Wilhelm Liebknecht in 1885: "Won't you ever get it into your head that this semi-educated pack of literati can only spoil and adulterate the party? ... The petty-bourgeois element in the party is increasingly gaining the upper hand. They want to suppress Marx's name as much as possible. If things go on like this, there will be a split in the party, on that you may depend" (CW 47:258). In letters to Paul Lafargue, Sorge, and Bernstein later in the same year he stated that he would have favored an outright split were it not for the special circumstances of the Anti-Socialist Law (CW 47:290, 296, 300). After the law was repealed Engels appeared to be reasonably satisfied with the conduct of the SPD executive and the parliamentary party, at least until the disagreement over the 1895 introduction. However, Kautsky was surely justified in his opinion that if Bernstein had aired his arguments while Engels was alive, the latter would have insisted on his expulsion from the party (see Salvadori 1979, 79). The obvious problem with the "splitting" option was that it would immediately imperil the ability of socialist parties to make the sort of electoral advances that had made them a force to be reckoned with. Formalizing a split would, in effect, recognize that "reform or revolution" *was* a genuine contradiction, a conclusion Engels strongly resisted. There was also a danger that splitting would become an easy option, thereby fragmenting the workers' movement.

Engels's faith in the uncompromising socialist instincts of the mass of the workers was not based on firsthand experience or convincing empirical evidence. It was a common enough assumption and was rehearsed by Robert Michels in his study of the SPD before the First World War (Michels 1959). Marx had written a questionnaire in 1880 to obtain a clearer picture of the attitudes and social and working conditions of workers (CW 24:328–34), but this empirical approach was not taken up by his epigones. The first survey of workers' attitudes was not conducted in Germany until 1929–31, by Hilde Weiss and Erich Fromm (Fromm 1984). Engels was obviously impressed by the fortitude displayed by working-class activists in Germany during the period of the Anti-Socialist Law. Before the elections in Germany in 1884 he lamented that there were many "milksops" among the leaders, "but my faith in the masses is unshakeable" (CW 47:152). When the "philistines" constituted a majority of the parliamentary group as a result of those elections, Engels remained confident that they did not have the support of the masses (CW 47:268). He regarded this reformist "philistinism" as quite harmless due to the "wonderful common sense of our workers" (CW 26:427–28). Even in Britain, where he and Marx had often despaired of the moderation of the working class, he was prone to exaggerate the slightest sign of radicalism as a mass awakening. So, having complained to Sorge in December 1889 that a bourgeois sense of respectability had "grown deep into the bones of the workers" (MEW 37:321), he informed Sorge only a few months later that "the day is no longer far off when this mass will suddenly *find itself,* when it will dawn upon it that it is this colossal advancing mass" (MEW 37:394–95). This instinct was given some substance by the success of the May Day celebrations in London, prompting Engels to proclaim that the English working class had roused itself from forty years of hibernation and had "rejoined the movement of its class" (CW 27:61). The coordinated demonstrations in favor of the eight-hour day throughout Europe and the United States in 1890 elicited great enthusiasm from him: "[T]he European and American proletariat is reviewing its fighting forces, mobilized for the first time, mobilized as one army, under one flag, for one immediate aim: the standard eight hour working day to be established by legal enactment. . . . If only Marx were still by my side to see this with his own eyes!" (CW 27:60). Engels can hardly be blamed for his enthusiasm over the apparent rise of class consciousness across Europe and in the United States. The years between the deaths of

Marx and Engels witnessed a remarkable rise in the number and strength of socialist parties. But the assumption that this reflected a grass roots of sufficient power to prevent their leaders from drifting to the right was highly questionable. Socialism had won its historic battle with anarchism on the basis of its ability to organize and deliver tangible achievements. Successful reformism could also be popular, as Bernstein was soon to argue, and it could be combined with a number of authoritarian or conservative traits, particularly nationalism.

It was only in the last few years of his life that Engels became an enthusiastic advocate of electoral politics, and he embraced it with the excessive zeal of a convert. In a speech to Austrian Social Democrats in September 1893, he praised universal franchise as one of the most powerful weapons in the hands of the proletariat, the sole means for gauging the power and strength of the party, as the German experience had demonstrated (CW 27:406, cf. 442). To the Italians, early in 1894, he extolled the benefits that collaboration with radicals and republicans would bring if it succeeded in securing universal franchise (CW 27:439–40). He praised the efforts of the English socialists (the embryonic Independent Labour Party) for their success in winning parliamentary seats (MEW 38:393, 396) and urged the French Workers' Party to work hard to improve its representation (MEW 39:40–41). But it was the success of the SPD that inspired his enthusiasm and produced wildly optimistic estimates of the outcome of the struggle for electoral supremacy.

In *Socialism in Germany*, written in 1891–92, he listed the six favorable election results of the SPD and declared that the point had been reached "where it is possible to determine the date when it will come to power almost by mathematical calculation" (CW 27:239–40). This typically positivist delusion was manifested in a number of similar pronouncements. In an interview with *L'Eclair* in April 1892 he expressed his hope that the German Socialist Party would come to power in ten years time (CW 27:537), and in an interview with the *Daily Chronicle* in June 1893 he predicted a socialist majority in Germany between 1900 and 1910 (CW 27:553). The 1895 introduction to the *Class Struggles* asserted that the SPD would be the "decisive power in the land" by the end of the century (CW 27:522). He qualified this optimism by warning that the German Empire would not go quietly, but he simply could not resist the temptation to offer the promise of a fast track to socialism. By arousing expectations that the revolutionary goal was in reach, he was able to play down the danger of eternal reformism, but this was a politics of gesture rather than reason. His lack of political caution was contrasted sharply with the views of Marx, who is reported to have said late in his life that all great movements are slow and that the establishment of a republic in Germany would be for socialism what the "Glorious Revolution" of 1688 was for liberalism, a "mere stage on the road" (CW 24:581). Engels's rash forecasts of imminent socialism played an important role in encouraging the revolutionary impatience that infused the Left in the Second International.

Second Contradiction: The Army Versus the People

As an experienced observer of military affairs, Engels knew that the power of the modern army was a powerful constraint on revolutionary tactics. The embrace of the electoral road to socialism provided a means of developing socialist politics while avoiding a fight that they could not win. Accordingly, Engels advised socialists not to be provoked into violent action and to distance themselves from the anarchists because of their association with political violence. But a crucial problem remained unanswered. What was to stop the army from crushing the socialists in the wake of a constitutional victory? did it need the pretext of an insurrection or a violent strike? If revolutionary socialists could not outline a scenario in which the army was effectively neutralized, then long-term reformism became the only viable option.

Engels's first concern was to avoid offering a pretext for the state to unleash its army on the socialists. Accordingly he took up the cudgels against the left-wing groups that might be tempted to fall into the insurrectionist trap. There was continuity here with the struggles conducted by Marx and Engels against the anarchists in the First International. By the time the Second International was launched in 1889 the balance of power between anarchism and socialism had altered in favor of the latter because of their considerable organizational development and electoral success. While only the SPD could claim mass support, winning 1.4 million votes at the 1890 election, the electoral strategy held out the promise of winning from governments concessions on social policy in the short term, and of implementing socialist policies in the long term. In comparison, anarchism offered an "all-or-nothing" approach that was fraught with dangers. Anarchists ensured that the 1889 Paris Conference and the 1891 conference in Brussels were lively affairs, and Engels was determined to be rid of them. When he spoke at the Zurich Congress of 1893 on the occasion of his election as president of the International, he declared himself satisfied with the resolution aimed at excluding anarchists from the organization on the grounds of their refusal to endorse participation in constitutional politics. In fact, the matter was not settled decisively until their permanent exclusion at the London Congress of 1896 (Braunthal 1966, 249–54). At first sight it might seem unexceptional for Engels and the majority of the socialist movement to refuse to have anything to do with the anarchists. The terrorist tactics used by some anarchists were an open invitation to the state to apply coercive measures against all socialists and trade unionists. But only a minority of anarchists supported terrorism, and their disavowal of parliamentarianism did not seem sufficient grounds for expulsion to many of the moderate British delegates at the 1896 congress.

The anarchists were not the only group with the potential to ignite revolutionary action. Every socialist party had a "far-left" element that might also trigger hasty and ultimately suicidal action. Although Engels was openly critical of certain leftist tendencies only sporadically, one episode is particularly revealing. It occurred in 1890 when three young activists condemned the rightward drift of the SPD leadership and suggested that it was effectively renouncing the revolutionary socialism represented by Engels. Infuriated by the implication that he had endorsed their criticisms, Engels responded by suggesting that these "academically educated" young men had more to learn from the workers than the workers had to learn from them (CW 27:71). Furthermore, the threat of the Right ("a petty bourgeois" group) was not as dangerous as that of "a clique of loud-mouthed men of letters and students" (CW 27:84–85). In a letter to one of the left-wing activists, the playwright Paul Ernst, he denied that the reformist elements in the SPD leadership constituted a majority and argued that in the course of the "joyful proletarian struggle" against the Anti-Socialist Law the Left had grown more powerful (CW 27:84–85). Ernst was expelled from the party in 1891. The "class-stereotype" vitriol displayed in this episode set the pattern for decades of mudslinging within socialism. The elements moving toward consistent reformism were dubbed "petty bourgeois", and the critics on the Left (who were merely exposing what at other times Engels was willing to admit) were denounced as intellectual dilettantes. Marx, of course, was not averse to using stinging invective, but he did not substitute name-calling for reasoned criticism. The 1879 circular letter written by Engels and Marx to the German party leaders, which complains about the right-wing stance of the editors of the party newspaper, is far more restrained in its tone than Engels's later pronouncements (CW 24:253–69).

Engels issued frequent warnings to socialist activists not to be provoked into revolutionary violence, which would give the state a pretext to crush the party, but he advised them to be prepared to take action if a clash became unavoidable. In 1884 he wrote to Bebel saying that the socialists should not go into action until the military power "ceases to be against us" (CW 47:223). In other words, although Engels knew that there was little chance of achieving power through insurrection, he was convinced the workers' movement might well have to defend itself in a political crisis. In 1890 he suspected Bismarck's government of provoking an uprising so that the Anti-Socialist Law could be reinstated, but he was confident that the workers would retain their self-discipline, particularly since so many of them had by this time gained military experience (CW 27:10). Later in the year he repeated his appeal for restraint in the face of provocation, stating that although the SPD represented "a very respectable" 20 percent of the vote, this meant that they were opposed by 80 percent, "and the army on top of that," spelling certain defeat and the loss of all the gains of the previous twenty-five years (CW 27:78–79). To Paul Lafargue in 1891 he warned of the danger of being provoked into rioting, since "we are still far from being able to withstand an open fight." He concluded that the SPD's strength lay in its very existence and its "slow, steady, irresistible progress" (MEW 38:20). In effect, Engels was expressing a confused position of "slow and steady but not *too* slow and steady."

The advice given by Engels on avoiding a bloody battle was judicious. Far more controversial was his view that the influx of class-conscious recruits into the army would weaken its reliability as an instrument of class oppression. This has been described by Martin Berger as the "Vanishing Army" formula (Berger 1977, 154–70; 1987, 227–29). Engels needed to assure the socialists that the modern state was not omnipotent, but in attempting to do so, he drifted dangerously into wishful thinking. The first hint of his idiosyncratic views on the army came in a piece published in 1876 entitled "Prussian Schnapps in the German Reichstag." Here he argued that Prussian schnapps production would be undercut by its rivals in Russia, resulting in the collapse of the Junker social system in eastern Germany and thereby undermining the social basis of the army. A new defeudalized social system would produce an army more disposed to support the social democrats than the state (CW 24:126–27). In *Le Socialiste* in 1887 he argued that if a state were to abandon the Prussian model of a standing army and replace it with a "popular army," it would double its military strength and halve its war budget. He recommended the adoption of the Swiss model, in which every citizen keeps his rifle and equipment at home. The advantages would be that the army would be overwhelmingly suited to defensive, rather than aggressive, purposes, and that in the face of the armed people, the state would not dare "lay a finger on civil liberties" (CW 26:444). But these were advantages for socialists, not for a bourgeois state. Four years later he published another article in the same journal, arguing that the mass recruitment of workers had led to the army's becoming "less secure" as a means of repression, so that state leaders "foresee with terror the day when soldiers under arms will refuse to butcher their fathers and brothers" (CW 27:177). In "Socialism in Germany," written in 1891–92, he asserted that "the German army is becoming more and more infected with socialism" (CW 27:240). In an interview with *Le Figaro* in May 1893 he extrapolated from the growth of electoral support given to the SPD the dubious conclusion that soon "we shall have half the army" (CW 27:547). This was repeated in the famous 1895 introduction to the *Class Struggles*, in which he forecast that by 1900 the army would have a socialist majority (CW 27:240).

The publication of *Can Europe Disarm?* in 1893 must rate as the nadir of his long career as a political commentator. It is written from the viewpoint of a dispassionate citizen and expert on military matters rather than that of a revolutionary socialist. He had adopted a "neutral" persona years before when writing on wars for the *Manchester Guardian* and the *Pall Mall Gazette,* which earned him the nickname of "the General" in the Marx household (Carver 1989, 227–28), but this time he was not so much "neutral" as utterly confused. In *Can Europe Disarm?* he appealed to all governments to agree to a limitation on the length of military service as a means of moving toward a militia. He had now moved away from the Swiss model by making provision for "the physical and military training of all male youths as an essential condition for the transition to the new system" (CW 27:372). The professional noncommissioned officers from the existing system could then become schoolteachers in the new model—teaching gymnastics and drill—to the mutual benefit of soldiers and boys (CW 27:380). This extraordinary pamphlet is flawed on several counts. As he made clear in a letter to Lafargue, his scheme was designed to meet objections from the bourgeoisie and the military (MEW 39:191), but this is a ludicrous claim. In the first place, the Prussian model of the professional army was popular because of its spectacular successes in the Austro-Prussian and Franco-Prussian wars. There was therefore no possibility of any state's voluntarily moving toward a militia system. But let us suspend disbelief and consider that the proposal could have some benefits in terms of military effectiveness and budget savings. The argument that the army would be less dependable as a means of repression would, however, hardly endear the model to state leaders. Nor, of course, would the diminution of offensive capacity appeal to any military mind. Finally, where was the evidence that working-class participation in the armed forces in any way mitigated the reactionary nature of those forces? Why did Engels not consider the alternative possibility that immersion in the army would bind the working class to the cause of the nation rather than the cause of the class? Engels was simply grasping at straws and, in the process, revealed a hideous ideal of the militaristic education of boys, which was later taken up in an exaggerated form by the Nazis.

Engels had another and more convincing scenario for the neutralization of the army—defeat in war. In an 1885 letter to Bebel he predicted a devastating carnage that would produce the end of the class state, a deluge after which "it's we who shall come and only we" (CW 47:354). In 1887 he predicted an intense war lasting three or four years extended over the entire continent, bringing famine and disease in its wake and causing "the universal lapse into barbarism." He predicted, again with accuracy, that "crowns will roll into the gutters by the dozen," but his strongest prediction was that these conditions would guarantee the ultimate victory of the working class (CW 26:451).

Clearly defeat in such a war would bring the state to its knees and open up the possibility of revolution, and that is precisely what happened in Russia in 1917 and Germany in 1919. Engels appeared to assume that socialists everywhere would stand apart from the hostilities and resume their international destiny when the class enemy was prostrate. But what if socialists became involved in hostilities as willing accomplices to their national ruling classes?

Third Contradiction:
Nationalism Versus Internationalism

As early as 1846 Marx and Engels had argued that communism was possible only on an international scale (CW 5:49), and Engels reiterated this forcefully in his *Principles of Communism*, referring to the necessity of simultaneous revolutions in at least England, France, Germany, and America (CW 6:352). As late as 1892, in the introduction to the English edition of *Socialism: Utopian and Scientific*, he argued that the triumph of the European working class "can only be secured by the cooperation of, at least, England, France, and Germany" (CW 27:301–2). However, as Marx and Engels had admitted in *The Communist Manifesto*, the class struggle was international only in substance, not in form; that is to say, political power was wielded within nation-states, and the proletariat of each country would "first of all [have to] settle matters with its own bourgeoisie" (CW 6:495). This form-substance distinction was brought up again by Marx in his *Critique of the Gotha Programme*, in which he flayed the proposed program of the SPD for foreswearing internationalism (CW 24:89–90). Marx was unwilling to accept that the distinction was a contradiction, but at the time, three years after the collapse of the First International, he was unable to provide more specific advice on how internationalism could be embodied in socialist politics.

The loss of the International, a central coordinating body for international socialist activity, came at a time when socialist politics began to take on its modern organizational form. The extension of the franchise in the major European states encouraged the growth of socialist parties and their participation in constitutional politics. The state machinery was also expanding to provide elementary education and a contribution to social welfare. In other words, working people might begin to see the state as a provider and be more inclined to identify with the national interest as defined by the ruling classes. Inevitably, socialist parties began to be drawn into debates concerning the "national interest," and it was not always easy to insist, as Marx and Engels had in the *Manifesto*, that "the working men have no country" (CW 6:502). Engels was involved in one such debate with comrades in the SPD, over the Steamship Subsidy Bill of 1884–85. The SPD parliamentary group was divided over whether to support a subsidy proposed by Bismarck's government for the building of postal steamships. Many SPD deputies were originally happy to support the measure, but Bebel and others were opposed. Engels suggested offering the government a compromise, asking for a similar amount of money to be given for the establishment of worker cooperatives. Although there was not the slightest chance of the government acceding to this, it implied a willingness to compromise rather than to declare outright principled opposition. A different sort of compromise was eventually attempted (without success), calling for the ships to be newly built in German yards while opposing their use on lines to the newly acquired African colonies (Lidtke 1966, 194–204). Engels thought that if the socialists simply opposed the bill on principle, they would be seen to be opposing a measure that would give work to German labor—hence the need to offer a compromise. However, in so doing the SPD was acknowledging that what the state was doing *was* in some way in the national interest. Decades of such compromise might bind the party to German nationalism.

The founding of the Second International in 1889 offered the hope of a new forum for the realization of socialist internationalism, and Engels greeted it as such. However, it lacked the executive powers granted to the general council of the First International, nor was it open to direct individual membership. It was really no more than a loose federation of national bodies, and it did not have even its own bureau during Engels's lifetime (Michels 1959, 193–96; Braunthal 1966, 243–45). Engels was aware that a strong International was essential to advancing the goal of social revolution, but his chief concern was ensuring that the majority favored a loyal "Marxist" line. He talked down its potential for coordinated international political action, praising the 1891 congress for rejecting the resolution proposed by Ferdinand Domela Nieuwenhuis that the International should call a European general strike in the event that war was declared (CW 27:233). Nieuwenhuis, one of the leaders of the Dutch Socialist League, moved his general-strike motion once more at the 1893 Zurich Congress, again without success. Engels justified his opposition to a general strike in the event of war by appealing to reality—it was a sign of maturity not to be overcome by the "resounding phrase" but to face the "facts" and realize the limitations of the power of the new organization (CW 27:233). As it happened, the general war did not break out for more than twenty years, and the decisions at these early congresses did nothing to urge the International to work for ways of applying pressure on their national governments. Gustav Mayer cites Nieuwenhuis's complaint that opposition to his motion was rooted in jingoism and was far from the principle of internationalism, and concludes with justification that Nieuwenhuis judged "more truly" developments that Engels "always explained away" (Mayer 1936, 291, 306).

If the success of socialism rested on international cooperation, it would appear obligatory for socialists to take a principled stand against the war efforts of their respective countries. However, Engels took the view that each case had to be viewed on its merits, and in particular that any struggle against Russia, the most reactionary state, should be supported. In "Socialism in Germany" he argued that German socialists would be forced to take up arms in a defensive war against the French if France sided with reactionary Russia (CW 27:244), a view he repeated in the interview with L'Eclair (CW 27:537–38). This was going much further than acknowledging that socialists lacked the power to prevent a war, and his position could later be cited to legitimize the decisions of the major socialist parties in 1914 to support the war efforts of their governments. Their leaders clearly calculated that they had far too much to lose by resisting the tidal wave of nationalism. Engels's optimism that the socialists could take advantage of the catastrophe of total war simply overlooked the logical outcome of their involvement in hostilities—the destruction of the International and splits within national parties.

Conclusions

When Engels wrote in 1893 that "things are going well everywhere" (MEW 39:41), it appeared to be a perfectly reasonable estimation of the prospects for socialism. The young socialist parties were making rapid and measurable progress, and there were growing signs of industrial militancy. The Second International had begun the task of bringing together the major socialist parties across Europe. These developments, however, masked the depth of the divisions within the socialist movement and the structural contradictions that were eventually to explode in 1914. It would be foolish to lay the responsibility for these contradictions at the door of Engels, but his revolutionary electoralism was riddled with delusion and evasion. Propagating the view that the socialists in Germany were on the verge of achieving political power contributed to the false expectations of swift social transformation that pervaded left-wing Marxism and played its part in the premature revolutionary actions of 1917–19. Although he was undoubtedly correct to warn that the state machines would be prepared to use their armies against socialists, the expectation that the further advance of socialist movements would cripple the reactionary discipline of those armies was a dangerous delusion. Only with socialist control over the state apparatus for a protracted period of time could there be a possibility that the army might be "neutralized." His idea of bringing the army closer to the people by militarizing the education system was hopelessly misguided. His opposition to using the Second International to mobilize strike action against the outbreak of war was an important and unfortunate concession to nationalism, almost certainly governed by his concern with settling old scores with the anarchists. Finally, his willingness to contemplate a scenario in which socialists from different countries could justify killing each other laid the groundwork for the actions of the socialist leaders in 1914.

Engels coined the phrase "scientific socialism," but there was little science in his politics. He made his political judgments without reference to empirical socioeconomic investigation, and he did not encourage others to engage in such work. He very much accepted the traditional liberal separation of politics from economics, despite working from a theoretical framework that was largely economistic. On the rare occasion in which he drew political conclusions from a socioeconomic study, his article on Prussian schnapps, the result was crudely deterministic and wholly unsupportable. His politics was reactive, impressionistic, riddled with wishful thinking, and frequently conducted in abusive rhetoric employed as a substitute for rational argument. Here we find the origins of twentieth-century Marxist invective, with contemptuous dismissals of socialists for being petty bourgeois, opportunists, careerists, philistines, dilettantes, and the like. Within a year of his death the argument about political strategy embroiled the entire SPD, following the publication of Bernstein's "revisionist" articles in *Die Neue Zeit.* Kautsky led the defense of orthodox Marxism against the revisionist position, which was condemned by a huge majority at the Hanover Congress of 1899 (Townshend 1996, ch. 2). The theoretical position of Engels was thereby preserved by resolution, but the contradictions in which it was mired remained stubbornly in place.

References

Berger, Martin. 1977. *Engels, Armies, and Revolution: The Revolutionary Tactics of Classical Marxism.* Hamden, Conn.: Archon.

———. 1987. Revolutionary Tactics and the Importance of Engels. In *The Crucible of Socialism,* ed. Louis Patsouras. Atlantic Highlands, N.J.: Humanities Press.

Braunthal, Julius. 1966. *History of the International, 1864–1914.* London: Nelson.

Carver, Terrell. 1983. *Marx and Engels: The Intellectual Relationship.* Brighton, East Sussex: Harvester/Wheatsheaf.

———. 1989. *Friedrich Engels: His Life and Thought.* London: Macmillan.

Fromm, Erich. 1984. *The Working Class in Weimar Germany.* Leamington Spa, Warwickshire: Berg.

Kautsky, Karl. 1971. *The Class Struggle.* New York: W. W. Norton.

Levine, Norman. 1975. *The Tragic Deception: Marx Contra Engels.* Santa Barbara, Calif.: Clio.

———. 1984. *Dialogue Within the Dialectic.* London: Allen & Unwin.

Lidtke, Vernon. 1966. *The Outlawed Party: Social Democracy in Germany, 1897–1890.* Princeton: Princeton University Press.

Luxemburg, Rosa. 1971. *Selected Political Writings.* New York: Monthly Review Press.

Mayer, Gustav. 1936. *Friedrich Engels: A Biography.* London: Chapman & Hall.

Michels, Robert. 1959. *Political Parties.* New York: Dover.

Rubel, Maximilien. 1977. Friedrich Engels—Marxism's Founding Father: Nine Premises to a Theme. In *Varieties of Marxism,* ed. Shlomo Avineri. The Hague: Martinus Nijhoff.

Salvadori, Massimo. 1979. *Karl Kautsky and the Socialist Revolution, 1880–1938.* London: New Left Books.

Steenson, Gary. 1981. *"Not One Man, Not One Penny": German Social Democracy, 1863–1914.* Pittsburgh: University of Pittsburgh Press.

———. 1991. *After Marx, Before Lenin: Marxism and Socialist Working-Class Parties in Europe, 1884–1914.* Pittsburgh: University of Pittsburgh Press.

Tegel, Susan. 1987. The SPD in Imperial Germany: 1871–1914. In *Bernstein to Brandt: A Short History of German Social Democracy,* ed. R. Fletcher. London: Edward Arnold.

Townshend, Jules. 1996. *The Politics of Marxism: The Critical Debates.* New York: Leicester University Press.

10

Engels and "Scientific Socialism"

Paul Thomas

Engels claimed in 1892 that his *Socialism: Utopian and Scientific* (three chapters excerpted from his longer and more difficult *Anti-Dühring*) was circulating in ten languages. "I am not aware," he wrote (rather Germanically), "that any other socialist work, not even our *Communist Manifesto* or Marx's *Capital,* has been so often translated. In Germany it has had four editions of about 20,000 copies in all" (Marx and Engels 1962, 2:94–95; Carver 1981, 46). This is a sobering, even alarming, claim. It suggests that significant numbers of interested readers were receptive, not necessarily to Marx in any direct sense, but to a Marxism whose scope was self-consciously extended—but also narrowed—by Engels. As he himself condescendingly put it in the privacy of a letter, "Most people are too idle to read thick books like *Capital,* so a little pamphlet does the job much more quickly" (CW 35:396; see Carver 1983, 132). In what follows I argue that this extension—and narrowing—needs urgently to be interrogated. The notion that *Socialism: Utopian and Scientific* "does the job" of *Capital* is an instance of breathtaking hubris. I argue further that Engels's arguments in *Socialism:*

Utopian and Scientific are in significant respects at variance and plainly incompatible with what Marx had said, and that the wide dissemination of Engels's arguments as surrogates for Marx's own has had effects—not just on the reception of Marx's doctrines but on the development of Marxism as a political movement—that were little short of disastrous.

The Effects of Distortion

The development of historical materialism over the late nineteenth and early twentieth centuries established a canon of theoretical writings within which Engels's offerings occupied a hallowed place. The existence of a canon, which at first was not imposed, points to a thirst for theory among German Marxists, as does the publication history of the texts that made it up, few of which were Marx's. "In Germany," writes Eric Hobsbawm (1982, 331), "the average number of copies per edition printed of the *Communist Manifesto* before 1905 was a mere 2,000 or at most 3,000 copies, though thereafter the size of the editions increased. For a comparison, Kautsky's *Social Revolution* (Part I) was printed in an edition of 7,000 in 1903 and 21,500 in 1905. Bebel's *Christenthum und Sozialismus* had sold 37,000 copies between 1898 and 1902, followed by another edition of 20,000 in 1903, and the [German Social Democratic] party's *Erfurt Programme* (1891) was distributed in 120,000 copies."

The reputation and influence of these works, which at one time was considerable, did not survive the First World War and the unexpected triumph of the Bolshevik Revolution in Russia (1917). What did survive these developments was the canonical status of Engels's works, works either like *Anti-Dühring* and *Socialism: Utopian and Scientific,* which were given a new lease of life by the Russian Revolution, or works like *Dialectics of Nature,* which were published for the first time in its wake. Engels failed to complete and publish *Dialectics of Nature* in his own lifetime. It was published and translated in short order in the Soviet Union and diffused widely, there and elsewhere, even though its editor, David B. Riazanov, the director of the Marx-Engels Institute (note the name), had believed, quite correctly, that much—some would say most—of what Engels had to say about natural science in the 1870s (when he put aside work on the book in order to write *Anti-Dühring*) was now obsolete. Nevertheless, it happened to fit into "the 'scientistic' orientation of Marxism which, long popular in Russia ... was reinforced during the Stalin era" (Hobsbawm 1982, 336)—a "scientistic" orientation, we might add, that Engels's already-published offerings played no small part in inspiring. Engels, that is to say, emerged over time as "the father of dialectical and historical materialism, the philosophical and historiographical doctrines ... [that] became the basis of official philosophy and history in the Soviet Union and in most other countries that declare themselves Marxist" (Carver 1981, 48). To the extent that Marx's early writings did not jibe with the canonical works—and we should remember that the Soviet canon, unlike the SPD canon, was state-imposed—these early works were all too frequently marginalized, and their links with Marx's later writings remained uninvestigated, save by mavericks writing in the West.

Yet selectivity had its limits. The CPSU's far-from-grudging imprimatur, its desire to put *Dialectics of Nature* into print in the shortest possible order, indicates that this same Soviet canon proved mightily hospitable to Engels's writings.

> The Russian Revolution ... transferred the center of Marxian textual scholarship to a generation of editors who no longer had personal contacts with Marx, or more usually with the old Engels. . . . This new group was therefore no longer directly influenced either by Engels' personal judgments on the classic writings or by questions of tact or expediency ... which had so obviously influenced Marx's and Engels' immediate literary executors [Eduard Bernstein, Karl Kautsky, August Bebel]. . . . [C]ommunist (and especially Russian) editors tended—sometimes quite correctly—to interpret the omissions and modifications of earlier texts by German Social Democracy as "opportunist" distortions. (Hobsbawm 1982, 332)

Yet it never entered the minds of the same Russian editors and Party stalwarts, who derogated German Social Democrats as "opportunists," to disparage Engels in anything like the same way. To the contrary, the theoreticians of the Marx-Engels Institute in Moscow presented Engels—his own disclaimers notwithstanding—as someone he had never claimed to be, someone on equal footing with Marx himself as a "classic" theorist and founding father.

The Marxist notables of the SPD and the Second International (1889–1914) had taken Engels, who had never claimed to be Marx's intellectual equal, at his word. They treated him personally as he treated himself, as Marx's junior partner. Russian Marxists, who did not have to deal at first hand with Engels's principled protestations, were governed instead by their own need to establish continuities—between Marx and Engels and thus among Marx, Engels, Lenin, Stalin, and whoever else was in vogue at the time. We have no way of knowing with any certainty whether Engels would have welcomed or approved such a development—if indeed "development" is the right word to employ, given the intellectually downward slope of the sequence. But what we can establish with some certainty is that Engels, whatever his intentions might have been, did much to make this sorry sequence possible. There is at least one sense in which the first believer in the mythic joint identity of Marx and Engels was none other than Engels himself (Carver, 1981, 73–76). To the extent that he appointed himself the posthumous alter ego of Marx (Marx's literary executor, one might say, in more senses than one), Engels is responsible for creating some of the conditions in which this same myth could take root and flourish, and in which there could be an *E* in the MEGA (the *Marx-Engels Gesamtausgabe*, the edition of their complete works that was to have been published in the Soviet Union before Riazanov's purge).

It is with Engels's canonical status in mind, his canonical status both within the SPD and—there is something remarkable about this double service—within the CPSU, that we should reexamine Engels's immense productivity, as theorist as well as *éminence grise*, between Marx's death in 1883 and his own in 1895 (the very period, on his own admission, when *Socialism: Utopian and Scientific* began to circulate widely). For he labored prodigiously, setting himself up as "the custodian not only of Marx's works but of the relationship [between Marx and Engels] itself" (Carver 1983, 118). He once complained that the translator of his *Condition of the Working Class in England*, Florence Kelly Wischnewetzky, "translates like a factory," but he produced texts like a factory himself. "In the years after Marx's death ... Engels produced prefaces to new editions of their *Communist Manifesto* (five editions), one of his own *The Condition of the Working Class in England* (two editions), and of (several) works by Marx, *The Poverty of Philosophy, Wage-Labor and Capital, The Communist Trial in Cologne,* and *The Class Struggles in France.* To these works he contributed editorial notes and changes, but his principal projects as editor were the second and third volumes of *Capital* (with prefaces)" (Carver 1981, 42–43). Engels put together *Capital* from Marx's scattered unpublished notes and drafts: it "has come down to us not as Marx intended it to, but as Engels thought he would have intended it to ... [even its] first volume is also a text finalized by Engels and not by Marx" (Hobsbawm 1982, 330). This means at one level that some of Marx's writings were made more widely available than ever before, thanks to Engels's diligence (and, for the record, that of Kautsky, who edited *Theories of Surplus Value,* and Bernstein, who edited Marx and Engels's correspondence). At another level, however, these were, in Hobsbawm's words, "a corpus of 'finished' theoretical writings [that were] intended as such by Engels, whose own writings attempted to fill the gap left by Marx and bring earlier publications up to date" (1982, 330).

Marx's writings, which often took the form of "penetrating but convoluted critiques" and which contain more than their fair share of cryptic or gnomic utterances, could well be regarded as complex and in need of the kind of simplification and popularization that Engels was not alone in bringing to bear. Engels's most recent English-language biographer points to a "steady focus on intended audience, quick publication and immediate effect" as characteristics of Engels's—though certainly not of Marx's— writings. Engels did not share Marx's "penchant for overblown satires," satires that were often mordant and heavy-handed into the bargain (Carver 1989, 181). However *terrible* he might have been—and he makes an unlikely villain—Engels was very much the *simplificateur.* But for all this, Hobsbawm's further point begs the question whether Marx would have agreed that what he had not covered in his own work left "gaps" of the kind that needed to be "filled" by others. This is a question to which I shall return.

Engels's relentless industriousness was not restricted to the reproduction or updating of Marx's texts. He also produced a large number of his own, which (we should remember) circulated, by and large, much more widely. Their scope and variety is at first glance impressive. Engels's *Peasant War in Germany* could well be regarded as "the first Marxist work of history"; Engels also could well be regarded as the first Marxist anthropologist on the basis of *The Origin of the Family, Private Property, and the State* and his manuscript on "Labor in the Transition from Ape to Man" (an early, prototypical attempt—the first of many—to combine Marx and Darwin). Nor is it too much to identify Engels as "the first Marxologist," for in writing *Ludwig Feuerbach and the Outcome of Classical German Philosophy* in 1888 (and by adding Marx's hitherto-unpublished "Theses on Feuerbach"— in an edited form—as an appendix) Engels "launched the first enquiry into the young Marx, tracing influences upon him, primarily philosophical, and searching in the earlier works for enlightenment concerning the origins and meaning of the later ones" (Carver 1981, 53). That *Feuerbach* is evidently a skewed account of Marx's development (see Carver 1983, 137–39) may be less important than what the book stood for. It established a modus operandi for dealing with Marx's development as a theorist, one that is still, in its broadest sense, followed today. There is more than one sense in which "the study of Marx has been footnotes to Engels" (Carver 1984, 256).

These are achievements of some moment, but whose moment depends, in large measure, on the assertion of a joint identity between Marx and Engels that accompanied them into the canon; Engels referred self-consciously to "our doctrine" on several occasions. Engels, in *Anti-Dühring*, tried to produce an "encyclopaedic survey of our conception of ... philosophical, natural, scientific and historical problems" (CW 36:136). But his use of the first-person plural is misprized. There is no evidence for *any* joint doctrine outside of Engels's insistence that it was somehow—or had to be—"there." Let us be plain. Engels's post-Marxian doctrines owe little or nothing to the man he called his mentor. Historical materialism—Engels's term—was something left to us not by Marx but by Engels (even though he originally credited it to Marx). Even if—or precisely because—Engels "brought Marxism into existence" and "put Marxism on the map" (Carver 1981, 38), Engels's Marxism had an improperly scientistic aspect that is radically, and demonstrably, at variance with Marx's approach, method, and even subject matter.

Engels claimed, in *Socialism: Utopian and Scientific* and elsewhere, that Marx's method produced a law of historical development of the kind that invited comparison with Darwinian biology. He proceeded blithely but fatefully to make claims about the certitude and universality of this "law" that have no counterpart in any of Marx's writings. "Just as Darwin discovered the law of development of organic nature," Engels declaimed at Marx's graveside, "so Marx discovered the law of development of human history" (Marx and Engels 1962, 2:167)—a law that is, however, nowhere to be found in Marx's writings. Marx's laws of capitalist development—which are tendential lawlike statements rather than anything else—were never intended to have any application outside the capitalist mode of production. Marx, unlike Engels, never equated these laws with the laws of matter in motion, laws that he never even discussed. Engels, not to put too fine a point on it, departed from Marx in claiming that he had found a historical law in accord, in some ultimate causal sense, with all events. Neither Engels's view that one, unitary set of dialectical laws accounts for all phenomena nor his view that "dialectical philosophy itself is nothing more than the mere reflection of this process in the thinking brain" (Marx and Engels 1962, 2:363) appeared in print before Marx's death. Moreover, "by interpreting 'material life' [Marx's phrase] to imply the materialism of the physical sciences, Engels glossed Marx's view of [individuals and their] material productive activity out of all recognition" (Carver 1981, 68).

Indeed, Engels's unwarranted extraction from Marx of a scientistic historical materialism "gave the impression that Marx was merely reflecting an historical course" in his own theoretical writings, rather than doing what he said he was doing: "subjecting a body of economic theory (*Capital*'s very subtitle is "Critique of Political Economy") to logical, philosophical, mathematical, social, political, and historical analysis" (Carver 1981, 40).

This impression, wrongheaded though it was, became readily, indeed eagerly, seized upon by others—either by those in Germany who were intent on developing Engels's historical materialism into a *Weltanschauung* (or worldview), or by those in Russia to whom historical materialism so understood (and shorn of its "opportunistic" aspects, to be sure) needed assimilation within that Soviet monster, dialectical materialism. The implications of such seizures both for the reception or understanding of Marx's thought and for Marxism's subsequent, and consequent, degeneration into an ossified dogma were, in a word, disastrous. Marxism in short order became what it has been ever since: a galaxy of contending creeds within which Marx's thought, effectively marginalized in the jostle at the very point where it should have been most useful, occupies an ambiguous place. Historical materialism perforce turned into what was not so much a means of explanation as an object of study in its own right—by which point the damage was well and truly done. Even before the Bolshevik Revolution set it in stone, historical materialism had become "an object of exegesis independent of the complexities it was designed to summarize" (Carver 1981, 63).

Engels was of course by no means the sole person to blame for this sorry story of confusion worse confounded. But he bears a degree and kind of responsibility for it, in the sense that his misrepresentation of Marx's legacy made possible or sanctioned in advance later, worse misrepresentations, which came almost to feed on one another exponentially. Even though a fateful degree and kind of distortion of Marx's views can be laid, for this reason, fairly and squarely at Engels's door, mendacity and perfidy cannot. (Would that we could say the same of his successors, who garbled Marx's message even further.) Even though Engels never claimed to have familiarized Marx with the arguments of *Dialectics of Nature*, it probably never occurred to Engels that his accounts of what Marx had really meant—or must have meant—could conflict with Marx's insights, or that his extensions of what he took to be Marx's method into uncharted regions were in any way out of line or incompatible with what Marx had accomplished (Carver 1981, 60). That Engels was anything but the last of the true believers in the mythical joint identity of Marx and Engels speaks to and impugns the ulterior motives of later theorists, stalwarts, and doctrinaires whose utterances neither Marx nor Engels could possibly have foreseen. But if the employment of Marx's resources was dogmatic and slanted from the outset, and if, as seems clear, not all of this was Engels's responsibility, he still has a lot to answer for. By making of Marxism a more universal, more scientistic theory than Marx had ever wanted it to be, Engels left behind the impression that Marx had provided posterity with a key to unlock every door—which leaves Marx himself as a historical figure high and dry.

The disservice done to Marx by the orthodox Marxist-Leninist worldview is to have turned his thought into the kind of overarching theory that Marx never intended to provide. Marxism-Leninism constructed around Marx's writings, to the extent that these were made available, a grand theory concerned with the ultimate laws and constituents of the universe, the natural as well as the social world, even though Marx himself had maintained discretion on such cosmic questions. Naturalism and cosmology were distant from, even alien to, Marx's brief, the critique of political economy. Worse still, it was in a sense precisely because Marx had remained reticent on these issues, while claiming a more limited scientific status for his more narrowly defined field of inquiry, that his admirers and followers—to whom Marx's reticence evidently seemed strange and unnerving—felt the need to fill in the "gaps" and construct a coherent, comprehensive system of materialist metaphysics. Yet Marx's sustained silence about many of the issues that came to be held to constitute his "system" denoted not a failure of scholarly nerve but a well-judged reluctance to extend his arguments into the domains of nature and physical science, domains to which his arguments could have no meaningful application. When we ask ourselves who thought that Marx's arguments could and should be extended in such untoward directions, and who regarded natural science and the laws of thought as "gaps" needing to be "filled" with Marxist argumentation, Engels is the earliest theorist to snap into focus.

Eric Hobsbawm claims that *Anti-Dühring* was the book "through which, in effect, the international socialist movement was to become familiar with Marx's thought on questions other than political economy" (1982, 2:328). But quite apart from the probability that this honor should be claimed, not by the ponderous and elephantine *pièce de circonstance* that was *Anti-Dühring*, but by *Socialism: Utopian and Scientific* instead, Hobsbawm's claim is disingenuous. Marx, by 1877–78, when *Anti-Dühring* first appeared, had written very little on "questions other than political economy," at least according to his own rather broad understanding of the term, and in future years was to add even less. This means that the international socialist movement had perforce to be made "familiar" with something having little real existence. Small wonder, perhaps, that such familiarity was quick to breed contempt among readers who were not predisposed to accept socialism of any stripe but who were nevertheless content for this very reason to credit *Anti-Dühring* as a definitive statement of Marx's doctrine —the very thing it was not.

The Pattern of Distortion

In the words of Lezsek Kolakowski, "[It] does not appear that the philosophical bases of Marx's Marxism are compatible with belief in general laws of nature having, as particular applications, the history of mankind and also the laws of thought, identified with psychological or physiological regularities of the brain." But such laws, rules, and regularities are the very *Leitmotiv* of *Anti-Dühring* and *Socialism: Utopian and Scientific* alike. Kolakowski, here at least, is under no illusion. There is, he goes on to say, "a clear difference between the latent transcendentalism of Engels's dialectics of nature and the dominant anthropocentrism of Marx's view," an anthropocentrism that can and should be contrasted with Engels's "naturalistic evolutionism." Whereas "Engels, broadly speaking, believed that man could be explained in terms of natural history and the laws of evolution to which he is subject, Marx's view was that nature as we know it is an extension of man, an organ of practical activity" (Kolakowski 1978, 401–2, 405; see Thomas 1976, 1988).

Engels maintained that "our mastery of nature consists in the fact that we have the advantage over other beings of being able to know and apply its laws," and that "we are more and more getting to know, and hence to control, even the more remote natural consequences ... of ... our productive activities" (Engels 1940, 292–30). This is a much more Baconian-Promethean notion than anything we encounter in Marx (Thomas 1988, 487–88). The relation of theory to practice Engels proffers is straightforwardly instrumental. The laws of physical nature, because they *are* laws as Engels understands the term, admit only of being applied for the sake of control. Such control can be either of nature or of society. Natural science and social management exist for Engels—not for Marx—on the same continuum. Engels effected a shift "from Marx's view of science as an activity important in technology and industry, to seeing its importance for socialists [as] a system of knowledge, incorporating the causal laws of physical science and taking them as a model for a covertly academic study of history, 'thought' and ... current politics" (Carver 1983, 157). Human beings in Engels's view are in the last analysis physical objects whose motion is governed by the same general laws that regulate the motion of all matter. Alfred Schmidt tersely observed, apropos of Engels, that "the fact that human history is made by beings endowed with consciousness is nothing more than a factor that tends rather to complicate matters" (Schmidt 1971, 191). Engels would not admit this as a criticism; he himself said much the same thing about human consciousness without any discernible irony. Purpose, practice, and human thought itself are in Engels's view complex forms of motion, about which lawlike statements may be made. The "law of the negation of the negation" Engels regarded as "an extremely general—and for this reason extremely far-reaching and important—law of development of nature, history, and thought; a law which holds good in the animal and plant kingdoms, in geology, in mathematics, in history, and in philosophy" (Engels 1969). How such a "law" could possibly admit of so broad a purchase is something Engels never took it upon himself to demonstrate in any adequate sense—unsurprisingly, since in passages like this one (there are examples aplenty) he was clearly out of his depth. Be this as it may, human history and human thought are on Engels's account nothing but special fields of play for nature's general laws of motion and development. This is why, on the one hand, the "government of persons" (in the Saint-Simonian phrase Engels so readily appropriated) can give way without undue difficulty to the "administration of things" (Engels 1969, 333; Carver 1981, 60)—a shift that also, far from incidentally, may be encountered in the writings (if not the practices) of Lenin (Thomas 1994, 129).

The "government of persons" and the "administration of things" are both simply matters of technique. Slippage from one to the other is unproblematic because each is viewed instrumentally. Either we control nature or nature controls us; subjection or subjugation of people to nature gives way, sooner or later, to their domination of nature, this being what human history finally comprises. "Master demons" in due course become "willing servants" (Engels 1972, 68).

Engels even manages to combine the apocalyptic dualism evident in such formulations with what Kolakowski identifies, correctly, as Engels's "naturalistic evolutionism." This unlikely alliance does nothing to make Engels's thought more palatable, or more compatible with the writings of

Marx, in whose name Engels took care to advance it. "The whole sphere of the conditions of life which environ man," declaims *Socialism: Utopian and Scientific*, "and which have hitherto ruled man, now comes under the dominion and control of man, who for the first time becomes the real, conscious lord of nature, because he has become master of his own social organization.... Man, at last the master of his own form of social organization, becomes at the same time the lord over nature, his own master—free" (Engels, 1972, 72, 75). If domination-and-control philosophies of nature all too readily lead into domination-and-control philosophies of human nature and vice versa—and I see no reason to doubt this general proposition—then Engels's views have repressive, authoritarian implications (though he sometimes sugared these with gradualist, evolutionary coatings, which in fact sit ill with the apocalyptic side of his thought—deep coherence was not Engels's strong suit). Terence Ball has argued persuasively that "there is a logical link between positivist meta-science and the view that social relations are best managed by technical experts and administrators" (Ball and Farr 1984, 236). This at root is why the task of disentangling Marx's writings from those of Engels is a task that matters. Since the historical links between post-Marxian Marxism and authoritarianism are not in doubt, there is every reason to question the extent of their intellectual grounding in Marx's writings.

Briefly put, Marx, in *Capital,* excoriated what he called "the abstract materialism of natural science" (Marx 1976, 272 n. 2). The truths of natural science, far from being logically prior to history and society, and far from providing any truths about society, are themselves dependent on the social purposes that provide the climate and context for the scientist's enterprise. Nature to Engels was by contrast necessitarian; freedom could only be freedom from it or over it. Marx saw nature very differently, and was a much less apocalyptic theorist than Engels. For Marx the continuum of nature does not stop short at the arbitrary barrier of the human senses and cognitive faculties. The implications of this for our understanding of the ontological basis of natural science lend no credence to Engels's apocalyptic and necessitarian claims. Natural science on Marx's view of it *cannot* be what Engels thought it *must* be: the observation of, and drawing of lawlike conclusions about, an external, material reality that exists independently of the observer it confronts. If nature is not independent of human aims, projects, and purposes in the sense Engels requires it to be, then scientific truth cannot be a matter of a correspondence between human perceptions and judgments, on the one hand, and an independently existing "reality," on the other. People's various observations and adaptations of nature are not, on Marx's view, to be regarded as forays into the uncharted territory of a categorically separate realm ("reality") that operates according to its own, necessitarian laws—laws we can but confront, interpret, and apply within our own, social realm.

Engels, who did regard our observations and adaptations in that very way, is often credited for having belatedly seen into print Marx's "Theses on Feuerbach." In so doing, however, Engels—whose own thought, let it be said, remains firmly and unambiguously within the confines of the "old materialism" that the "Theses" excoriate—seems not to have reflected very much about their meaning. He seems never to have discerned that if, in the words of the Second Thesis, "the dispute over the reality or non-reality of thinking that is isolated from practice is a purely scholastic question," then this admonition may be as true of scientific thinking as of any other kind. The constitutive function of human thought and action on the world arises not from anything in the realm of thought, as Hegel and the Young Hegelians had believed, but from people's life *in* the world. Nature, on this view, cannot be regarded as Engels evidently regarded it: as an inhuman, necessitarian realm to whose laws people are subject until they can "master" them. Nor can the world be regarded as Engels regarded it, as a kind of screen on which we as supine spectators can or should watch natural processes unfold. Engels, to reiterate, understood "dialectics" to be "the science of the general laws of motion and development of nature, human society and thought," considered in all seriousness as constituting a seamless web. He believed that "the dialectic going on in our heads is in reality the reflection of the actual development going on in the world of nature and of human history in obedience to dialectical forms." People's cognitive links with nature consist in their subjection to general laws of nature, of which human history and the "laws" of thought are but particular expressions. Thoughts are identified as physiological regularities of the brain; everything in the last analysis is an instance of matter in motion. Since "the unity of the world consists in its materiality," we can deduce the "dialectics" of society from the "dialectics of nature" by using "a 'system of nature' [like that of the eighteenth-century French *Aufklärer* d'Holbach, but] sufficient for our time" (Marx and Engels 1962, 2:504; Engels 1940, 314, 179; Marx and Engels 1975, 590; Marx and Engels 1962, 2:65, 136–137; Marx and Engels 1968, 622).

It should be clear how distant such thinking is from Marx's. It differs not just in degree but in kind, not just in emphasis but in principle. Marx and Engels are separated by a conceptual chasm that should have resisted all attempts at papering it over.

The Nature of Distortion

Yet there have been many such attempts. We have been told, for over a century now, that Marx and Engels occupy common ground—and there are still people who subscribe to such a belief (there are to this day chairs of the dialectics of nature in Chinese universities). Investigation of their reasons for subscribing to it would take this essay too far afield; we must remain content with an outline of the textual evidence, which, unless it proceeds from Engels after Marx's death, all points in a different direction. Engels claimed in 1885 that he had read *Anti-Dühring* to Marx—a curious claim, since Marx was not incapacitated or bedridden at the time it was written, and listening to a recitation of its ponderous contents would have taxed the patience of Job—and that it was issued with his knowledge (a much weaker claim, which, as far as it goes, is presumably true but means little). "It was self-understood between us," wrote Engels, "that this exposition of mine should not be issued without his knowledge" (Engels 1969, 13). The implication here, seized upon by later true believers, is that Engels, in writing *Anti-Dühring*, was faithfully fulfilling his part in what was an agreed-upon division of labor, according to which Engels produced texts that were interchangeable with Marx's on some subjects and supplementary to, but always compatible with and true to, Marx's work on others. The trouble is that there is no direct textual evidence anywhere in Marx's writings—and most of these are by now available—that he agreed with Engels's ambitiously comprehensive "laws" as set out in *Anti-Dühring*, or with Engels's overall deterministic materialism and teleological "dialectics." "We do not find in Marx's works the confusing, windy and ambiguous philosophizing that we find in Engels" (Carver 1984, 251). Only after Marx's death did Engels write that "Marx and I were pretty well the only people to rescue conscious dialectics from German idealist philosophy and apply it in the materialist conception of nature and history.... [I]n nature, amid the welter of innumerable changes, the same dialectical laws of motion force their way through as those which in history govern the apparent fortuitousness of events; the same laws that simultaneously form the thread running through the history of the development of human thought and gradually rise to consciousness in the mind of man" (Engels 1969, 15–16).

Engels's claims in the first (1878) preface to *Anti-Dühring* are appreciably more modest. He refers there to "my views" or "the various views which I have advanced." Even with these, Marx is nowhere on record as having agreed. And why should he have, since the views were so radically at variance with his own? The wearisome argument we have all heard, over and over again—that Marx must have agreed with Engels about science because he never expresses disapproval of Engels's views in the surviving correspondence—is weak, argues from silence, and strains credulity. Carver observes wryly that "it is not really possible to agree or disagree with Engels's dialectics" anyway, "because they are supposed to underlie everything" (Carver 1984, 256). Quite apart from this, sustained epistolary exchanges between friends need to be treated with considerable caution. It is likely that each correspondent will, at times, write what he expects the other to hear, and will humor or even indulge him when nothing pressing or urgent is at stake. Over and above this, it has been noted that "in correspondence on dialectical subjects as Engels understood them Marx was stand-offish or evasive" (Carver 1984, 252; Stanley and Zimmerman 1984, 242–43) rather than supportive. It is not hard to see why he adopted so markedly "perfunctory and non-committal" an attitude (Carver 1983, 128–29).

Engels wrote a postscript to Marx on 30 May 1873 that, as Helena Sheehan points out (1985, 64), was omitted from the English-language *Selected Correspondence* (one suspects the usual chicanery and legerdemain). "If you think there is anything in it," wrote Engels, "don't say anything about it just yet, so that no lousy Englishman will steal it on [*sic*] me. It may take a long time yet to get it into shape" (CW 33:81). The "it" in Engels's postscript refers to the following:

> This morning while I lay in bed the following dialectical points occurred to me: the subject-matter of natural science—matter in motion, bodies. Bodies cannot be separated from motion, their forms and kinds can only be known through motion; of bodies out of motion, out of relation to other bodies, nothing can be asserted. Only in motion does a body reveal what it is. Natural science, therefore, knows bodies by examining them in relation to one another, in motion. The knowledge of the different forms of motion is the knowledge of bodies. The investigation of these different forms of motion is therefore the chief subject of natural science. (CW 33:80–81)

From all appearances Marx did indeed maintain a discreet silence—and presumably an embarrassed one—about this instance of scholarship in majestic stride. Marx's doctoral dissertation, we might recall, had been about Democritus and Epicurus, either of whom takes us much further than Engels's amateur peregrination does. Engels had admitted to Arnold Ruge in 1842 that he was an *Autodidakt in der Philosophie* (Carver 1989, 93). He still was. One is hard put not to admire Marx's forbearance in not pointing out to his friend that there is nothing remotely dialectical (or even profound) about Engels's presumed insight. "Perhaps Marx felt it easier, in view of their long friendship, their role as leading socialists, and the usefulness of Engels's financial resources, to keep quiet and not to interfere with Engels's work. After all, *Anti-Dühring* went out under Engels's name alone, Engels stated in the preface that the work contained 'my views,' and neither Engels nor Marx seems to have revealed publicly during Marx's lifetime that Marx contributed to the chapter on political economy," or that Marx's "rather distant" preface to *Socialism: Utopian and Scientific* was published under Paul Lafargue's name. In general, "Engels, it seems, was canny enough to avoid creating disagreements with Marx. And Marx seems to have been similarly canny in not pressing Engels on his work" (Carver 1983, 129–32). The fact remains that, overall,

> [t]he surviving Marx-Engels correspondence fails to support the picture painted by Engels in the 1885 preface to *Anti-Dühring*. Marx did not discuss Engels's dialectical laws, even after prodding, nor did he say anything to substantiate the contention that he and Engels were the joint expositors of a universal materialism predicated on the natural sciences, understood as the study of matter in motion. Marx said nothing to confirm Engels's claim that he was familiar with the lengthy text of *Anti-Dühring*, much less that he endorsed it.... the diffidence, lacunae, and artful evasion displayed in Marx's replies to Engels does not illustrate a perfect partnership on theoretical issues. (Carver 1983, 128–30)

The Stakes of Distortion

Yet this is not how the Marx-Engels intellectual relationship has come down to us. It has come down to us in mythic form as a story of complete agreement expressed in interchangeable works or an agreed-upon division of labor within a perfect partnership. It has come down to us in this mythic form in large measure because Engels wanted it to and because, mainly in the 1883–95 period, he bent to the task of "setting Marx's work in an academic and philosophical context, drawing out its implications as a universal methodology, and adding what was declared in advance to be consistent with it, a positivist account of natural science" (Carver 1983, 156). To rehearse the long and weary story of how this myth found so many subsequent takers, and why it found so many adherents, would take us too far afield. Suffice it to say that the myth set the terms of its own acceptance—again, in large measure because Engels wanted it to do so. Leonard Krieger (one of the best commentators on Engels as a historian) referred in 1967 to "the delicate surgery of detaching Engels from Marx" (Krieger 1967, xii). I cannot forgo the observation that such surgery has needed to be "delicate" in large measure because Engels wanted it to be "delicate." He has to this day given us a great deal of work to do, work that is uphill and ought to have been needless. But in saying this we are by no means done with irony.

It is arguable that Engels's best and most original works—*The Condition of the Working Class in England* is a minor masterpiece, if ever there was one—were those which owed least to Marx. This is not an idle observation. One could write—many people by now have written—about Marx without much emphasis on Engels. That one could write about Engels without reference to Marx is, however, much less clear. Engels in his manner may have been perfectly aware of this. His adoption of Marx's mantle, conscious or unconscious as this may have been, was certainly *self*-conscious. Without invoking or even (to a considerable extent) inventing the adjectival status of Marx's name, would he have been listened to? Would he have found as many takers for ideas that were his and his alone? The question is at the very least an open one. I rather suspect that Engels himself knew in his heart of hearts that the answer to it has to be no.

References

Ball, Terence, and James Farr, eds. 1984. *After Marx*. Cambridge: Cambridge University Press.

Carver, Terrell. 1981. *Engels*. Oxford: Oxford University Press.

———. 1983. *Marx and Engels: The Intellectual Relationship*. Brighton, East Sussex: Harvester/Wheatsheaf.

———. 1984. Marx, Engels, and Scholarship. *Political Studies* 32:249–56.

———. 1989. *Friedrich Engels: His Life and Thought*. London: Macmillan.

Engels, Friedrich. 1940. *Dialectics of Nature*. New York: International Publishers.

———. 1969. *Anti-Dühring*. Moscow: Progress Publishers.

———. 1972. *Socialism: Utopian and Scientific*. New York: International Publishers.

Hobsbawm, Eric J. 1982. *The History of Marxism.* Vol. 1, *Marxism in Marx's Day.*
    Bloomington: Indiana University Press.
Kolakowski, Leszek. 1978. *Main Currents of Marxism.* Vol. 1, *The Founders.* Trans. P. S.
    Falla. Oxford: Oxford University Press.
Krieger, Leonard. 1967. Introduction to *The German Revolutions,* by Friedrich
    Engels. Chicago: University of Chicago Press.
Marx, Karl. 1976. *Capital.* Vol. 1. Harmondsworth, Middlesex: Penguin.
Marx, Karl, and Friedrich Engels. 1962. *Selected Works in Two Volumes.* Moscow:
    Progress Publishers.
———. 1968. *Selected Works in One Volume.* New York: International Publishers.
———. 1975. *Selected Correspondence.* Moscow: Progress Publishers.
Schmidt, Alfred. 1971. *The Concept of Nature in Marx.* London: New Left Books.
Sheehan, Helena. 1985. *Marxism and the Philosophy of Science.* Vol. 1, *The First Hun-
    dred Years.* Atlantic Highlands, N.J.: Humanities Press.
Stanley, John, and Ernest Zimmerman. 1984. On the Alleged Differences Between
    Marx and Engels. *Political Studies* 32:226–48.
Thomas, Paul. 1976. Marx and Science. *Political Studies* 24:1–23.
———. 1988. Nature and Artifice in Marx. *History of Political Thought* 9:485–503.
———. 1994. *Alien Politics: Marxist State Theory Retrieved.* New York: Routledge.

nation as a form of solidarity, nor did he see it in overly economic terms. If his approach to the national question sometimes lacked coherence, this was due to the fact that two theoretical strands coexisted uneasily in his work. The first was rooted in the critical theory of capitalism that resulted from his collaboration with Marx. The other was rooted in Engels's own radical republicanism. Both were guided by the political necessity of constructing a discourse that appealed to workers in terms of an internationalist class-based solidarity.

Capitalism and Nationalism

The critique of capitalism—in the elaboration of which Engels played such a significant role—bore the imprint of the main intellectual currents of the age: the utopianism of the French socialists, the historical and philosophical sophistication of German idealism, and the liberalism of English political economy. Yet, though the point of this critique was to change the world, certain historical events also played a key role. The French Revolution of 1789, for example, provided much of the political language, imagery, and many of the symbols for socialist discourse well into the late nineteenth century. For Engels, in particular, the first republic that emerged from the great revolution exemplified the potential and the limits of bourgeois democracy. Beyond this, the battles of 1848 served to demarcate new lines of conflict and to offer practical experience. It was then, for example, that Engels participated in combat in his native Wuppertal, and Marx was also involved in agitation, leading to his arrest and trial in Cologne (Hammen 1969). Later, the rise and demise of the International Working Men's Association (IWMA) provided an institutional referent for the internationalist position.

What resulted was a theoretical apparatus that included a perspective on the nation that combined the language of the French Revolution with an assessment of the situation confronting the new democratic force, the class of wage workers. It was this new force, well organized in England and politically significant in France and the Low Countries, but barely in its infancy in Germany, that would pick up the struggle for democracy and human emancipation, which the bourgeoisie had dropped in 1848 (Bronner 1990, 7–14). Along with Marx, Engels discerned a contest between a capitalism that was becoming global and a working class whose allegiances were properly internationalist. Later, he saw in the First International an

organization that furthered the proletarian cause by fostering international solidarity over nationalist concerns: the proletariat came into being
in a national context, but its struggle had a cosmopolitan purpose and an
international practice. Marx and Engels remained unshaken in this conviction even after the demise of the IWMA, as Engels reiterated during
the early years of the Second International: "[T]hat eternal union of the
proletarians of all countries created by [the IWMA] is still alive and lives
stronger than ever ... [b]ecause today ... the European and American proletariat is reviewing its fighting forces, mobilized for the first time, mobilized as *one* army, under *one* flag ... as proclaimed by the Geneva Congress
of the International in 1866, and again by the Paris Workers' Congress in
1889" (CW 27:60).

Already in *The Communist Manifesto,* Marx and Engels had argued that
the struggle against the bourgeoisie had to be carried out in international
solidarity and informed by a cosmopolitan perspective. They held that
the industrial bourgeoisie was rapidly transforming the planet and that
the old political borders were not enough to contain a capitalist system in
which "national industries ... are daily being destroyed. They are dis-
lodged by ... industries that no longer work up indigenous raw material,
but raw material drawn from the remotest zones; industries whose products are consumed ... in every quarter of the world.... In place of the old
local and national seclusion and self-sufficiency, we have intercourse in
every direction, universal inter-dependence of nations." In effect, the
authors of the *Manifesto* were proposing that the long-term trend pointed
in the direction of what today we term globalization, a process by which
capitalism would universalize itself, that is, would cause "all nations, on
pain of extinction, to adopt the bourgeois mode of production." This
drive would bring capitalist accumulation to the most isolationist countries and the most remote corners of the planet: the bourgeoisie would
"creat[e] a world after its own image" (Marx and Engels 1978, 476–77).

Yet this was not a simple linear development. Internationalism was not
the only product of the extension of capitalist relations. Despite the "cosmopolitan character" the bourgeoisie had given to production, this class
had also created, or at least conquered, the modern representative state
to match its modern industry. It was through this state, or, rather, through
its executive, that the bourgeoisie "manag[ed] its common affairs" (Marx
and Engels 1978, 475). The state, in this case, was to be a republic where
the nation would be formally represented, thereby setting the stage for the
battle of democracy, which the proletariat had to win. This was a position
Engels held to for the remainder of his life. For example, in an 1892 essay

on the socialist position on democracy in Italy, he wrote that "the democratic republic is the only political form in which the struggle between the
working class and the capitalist class can first be universalized and then
culminate in the decisive victory of the proletariat" (CW 27:271).

Of course, the democratic republic was far from common when Engels
collaborated with Marx on the *Manifesto*. At the time, they could claim that
the "working men have no country" precisely because universal men's
suffrage had not been achieved anywhere. It was by achieving political
rights that the proletariat could "acquire political supremacy ... constitute
itself *the* nation" (Marx and Engels 1978, 488). In the meantime, nationalist appeals were appeals to interests contrary to those of the proletariat. It
is important to note, in this respect, that contrary to the common assumption that the authors of the *Manifesto* claimed that all cultural distinctions
would disappear, Marx and Engels were in fact relatively silent on the cultural composition of the nation. The reason for this is that they saw nations
as political, rather than cultural, entities. After Marx's death, in 1883,
Engels sought to clarify this in a series of notes on the relationship
between the decline of feudalism and the emergence of national states
(CW 26:556–65).

Nations and History

Engels's treatment of the decline of feudalism and the emergence of
national states relied on linguistic and anthropological evidence and was
largely consistent with the approach to the history of the Germans that
he took in his 1878–82 notes on the topic (CW 26:5–107). In both pieces,
Engels traced the development of German nationality by following linguistic evidence as presented by Roman historians and nineteenth-century
linguists. The latter suggested that the geopolitical divisions of the eighteenth and nineteenth centuries largely corresponded to Roman boundary lines. Yet, in theoretical terms, Engels went beyond them in arguing
that "modern nationalities are ... the product of the oppressed classes"
(CW 26:559). The oppressed classes in question were the peasantry and
the emergent bourgeoisie, while the connection Engels drew to language
boundaries suggests something akin to Weber's notion of "elective affinity,"
rather than outright economic determination. This is to say that, although
Engels placed much of the explanatory burden on the development of the
forces and relations of production, he saw the outcome as conditioned by

the availability of cultural-historical elements for new purposes. As early as the ninth century, Engels held, the emerging feudal states followed roughly the boundaries of language: "[I]t was natural for the linguistic groups to serve as the existent basis for the formation of states; for the nationalities to start developing into nations" (CW 26:560). It was natural, not because cultural and linguistic groups were entitled to become states, but because, at the political level, the historical task of monarchs was to forge national unity by confronting the nobility and rival monarchs with the aid of the emerging urban classes, so that by the sixteenth century there were only two countries, Italy and Germany, "in which the monarchy and the national unity that was then impossible without it, either did not exist or existed only on paper" (CW 26:565).

Engels's concern here remains an important question in modern historiography: the emergence of the system of states associated with the Peace of Westphalia. The treaties by which the European states ended their hostilities and regulated their behavior after 1648 ratified an arrangement whereby states were deemed juridically equal and sovereign within their territories. The historical uniqueness and spread of this system, and its relation to capitalist development, have been amply documented and closely examined by contemporary historians (e.g., Arrighi 1994; Kennedy 1987; Tilly 1975). Engels's notes were an important and unfortunately incomplete effort to address these questions.

As both Arrighi (1994, 85–158) and Kennedy (1987, 16–72) argue, the emergence of the European system of states was in good measure a function of military conflict and of the ability of institutional clusters to capture and wield resources. Nearly a century earlier, Engels also saw this, and in some ways went beyond to offer explanations for why one particular set of arrangements and borders, rather than some other, resulted from the conflicts that marked the end of the Middle Ages. Why did states associated with certain population groupings emerge? Why, for example, not multinational states? Some, such as the Habsburg Empire, did in fact endure. However, they were unstable and in good measure owed their position to the need that other, more powerful states had for them in the balance-of-power diplomacy that evolved. Similarly, why did some peoples provide the bases for the establishment of monarchies, while others did not? Engels's answers to questions such as these may be unsatisfactory, but one virtue of his approach is that it permitted him to ask them. Two elements turn out to be crucial here: the significance Engels attributed to force, and the distinction he drew between nationhood and nationality or ethnicity.

Although the emergence of merchant capitalism played a crucial role in the development of the Westphalian system and its component states ("the Burghers of the towns had already become more indispensable to society than the feudal nobility," CW 26:556), the central dynamic was political power. The burghers, with their monetized wealth, constituted an ally and a resource for the monarchy, which "stood for order amid disorder, the nation in the process of formation as opposed to disintegration into rebellious vassal states," and was, consequently, "the progressive element" (CW 26:561). The monarchy offered a focus of solidarity against the centrifugal forces embodied in the feudal nobility, and, once new military technologies gave infantry the upper hand, it was able to triumph by tapping into the resources of the burghers. As it turns out, one of the main factors that made the monarchy function as the new focus of solidarity was its ability to shape preexisting linguistic entities into nations. In fact, in Engels's view, the historical function of absolutism consisted precisely in the creation of national states.

Engels returned to these themes, with greater specificity, in an 1887–88 manuscript, posthumously published in *Die Neue Zeit* and known as "The Role of Force in History." The main purpose of this piece was to "apply our theory to contemporary German history and its use of force, its policy of blood and iron," in short, to explain why Bismarck had to invade France to unify Germany. Engels argued that the arrangements of the Congress of Vienna (1815) went against the long-term tendency to form "a Europe composed of large national states," where the bourgeoisie could rule in constitutional republics and prepare the way for the "establishment of harmonious international co-operation between peoples, without which the rule of the proletariat is impossible." Consequently, the division of Germany and Italy into small states, the subjugation of Hungary, and the partition of Poland stood in the way of history and peace. Peace in fact was the victim of national friction. Thus, Engels held that "each people must be independent and master in their own house" (CW 26:455).

From these premises, Engels went on to argue that the unification of Germany was the product of larger historical trends that worked themselves out both through and in spite of the specific arrangements of the Congress of Vienna as Bismarck manipulated them to Prussian advantage. The emergent bourgeoisie's need for larger markets and national consciousness, awakened by the Napoleonic invasions, had run into the persistence of two conflicting states, Prussia and Austria, and the broader demands of a proletariat that had made its presence felt in the revolutions of 1848 and, after 1869, through its own industrial and political organizations. Of course, already by 1846 the bourgeoisie had chosen to cast its lot with Prussia because of the latter's relation to the Customs Union and because it had "two good institutions ahead of other large states: universal conscription and universal compulsory education" (CW 26:470). Universal conscription, and the rational organization of its army, gave Prussia the upper hand within German lands, as it demonstrated first against Denmark, then against Austria, finally against France. Universal public education made a large number of people available to resolve one the key barriers to German industrialization (as the bourgeoisie perceived it)—the shortage of qualified personnel to fill supervisory positions (CW 26:471). Finally, the political weakness of the German bourgeoisie meant that, despite its dominant economic position, it had been unable to triumph over Bismarck, so it had to settle for "the revolutionizing of Germany from above" (CW 26:499).

Nations and Class Struggle

Thus the development of the bourgeois mode of production in Germany and the political history of Europe both called for a sovereign national state, yet the bourgeoisie was unable to produce this result on its own. As a consequence, the task of nation building fell to Bismarck, who took it on as a process of annexation rather than consolidation. This meant that a number of issues—not least, cultural ones—were left unresolved. Of special importance in this respect was Bismarck's effort to ensure that the German lands would be Prussianized under Junker leadership. This, according to Engels, would require that the Junkers be transformed, despite their own inclinations, into the core of a party with a national ideology, something they lacked and that Bismarck attempted to provide through a policy of *Kulturkampf* (1871–75), whereby he initiated an attack on separatist elements associated with the Catholic Church and the Center Party, an attack he subsequently had to break off in order to confront the even more radical working-class forces then emerging (CW 26:508–10).

Unfortunately, "The Role of Force in History" ends at this point, and we are left in the dark regarding how a national policy was to have emerged and what the consequences of its failure to develop actually were. There are, however, a number of indications of where Engels might have gone with this argument. The development of capitalism, of course, remained the main factor; however, other elements were also important, not the least of which, given our current concern, was nationality. This was important not because nationalism was a completely autonomous force, but because it provided elements on which bourgeois states could be built. To understand this, we need to go back to Engels's early work.

Capitalism brought about change not only because its products undermined domestic industries, but mainly because it was a new way of life that changed basic social relations and brought different peoples into contact, thereby undermining customs, transforming the very experience of everyday life, and producing conflict at every level. Already in 1845, before his association with Marx, Engels had explained the migration of the Irish and highlighted the ethnic tensions it produced in England by referring to the expansion of British industry. The Irish, he held, constituted "a reserve of labor," living in dire poverty and consequently available at significantly lower wages than the English workers with whom they competed for jobs. Thus poverty pushed the Irish out of Ireland, and the relatively higher wages prevailing in England pulled them there. Their presence in the factories, in turn, made for a shared interest with English workers, but it also depressed the latter's wages and drove them to degraded living conditions and habits that matched those of the immigrants, thereby fueling resentments between English and Irish workers. Meanwhile the English migration to Ireland was replacing the stagnant agriculture prevalent there with a more productive commercial agriculture. Yet these changes did not relieve the misery of the Irish, but rather, by exploiting them "in a brutal fashion," only accelerated their impoverishment. Ireland, he continued, "has no cause to be grateful to the English immigrants. On the other hand the Irish immigrants in England have added an explosive force to English society which will have significant consequences in due course" (Engels 1958, 309; generally 104–7, 306–10).

The transformation of Ireland, and for that matter so many other countries, was part of the process by which the bourgeoisie created a world in its image. This new world was not simply an extension and intensification of arms-length trade relations. By 1848 Marx and Engels had already discerned that the emerging ties between nations were having a deep impact upon their social structures, their customs, their "civilizations," in short, their cultures and modes of existence. In Europe, the remnants of feudal relations and traditional communal ties were giving way before the modern state, the machine, the commodity, and the wage contract. Even long-assumed "[d]ifferences of age and sex [had] no longer any distinctive social validity *for the working class*. All [were] instruments of labor" (Marx and Engels 1978, 475, emphasis added). The same held for differences between nations. National distinctions had no social validity for a working class that had no country because it nowhere controlled a state. This was not to say that the working class was automatically antinationalist, only that its cause was. An internationalist practice and a cosmopolitan perspective became "the first conditions for the emancipation of the proletariat" quite simply because its cause was rarely well served by loyalty to states controlled by other classes (488).

Nations and Nationalities

At this point it is important to clarify a the distinction between the *nation,* as a problem for proletarian solidarity across state borders, and *nationalities,* as a problem of cultural minorities within a state. As Rosdolsky (1965) has argued, in *The Communist Manifesto* the terms "nation" and "national" refer to the populations of sovereign states, while "nationality" may be synonymous with citizenship, as is usually the case in English and French usage, or may "designate a *mere community of descent and language* (a 'people' or *Volk*)" (332). It is in the latter sense that Germans and eastern Europeans have often conflated nation and nationality into *Volk.* Engels's own usage, as we will see in a moment, followed the English and French conventions in that he more or less explicitly drew these distinctions and concentrated on the freedom of nations rather than nationalities (ethnic communities).

In fact, Engels backed many projects of national liberation when he thought they would further the fortunes of the proletariat by establishing democratic republics, particularly in Ireland, Italy, and Poland. For historical and theoretical reasons, Engels's lifelong position on the Polish question expressed this relationship most clearly. The reestablishment of Poland's independence had been an important issue and a marker of radicalism since the late eighteenth century. The partitions of Poland had led to valiant attempts to secure its independence, and the failure of these attempts had produced a significant émigré population that kept the issue alive in radical circles (see Hobsbawm 1962, 161). Like most European radicals, Engels supported Polish independence. Already in 1847, he had argued that it was indissolubly linked with the struggles for democracy and communism elsewhere in Europe. Yet it is crucial to note the terms in which he supported this position: his was not an unconditional defense of a politics of national liberation. Rather, he thought that Polish independence would mean the establishment of a democratic republic and the beginning of the end of the most reactionary powers in Europe, the empires of the Habsburgs and the Romanovs. This, in turn, would ease the way for bourgeois republics elsewhere in central Europe while depriving the Western ruling classes of their gendarmes (CW 6:391–92, 549–52). As he wrote to Walery Wróblewski on 4 December 1875, "I shall always regard the liberation of Poland as being one of the foundation stones of the ultimate liberation of the European proletariat and, in particular, of the liberation of the other Slav nationalities" (CW 45:112).

It is nonetheless important to note that, for Engels, claims about the emancipatory quality of national liberation projects were always premised on a civic republican conception of the nation, that is, of a people politically organized as a state rather than of a community of descent. Engels drew this distinction most forcefully in a series of still controversial articles known today under the title "What Have the Working Classes to Do with Poland?" and published early in 1866 in *Commonwealth*. He wrote them at Marx's request and in support of section 9 of the instructions to the delegates to the Geneva convention of the IWMA. The continuing opposition of the Proudhonist delegates, who held that the goal of the IWMA was economic, while Polish independence was purely a "question of nationalities," made a response necessary (Puech 1907, 101–3, 112–50; Braunthal 1967, 121–33). To this end, Engels argued that there was a great deal of "difference between the 'principle of nationalities' and the old democratic and working-class tenet as to the right of the great European nations to separate and independent existence" (CW 20:157).

The Proudhonists and other elements of the international labor movement opposed the "principle of nationalities" in good measure because of its association with Louis Bonaparte, who had reputedly coined the term to suggest the communal origin of state authority and the proposition that ethnicity was an a priori claim to statehood. Consequently Engels sought to remove the position Marx had endorsed from the shadow of the Second Empire. As the Bonapartist principle proclaimed support for ethnicity-based movements, Engels, who had never been sympathetic to the politics of ethnic identity, countered with the argument that the "restoration of Poland mean[t] the re-establishment of a State composed of at least four different nationalities," rather than an "appeal to the principle of nationalities" (CW 20:159). In contrast to the claims of the advocates of this principle, Polish speakers, Lithuanians, White Russians, and Ukrainians inhabited Polish territory, and the IWMA would support the establishment of one state on this territory in accord with the principles of radical democracy.

Most important, Engels held that the principle of nationalities was anti-democratic and, in any case, derivative of Pan-Slavism, the tsarist ideology that justified the partition of Poland. That Engels was wrong about the genesis of Pan-Slavism does not affect the thrust of his analysis, which is to draw a distinction between nations and nationalities, between citizenship and ethnicity. (He had written that "Pan-Slavism did not originate in Russia or Poland, but in Prague and in Agram [Zagreb]" [CW 8:233]; on Pan-Slavism see Kohn 1953.) His larger point was that nations were political entities, states, not cultural phenomena. He noted that all the major countries of Europe included more than one nationality, while most nationalities were part of more than one nation. Indeed, "no state boundary coincid[ed] with the natural boundary of nationality, that of language." As a result of ten centuries of European history, most great nations had lost some of their elements, and "the various nations, as *politically constituted,* have most of them some foreign elements within themselves, which form connecting links with their neighbors, and vary the otherwise too monotonous uniformity of the national character" (CW 20:156–57, emphasis added). Indeed, the newly emerging political entities, the sovereign nations, were political structures that included, and ought to include, a variety of cultural communities, themselves spread among a multiplicity of political entities.

Nations and Cultures

None of this was meant to indicate that the cultural community played no role. Culture mattered, but the goal of democratic politics could not be the further differentiation and separation of cultures. The point, rather, was to support the kind of political arrangements within which the goals of the working class could best be expressed. These goals included, as the French delegates would certainly agree, the improvement of the living conditions of working people, not a program of national liberation for ethnic Poles, Italians, or any other nationality so understood. Yet if the improvement of social and economic conditions depended in good measure upon the political conditions in which they were pursued, then these goals called for sovereign democratic republics. Consequently, in Engels's view, the appropriateness of supporting the democratic project of Polish patriots was evident. The establishment of an independent Poland was a political project to free a great nation and so to counter the reactionary kind of nationalism that the French delegates so feared.

Engels's reference was to the revolutionary French concept of the great nation, *la grande nation*. This was an expansive idea that referred to the notion of *fraternité* and aimed to grasp (and propagate) the proposition that any community with democratic aims was welcome to join the Republic. Unfortunately, with Engels, this conception decayed into a dichotomy between the great nations and the infamous "peoples without history." This distinction, however, was not a question of size or of economic reductionism, as some interpreters have held (Schwarzmantel 1991, 59–76). Of course, Engels did argue on at least one occasion that the trend in Europe was toward the formation of large national states (CW 26:455, 470), but in this case the observation referred to the requirements of markets and the exercise of military force, not to ethnic identity. Yet, even given this distinction, his appeal to the ideas of historical and nonhistorical nations requires further consideration.

Engels, of course, did not himself introduce the formulation. Some variation of the phrase "historical nation" had been in use for nearly half a century as part of the debates of the "spring of nations" and ironically enough among the proponents of Pan-Slavism (Anderson 1991, 103, 195). No less than them, Engels derived his approach to this matter from a Hegelian notion that linked a people's relation to world history to the presence of a state.

Hegel (1956) saw in World History the unfolding of the human spirit through time and space. In his view, a select few peoples, possessing arts, literature, an awareness (however abstract) of freedom, and the energy to carry out great projects, were agents through which World History achieved concreteness. Through them, universal human freedom unfolded in the concreteness of states as the World Spirit moved westward from China. Those through whom the great principles had achieved concreteness, however temporarily, were the "world-historical peoples." In Hegel's view, they provided the material and the stage for the unfolding of freedom, while the rest were forgotten or left behind. Engels, like many of his contemporaries, reversed the formulation to refer to those nationalist movements that stood in the way of the establishment of democratic republics and their great nations.

Engels first used the Hegelian notion in a series of *Neue Rheinische Zeitung* (*NRZ*) articles published between 1848 and 1850, and he returned to it sporadically in the mid-1850s and 1860s. The occasion for the *NRZ* writings was the series of revolutions that swept Europe at midcentury and the success of counterrevolutionary appeals to the ideologies of Pan-Slavism and nationalism. With Hungary in revolt, then, the supporters of

Habsburg rule defended themselves by calling on Europe's gendarme, Tsar Nicholas I, by raising armies staffed primarily by Southern Slavs, and by offering reconciliation to Western Slavs (Poles excluded, of course). In January of 1849 Engels reacted angrily, asking, "Is there a single one of these races, not excluding the Czechs and Serbs, that possesses a national historical tradition which is kept alive among the people and stands above the pettiest of local struggles?" (CW 8:234; for the juxtaposition between nationalist and democratic aspirations and its importance for Marxian thought, see Lichtheim 1965, 76–89).

Engels distinguished between the Poles and other Slavic peoples. Poland had attempted a democratic revolution (CW 8:371; 20:158–60). By contrast, the smaller Slavic peoples (Czechs, Croatians, Serbs, etc.), much like the Gaels, Bretons, Basques, and many others, had been "suppressed and held in bondage by a nation which later became the main vehicle of historical development." Their own national spirit had been plundered, and, he claimed—appealing to Hegel—under such circumstances "the residual fragments of peoples always become fanatical standard-bearers of counter-revolution and remain so until their complete extirpation or loss of their national character, just as their whole existence in general is itself a protest against a great historical revolution" (CW 8:234). The non-historical peoples, then, were those that had fallen at the slaughter bench of history. As *historical subjects* they were destined to disappear because they could not sustain states. In the meantime, they were available for counter-revolutionary purposes. Whether or not they had a past, they had no historical future.

Undeniably, there was more than a hint of prejudice, chauvinism, and ignorance of actual conditions in eastern Europe in this account. It is just as certain, however, that the discussion of the "peoples without history" points to the limitations of the critics of Marxian views on the nation, precisely because it occurs in a context where Engels had diverged from Marxian analysis. The fact is that Engels's appeal to the concept of the "peoples without history" both reveals a serious concern with the dangers of nationalism and gives the lie to commonplace charges of economic reductionism. It also points to the weakness of approaches to the national question that do not address history and structure. If anything, Engels, in his discussions of central and eastern European nationalism, had strayed from the method he and Marx had developed and so had fallen back on essentialist cultural metaphysics (for a more elaborate discussion of this theme, see Forman 1998, 48–58, 62–64; Benner [1995, 163ff.] makes a parallel argument).

Inasmuch as it aimed to draw transhistorical conclusions, the proposition of the nonhistorical peoples was certainly a metaphysical one. As Roman Rosdolsky has argued (1986, 128), Engels's evaluation "stood in contradiction to the *materialist conception of history* which Engels himself helped create." Rosdolsky demonstrates through close commentary on the *NRZ* articles that Engels did not apply the Marxian method of social and economic historical analysis in those pieces. For instance, instead of examining structural factors, such as the relationship between ethnicity and land distribution that made Croatian nationalists into opponents of Kossuth's Hungarian republic, Engels delved into their centuries-old inability to maintain a Croat state and concluded from this that their time had forever passed. Thus, by making the Southern Slavs into "counter-revolutionary nations," an assessment he later dropped (CW 27:47, 398, 403), Engels was moving away from one of the main tenets of *The German Ideology*, the proposition that the very understanding of history must begin with "real premises . . . real individuals, their activity and the material conditions of their life," because history begins with "the production of material life itself" (CW 5:32, 42).

Indeed, as Otto Bauer argued some years later, Engels had taken the Southern Slavs as he had found them, and, considering their past a closed book, he had concluded that they had no future. He had turned them into abstract categories. Bauer's contention was that Engels was unable to explain subsequent developments, because he lacked an adequate notion of nationality that would link the emergence of capitalist relations with the political, cultural, and historical context of a multinational polity (1924, 190–216). In fact, Engels's formulation of the national question focused on its political constitution, and he did not much concern himself with the coexistence of ethnic minorities within a polity, let alone within the working-class movement.

National Identity and Class Solidarity

The fact is that for Engels solidarity always meant the unity of the political project of the working class rather than a problematic of identity. The working class was not a community of descent, and it did not hang together in the absence of political action. Rather, what made the proletariat into a class, an international class, were the commitments and projects for which it organized and struggled. In his 1885 essay on the history of the Communist League, Engels made this plain by recounting that the old motto of the league had been "All Men Are Brothers" and that he and Marx had been instrumental in replacing such a proposition with "the new battle cry, 'Working Men of All Countries, Unite!' which proclaimed the international character of the struggle" (CW 26:322). The difference between the two statements, and a third possibility that we might formulate as "All Working Men Are Brothers," is that the Marxian coinage both recognizes the reality of juridico-political barriers and calls for a practice to overcome them.

Similarly, in Engels's estimation, the nation was very much a political entity that could not exist without a practice, the state. In the first major work he published after the death of Marx, *The Origin of the Family, Private Property, and the State,* Engels made the point as part of his considerations on the relationship between juridical forms and the changing division of labor. In ancient Athens, for example, Theseus's constitution had centralized authority, thereby fusing the tribes "into one single nation" sharing a civil law that "stood above the legal customs of the tribes and gentes [clans]" (Engels 1972, 172). Similarly, the presence of increasingly differentiated dialects following the collapse of the Roman Empire resulted from the rise of the "elements of new nations" that nonetheless lacked the "strength to fuse these elements into new nations" (208). What was needed was a certain level of development in the division of labor. When this level was attained, there was a "cleavage of society into classes," which, in turn, called the state into being as an organization "grouping its members on a *territorial basis*" and instituted as "a *public force* . . . no longer identical with the people's own organization of themselves as an armed force." The state, then, was not rooted in a moral idea or a set of customs but in irreconcilable social differences that it sought to contain as it fused its population into a nation. It was not custom or language that had made nations and underpinned states, but states that had made nations (228–30).

Understood this way, Engels's strongest claims about, for example, the primacy of material life are readily explicable because the solidarity of the proletariat as a class was always in question. It was something that had to be sustained through political action and ideological intervention, much as, for example, the faith of the ancient Christians—before the Church was victorious—had "survive[d] only through active propaganda, unrelenting struggle . . . the proud profession of the revolutionary standpoint before the heathen judges" (CW 27:468). Similarly, internationalism was not the automatic product of a shared position in the relations of production, it was a theoretical endeavor and a practical one. Internationalism was also vulnerable to appeals to prejudices and commonalities of descent that really did not further the interests of working people. Thus, writing about anti-Semitism in 1890, Engels could say both that it had lost its social validity in places where "old social distinctions resolve themselves in the one great antithesis—capitalists and wage laborers," and that it "is merely the reaction of declining medieval social strata ... so that all it serves are reactionary ends under a purportedly socialist cloak" (CW 27:50–51). Appeals to prejudice and ethnicity only served to misdirect proletarian energies, so the only national claims Engels could support were rational-legal ones.

In any case, nationality, understood in terms of ethnicity, was not the necessary basis for a nation. Most great nations, in fact, included more than one nationality, and the version of the national question Engels was concerned with was the claim to the loyalty of their citizens that states made. It was unavoidable, particularly in the view of the older Engels, that workers would be attracted by these appeals as long as they forgot the class nature of even the democratic republic. In fact, the democratic republic was the "highest form of the state," where the "possessing class rules directly by means of universal suffrage," relying on the cooperation of the working class as long as it remained immature (Engels 1972, 231–32). Yet it was precisely in the democratic republic that working people were most susceptible to the appeal of national, as against class, solidarity. At the same time, the democratic republic remained a desirable form not only because it opened up new possibilities for the pursuit of the class struggle, but also because the very idea of the sovereignty of the citizens was necessary for the expression of the universality of the proletariat's interests.

Conclusions

One of the most important among Engels's contributions to Marxism was an effort to understand the modern nation and its appeal as a form of solidarity. The theory that emerged from this was intimately related to the political struggles of the working class and its internationalism. The latter, as he wrote to Eduard Bernstein on 22 and 25 February 1882, was the main point of reference for political judgment: "We must co-operate in the work of setting the West European proletariat free and subordinate everything else to that goal" (CW 46:205). The proletarian struggle also required great nations, that is, political units constructed along the lines of republican citizenship, for, as he informed the younger Kautsky on 7 February

1882, "an international movement of the proletariat is possible only as [*sic*] between independent nations" (CW 46:191–92).

This view only made sense because Engels saw the nation as the political community of citizens, that is, much as it had been proclaimed by the first French republic. From this perspective, national freedom presupposed not only sovereignty, but a republican form of government: "A sincerely international collaboration of the European nations is possible only if each of these nations is fully autonomous in its own house" (CW 27:274). Full autonomy, in this context, meant not only independence but also democracy. A Poland governed by a dictator or an autocrat, for example, was no freer than a partitioned Poland. The point, for Engels, was never to establish states in the name of human groupings defined around descent, language, race, or any other such characteristic. Rather, it was to institute democratic republics where workers could best pursue their struggles. Since Engels perceived the nation as a society exercising political power, as a nation-state, its political form was of great importance. In practice, this meant that nationalities, that is, nations understood in terms of shared orientations emerging from an organic development out of a common history, had no a priori claims to the support of progressive forces. Working-class internationalism did not aim to establish ethnic states. If its goals coincided with those of a particular national liberation movement, this was due to the democratic tendencies of this movement.

In sum, Engels considered the nation a political phenomenon to be understood in a broader social and historical context. This broader context was the capitalist mode of production; among its characteristics was the tendency to universalize itself as it revolutionized societies. In remaking the world in its own image, the bourgeoisie was creating a system of territorial nation-states and a global economy. Thus it both divided the working class and forced its struggle onto the global level. The globalization of capital pitted the working class of any one country against those of others, and proletarian victory was only conceivable with the global overthrow of the bourgeoisie and its allies. Consequently internationalism and the International were fundamental. Yet this internationalism was not about solidarity between nations. It was instead about principled solidarity among wage workers and strategic solidarity with political forces whose democratic projects furthered the advancement of the proletariat and its project, the extension of democracy into civil society—that is, socialism.

References

Anderson, Benedict. 1991. *Imagined Communities: Reflections on the Origin and Spread of Nationalism.* Rev. ed. London: Verso.

Arrighi, Giovanni. 1994. *The Long Twentieth Century: Money, Power, and the Origins of Our Times.* New York: Verso.

Bauer, Otto. 1924. *Die Nationalitätenfrage und die Sozialdemokratie.* Vienna: Volksbuchhandlung.

Benner, Erica. 1995. *Really Existing Nationalisms: A Post-Communist View of Marx and Engels.* New York: Oxford University Press.

Braunthal, Julius. 1967. *History of the International.* Vol. 1. Trans. Henry Collins and Kenneth Mitchell. New York: Praeger.

Bronner, Stephen Eric. 1990. *Socialism Unbound.* New York: Routledge.

Carver, Terrell. 1983. *Marx and Engels: The Intellectual Relationship.* Bloomington: Indiana University Press.

Cummins, Ian. 1980. *Marx, Engels, and National Movements.* New York: St. Martin's.

Engels, Friedrich. 1958. *The Condition of the Working Class in England.* Trans. W. O. Henderson and W. H. Chaloner. Stanford: Stanford University Press.

———. 1972. *The Origin of the Family, Private Property, and the State.* Ed. Eleanor Burke Leacock. New York: International Publishers.

———. 1993. Speech on Poland. In Karl Marx, *The Revolutions of 1848,* ed. David Fernbach, 105–8. New York: Penguin.

Forman, Michael. 1998. *Nationalism and the International Labor Movement: The Idea of the Nation in Socialist and Anarchist Theory.* University Park: Pennsylvania State University Press.

Hammen, Oscar J. 1969. *The Red '48ers.* New York: Scribner.

Hegel, Georg Wilhelm Friedrich. 1956. *The Philosophy of History.* Trans. J. Sibree. New York: Dover.

Herod, Charles C. 1976. *The Nation in the History of Marxian Thought: The Concept of Nations With History and Nations Without History.* The Hague: Martinus Nijhoff.

Hobsbawm, Eric J. 1962. *The Age of Revolution: 1789–1848.* New York: New American Library.

International Workingmen's Association. 1962. *La première Internationale.* Vol. 1. Ed. Jacques Freymond. Geneva: Droz.

Kennedy, Paul. 1987. *The Rise and Fall of the Great Powers.* New York: Random House.

Kohn, Hans. 1953. *Pan-Slavism.* Notre Dame, Ind.: University of Notre Dame Press.

Levine, Norman. 1975. *The Tragic Deception: Marx Contra Engels.* Santa Barbara, Calif.: Clio.

Lichtheim, George. 1965. *Marxism: A Historical and Critical Study.* New York: Praeger.

Marx, Karl. 1992. *The First International and After.* Ed. David Fernbach. New York: Penguin Classics.

Marx, Karl, and Frederick Engels. 1978. *Manifesto of the Communist Party.* In *The Marx-Engels Reader,* 2d ed., ed. Robert C. Tucker, 469–500. New York: W. W. Norton.

Nimni, Ephraim. 1989. Marx, Engels, and the National Question. *Science and Society* 53:297–326.

————. 1991. *Marxism and Nationalism: The Theoretical Origins of a Political Crisis.* London: Pluto.

Puech, Jules. 1907. *Le Proudhonisme dans l'association internationale des travailleurs.* Paris: Alcan et Réunis.

Rosdolsky, Roman. 1965. Worker and Fatherland: A Note on a Passage in the *Communist Manifesto. Science and Society* 29:330–37.

————. 1986. *Engels and the "Nonhistoric" Peoples: The National Question in the Revolution of 1848.* Trans. and ed. John-Paul Himka. Glasgow: Critique.

Schwarzmantel, John. 1991. *Socialism and the Idea of the Nation.* London: Harvester/Wheatsheaf.

Tilly, Charles, ed. 1975. *The Formation of National States in Western Europe.* Princeton: Princeton University Press.

Traverso, Enzo, and Michael Löwy. 1990. The Marxist Approach to the National Question: A Critique of Nimni's Interpretation. *Science and Society* 54: 132–46.

12

Engels's *Origins:*
A Feminist Critique

Carol C. Gould

Frederick Engels's 1884 work *The Origin of the Family, Private Property, and the State* was one of the first major contributions to the theoretical analysis and critique of women's oppression and to the argument for their equality, along with John Stuart Mill and Harriet Taylor Mill's work *On the Subjection of Women.* Basing his essay on Marx's unpublished notes on his reading of the American anthropologist Morgan's work concerning the Iroquois and other societies, Engels attempts to explain the emergence of the modern family and the oppression of women from earlier stages of social and economic organization in terms of the crucial role played by the development of private property and class society. Pivotal to his explanation is the introduction of the herding of cattle as a male activity in the historical division of labor and the attendant accumulation of wealth in the hands of men, who subsequently needed to establish a system of assured paternity in order to bequeath this wealth to their children. Engels marks off this transition from earlier forms of matrilineal descent and matriarchy (in societies based on what he calls "group marriage" and then the "pairing family") as "the world historical defeat of the female sex" (Engels 1972, 120). Thus Engels links the modern oppression of women to the development of the institution of private property. Correlatively, he argues that the economic system of capitalism draws women into the public workforce and thus sets the conditions for their equality. But he holds that full emancipation would require the socialization of domestic functions and the abolition of capitalist private property in some sort of communal society of the future.

Criticizing Engels

Feminist theorists, early in the development of the contemporary feminist movement, criticized Engels's approach as one-sidedly economic, and introduced the concept of patriarchy as essential for understanding the origins and continued existence of women's oppression. The system of patriarchy, which antedated the emergence of private property, was characterized by gender hierarchy, in which practices of male authority and domination over women were institutionalized (see Rubin 1975; Hartmann 1981). Even among feminist theorists sympathetic to historical materialist approaches, Engels's explanation has been seen as narrowly economistic in the causal priority attributed to the production process and the decisive part played by the introduction of technologies in the means of production, for example, the iron plow in agriculture, by contrast to the relative disregard of social relations of oppression (Mitchell 1971, 97; Rowbotham 1974, 69–70; Nicholson 1986, 92–93). This critique is already present in Simone de Beauvoir's *Second Sex,* where she argues against what she calls Engels's "economic monism" as reductive (de Beauvoir 1989, 60). She proposes a theory of woman as "Other," which involves men's desire for mastery and adds to the economic factors an emphasis on women's role in childbirth and childrearing (54–60, 77–78).

De Beauvoir also points to what we might call the ad hoc character of Engels's explanation. She remarks that "it is not clear that the institution of private property must necessarily have involved the enslavement of women. Historical materialism takes for granted facts that call for explanation: Engels assumes without discussion the bond of interest which ties man to property; but where does this interest, the source of social institutions, have its own source?" (de Beauvoir 1989, 56).

In an early essay (1974), "The Woman Question: Philosophy of Liberation and the Liberation of Philosophy," I develop a related criticism of the

11

Engels's Internationalism and Theory of the Nation

Michael Forman

There are at least two reasons for examining Engels's intervention in the nineteenth-century debates on the national question. The first is that the originality of his own contribution to Marxism is clearest in this area. While there is some dispute regarding the extent to which Marx shared a number Engels's ideas, it is generally accepted that Engels played the main part in this area and that Marx never expressed disagreement with his views on the national question (Nimbi 1989, 375; Herod 1976, 18–20; Traverso and Löwy 1990, 139–41; Cummins 1980, 176–78; Carver 1983; Levine 1975). However, the more important reason to examine Engels's efforts to address the national question and its relationship to internationalism is substantive. His contribution merits attention because, in contrast to the claims of many of its critics, and even of some of its supporters (e.g., Nimni 1991; Schwarzmantel 1991), socialism has given rise to a significant body of theoretical work on the subject (Forman 1998). In this tradition, Engels stands as one of first to examine the implications of nationalism for the working-class movement. Neither was he oblivious to the appeal of the ad hoc nature of Engels's explanation, focusing on his narrow understanding of economic production itself. I write there that "for much of political economy, production in the narrow sense, understood in terms of the activity of men, has been taken as the model of universal human economic activity. Indeed, political economic theories often omit entirely the broader sense of production in which domestic labor might be considered productive." This narrow understanding of production is manifest even in Engels's *Origin of the Family, Private Property, and the State,* and in this case leads to distortion in the theory. For, as we shall see, Engels does not show why it became dominant, except for the reason that it was male. That it was both male and dominant is a matter of historical fact. But Engels's explanation of this fact begs the question. Thus Engels attempts to explain how, with the domestication of animals, property rights fell to the man; he writes, "To procure the necessities of life had always been the business of the man; he produced and owned the means of doing so" (Engels 1972, 134).

But we may wonder why "procuring the necessities of life" is accomplished through food *getting* rather than food *processing.* Indeed, Engels goes on to define the "getting" labor as socially productive, whereas he claims that domestic labor is not. Why are domestic utensils not also regarded as means of production? Moreover, Engels gives no reasoned argument why one should regard as "nonproductive" the curing of meat, the dressing of hides, and the transforming of raw material into food. Following this line of reasoning, we wonder why the herding of sheep is to be considered any more a claim to property rights in the herd than the processing of milk, carding of wool, and so forth. Instead, it would appear that the "property rights" associated with the surplus produced by the domestication of animals has no more intrinsic or social source in the male activity than in the female (domestic) activity. The claim to that property does not seem to lie in some intrinsic distinction between "procuring the necessities of life" as herding and the like or "procuring the necessities of life" as domestic processing (Gould 1973–74, 24).

Another set of criticisms may be made concerning Engels's explanation of the crucial transition from mother right and communal property to patrilineal inheritance and private property, which, according to him, brings about the oppression of women. He presents this transition as having an economic basis. But the curious thing is that in fact the most significant factor in Engels's account of this transformation is perhaps the man's desire to bequeath his property to his children, which in turn requires a guarantee of paternity and therefore the overthrow of matrilineal descent, or mother right. But this desire to bequeath and to guarantee paternity is not evidently economic in itself, but rather involves the continuance or preservation of one's authority, power, or social status, beyond one's death, by passing it to one's immediate descendants. Thus, although it may be that the emergence of this mode of preserving social power through the paternal line is occasioned by the development of an economic surplus as the property of the male, the motivation for this preservation, which is crucial to the explanation, would seem to have noneconomic sources. This observation significantly qualifies the claim that the introduction of the economic category of private property is historically decisive.

In addition, other factors remain mystifying in Engels's account of this transition. There is first of all the sudden appearance of acquisitiveness with the development of herding, whereas it seems not to have played a role at an earlier stage. Engels attributes this to the emergence of a surplus. But we may wonder about the unexplained absence of any sharing of this emerging surplus by the male with his female partner, instead of its remaining the exclusive possession of the male. Further, as I suggested earlier, there seems to be no more reason for private property to have developed with respect to the domain of herding in the division of labor than for it to have developed with respect to the instruments within the domain of women's work, for example, scraping, piercing, and sewing tools, cooking and storing utensils, and so forth. All of these various criticisms, then, suggest that there is a strong ad hoc element in Engels's explanation and that he sometimes posits explanatory hypotheses that beg the question or that are at odds with his stated economic theses (for further criticisms, see Carver 1985, esp. 487).

A more general methodological point can be made from the standpoint of a feminist critique of Engels. In keeping with the thesis of historical materialism, at least as it is expressed in *Origins,* the explanation that Engels proffers of the oppression of women attempts to go from the material conditions (of the development of private property) to the social relations of women's oppression. As noted, in reaction to this, feminists have introduced the supplementary (or alternative) notion of patriarchy as necessary to account for this oppression. There is, however, a third way of looking at this linkage between the oppression of women and the nature of capitalist economy (as well as the state): that is, to recognize that the oppression of women has had considerable effect on the character and functioning of the economy and the state. Thus, in fact, the causal relation (if it is relevant to talk about causality at all in this case) could just as well work the other way round. Modern capitalist economies may well have been shaped by the history of women's oppression. To the degree that women were excluded from the public sphere of the state and economic institutions, this public domain came to embody the historically dominant "male" characteristics, for example, of acquisitiveness, war, and aggression. Engels does not explore this alternative direction of historical construction.

This gap is reflected as well in Engels's argument that full equality of women can be achieved only with the abolition of class society. The converse argument seems equally persuasive, namely, that the abolition of class society and private property as he defines them (i.e., of exploitative social relations) requires as its condition the achievement of women's equality, as well as the introduction into the public sphere of those characteristics historically associated with the "female," such as supportiveness and caring (see Gould 1984).

A final point by way of criticism (here, with the benefit of hindsight) is the incompleteness of Engels's analysis in yet another respect. Though his analysis links sexual oppression to class oppression, it ignores the relation of both of these to questions of culture, race, nationality, and ethnicity. This criticism concerns more than the obvious defect of the Eurocentrism of Engels's theory, a feature that he shares with almost all social critics of his time. This Eurocentrism can be found in the theory of stages of development, where the normative end point is seen as the culmination of European history and the development of European forms of political economy to a socialism that distinctively emerges from it. History becomes a retrospective reconstruction of earlier stages leading to that end state, where such unfortunates as the inhabitants of the Western hemisphere do not make it past barbarism, except through the forcible introduction of European civilization by the colonizers. But the point I want to make here is a bit different. There is a need, I think, for the development of a theoretical understanding of the role of women and of the family in maintaining cultural continuities and identities, whether in terms of race, ethnicity, or nationality, as well as cultural affiliation more generally. Through mothering, or parenting, feelings of belongingness to larger groups are established, as is the more negative notion of the exclusion of others. Whereas these connections have been studied to some degree in the limited domain of kinship systems, they have played an important role in modern and contemporary societies, a role that has recently come to be sharply recognized. I believe we can discover close connections between the oppression of women and what we may call cultural injustices, and positive links between the role of women and certain features of family life also set the conditions for cultural expression and development. But these will need to be worked out as a research program.

Reclaiming Engels

Despite the range and force of these criticisms of Engels's *Origins*, several aspects of his argument remain particularly important. The first is that his account of the basis and development of the subordination of women is not biologistic; that is, it does not depend on some notion of a natural tendency of males to dominate or of women to be subordinate. Rather, he regards oppression and to some degree even gender itself as socially and historically constituted or constructed (Nicholson 1986). This orientation is in keeping with much of contemporary feminism, and not only with those sympathetic with Marxist feminism. Another useful aspect of Engels's analysis here is that it does not pretend to a notion of simple linear historical progress. Rather, it suggests a more complex history in which not all past societies were equally oppressive, and indeed in Engels's version (which has been challenged), early societies afforded greater equality and social freedom to women until the hypothesized overthrow of matriarchy. In this respect, his account is not universalistic in adducing some essential human nature that maps gender differences into history.

Engels's specific alternative to a biologistic approach, as we have seen, is a focus on economic activity and its resulting forms of social relations. Though Engels has been soundly criticized by feminist theorists for his one-sided emphasis on the role of economic factors, we can appreciate the importance of taking such factors seriously into account. In fact, I would suggest that this would be a useful theme to reemphasize, in a properly nuanced and noneconomistic way, in contemporary discussions of feminist theory. Although there was an intensive consideration of the political economy of sexism, especially in the 1970s, focusing on housework or domestic labor and on the relations of the exploitation of women to class exploitation, this ran into the problems of attempting to contain the phenomena of women's oppression within the categories of classical Marxist political economy and of disregarding the crucial role played by patriarchy.

Perhaps in an overreaction to these criticisms, at present there is relatively little theoretical analysis of the economics of gender hierarchy beyond the accepted analysis of liberal theory, for example, equity theory concerning pay differentials, "pink-collar workers," and the relation of intrahousehold stratification to gender stratification outside the home. Further, the economic study of women's work that does exist has tended to remain separated from the main trends in feminist theory more generally. The interesting concept of comparable worth was introduced not only as a theoretical term but as a program of action, but it was dropped for political reasons. There is of course a substantial analysis of women and poverty and recently of the gendered nature of welfare, but a fuller theoretical analysis and critique is needed of how gender oppression functions in the economies of advanced capitalist societies. Is the differential economic treatment of women of any functional moment to so-called liberal capitalism, beyond the obvious benefits that derive from taking advantage of women's residual historical vulnerability? That is, is this benefit or utility simply a matter of exploiting gender difference for the sake of cheap labor and a so-called reserved army of the unemployed, where women would simply be like any other relatively disadvantaged group; or is there a special character to the continuation of gender inequality in economic contexts? In addition, in the new multinational world labor market, does the impoverished and vast population of unemployed and underemployed women further intensify the already intense exploitation of cheaper labor by corporations, undercutting the cost of the home labor force? Further, does the especially impoverished and sexually oppressed status of women worldwide provide a vast resource of cheap labor in competition with the workers—male and female—in the advanced industrial nations? These kinds of studies, as I suggested earlier, need to be carried out with an awareness of the interaction between gender oppression and economic structures, an acknowledgment of the affect the treatment of gender has on the economy and not just the reverse.

Finally, another important aspect of Engels's *Origins* is its normative framework for future developments. Like John Stuart Mill and others writing roughly contemporaneously, Engels projects as an aim for the future a society in which true love can take its place freed from the constraints of economic dependency or male domination, and in which women work outside the home in full equality with men. Features of his account are clearly laudable, as is his implicit idea of the degendering of family roles. The latter conception has been a bit controversial among feminists in the past few years, but I myself think that such a degendering, for example, in shared parenting as well as in economic roles, is a good thing. This is wrongly taken if it is thought to imply the elimination or repression of differences. Rather, it would entail that differences be matters of personal choice rather than of given role expectations.

A question one can raise about Engels's account here, however, concerns his view that these transformations require the full socialization of family functions, including not only housework but also childraising. Further, he speaks of the abolition of the family as an economic unit, no longer required by the emergent communal forms of social life. This seems to mean that childraising would necessarily be communal rather than parental, and this does not seem to me particularly desirable. Similarly, Engels does not appear to appreciate the importance of family privacy. As long as one is living in an industrialized public world, some protection of the privacy of interpersonal relations is indispensable. Likewise, the family (however precisely defined) plays an important role in providing the security for childraising, and this function as well seems to me of continuing significance. These, I would suggest, are the crucial factors of "family values," if I may use the term, which need to be preserved or enhanced. But this does not commit us to the preservation of all features of the contemporary family, some of which are problematic or even dysfunctional. But further discussion of the future will have to wait for the future.

References

Carver, Terrell. 1985. Engels's Feminism. *History of Political Thought* 6:479–89.
de Beauvoir, Simone. 1989. *The Second Sex*. New York: Vintage.
Engels, Frederick. 1972. *The Origin of the Family, Private Property, and the State*. Ed. Eleanor Burke Leacock. New York: International Publishers.
Gould, Carol C. 1973–74. The Woman Question: Philosophy of Liberation and the Liberation of Philosophy. In *Women and Philosophy*, ed. Carol C. Gould and Marx W. Wartofsky, a special double issue of *Philosophical Forum* 5.
———. 1984. Private Rights and Public Virtues: Women, the Family, and Democracy. In *Beyond Domination: New Perspectives on Women and Philosophy*, ed. Carol C. Gould. Totowa, N.J.: Rowman & Allanheld.
Hartmann, Heidi. 1981. The Unhappy Marriage of Marxism and Feminism: Towards a More Progressive Union. In *Women and Revolution*, ed. Lydia Sargent, 1–41. Boston: South End Press.
Mitchell, Juliet. 1971. Women: The Longest Revolution. In *From Feminism to Liberation*, ed. Edith Hoshino Altbach. Cambridge: Schenkman. (Originally published in *New Left Review*, no. 40 [1966]: 11–37.)
Nicholson, Linda. 1986. *Gender and History*. New York: Columbia University Press.
Rowbotham, Sheila. 1974. *Women, Resistance, and Revolution*. New York: Vintage Books.
Rubin, Gayle. 1975. The Traffic in Women: Notes on the Political Economy of Sex. In *Toward an Anthropology of Women*, ed. Rayna R. Reiter. New York: Monthly Review Press.

13

Engels, Dewey, and the Reception of Marxism in America

James Farr

In a revelatory letter to Franz Mehring in 1893—ten years after Marx's death and two before his own—Engels took the long view of his relationship with his famous friend. "When one has had the good fortune to work together for forty years with a man like Marx, one does not during his lifetime receive the appreciation one believes he deserves. But just as soon as the greater of the two dies, the lesser is easily overrated. That seems to be true for me now. History, however, will take care of all that" (translated in Hook 1933, 340).

Reading Engels as Marx

"History"—as it turns out—did not take the care that Engels imagined. Instead of being underappreciated and then overrated, Engels came to be virtually identified with Marx. Their works were merged into a single canon, out of which emerged a system of science and philosophy. Engels supplied the authoritative interpretations of this canon, as well as the striking phrases of its system—"scientific socialism," "historical materialism," and "dialectics of nature." In this way, for friend and foe alike, Engels exerted a uniquely powerful influence over the meaning of Marx's works and the trajectory of Marxism.

The power of Engels's influence finds ample testimony in the subsequent development of Marxism, of course. This is true even in the United States, where Marxism had the least success among modern nations in taking root. America's most original interpreter of Marx's writings, Sidney Hook, remembered the 1920s as a period when "the works of Engels ... were accepted by the faithful as part of the sacred canon, along with those of Marx. Engels discoursed on almost all areas of knowledge, and the positions he defended in these fields, from anthropology to physics and zoology, were accepted by many young readers as the correct Socialist view." Hook is a reliable witness on this point, despite his editorializing that Engels's influence proved to be "retrograde," especially on "the uncritical-minded" and on "those who did not pursue their studies in depth" (1987, 35). But mentioning Hook, America, and the uncritical-minded opens the door to more intriguing testimony of the power of Engels's influence in the reception of Marxism. For it was Hook's teacher and America's greatest philosopher, John Dewey, who reacted negatively but uncritically to Marx and Marxism. He used the name Marx to cover all that passed for Marxism. He failed to distinguish texts or to make distinctions between Marx, Engels, or various Marxists, even when these were insisted upon by Hook himself. And Dewey seemed unmoved by Hook's further, far-reaching suggestions that Dewey's pragmatism and Marx's critical philosophy were essentially the same. Instead, Dewey rejected Marxism. Some of his reasons were political ones that reflected his reaction to Communist agitation in the United States and to totalitarian tendencies in Soviet Russia, both of which were profoundly undemocratic. But there were also philosophical reasons that turned upon science, dialectics, and historical interpretation. The Marx(ism) that Dewey rejected—especially in *Freedom and Culture* (1939), his most important work on the topic—bore the unmistakable marks of Engels's interpretation and subsequent influence. Dewey's later confessions that he neither understood Marx's theories nor even read his writings—confessions that have confused or bemused his commentators—are telling. They point to an important, if unconscious, truth: it was Engels or an Engelsified Marxism that Dewey read and rejected.

Here, then, is a case study in the American reception of Marxism in the form of John Dewey's reading of Engels-as-Marx. It provides testimony to the doctrinal power that Engels exercised in America, long after his death. His dialectical and materialist system of nature and history was at the same time both imposing and simple. It earned Marxism many of its American adherents. But it also earned it its philosophical foes, John Dewey foremost among them. Dewey's antipathy was by no means ingrained or crudely ideological, for he was as open-minded, progressive, and socialistic a liberal democrat as America would produce. He proved sympathetic to the humanistic goals of Marxism, and came to share much of its critique of capitalism. He reported favorably on developments in Russia when he traveled there in 1928, and he would later lead the commission that vindicated Leon Trotsky. But, doctrinally, he could not abide the dialectics, the materialism, or the pretensions to science. He also could not see through—or refused to see through—the system, to disaggregate Marx from Engels, to distinguish founding figures from later epigoni, or to follow leads laid out for him by Hook. While Dewey is unique in the American reception of Marxism because of his stature, he was in this way strikingly typical. To use Hook's words, Dewey too did not pursue his studies in depth. For all but a tiny handful of Americans (like Hook, and then only for a while), Marxism was what Engels and his philosophical followers made of it.

This chapter focuses, then, on John Dewey's engagement with the figure he called Marx and the system he called Marxism—with Engels and Engels's legacy hovering spectrally over them. Dewey's critique of Marx(ism), against the backdrop of identifiable similarities, has been well served by a few previous commentators (especially Cork [1950], Campbell [1988], Manicas [1988, 1989], Westbrook [1991], and Ryan [1995]). For its part, this chapter problematizes Engels in a way not done before, and it develops leads out of Hook (which remain interpretively promising). In constructing a narrative based largely on Dewey's expressed views, it also deploys extensive textual documentation. A broader study would have to do more of this, as well as to consider a larger debate that included, among others, another student of Dewey's, Max Eastman (for beginnings in this direction, see Eastman 1926, 1937, 1941b; Diggins 1994b; Wald 1987). The chapter begins with a brief glance at the later Engels's shaping of Marxism, as well as his stature among American Marxists. The second section turns to Dewey, tracing his fitful reaction to Marxism through the late 1920s, when he went to Soviet Russia. The third attends to Hook's "discovery" that Marx's critical philosophy was wrongly systematized and scientized by

Engels, a discovery that was essentially ignored by Dewey during the 1930s, when Communist agitation and the Moscow trials dominated his judgments of what Marxism meant. Whereas the second and third sections mainly chronicle, the fourth looks more closely and analytically at Dewey's most sustained critique of scientific Marxism in *Freedom and Culture.* The chapter concludes with some final thoughts about Dewey and the American reception of Marxism after Engels.

Marxism in America

To say that Engels contributed to Marxism—or even that he was one of its founding figures—understates the imaginative power he exercised over the legacy that bore Marx's name. He virtually "invented" it (Carver 1981, 1983, 1989). (For variations on or dissensions from this view, see Ball and Farr 1984, Hobsbawm 1982, Rigby 1992, and essays in Arthur 1996.)

Engels's "invention" of Marx went far beyond his own theoretical inventiveness of the 1840s, 1850s, and 1860s, when he galvanized attention to the condition of the working class in England or helped place the category of production at the center of socialist economic doctrine. It certainly went beyond his co-authorship of *The Communist Manifesto* or *The Holy Family,* or all the items of his journalistic talents that issued forth under Marx's byline. No, Engels's invention vaulted well over the sum total of his early creative work; it even vaulted over what Marx himself had written, despite intimations in Marx's own work. It was a system of scientific socialist doctrine that brought nature and history together under an overarching dialectical and materialist framework. Class struggle, the transmutation of chemical elements, matter-in-motion, and everything else went into a *Weltanschauung* that was ready-made for socialist activists.

Marxism, in this systematic version, was the labor of Engels's later years. His energies were prodigious. He assembled and edited Marx's unfinished works and introduced or prefaced new editions of older ones. He kept up the drumbeat of criticism not only against capitalists but against faux socialists. He sustained his own prodigious writing agenda, some of it on works of popularization or polemic, the rest on works of philosophy, anthropology, and natural science. He wrote lucidly and well, making complex points simple and at times simplistic. He cribbed his own work, as, for example, *Socialism: Utopian and Scientific* out of *Anti-Dühring,* the better to put the accessible bits before a wider audience. He had a knack for the telling title or phrase. With "historical materialism," he rechristened the set of historical studies that he and Marx, separately and together, had undertaken. He then placed that interpretation so named under a banner of "scientific socialism" and a broader ontology whose defining feature was dialectical and whose scope encompassed the whole of nature. A "dialectics of nature" was thus coined, and Marxism completed as a systematic worldview. As a final touch, Engels stood down, attributing it all to Marx.

Engels was accorded "unrivalled prestige" (Stedman Jones 1982, 291) among Marxists not only during his closing years, but well through the Second International and after. *Socialism: Utopian and Scientific*, in particular, proved to be "the work from which millions of conversions to Marxism were made, and it was Engels's greatest achievement as a publicist for Marx" (Carver 1989, 250). Engels's prestige continued unabated in the new Soviet Union, where his own systematizations and simplifications underwent more of the same by self-styled dialectical materialists. But the line was direct and acknowledged by Plekhanov, Bukharin, and Lenin. In America, too, where Marxism and other Continental socialist ideas played a much smaller role in framing national debates, Engels was the preeminent Marxist.

Through the second half of the nineteenth century, Engels wrote about America, especially the Civil War, for European and American newspapers, much of the work signed by Marx. Along with Marx, he maintained an extensive correspondence with émigrés to the United States who, like Joseph Weydemeyer, formed the nucleus of the American Workers League, the first Marxist organization in the United States. Engels continued contact with the American Marxists in the International Working Men's Association, especially after it came to New York in 1872. The general secretary of the First International when in America was Friedrich Sorge, who was also instrumental in creating the Socialist Labor Party in 1877 and serving as "Engels's emissary" (Bell 1996, 39) to the party through 1890. It was to Sorge in 1882, after publication of the German edition of *Socialism: Utopian and Scientific*, that Engels wrote, thinking perhaps especially of his American readers, that "most people are too idle to read thick books like *Capital*, and so a pamphlet does the job more quickly" (in Carver 1989, 250). At least some Americans, however, liked their books thick. Daniel de Leon, for one, was "converted to Socialism" by reading *Anti-Dühring* in tandem with the anthropological writings of Engels's American authority, Lewis Henry Morgan (Buhle 1991, 55). De Leon would join and soon dominate the Socialist Labor Party. Among his first activities was to edit the new English-language weekly *The People* ("Published in the Interests of the Toiling Masses every Sunday Morning"). *The People* brought out an English translation of *Socialism: Utopian and Scientific* (under a slightly different title) in 1892, the same year as Edward Aveling's authorized translation. Engels, meantime, continued his contact with the Socialist Labor Party, encouraging it to downplay its German connections and hoping (in vain, alas) that it would achieve revolutionary successes "compared with which we in Europe shall be mere children" (Marx and Engels 1975, 420).

After his death in 1895, Engels would play the posthumous role of Marxist theorist, mainly as author of works now published in English and a dozen or so other languages. The Charles H. Kerr Company in Chicago would begin publishing socialist writings at the turn of the century, including the first American reprint of the authorized translation of *Socialism: Utopian and Scientific* in 1900 and works cut in its mold, like Charles H. Vail's *Principles of Scientific Socialism* (1899). They also published the first English translation of Engels's host book in 1907 under the title *Landmarks of Scientific Socialism: Anti-Duehring*. In the next year, the original plates of *Socialism: Utopian and Scientific* having been used up, Kerr brought out an improved edition. The publisher himself took note of Engels's claim that the sales of the German edition between 1883 and 1892 had amounted to twenty thousand copies. "Our own sales of the book in America from 1900 to 1908," Kerr boasted, "were not less than 30,000" (1908, 7). Moving off business, he editorialized that "Frederick Engels is second only to Karl Marx among socialist writers, and his influence in the United States is only beginning" (8).

The fate of Engels's influence turned, of course, on more than his theoretical acumen. The Russian Revolution changed everything, and the vast majority of self-styled Marxists turned toward the Soviet Union for guidance in theory and practice. Engels would lose none of his authority with Communist Party ideologists, beginning in the early 1920s, when, among other things, International Publishers would issue its own editions of Engels's work. The Socialist Labor Party, estranged from the Socialist Party that had emerged out of it and from the new Communist Party, would still turn to Engels, including him in fights with anarchists and "physical-forcists" over the question of violence. In 1922, for example, it published *The Revolutionary Act*, Engels's much earlier introduction to Marx's *Class Struggles in France*. Of "Marx's life-long co-worker" the translator (Kuhn 1922, 7) would ask rhetorically, "who is more fit to interpret Marxism than he?" Remarks like these were not consigned exclusively to partisan presses. They formed the backdrop of debates among those soon dubbed "New York intellectuals" (Wald 1987), as well as of Sidney Hook's own initiation to and later remembrance of "the sacred canon." They also formed the backdrop for those American intellectuals like John Dewey, who would take a very different measure of the canon.

Dewey and Marxism

Anti-Dühring was originally published in 1878, the year that John Dewey became a senior at the University of Vermont and began his course of study in moral philosophy. Political economy was one of the subtopics in the old Scottish-styled curriculum, and it is likely that Dewey first heard of Marx and Engels in that setting. Doubtless, what he heard was unflattering. Given his upbringing (Coughlan 1975, Rockefeller 1991), he would have reacted against the Marxism for undergraduates (of the Woolsey 1880 type) that caricatured and stigmatized materialism, atheism, free love, and class war. However, there were more sympathetic resonances to be heard between Marxism and New England Transcendentalism (Herreshoff 1967); and Dewey's early interests in Kant and Hegel, as well as social reform, set him on a course destined to intersect with the philosophical and political doctrines of Marxism. Upon graduation, he published an article critical of the metaphysical assumptions of materialism (1882) in the Hegelian *Journal of Speculative Philosophy*. The incipient Hegelianism of his critique became full-fledged during graduate study at Johns Hopkins, only to drift away as his pragmatic philosophy of inquiry matured. Although Hegelianism would leave a "permanent deposit" on his thinking, Dewey would come to reject not only its "form" and "schematism" but, tellingly, its "mechanical dialectical setting" (LW 5:154).

Dewey mentions Marx—as an "economist" (EW 4:215)—for the first time in his published writings in an 1894 review of James Bonar's *Philosophy and Political Economy in Some of Their Historical Relations* (1893). In preparing his review, Dewey would have been treated to a remarkably sane and temperate assessment of *Capital* and *The Poverty of Philosophy*. He would also have seen that Bonar thought that Engels was "the chief prophet of the school" and had "the last philosophical word" on socialism at this stage of its history. In Bonar's view, Engels, who was then still alive, was also suspiciously unforthcoming about his own work. With respect to *The Origin of the Family, Private Property, and the State*, for example, he noted that "Engels is never beyond suspicion of allowing his modesty to wrong him, a generous fault which might be counted a virtue if it did not hinder his critics from being sure whom they are criticising" (1893, 328, 346, 349). To judge by his review, which failed to name Engels, as well as by his subsequent writings, Dewey was indeed the sort of critic hindered by Engels's claim only to be executing a plan of Marx's design.

The first indications of Dewey's taking on the labor theory of value and what by then was universally known as historical materialism occur in his lectures on ethics in 1898 and 1901, respectively. Dewey's grasp was not very firm in either case. For the one, Dewey substituted "'socially available' labor" for socially useful labor, and then blamed Marx for begging the question about what made labor valuable (1976, 400). In the other, he missed the centrality of production: "The socialists who follow Karl Marx have interpreted history from a materialistic standpoint, making ... distribution of food and maintaining life that out of which artistic life, social life, and all the rest of it have grown" (Dewey 1991, 373; cf. the later, correct view in MW 14:207). These accounts are so wildly inaccurate that we must presume that Dewey, scrambling to prepare undergraduate lectures, was badly paraphrasing some secondary source. His practice of taking Marx at second hand, however, was in any case established here. Yet, it is significant and retrospectively important for understanding Deweyan pragmatism that, in front of his University of Chicago students, he admitted that many of the "scientific and practical aspects" of Marxism were "quite close" to his own views (Dewey 1991, 373).

Over the course of the next three decades—spanning World War I, the Bolshevik Revolution, and his own travels to Soviet Russia—Dewey was to return periodically to themes he attributed to Marx and that passed for popularized Marxism. In the course of his own rethinking of Hegelianism, metaphysics, and scientific inquiry, Dewey fixed upon the claims made by or about Marxists that their doctrines were "scientific" and their worldview "materialist" and "dialectical." Ever wont to emphasize the animating power of human ideas and the freedom of action, he roundly rejected historical inevitability and the epistemological howler that ideas were copies of things in the material world. These elements came together, for example, in *German Philosophy and Politics* (1915), Dewey's first work of political theory that centered mainly on Kant, Hegel, and their philosophical descendants. Therein lay the connection to Marx, for "the materialist interpretation of history was but the Hegelian idealistic dialectic turned upside down." While Marx and the Marxists expressly wished to set the old philosopher upright, not turn him upside down, Dewey at least properly worried that Marxists were not offering real history so much as "another philosophy of history." He complained further that "our strictly scientific economic interpreters will have it that economic forces present an inevitable evolution." But he countered that "even highly abstract theories" like Marxism itself "are of efficacy in the conduct of human affairs." Since ideas are plans of action, not copies of anything, they have causal force and belie any inevitability. "Even if we went so far as to say that the reigning philosophies simply reflect as in a mirror contemporary social struggles, we should have to add that seeing one's self in a mirror is a definite practical aid in carrying on one's undertaking to its completion" (1915, 5–6, 123; cf. MW 14:187).

The texts that prompted Dewey's responses are not specified by him, an unfortunate habit that would persist in his subsequent discussions of Marx and the Marxists. Dewey's personal and professional library (Boydston 1981) offers no help with respect to his early references, and not much more for later ones. His estate bequeathed to the Morris Library at Southern Illinois University, among numerous other books, a 1932 edition of *Capital* (edited by Max Eastman), as well as the 1926 edition of *Selected Essays* (translated by H. J. Stenning). No works of Engels were included, although an undated edition of Plekhanov's *Fundamental Problems of Marxism* and a 1937 edition of Trotsky's *History of the Russian Revolution* were. Except for Eastman's *Marx, Lenin, and the Science of Revolution* and Hook's *Reason, Social Myths, and Democracy* (which reproduced the stinging critique of *Dialectics of Nature*), none of their other works on Marx or Marxism were in Dewey's collection.

Dewey's early habit—of not specifying texts—was tied to another, that of indifferently lumping together different thinkers. This violated a maxim of interpretation that Dewey himself formed during these years. Complaining of an author who made a "forced assemblage" of theorists, Dewey dictated that "nothing accurate or intelligible can be said except by specifying the interest and purpose of a writer, and his historical context of problems and issues" (LW 2:42). In any case, a preface to *Capital* had tried to set Hegel upright; and Engels repeated the "upside-down" image in several texts, including *Socialism: Utopian and Scientific*, where he also criticized Hegel for failing to think of ideas as "abstract pictures of actual things and processes" (1908, 86, cf. 97). (To its great credit, however, in Engels's view, the "Hegelian system" did develop the logic of contradiction and helped make possible the correct worldview that "nature is the proof of dialectics" [83]). *The Communist Manifesto* had announced the inevitable fall of capitalism, which was philosophically innocuous but rhetorically moving. In this and most other respects, the *Manifesto* transcribed points to be found in Engels's catechistic *Principles of Communism*.

But by 1915 these were all stock phrases of popular Marxism. Only one note to a passage discussing the "bird [*sic*] of Minerva" taking flight at dusk suggests any particular text. In an evident (but uncited) reference to the introduction to the *Critique of Hegel's "Philosophy of Right,"* Dewey notes that "Marx said of the historic schools of politics, law and economics that to them, as Jehovah to Moses on Mount Sinai, the divine showed but its posterior side" (1915, 110n). Dewey's source of this quite specific reference is fugitive, though it had been published in the *Deutsch-Französische Jahrbücher* in 1844, the *Berliner Volksblatt* in 1890, *Le Devenir Social* in 1895, and Franz Mehring's *Aus dem Literarischen Nachlaß von Karl Marx und Friedrich Engels* in 1902. The passage occurs in the course of Marx's critique of religion, and his programmatic claims about the powers of critique. God's backside notwithstanding, emphasis on criticism resonated with Dewey's own conception of philosophy, as he would articulate it most forcefully in *Experience and Nature* (1925).

By 1918, Dewey's reading of Marxism was being presented in terms that almost wholly reflected Engels's popularized terminology (especially from *Socialism: Utopian and Scientific*). The problem of reading it, however, had been dramatically transformed because of world war and the Russian Revolution. World War I, he thought, "ought to give a final blow to that myth still current in Marxian circles that a new era will be ushered in by the breakdown of the present regime of capitalism." He went on in terms recognizable to the generation of the erstwhile Second International: "The doctrine smacks, of course, of the Hegelian dialectic of opposites. But that is only its formal aspect. Its subject matter is the belief in a catastrophe ... to be followed by a millennial period." Given the lack of any evidence or careful theorizing about the future, the "adoption [of this doctrine] into 'scientific socialism' is merely a confession of the absence of science." To make matters worse, Dewey feared that such notions would fuel a "red scare" in America, where "some Bolsheviki" would be blamed for any attempt at progressive social change (MW 11:91, 96).

Red scares would haunt American public opinion over the course of the twenties and well after. Dewey would alert his readers to them, especially when prompted by "American reactionaries," who, in the case of China in 1920, overreacted to "the Marxian doctrine of a sudden revolution" (MW 12:20). But if a Chinese revolution along Marxist lines was then only imaginary, the Russian Revolution was established fact. In 1928 Dewey went to see for himself, sending back his "Impressions of Soviet Russia." The impressions turned out to be almost uniformly positive (prompting a friend to observe that they were "99% John Dewey and 1% Russia" [in

Westbrook 1991, 477]). He ended up admiring the cooperatives, the schools, the public art, and especially "the courage, energy, and confidence" of the Russian people. A revolution of "incalculate significance not only for that country, but for the world" had been accomplished. It was a progressive pragmatist's dream, "an enormous psychological experiment in transforming the motives that inspire human conduct." All of this, however, gave the lie to the "stereotyped formulae" of Marxism (in its indigenous form as "Bolshevist Marxianism"). Russian facts undermined Marxist science. Unlike genuine science, Bolshevik doctrine "smells of outworn absolutistic metaphysics and bygone theories of straight-line one-way 'evolution.'" Dewey introduced his objection to a theme sounded repeatedly in Engels's later writings and absorbed into Bolshevism as the calling card of "economic determinism," namely, that there was "a single and necessary 'law' of historical change." If any of this dogma were true, the Russian Revolution would not have happened. Dewey pressed his point by spoofing the dialecticians and their theory of contradictions. "One hears all the time about the dialectic movement by means of which a movement contradicts itself in the end. I think the schools are a 'dialectic' factor in the evolution of Russian Communism." More stingingly: "In the dialectic of history, the function of Bolshevism is to annul itself" (LW 3:205, 207, 221, 243, 249).

Dewey and Hook

Dewey's impressions embroiled him in the public debate over the nature of the Soviet experiment and the American reaction to it. One of the more important responses to Dewey came from his prize student, Sidney Hook. Hook had completed his dissertation on pragmatism under Dewey, and in his first published article had criticized Lenin for "overly literal appropriation of Engels" and had argued that "dialectical materialism must take its cues from the scientific pragmatism of Dewey" (1928, 34). In 1928 and 1929 Hook was in Berlin working on post-Hegelian philosophy, meeting Georg Lukács, and falling under the spell of Karl Korsch—the two most important figures to challenge the Engelsian orthodoxy into which Second and then Third International Marxism had settled. Soon, Hook would go to the Marx-Engels Institute in Moscow by invitation of David Riazanov and be among the first American scholars to have access to the definitive editions and source materials being released there. He would

go on to write *Towards the Understanding of Karl Marx* (1933), the most creative and scholarly interpretation of Marx's philosophy written by an
American through that time, and arguably since. From Berlin, on 9 January 1929 (paraphrased and misdated in Diggins 1994a, 82), Hook wrote to
Dewey on the occasion of having read *The New Republic* essays on Russia—
which he thought "kind of apologetic for the enthusiasm they did contain"
but deserving "the gratitude of every lover of truth and friend of Russia"
(1929). But he was more keen to share his discoveries about the founding
figures of Marxism.

> With Marx I am on surer ground. I have come to the conclusion
> that in its original form Marx's thought was not in the least an
> expression of a system but rather a thorough criticism all along the
> line of the current "presumably" presuppositionless economics,
> presuppositionless history, philosophy, etc. His whole endeavor was
> to show that the so-called "external truths" were vicious inversions
> of conditional, temporal and partial social interests. I have no time
> to develop the theme here but will call attention to one external
> consideration which has never been sufficiently reflected upon.
> Almost every one of Marx's writings from 1842 on, was entitled a
> critique of something or other! The list of these "critiques" is a very
> imposing one. They are directed against all those who are uncon-
> scious of the fact that their categories have relevance (meaning),
> validity as well as the limits of that validity in a world developing in
> time. What about Capital? you will ask. Just look at the sub-title, "a
> critique of political economy." And as I understand it, that is just
> what Marx's economic theories are. They are a protest against false
> abstractionism in economics—against "the fetishism of commodi-
> ties." This section on the "fetishism of commodities" is the heart
> of Capital. It was Engels who attempted for good but insufficient
> reasons to make a system out of Marx. But Marxism is no more a
> system than is pragmatism!

Having decried system, equated philosophy with criticism, and expressed horror as early as 1899 at "the monstrous fetishism" (MW 1:128) of
the age, Dewey understood Hook's speech-act. Hook was hoping for
Dewey's imprimatur for a Korschian interpretation of Marx(ism) and for
a synthesis of Marx and Dewey himself. (In finding connections between
pragmatism and Marxism, Hook was preceded by Walling [1913]—as discussed in Pittenger 1993 and Lloyd 1997—and followed by Cork [1950]

and Kolakowski [1968].) It is hard to imagine that Hook and Dewey had not talked earlier about the proposed synthesis—toward a Red pragmatism, as it were—or even about the differences that separated Marxists, including Marx and Engels. But by this letter of 1929, in any case, Dewey was apprised what a trustworthy pragmatist and first-rate scholar was concluding about these matters. Dewey responded by acknowledging that Hook's labors showed at least one version of "how Marx should be interpreted, not what he 'really meant'" (in Phelps 1997, 58). Any lingering doubts would be settled by Hook's writings over the next few years (1933, 1936, 1940), as well as in the many forums into which Hook drew Dewey. Dewey learned from Hook how to sharpen his critique of Marxism, and many of Hook's critical phrases became Dewey's. Yet, for reasons he would later only hint at, he failed or refused to disaggregate Marxism or to take up the cause of pragmatizing it.

The year 1930 began a decade that forced Dewey to attend even more closely than he had to Marxism. The Great Depression, the New Deal, and the frightening prospects of an American fascism set the scene, as did the agitations of domestic Communists and the machinations of the Soviet Union. Marx, Dewey admitted, was "the prophet of just this period of economic consolidation" whose "ghost hovers above the American scene" (LW 5:90). Yet, stunningly, he also confessed in 1930 that "I do not know enough about Marx to enter into the discussion concerning his philosophy" (LW 5:367)! This contained more than a grain of truth, and perhaps Dewey was acknowledging the far superior understanding of someone like Hook. But this did not stop Dewey from making further references to "Marx" in that year or the coming decade.

Dewey's confession came at the end of a symposium called "Marx and Social Change" first published in *Modern Quarterly* (1930). In his short contribution, Dewey rearticulated his views of human action as intelligent problem solving in inherited contexts, as well as of the present need to understand how these contexts had been formed historically. (Reproducing his dictum from *Democracy and Education* [1916, 214], he averred that "significant history is history of the present.") In the present period, in which economic problems dominate, historical understanding must be primarily economic. Here, then, was Marx's "immense significance," Dewey thought. On grounds of his own ignorance, he might beg off with regard to matters of interpretation, but he persisted with one of his main complaints. "Those who interpret [Marx's] philosophy, whether correctly or incorrectly, as one of an automatic working of historical forces not only have, as it seems to me, an entirely false conception of the relation of the past to the present and its future, but they are virtually accomplices in the policy of drift" (LW 5:365, 367).

Another symposium, organized by Hook in 1934, gave Dewey the chance to admit, in the word's of his contribution's title, "Why I Am Not a Communist." Hook's contribution to the symposium was the lengthy piece "The Meaning of Marx" (which Ryan [1995, 300] finds to be "as intelligent and articulate an account of the intellectual dynamics of Marxism as any American produced in those years or for many years after"). In Dewey's view Marx's meaning should be found in his "own writings and manuscripts" as opposed to "the way in which people who have not even taken the trouble to read him carefully bungle with it—like children playing with their grandfather's sword" (Russell et al. 1934, 60–61). Hook compressed the points he had made so brilliantly the previous year in *Towards the Understanding of Karl Marx* (1933), in which he had decried orthodoxy, rejected inevitabilism, and equated the dialectic with scientific method properly understood. Dewey, if not the other symposiasts, Bertrand Russell and Morris Cohen, would have known the essentials of Hook's views, especially those distinguishing Marx from Engels and the orthodox Marxism that prevailed between 1895 and 1917. This period, Hook had argued, witnessed "an emasculation of Marx's thought." His "philosophy of action" and "method of revolutionary criticism" had been transformed into "a monistic system." Beginning with *Anti-Dühring*, Engels was behind this transformation. He had formulated a "simplified materialism called dialectical but in reality mechanical." He had substituted a "carbon-copy" epistemology for the "active practical element in the Marxian theory of knowledge." He held "unclear absolutistic views" regarding space and time. He was more concerned with the rate of profit than the fetishism of commodities. His application of historical materialism was "rigid and mechanical," especially when explaining how "history" calls forth "great men" like Caesar or Napoleon when deeds needed doing. (Kautsky would further rigidify this "logically infantile" maneuver, and later Marxists like Plekhanov and Bukharin would "play the game of follow your master with amazing fidelity.") Not all of Engels's contributions to Marxism were objectionable, and Hook seized upon select passages to underscore his own pragmatist, activist theory of history and revolution. In particular, he played upon Engels's concessions, made famous in letters of the 1890s and first translated by Hook, that it was only "in the last instance" that economics dominated social relations. But the "characteristic emphasis" he had given to Marx's doctrine regarding science, dialectics, and materialism had "far-reaching consequences ... in the hands of the official party theoreticians" (Hook 1933, vi, ix, 29–32, 170–71, 252).

Dewey thus had before him neither a promissory indication that there were differences between Marx and Engels nor a vague admonition that care should be taken in speaking about Marxism *tout court*. He had the sustained case, in great and scholarly detail. If Hook's interpretation was correct, his own critique of Marx and Marxism was mainly a critique of Engels or his orthodox legacy. In the symposium of 1934, Dewey again did not take up the challenge or opportunity to admit any of this or to disagree publicly with Hook, if in fact he disagreed with him. He sidestepped the broader issue by saying that he was no Communist if that meant being a member of an organized party. Whatever prospects there were for "small-c" communism as a popular movement, Dewey was settling scores with his more positive and naive views of Russia five years earlier. If the Russian people still deserved his praise, the Communist Party leadership had drained him of the energy to say so. Theoretically, Dewey echoed Hook's and his own earlier complaint about supposing a "monistic and one-way philosophy of history" that was inattentive to historical particularities. In the United States, this meant attending to the absence of a feudal past and the ideology of individuality. "Dialectical materialism" had been more imposed than argued in the various national parties of the Third International; even then it had to "undergo frequent restatement in accordance with the exigencies of party factional controversy." Dewey admitted the importance of class conflict while doubting the wisdom of using class war as "the means" of social change (Russell et al. 1934, 86–90). On other matters of Marxist theory he deferred to the others, naming Russell.

Dewey raised one final issue that had nothing to do with the founding figures of Marxism but that played an evidently powerful role in his views. It was the "repugnant" conduct shown by American Communists regarding "fair play" and "elementary honesty" in dealing with facts and the opinions of others.

> The systematic, persistent and seemingly intentional disregard of these things by Communist spokesmen in speech and press, the hysteria of their denunciations, their attempts at character assassination of their opponents, their misrepresentation of the views of the "liberals" to whom they also appeal for aid in their defense campaigns, their policy of "rule or ruin" in their so-called united front activities, their apparent conviction that what they take to be the end justifies the use of any means if only those means promise to be successful—all these, in my judgment, are fatal to the very end which official Communists profess to have at heart. And if I read the temper of the American people aright, especially so in this country.

Dewey's remarks were personal as well as political. His (and Hook's) own Teacher's Union Local no. 5 had been a casualty of domestic agitation (see LW 3:273). The *Large Soviet Encyclopedia* of 1931 had said that "the philosophy of Dewey is a philosophy of war and fascism" (in Westbrook 1991, 482). The *Daily Worker* and other organs of the Communist Party in America dutifully repeated the accusation at opportune moments (see Hook 1940, 74n).

After such condemnatory remarks, it is surprising that America's preeminent liberal would soon consent to aid in yet another "defense campaign," especially one for a Communist known for justifying "any means." But this is precisely what Dewey did in 1937, thanks again to the offices of Hook, who had just completed an essay for the *Marxist Quarterly* (1937) devastating Engels's *Dialectics of Nature* for harboring "monism" and giving "comfort to contemporary positivism." (He also noted that "the philosophical writings of Plekhanov, Kautsky, Lenin, Trotsky, and Mehring and the minor figures in the orthodox tradition contain little on these themes not already to be found in Engels" [as reprinted in Hook 1940, 184, 193–94].) Knowing Dewey's view of Trotsky's "abstract ideological fanaticism" (in Phelps 1997, 152), Hook convinced Dewey to head the American Committee for the Defense of Leon Trotsky because of the liberal and democratic principles at stake. The committee morphed into the Preliminary Commission of Inquiry into the charges (of counterrevolution and murder) made against Trotsky in the Moscow trials. (On the commission, see Farrell 1950; Deutscher 1963, 371–82; Wald 1987, ch. 5; and LW 11:326–36.) The preliminary commission (1938) found Trotsky not guilty and confirmed Dewey in his judgment of Stalin's "epoch of terrorism" (LW 13:348). Dewey found it "the most interesting intellectual experience" of his life (in Hook 1987, 244). Yet, the precise intellectual dimensions of the experience were kept to himself during the hearings. Excepting a few questions about party democracy and international revolution (Preliminary Commission of Inquiry 1937, 356, 432), Dewey refrained from theoretical or political intervention with Trotsky during the intense week in Mexico City. However, the occasion arose almost immediately after, when Trotsky offered up "Their Morals and Ours" in the *New International* (1938). Ready for an "open polemic" with liberals, Trotsky noted that "my article on morals provoked great dissatisfaction in Dr. Dewey, Sidney Hook, and others, and that they intend to smash my bad philosophy. I am very glad to hear this" (1976, 370). Dewey responded with "Means and Ends."

With the exception of a brief line in the 1934 symposium, Dewey's response provided him with the first occasion to take up the question of moral theory in connection with Marxism. This topic had never been a strong suit of Marxist theory, and indeed only a few pages in *Anti-Dühring* seemed to offer any guidance from a founding figure. Even then, the debate over morals, in Dewey's view of Marxism, turned upon the allegedly "scientific" claims of "dialectical materialism" and especially its account of (in Trotsky's words) "class struggle, the law of all laws." Agreeing with Trotsky's sweeping claim that "the end justifies the means"—what else could, if they were interdependent?—Dewey claimed that the end (in his terms, the "end-in-view" as anticipated consequences) did not justify any means whatsoever. This was simply an improper "deduction" and "another kind of absolutism" that "closes the door to further examination of history." Dewey concluded: "To be scientific about ends does not mean to read them out of laws, whether the laws are natural or social. Orthodox Marxism shares with orthodox religionism and with traditional idealism the belief that human ends are interwoven into the very texture and structure of existence—a conception inherited presumably from its Hegelian origin" (LW 13:351, 353–54).

Hegelian origins and scientific inadequacies were also on Dewey's mind, apart from Trotsky's casuistry. For he was just then finishing for publication *Freedom and Culture*, his final and most thorough encounter with Marxism.

Dewey's Critique

Published in 1939, *Freedom and Culture* brought to culmination four decades of Dewey's confrontation with Marxism. The work was not only a confrontation with Marxism, but with fascism, utilitarianism, laissez-faire liberalism, corporate capitalism, even "Americanism" (LW 13:131). It was also not so much a confrontation as a continuation of Dewey's own programmatic project of articulating a democratic political philosophy for a humanistic culture dedicated to free inquiry most fully exemplified in the ideals of science. Yet, Marxism was the most formidable opponent of this philosophy, since it too claimed to value science and humanistic culture, as well as freedom and democracy. Dewey placed his critique of Marxism in the center of his book, in the longest chapter.

The title of chapter 4—"Totalitarian Economics and Democracy"—lent the discussion political currency at the end of the 1930s, with another world war in the making. Dates and debates of the previous decade came into view, including those that had embroiled Dewey personally. Murderous "trials" (LW 13:127) were still on Dewey's mind, as were domestic slings and arrows. "Verbal abuse in countries like the United States is the substitute for the physical power exerted where dictatorship exists, the mildest epithet being that of Fascist or friend of Fascism" (129). References to "socialism in one country" and to how "Moscow determines that Mendelism is scientifically false" picked out Stalin (135, 158). Those references to "the moral . . . question of values and ends" (184) recalled Dewey's own recent controversy with Trotsky. In the main, however, the focus of *Freedom and Culture* was squarely on what he took to be time-honored Marxist doctrine—on science, dialectics, and historical materialism. The phrases that most offended—"utopian socialism," "transmutation of chemical elements," "the negation of negation"—or those that intended to give most offense—"monistic," "absolutistic," and "uniformitarian"—had Engels written all over them, at least as Hook had so insistently read the body of Marxism.

Since the presentation in *Freedom and Culture* is, as one reviewer said (Merriam 1940, 342), somewhat "disorganized" and "repetitive"—which Dewey, too, admitted—we may reconstruct five principal arguments. Even these are portmanteau, overlap, and recall earlier charges. They issue forth from Dewey's "empirical, pluralistic, and pragmatic method" (LW 13:131). They culminate in his charge that Marxism "has violated most systematically every principle of scientific method" (135), which is also to say every principle of democracy.

First, Marxist doctrine is "uniformitarian" (132). Not only does it rely upon so-called objective uniformities, it holds to a species of determinism —"without which its 'materialism' is meaningless"—that denies causal efficacy to human action, unless such action is in turn "previously determined" by productive forces (133). Such a materialism "reduces the human factor as nearly as possible to zero" (117), and it fuels the rhetoric of inevitability, especially the contention that social developments are "inevitable because scientific" (122). Dewey wastes no time in showing that productive forces are themselves prompted and kept going by human needs, which concedes the point that there is causal interaction between humans and nature. Moreover, counterfactually, if the doctrine were true, it would render pointless an "imperatively required condition of Marxist theory" (133), namely, that the emerging class of proletarians must have its consciousness raised and mobilized. But this plainly depends upon "the operation of psychological factors which are not mentioned—and which the theory rules out" (134). Marxism as a revolutionary doctrine arming the proletarian with the weapons of theory cannot be squared with its uniformitarian materialism.

Second, Marxist doctrine—especially dialectical materialism—is "absolutistic" (117, 122, 184). Not only does it affirm an "absolute necessity" (120) attendant to uniformitarianism, but that necessity is stated in "absolute terms" (116). This is true of its claims about history, but also of those about nature. In transforming "dialectical idealism into dialectical materialism," Marx (in Dewey's old image reversal) "stood Hegel on his head" (119, 120). Yet, the rest of the Hegelian apparatus remained intact, including the law of contradiction, the negation of negations, and the unity of opposites (119, 122, 125). So too did the claim that this dialectical philosophy holds good for nature, including, paradigmatically, the conservation of energy, its transference through friction, and the transmutation of chemical elements (123, 124). (It is hard to believe that with these as his precise and sole examples Dewey did not have ready to hand *Anti-Dühring* in any of the languages he spoke, the *Dialectics of Nature* in its German edition of 1927 or some gloss on it [the English translation being in press at just that moment], or Hook's 1937 essay "Nature and Dialectics.") These examples are not what they seem to be, Dewey avers; thus, the transmutation of chemical elements "does not wipe out the differences of quality" (124). But, more fundamentally, the whole dialectical business is "metaphysical and *extra*-scientific" (123). The aspiration to include nature as well as society and history in the object field of scientific method is not objectionable. What is objectionable is the metaphysical view that a dialectical "science" sews up the universe in some absolute scheme, with nature its proof. But science is "not a competitor with theology for a single ultimate explanation" (123). It is about multiple and changing explanations. The "experimental method of science" (131) explores and enters into an open universe, whose tools of inquiry themselves undergo change as more is discovered about nature. Here is but a higher-order form of the human interaction with nature. In search of the absolute, Marxism misunderstands nature and the contingent character of scientific inquiry into it.

Third, Marxist doctrine is positivistic. While it does not make objectionable claims about sensations or verification associated with certain strains of positivism (LW 12:511), it is positivistic in at least two ways. On the one hand, Marxist doctrine entails a program of reduction, in particular the reduction of human science to physical science. This follows from the previous two positions, both in denying effective causal agency to human actions and in trumpeting an absolutism that covers the whole of nature.

Thus Dewey speaks of the "fallacy" "that there is an economic or 'material-istic,' dialectic of history by which a certain desirable (and in that sense moral) end will be brought about with no intervention of choice of values and effort to realize them. As I wrote some years ago, 'the assimilation of human science to physical science represents only another form of abso-lutistic logic, a kind of physical absolutism'" (LW 13:184). Dewey does not inform the reader that he first wrote these words in *The Public and Its Problems* (1927, 199) in evident reaction to physicalism, one of the central doctrines of midcentury positivism. There he also criticizes the other sense in which Marxism is positivistic: its fixation on laws. Here Marxists continue the legacy of the positivists Comte and Spencer (LW 13:121) in aspiring to "laws for all social phenomena" (120). "Still more wonderful," Dewey digs, Marxism puts "forth one law working with absolute necessity" (120). But this just shows how "Marxism is 'dated'" (123). Laws have no necessity and indeed not so important a place in science as actually prac-ticed. So-called laws are but restricted generalizations that hold under limited conditions. They function as provisional, ever-changing tools of inquiry or rules of inference. They are no more to be accumulated in a fixed science than is human science to be reduced to physical science.

Fourth, Marxist doctrine is "monistic" (126, 127, 134). It is so with respect to the categorical framework of its social theory. In contrast to a "pluralistic" theory (74), Marxism emphasizes "one factor" in social devel-opment, namely, "the forces of economic productivity at a given time" (118). This "Marxist simplification" (118) in turn finds expression in another monistic formulation, alluded to in the above reference to "one" law, thus committing Marxism to a "monistic block-universe theory of social causation" (126). This is the "single all-embracing law" of class strug-gle (119). Dewey, naturally, is critical of this law, as he had been for many years. But he is not concerned to criticize the importance of classes or class struggle in modern society (Campbell 1988; Manicas 1988). Indeed, he believes in their contemporary centrality, and had stated his beliefs quite forcefully in *Liberalism and Social Action* (1935) and earlier. In the context of 1939 he admits that this is "taken for granted" (117). But "the proposi-tion that serious strife of economic interests exists"—which Dewey holds— must be contrasted with "the genuine Marxist thesis that it is the sole agency by which social change is effected" (124). Besides sharing in the infelicities of law-aspiring positivism, this all-embracing law issues illicitly out of the font of Hegelianism. This of course is Dewey's allegation, but in making it he follows a distinct structure of argument or pattern of pres-entation familiar to orthodox Marxism since *Socialism: Utopian and Scien-tific* (Engels 1908, 85–93). "This 'law' was not derived nor supposed to be derived from study of historical events. It was derived from Hegelian dialectical metaphysics" (LW 13:119). Beyond its extrascientific derivation, the alleged law claims far too much in explanatory power; it is unguarded with respect to the conditions under which it may be said to hold; and it discourages further inquiry. Indeed, "the inherent theoretical weakness of Marxism is that it supposed a generalization that was made at a particular date and place ... can obviate the need for continued resort to observation, and to continual revision of generalizations in their office of working hypotheses" (125). In contrast to monism, then, both as categorical framework and singular law in a "block-universe," Dewey stresses "the importance of ideas and of a plurality of ideas employed in empirical activity as working hypotheses" (131).

Fifth and last, Marxist doctrine is "monolithic" (122, 134). Insofar as the term differs from "monistic," it is used to underscore the massive, singular, rigid force of the doctrine in the practice of Marxist believers. It picks out the "practical" force that monism serves as "a fountainhead of inspiration to action, providing also rallying cries and slogans" (122). Moreover, Dewey seeks to call special attention to the dire consequences that he sees being drawn from a monistic social theory that, in its rigidity, settles things "in advance" and is critical of everything but itself. "Any monolithic theory ... tends to have a ready-made answer for problems that present themselves," and this "prevents critical examination and discrimination of the particular facts involved in the actual problem." Indeed it "prevents exploration of the problem as a problem" (134). This is true of the individual Marxist, psychologically speaking. But it is also true of the Marxist party to which the individual turns and which controls the means of problem formation. "A monistic theory is accompanied in its practical execution by one-party control of press, schools, radio, the theater and every means of communication" (127). It is a short "practical" step from here to suppressing speech, silencing opposition, even beheading "counterrevolutionaries" (135). Such examples are not "facts in dispute" (127), Dewey contends. Pointing them out to readers in 1939 underscored his considered judgment that Marxism had violated "every principle ... of scientific and democratic method" (135).

Conclusions

Within months of the release of *Freedom and Culture, Dialectics of Nature* was finally published in English translation and greeted by "uniform and uncritical celebration" by American Marxists (Buhle 1991, 167). The Soviets signed their nonaggression pact with Nazi Germany. And Sidney Hook came forth with a book on his other hero besides Marx, *John Dewey: An Intellectual Portrait* (1939). Hook proclaimed Dewey a socialist in all but name, hailed *Liberalism and Social Action* (1935) as *The Communist Manifesto* of the twentieth century, and proposed a convergence between pragmatists and "realistic Marxists." However, he made plain that, as things stood, Dewey rejected Marxism. But his rejection was not well informed, at least in that Dewey had "never moved to make an independent study of the theoretical writings." Like "most Americans of his time" he took little interest in "genealogical" questions. So, "Marxism for Dewey was what those who called themselves Marxists made of it" (Hook 1939, 161–62). Shortly thereafter, in an otherwise glowing account of his teacher, Max Eastman would pronounce that "there is one act of learning ... which Dewey never performed and whose neglect ... will stand against him in history." He never studied Marx. Worse yet, Eastman reported that Dewey had confessed to him that "I have never read Marx. ... I cannot speak with authority on the subject" (1941a, 682).

Hook must have felt disappointed, especially after his labors, that Dewey could not or would not make elementary but important distinctions; and Eastman was obviously astonished at Dewey's confession, especially in light of all that Dewey had written with apparent authority on a subject called "Marx." In 1950, Jim Cork, too, would find "astounding" Dewey's charges that Marx was (in our reconstruction) uniformitarian, absolutistic, and monistic. Marx was not "guilty" of these or related doctrines, as the briefest reading of his writings would confirm (Cork 1950, 335–37). But then, perhaps Dewey had not read them, as Eastman reported, or he had read only snippets out of them without theoretical attentiveness. Dewey certainly knew enough of Trotsky's views to hail his concluding speech in Mexico City as "literature of a high order" (in Phelps 1997, 157). He certainly knew enough of the phraseology of the Stalinists, who, as Cork reports, may have influenced Dewey with their "tiresome claim that they were the only legitimate descendants of Marx" (337). But of course Dewey had been around and critical of Marxism well before there were Stalinists, at a time when Old Bolsheviks and, before them, the orthodox theoreticians of the Second International had made their claims about dialectics, historical materialism, and scientific socialism. If Hook was right, the main lines went back to Engels. In the terms of Dewey's criticism in *Freedom and Culture,* Engels was not and could not have been party to making Marxism "monolithic." This was the work of the apparatuses and apologists of contemporary Communist Parties. But the lineaments of a philosophical system that was, in Dewey's and Hook's terms, uniformitarian, absolutistic, positivistic, and monistic were evident in Engels's writings, especially his later writings, as these had been popularized for half a century.

It was Engels's invention, if not his writings, to which Dewey responded with such spirit. Whatever one makes of it, this is testimony to Engels's theoretical influence, as well as to the orthodox systematizers that followed him. It is also testimony to Dewey's consequentialism, which he thought quintessentially American. What mattered were the consequences of ideas. It was what self-styled Marxists said and did that gave Marx's ideas their meaning. *Socialism: Utopian and Scientific* was as important as, or more important than, *Capital,* Party propaganda as important as *The Eighteenth Brumaire,* the Moscow trials as important as *The Civil War in France.* This is a coherent view, perhaps, and typical of the American reception of Marx and Marxism. It is certainly understandable given the personal and political travails Dewey underwent. But it must be said that Dewey could well have responded differently to Marx, Engels, and Marxism. As a philosopher who could split hairs with the best of his contemporaries and who justly complained about what some "pragmatists" made of pragmatism, he should have responded differently, even if his final judgments went unchanged. He could have read more closely and acknowledged what he read. He need not have so flagrantly violated his own maxim of interpretation, not to make "forced assemblage" of different thinkers or to deny them their interests, problems, and contexts. He certainly had no excuse —if not for following Hook's account of Marx, Engels, and Marxist orthodoxy—then at least for not acknowledging or disagreeing with it. He might even have given Engels credit for his own work, where it was (as it often was) creative, or where it was (as it also was) a system worth undoing. Had Dewey done any of these things, the American reception of Marx and Marxism would have been different, just because Dewey himself was such a famous participant in the American reception. More than Hook, Dewey would have drawn notice; and the debates would have been at least that much more refined and informed, whatever their final disposition.

Dewey never took up Marx or Marxism in any theoretical way after *Freedom and Culture,* though he lent his name to the causes of liberal anticommunism until his death in 1952. Hook ended up agreeing with Dewey: he ceded Marxism to the "Marxists" and turned on them all. It was another moment in the American reception of Marxism and a harbinger of the intellectual ossification of the Cold War. In his memoir, Hook remembered and at last agreed with the gist of a remark Dewey had made a half century earlier. "Regardless of the accuracy of my interpretation of Marx, it was largely an intellectual conceit: To the extent that ideas counted in the world, Marxism in our time ... was the state philosophy of the Soviet Union and its satellites" (Hook 1987, 140). This was a crucial concession to Soviet hegemony, not to mention a not-very-pragmatist view of the many different ways "ideas counted in the world." It was in any case a register of what Hook had abandoned, as he himself made clear looking back. His defiance of "the canon that Engels's philosophical views ... could be attributed to Marx" and his constructive efforts to forge a "pragmatic interpretation of Marx" and "a synthesis ... between Dewey and Marx" were over (111).

What a difference a decade makes. Marxism "in our time" is no longer the state philosophy of the Soviet Union for the obvious reason that the Soviet state is no longer. And in America, a "resurgence of pragmatism" is under way (Bernstein 1992). Whether resurgent pragmatists will revisit their own history—including the instructively complex relations that bound Dewey and Hook to Soviet statism, Engels's system, and Marx's critical philosophy—remains an open question.

References

References in the text to EW, MW, and LW, followed by volume number, refer to the respective volumes of Dewey's *Early Works, Middle Works,* and *Later Works.*

Arthur, Christopher J., ed. 1996. *Engels Today: A Centenary Appreciation.* New York: St. Martin's.

Ball, Terence, and James Farr, eds. 1984. *After Marx.* Cambridge: Cambridge University Press.

Bell, Daniel. 1996. *Marxian Socialism in the United States.* Ithaca, N.Y.: Cornell University Press.

Bernstein, Richard J. 1992. The Resurgence of Pragmatism. *Social Research* 59:813–40.

Bonar, James. 1893. *Philosophy and Political Economy in Some of Their Historical Relations.* New York: Macmillan.

Boydston, Jo Ann. 1981. *John Dewey's Personal and Professional Library: A Checklist.* Carbondale: Southern Illinois University Press.

Buhle, Paul. 1991. *Marxism in the United States: Remapping the History of the American Left.* New York: Verso.

Campbell, James. 1988. Dewey's Understanding of Marx and Marxism. In *Context over Foundation: Dewey and Marx,* ed. William J. Gavin, 119–45. Dordrecht: D. Reidel.

Carver, Terrell. 1981. *Engels.* New York: Hill & Wang.

————. 1983. *Marx and Engels: The Intellectual Relationship*. Brighton, East Sussex: Harvester/Wheatsheaf.

————. 1989. *Friedrich Engels: His Life and Thought*. London: Macmillan.

Cork, Jim. 1950. John Dewey and Karl Marx. In *John Dewey: Philosopher of Science and Freedom*, ed. Sidney Hook, 331–50. New York: Dial Press.

Coughlan, Neil. 1975. *Young John Dewey*. Chicago: University of Chicago Press.

Deutscher, Isaac. 1963. *The Prophet Outcast: Trotsky, 1929–1940*. New York: Vintage.

Dewey, John. 1915. *German Philosophy and Politics*. New York: Henry Holt.

————. 1916. *Democracy and Education*. New York: Macmillan.

————. 1927. *The Public and Its Problems*. New York: Henry Holt.

————. 1969–72. *The Early Works of John Dewey: 1882–1898*. 5 vols. Carbondale: Southern Illinois University Press.

————. 1976. *Lectures on Psychological and Political Ethics, 1898*. New York: Hafner Press.

————. 1976–83. *The Middle Works of John Dewey: 1899–1924*. 15 vols. Carbondale: Southern Illinois University Press.

————. 1981–90. *The Later Works of John Dewey: 1925–1953*. 17 vols. Carbondale: Southern Illinois University Press.

————. 1991. *Lectures on Ethics, 1900–1901*. Carbondale: Southern Illinois University Press.

Diggins, John Patrick. 1994a. *The Promise of Pragmatism: Modernism and the Crisis of Knowledge and Authority*. Chicago: University of Chicago Press.

————. 1994b. *Up from Communism: Conservative Odysseys in American Intellectual Development*. New York: Columbia University Press.

Eastman, Max. 1926. *Marx, Lenin, and the Science of Revolution*. London: Allen & Unwin.

————. 1937. *The End of Socialism in Russia*. Boston: Little, Brown.

————. 1941a. John Dewey. *Atlantic Monthly* 168:671–85.

————. 1941b. *Marxism, Is It a Science?* London: Allen & Unwin.

Engels, Frederick. 1892. *The Development of Socialism from Utopia to Science*. New York: Labor News Company.

————. 1907. *Landmarks of Scientific Socialism: Anti-Duehring*. Trans. Austin Lewis. Chicago: Charles H. Kerr.

————. 1908. *Socialism: Utopian and Scientific*. Chicago: Charles H. Kerr.

————. 1922. *The Revolutionary Act: Military Insurrection or Political and Economic Action?* Trans. Henry Kuhn. New York: Labor News Company.

————. 1939. *Anti-Dühring: Herr Eugen Dühring's Revolution in Science*. New York: International Publishers.

————. 1940. *Dialectics of Nature*. New York: International Publishers.

Farrell, James T. 1950. Dewey in Mexico. In *John Dewey: Philosopher of Science and Freedom*, ed. Sidney Hook, 351–78. New York: Dial Press.

Herreshoff, David. 1967. *The Origins of American Marxism: From the Transcendentalists to De Leon*. Detroit: Wayne State University Press.

Hobsbawm, Eric J., ed. 1982. *The History of Marxism*. Vol. 1, *Marxism in Marx's Day*. Bloomington: Indiana University Press.

Hook, Sidney. 1928. The Philosophy of Dialectical Materialism. *Journal of Philosophy* 25:113–24, 141–55.

————. 1929. Letter of 9 January to John Dewey. Dewey Papers, Morris Library, Southern Illinois University.

————. 1933. *Towards the Understanding of Karl Marx.* New York: John Day.

————. 1936. *From Hegel to Marx: Studies in the Intellectual Development of Karl Marx.* New York: John Day.

————. 1939. *John Dewey: An Intellectual Portrait.* New York: John Day.

————. 1940. *Reason, Social Myths, and Democracy.* New York: John Day.

————. 1987. *Out of Step: An Unquiet Life in the 20th Century.* New York: Harper & Row.

Kerr, Charles H. 1908. Publisher's Note. In *Socialism: Utopian and Scientific,* by Frederick Engels. Chicago: Charles H. Kerr.

Kolakowski, Leszek. 1968. *Toward a Marxist Humanism: Essays on the Left Today.* New York: Grove Press.

Kuhn, Henry. 1922. Translator's Note. In *The Revolutionary Act: Military Insurrection or Political and Economic Action?* by Frederick Engels. New York: Labor News Company.

Lloyd, Brian. 1997. *Left Out: Pragmatism, Exceptionalism, and the Poverty of American Marxism, 1890–1922.* Baltimore: Johns Hopkins University Press.

Manicas, Peter T. 1988. Philosophy and Politics: A Historical Approach to Marx and Dewey. In *Context over Foundation: Dewey and Marx,* ed. William J. Gavin, 147–75. Dordrecht: D. Reidel.

————. 1989. *War and Democracy.* Oxford: Basil Blackwell.

Marx, Karl. 1926. *Selected Essays.* Trans. H. J. Stenning. New York: International Publishers.

Marx, Karl, and Frederick Engels. 1975. *Selected Correspondence.* Moscow: Progress Publishers.

Merriam, Charles E. 1940. Review of *Freedom and Culture,* by John Dewey. *American Political Science Review* 34:339–42.

Novack, George. 1975. *Pragmatism Versus Marxism: An Appraisal of John Dewey's Philosophy.* New York: Pathfinder Press.

Phelps, Christopher. 1997. *Young Sidney Hook: Marxist and Pragmatist.* Ithaca, N.Y.: Cornell University Press.

Pittenger, Mark. 1993. *American Socialists and Evolutionary Thought, 1870–1920.* Madison: University of Wisconsin Press.

Preliminary Commission of Inquiry. 1937. *The Case of Leon Trotsky.* New York: Harper.

————. 1938. *Not Guilty.* New York: Harper.

Rigby, S. H. 1992. *Engels and the Formation of Marxism: History, Dialectics, and Revolution.* Manchester: Manchester University Press.

Rockefeller, Steven C. 1991. *John Dewey: Religious Faith and Democratic Humanism.* New York: Columbia University Press.

Russell, Bertrand, et al. 1934. *The Meaning of Marx.* New York: Farrar & Rinehart.

Ryan, Alan. 1995. *John Dewey and the High Tide of American Liberalism.* New York: W. W. Norton.

Stedman Jones, Gareth. 1982. Engels and the History of Marxism. In *The History of Marxism,* vol. 1, *Marxism in Marx's Day,* ed. Eric J. Hobsbawm, 290–326. Bloomington: Indiana University Press.

Trotsky, Leon. 1938. Their Morals and Ours. *New International* 4:163–73.

———. 1976. For an Open Polemic with the Liberals. In *Writings of Leon Trotsky, 1937–38,* ed. Naomi Allen and George Breitman. New York: Pathfinder Press.

Vail, Charles H. 1899. *Principles of Scientific Socialism.* Chicago: Charles H. Kerr.

Wald, Alan M. 1987. *The New York Intellectuals: The Rise and Decline of the Anti-Stalinist Left from the 1930s to the 1980s.* Chapel Hill: University of North Carolina Press.

Walling, William English. 1913. *The Larger Aspects of Socialism.* Chicago: Charles H. Kerr.

Westbrook, Robert B. 1991. *John Dewey and American Democracy.* Ithaca, N.Y.: Cornell University Press.

Woolsey, Theodore Dwight. 1880. *Communism and Socialism in Their History and Theory: A Sketch.* New York: Scribner's.

Select Bibliography

Engels is listed as Engels, F., since usage is sometimes Friedrich and sometimes Frederick.

Arthur, Christopher J., ed. 1996. *Engels Today: A Centenary Appreciation*. London: Macmillan.
Ball, Terence, and James Farr, eds. 1984. *After Marx*. Cambridge: Cambridge University Press.
Benner, Erica. 1995. *Really Existing Nationalisms: A Post-Communist View of Marx and Engels*. New York: Oxford University Press.
Berger, Martin. 1977. *Engels, Armies, and Revolution: The Revolutionary Tactics of Classical Marxism*. Hamden, Conn.: Archon.
Braunthal, Julius. 1966. *History of the International, 1864–1914*. London: Nelson.
Bronner, Stephen Eric. 1990. *Socialism Unbound*. New York: Routledge.
Carver, Terrell. 1981. *Engels*. Oxford: Oxford University Press.
———. 1983. *Marx and Engels: The Intellectual Relationship*. Bloomington: Indiana University Press.
———. 1989. *Friedrich Engels: His Life and Thought*. London: Macmillan.
Cummins, Ian. 1980. *Marx, Engels, and National Movements*. New York: St. Martin's.
Engels, F. 1935. *Ludwig Feuerbach and the Outcome of Classical German Philosophy*. New York: International Publishers.
———. 1958. *The Condition of the Working Class in England*. Trans. W. O. Henderson and W. H. Chaloner. Stanford: Stanford University Press.
———. 1968. *The Role of Force in History*. London: Lawrence & Wishart.
———. 1969. *Anti-Dühring*. London: Lawrence & Wishart.
———. 1969. *Germany: Revolution and Counter-Revolution*. London: Lawrence & Wishart.

———. 1972. *Dialectics of Nature.* Moscow: Progress Publishers.

———. 1972. *The Origin of the Family, Private Property, and the State.* Ed. Eleanor Burke Leacock. New York: International Publishers.

———. 1972. *Socialism: Utopian and Scientific.* New York: International Publishers.

———. 1977. *The Peasant War in Germany.* Moscow: Progress Publishers.

———. 1978. *Socialism: Utopian and Scientific.* Moscow: Progress Publishers.

Ferraro, Joseph. 1992. *Freedom and Determination in History according to Marx and Engels.* New York: Monthly Review Press.

Forman, Michael. 1998. *Nationalism and the International Labor Movement: The Idea of the Nation in Socialist and Anarchist Theory.* University Park: Pennsylvania State University Press.

Gould, Carol C. 1973–74. The Woman Question: Philosophy of Liberation and the Liberation of Philosophy. In *Women and Philosophy,* ed. Carol C. Gould and Marx W. Wartofsky, a special double issue of *Philosophical Forum* 5.

Gouldner, Alvin W. 1980. *The Two Marxisms: Contradictions and Anomalies in the Development of Theory.* New York: Seabury Press.

Hammen, Oscar J. 1969. *The Red '48ers.* New York: Scribner.

Henderson, W. O. 1976. *The Life of Friedrich Engels.* 2 vols. London: Frank Cass.

Hobsbawm, Eric J. 1982. *The History of Marxism.* Vol. 1, *Marxism in Marx's Day.* Bloomington: Indiana University Press.

Hunley, J. D. 1991. *The Life and Thought of Friedrich Engels: A Reinterpretation.* New Haven, Conn.: Yale University Press.

Jordan, Z. A. 1967. *The Evolution of Dialectical Materialism: Philosophical and Sociological Analysis.* New York: St. Martin's Press.

Kellogg, Paul. 1991. Engels and the Roots of "Revisionism": A Re-evaluation. *Science and Society* 55:158–74.

Kircz, Joost, and Michael Loewy, eds. 1998. Friedrich Engels: A Critical Centenary Appreciation. *Science and Society* 62 (special issue).

Kolakowski, Leszek. 1978. *Main Currents of Marxism.* 3 vols. Trans. P. S. Falla. Oxford: Clarendon Press.

Krieger, Leonard. 1967. Introduction to *The German Revolutions,* by Friedrich Engels. Chicago: University of Chicago Press.

Levine, Norman. 1975. *The Tragic Deception: Marx Contra Engels.* Oxford: Clio.

———. 1984. *Dialogue Within the Dialectic.* London: Allen & Unwin.

Lichtheim, George. 1961. *Marxism: A Historical and Critical Study.* New York: Praeger.

Manicas, Peter T. 1987. *A History and Philosophy of the Social Sciences.* Oxford: Blackwell.

Marcus, Steven. 1974. *Engels, Manchester, and the Working Class.* New York: Vintage.

Marx, Karl, and F. Engels. 1962. *Selected Works in Two Volumes.* London: Lawrence & Wishart.

———. 1968. *Selected Works in One Volume.* New York: International Publishers.

———. 1970. *The Communist Manifesto.* Harmondsworth, Middlesex: Penguin.

———. 1975. *Selected Correspondence.* Moscow: Progress Publishers.

———. 1996. *Later Political Writings.* Ed. and trans. Terrell Carver. Cambridge: Cambridge University Press.

Mayer, Gustav. 1969. *Friedrich Engels: A Biography.* New York: Howard Fertig.

McLellan, David. 1977. *Engels.* Hassocks, Sussex: Harvester Press.

Nimni, Ephraim. 1991. *Marxism and Nationalism: The Theoretical Origins of a Political Crisis*. London: Pluto.

Pierson, Stanley. 1993. *Marxist Intellectuals and the Working-Class Mentality in Germany, 1887–1912*. Cambridge, Mass.: Harvard University Press.

Plekhanov, George V. 1970. *Fundamental Problems of Marxism*. New York: International Publishers.

Riazanov, D. B. 1973. *Karl Marx and Friedrich Engels*. New York: Monthly Review Press.

Rigby, S. H. 1987. *Marxism and History: A Critical Introduction*. Manchester: Manchester University Press.

———. 1992. *Engels and the Formation of Marxism: History, Dialectics, and Revolution*. Manchester: Manchester University Press.

Rogers, H. K. 1992. *Before the Revisionist Controversy: Kautsky, Bernstein, and the Meaning of Marxism, 1895–1898*. New York: Garland.

Rosdolsky, Roman. 1986. *Engels and the "Nonhistoric" Peoples: The National Question in the Revolution of 1848*. Trans. and ed. John-Paul Himka. Glasgow: Critique.

Rubel, Maximilien. 1977. Friedrich Engels—Marxism's Founding Father: Nine Premises to a Theme. In *Varieties of Marxism*, ed. Shlomo Avineri. The Hague: Martinus Nijhoff.

Sayers, Janet, Mary Evans, and Nanneke Redclift, eds. 1987. *Engels Revisited: New Feminist Essays*. London: Tavistock.

Schwarzmantel, John. 1991. *Socialism and the Idea of the Nation*. London: Harvester/Wheatsheaf.

Sheehan, Helena. 1985. *Marxism and the Philosophy of Science*. Vol. 1, *The First Hundred Years*. Atlantic Highlands, N.J.: Humanities Press.

Stedman Jones, Gareth. 1973. Engels and the End of Classical German Philosophy. *New Left Review*, no. 79:17–36.

———. 1982. Engels and the History of Marxism. In *The History of Marxism*, vol. 1, *Marxism in Marx's Day*, ed. Eric J. Hobsbawm, 290–326. Bloomington: Indiana University Press.

Steenson, Gary. 1991. *After Marx, Before Lenin: Marxism and Socialist Working-Class Parties in Europe, 1884–1914*. Pittsburgh: University of Pittsburgh Press.

Steger, Manfred B. 1997. *The Quest for Evolutionary Socialism: Eduard Bernstein and Social Democracy*. Cambridge: Cambridge University Press.

Stepanova, Yelena. 1958. *Frederick Engels*. Moscow: Foreign Language Publishing House.

Tilly, Charles, ed. 1975. *The Formation of National States in Western Europe*. Princeton: Princeton University Press.

Townshend, Jules. 1996. *The Politics of Marxism: The Critical Debates*. New York: Leicester University Press.

Tucker, Robert C., ed. 1978. *The Marx-Engels Reader*. 2d ed. New York: W. W. Norton.

Tudor, Henry, and J. M. Tudor, eds. 1988. *Marxism and Social Democracy: The Revisionist Debate, 1896–1898*. Cambridge: Cambridge University Press.

Wilde, Lawrence. 1989. *Marx and Contradiction*. Aldershot: Avebury.

Index